ANDY GETS CONNED

A (Nerdy) Novel

MATTHEW T. MCKEAGUE

No part of this book may be reproduced, transmitted, or stored in any form or by any means except for your own personal use, without the express, written permission of the author. No part of the author should reproduce either, according to the general population.

This is a work of fiction. Any resemblance to actual persons, living or dead, or actual events is purely coincidental. Promise.

Cover Illustration by Fabio Sanna.
Copyright © 2020 Matthew T. McKeague.
All rights reserved. Matthew T. McKeague.
ISBN-13: 978-0-9997901-2-0

CHAPTER 1

Morning birds torturously chirped as sunshine shot onto Andy Gordon's face like a cancerous alarm clock. Nothing an extra dinosaur-patterned blanket couldn't stop, of course, yanked over his head quicker than the virtual victims he slayed the night before. Yet, after drifting back into dreams of intergalactic goddesses, he soon awoke again hearing four hurtful words. But no matter how hard he crossed his fingers, his desired coma never came...and the four dreadful words returned even louder.

"Andy, time for school!" Mom beckoned from the downstairs kitchen.

Yes, it was already that time of year, approximately one hour before Hell's doors re-opened for business after summer break. His sleep now battling an effective bird-sun-Mom trifecta, Andy's brain lost its nightly escape. Morning was here again.

After Mom's words pounded Andy's eardrums like aggressive cotton swabs, he unraveled his blanket cocoon. And he shuffled in wizard slippers to a fresh tankard of 'black magic' brewed by his bedside coffee maker. Andy then hopped on his skateboard to regain a few seconds, tardy today from last night's heroic tasks of the utmost importance. His quest to raise caterpillars in the latest *Space Fightin'* video game left him so tired that he slept through all alarms and was now 2.7 minutes behind schedule—a true butterfly effect. Andy now blasting down the hallway while making engine sounds with his mouth, his bulbous body dodged Renaissance weapons and geeky collectables spread all over the floor.

"Hurry up or you'll be late, dammit!" advised Mom. "Get your butt down here!"

With sounds of Andy crooning tunes of comedy singer Wacky Will Zimmerman in the shower, Mom knew that her shrill reminder worked and, ultimately, that her son wasn't dead today. She then returned to her coffee while reading *Geriatric Dating* magazine, the steam from her massive mug coming nowhere close to flattening her shellacked bouffant.

"What a wonderful swimsuit edition," growled Mom, then licking her finger and flipping the page. "Oh my. Hello there, Mr. Octogenarian October!"

Upstairs, Andy quickly toweled off. And then he put on his dress shirt and pants, both pre-hung on the door. This way, the shower's steam cut out all ironing time that'd be better spent elsewhere—like electronic caterpillar collecting, obviously. Not so much a fashion statement, but more so a friendship exam, his calculated accessories had to appeal to the possible dorks, geeks, nerds, misfits, and outcasts he'd see today. And those who didn't enjoy the references would fail Andy's fashion pop quiz, thus saving him significant time in the peer review process.

His Wacky Will watch came first, then cufflinks shaped like polyhedral dice displaying critical hit 20s. Soon after, his tie featuring zombified versions of historic figures dangled over a behemoth belly built from years of cheese curls and high-fructose corn syrup. This was the type of badass bling bound to repulse most women, but he liked it anyway.

Last on Andy's preparation list, he grabbed a professional video camera. And he slid it onto a mount at the front of his skateboard, starting the daily documentation of his entire existence. Inspired by all the dull videos of cats and police brutality online, he figured he could make something better and release it someday. Whenever the world was ready, and his videos were good enough to show to an audience larger than his action figures, he'd unleash his brilliance with a few clicks.

"Andy Gordon! Get down here now!" Mom yelled. "Final warning! You have 30 more seconds, or all your toys go in the trash."

"Be right there!" responded Andy.

Gaining speed with backward leg kicks, Andy skated down the hallway and slalomed through an assortment of plastic brick towns and robot vacuum parts. He then passed his Wacky Will doll shrine with a full set of hand-attachable accordion and rubber chicken accessories. Around the corner, Andy stepped off the recording skateboard, lodged it under his arm, rushed downstairs, and transitioned back to the skateboard when he struck the scotch-guarded ground. Yes, he knew this trip like the back of his hand knew how to waft away heat from a microwavable burrito—this was his terrain.

Now at top speed in the living room, anticipating his second cup of coffee and half a box of ginger snaps, Andy zoomed toward the kitchen. His retinas nearly exploded from a strange, natural sunlight reflecting off of the linoleum. And Andy lost balance inches away from breakfast. After regaining equilibrium for about two milliseconds, Andy lost it again, totally face-planting when his skateboard slid on an oddly slick section of floor.

Since Andy paid attention in science class, he could describe the reliable yet tragic physics propelling him forward across the glossy floor. Now more wrecking ball than human, Andy plowed into a cardboard block fort from the weekend's *Rejects & Reptiles* role-playing session. And then he wiped out its resident figures with a flood of flab, an event so catastrophic that its surviving metal elders would pass down the tale for centuries.

"Be careful, dear. I waxed the floor while I was waiting for you. And I opened the blinds to let some more light in here," Mom said, then looking up from the *Geriatric Dating* centerfold. "I'm sorry if I sound distracted right now. You'll understand once I show you the dangling set of grapes on this guy."

Emerging from the demolished fort, Andy Gordon poked his portly face through its blocks like a whale seeking fish guts. As he rubbed his throbbing noggin, messing his parted auburn hair, a large hanging pot fell from the cabinet and smashed his head and fingers. The

ANDY GETS CONNED

second pot didn't hurt as much because his scalp was already numb from the first, but the third and fourth pots definitely caused a bit of brain damage. Soon after, a dislodged cast-iron skillet could have qualified him for the Special Olympics, but that fortunately crashed onto his now-shoeless foot instead.

"I love what you've done with this place," Mom smirked. "The blocks are a nice touch. Women like men who can build things."

After Andy stopped yelping from the barrage of painful cookware, he detached his camera. And then he shambled to Mom as she finally put down her magazine.

"What a lovely surprise to see you again. In *my* kitchen," Andy said with a smile, recording the lady with body parts elastic enough to squeeze him out 34 years prior. "Drinking *my* coffee. Threatening to throw away all the toys that I purchased with *my* own paychecks."

"And you'll see me every morning until you fix *my* computer. It's been weeks. You were the one who got me hooked on the Internet, dear."

"These things take time. You had enough malware on this sucker to take down a government. You must have really screwed it up with all that porn you downloaded."

"I'm very careful with my viruses, both real and digital," chuckled Mom. "Please fix it. Please?"

"I will, Mom. Also, gross."

"And much like I said to your father, do you have to keep pointing that thing at my face?"

"Double gross. I'm trying to make magic with this camera. You could be a star someday."

"Your dad gave me those lines too."

"If you reference your sex life one more time, I'm changing the locks," Andy joked.

"So, you're still working on those home videos of yours? What was that word you used again? Flogging?"

"Video blogging, Mom. Some people call it vlogging. I've told you that about as many times as you've brought up horror stories about Dad's junk."

"Vlogging, yes. Now *that* sounds like something you get a virus from," Mom said, flipping another page in the wrinkle-filled magazine.

"Well, it might sound weird, but lots of people like this day-in-the-life, voyeuristic crap on the Internet."

"People watch...this?" Mom asked, alternating her pointer finger between her face and Andy's camera.

"Yeah, if I put this video up, we'd have a stalker in no time. People watch anything. There's a cornucopia of information spanning human history available at our fingertips, and everyone's busy watching everyone else's boring life all the time."

"Well, can I see this vlog when it's done?"

"Yes, when one of these passes my rigorous set of quality standards, I'll put it up. And if you're still alive by then, you'll see it."

The two, reverting to their morning breakfast rituals from Andy's childhood, performed juice pouring and toast making like they hadn't skipped an egg beat. Other than the scattered resin statues and increasing piles of toys, the decor didn't change much. The house looked like it was still in the 1950s with its droll color schemes,

ANDY GETS CONNED

lead-based paint, and clear lack of female input; the only estrogen this place saw since then was Mom's. Andy's diet didn't evolve since then either, as he now munched on ginger snaps and poured an entire box of cereal into a party punch bowl. For Andy, the serving suggestions were exactly that—suggestions only. Then chomping down on a thousand calories of delectably dyed sugar, Andy glanced at a pile of letters near Mom's spicy publication.

"My mail, I presume," Andy said, gesticulating with a ladle-sized spoon and grabbing the letters. "Oh, and look, it's already open. Did you do this or was it the creepy mailman again?"

"Oh hush, of course it was the new mailman. Well, he opened them first, and then I looked. He accidentally delivered these to my address this morning. Handsome guy, but he didn't know we had a separate mailbox for my apartment above the garage."

"Handsome? He reads our mail! Please don't tell me you tried to get his number."

"Tried? I *did* get a number—for his phone and bank account. He's too young to date, but your Momma still has the moves!"

"Okay, good. So, is anything in this stack worth opening a third time then?"

"Only this one," Mom said, sliding the top letter in front of Andy's sugary feast. "You're lucky I'm here. Now we can celebrate your big day together."

"What is it?" Andy asked, snatching the letter and proceeding to read it aloud: "You are invited to a special luncheon for your fine service at Bumble Ridge High

School. Please respond by...blah blah blah, shut your stupid letter face, I don't care."

"That's not what it says."

"I'm not interested. No pomp and circumstance for me. How's this a big day, Mom?"

"Read the bottom."

"We hope to see you at the school's budget-pending celebration honoring your *fifth* year of service?" gulped Andy. "Five years? I can't believe it. I told myself this was temporary. Five years!"

"Don't you worry, dear; it is temporary. You're only six or seven more of these 5-year letters away from retirement like me," Mom said, as every muscle in Andy's body locked up worse than the time he tried yoga. "And that's when you can follow your real dreams like I did with the flower shop."

Powerless and frozen, Andy lost grip of his oversized cereal bowl. And it plummeted, shattering across the formerly clean floor. Andy's robot vacuums then beeped, activating their fluid suction modes like a small island's tsunami warning. But Mom acted quickly, lifting her feet as an udder's worth of liquid lactose flowed across the tile.

"Andy, what's wrong?"

"Nothing," he said, still immobilized. "Nothing at all."

"There's a bowl of cereal on the floor, and you're not hyperventilating. Something is very wrong."

"No, it slipped, that's all," said Andy, shaking out of his trance. "I have to go. I'm even later now. I'm fine—late and fine, but I'll see you tonight, okay?"

"Do you want me to drive you to school?"

"No need. Why don't you relax while you watch the bots clean up? And leave a note in my room to finish your computer after work so I don't forget. I'll get her patched up and purring tonight, I promise."

"I'd love that."

"You'll be back to your online dating in no time. And therefore, out of my business in no time," joked Andy.

Andy kissed Mom's cheek and rummaged through the cardboard blocks until locating his backpack and missing shoe. His eyes then darted to the kitchen counter, focusing on a brown paper bagged lunch with the name 'Andy' written on it. Gussied up with a variety of markers, crayons, and dazzling rhinestones, the bag's exterior appeared as if Mom had blasted it with a craft store shotgun. He peeked inside, and its set of glued-on googly eyes spun around like two detached corneas at a sarcasm festival. With Andy's pain now paused by the bag's contents, his face beamed with childlike giddiness.

"Cheese curls?" Andy asked, then hugging Mom as tightly as possible without breaking her bones. "And these are Nielsen's, aren't they?"

"You bet. The only cheese curls fit for a king," recited Mom, reenacting the commercial Andy listened to on repeat as a child. "Fresh from the factory this morning."

"I love you, Mom...almost as much as these cheese curls," Andy said with a grin, putting on his extra-large hiking backpack never used for actual hiking.

With breakfast banter now behind him, Andy was off to school using a methodology incorporating a little bit of efficiency and a lot of avoiding the public. While duration and sidewalk smoothness both played a part in his preferred path, another factor was far more important—his chances of saying something stupid that he'd regret for days. He also avoided all dogs in case one would smell the processed meat scent that Andy's pores seemed to naturally produce. Though the detours added minutes to his morning skate, they were necessary; five years of perfecting this path gave Andy solid odds of a commute without any hospital visits, therapy sessions, or mindless chats about the weather.

Now gaining minutes back with a risky shortcut through the beekeeping company's parking lot, Andy was only a few seconds late. So he picked up the pace, skating down his school's sidewalk lined with science fair projects that nerds made over the break. After passing poster boards and some town yokels celebrating that Bumble Ridge High literally kept science out of the classroom, Andy blasted up the wheelchair ramp.

"Listen, all you clueless crusaders," shouted Andy, heading to Hell. "Evolution's real, the Earth's not flat, and using deodorant is highly suggested in this day and age."

Andy swung open the doors and rolled through as the school bell rang, security bars then slamming shut in front of a furious yokel crowd. Screams of 'I ain't no monkey' now muted behind him, Andy rocketed past the foreign exchange students getting their extra-invasive safety pat-downs at the entrance. Totally mismanaged, such defense spending took up 90 percent of the school's budget despite its crumbling architecture, underpaid staff, and scribe-copied textbooks from the 1400s. Seconds before the bell stopped blaring down the asbestos-lined hallways, Andy knew that his life was at risk. But the building's condition and fuming mob were nothing compared to Andy's biggest concern right now—what his students would do to his coffee cup without supervision.

Undoubtedly, the longer he left his students alone, the more likely his coffee cup would be slathered with laxatives, psychedelics, and whatever animal pooped in the schoolyard that morning; Andy couldn't mess around or else he'd have a far nastier mess on his hands, in his mouth, and coating every square inch of his desk. But perhaps even more worrying, the disturbing scent of vanilla protein bars now filled the hall. And this flooded Andy's brain with memories of juvenile jocks and beefy bullies from his pestering past. With Andy's summer now over, his next level of Hell was seconds away from starting...and minutes away from becoming even more unbearable than the last five years combined.

CHAPTER 2

"Mr. Gordon never misses class," said Emily in her seat, nodding enough to almost start a friction fire in her turtleneck sweater. "I'm sure he'll arrive any second, and we're legally required to stay here until he shows up or someone tells us he's dead. Or at least severely injured. And anyone who gives me a hard time about that will also wind up either dead or severely injured! Got it?"

Completely ignoring her threats, a pack of students scurried from their gum-covered desks to the exit. But Emily remained seated, still protecting the science fair project between her legs—a caged cricket with impeccable comedic timing. The front four rows of students escaped without issue, Billy and Bobby going first. Then went Barbara and Britney followed by Bentley and Bradley. Yes, most parents in the area seemed to be pretty dead set on first names starting with the letter B. This was intentional, of course, in hopes of increasing their kids' chances of landing jobs at the local beekeeping company, Bee's Needs. Shockingly, this tactic proved to be successful. Such odd hiring practices at Bee's Needs, though unethical, created a hive camaraderie within the business and town. Over the past 20 years, this company provided enough employment to nearly wipe out Bumble Ridge's record-breaking rates of welfare, crime, and hopelessness. So the town put up with B names for the company's pun-filled promotions—it meant that their kids could avoid perpetual poverty, after all.

Jockeying for their exit, Barney, Betty, Bernie, Bailey, and Barry blocked the door as if they were cholesterol clogging an artery. All were soon pushed apart like an angioplasty, however, by the bulldozer-sized, albino student B-Fred; he was perhaps the most blatantly stupid example of the strict B-naming policy. B-Fred now finding himself under public scrutiny yet again, plowed through the crowd while shaking his maracas in a Native American headdress and clopping in a pair of Dutch clogs. Likely a result of only skimming last week's school email, B-Fred had misread 'Cultural Appreciation Day' as 'Cultural Appropriation Day' and dressed accordingly. Thus, B-Fred headed for his locker to fetch new clothes, and the rest of Andy's B students successfully skedaddled. With nobody blocking them, the defiantly-named teens in the back now had their chance to escape an education that they desperately needed.

Marcus was next to try and skip out early, tightly gripping his portable whiteboard containing a mix of dystopian fiction quotes and basketball plays. As he walked, Marcus spun the dry-erase board atop his black-tipped fingernail like a lanky, Gothic grave trotter.

ANDY GETS CONNED

"Later, Em," he said, as whiteboard shavings rained down from his sharpened fingernail to the floor. "You coming, Fran?"

Marcus then crossed in front of Andy's desk containing *Rejects & Reptiles* figures and his biohazard coffee cup. Fran closely followed, trying to slink out under the radar. Since Fran was a 'little person' in size and age having skipped ahead two grades in school, she easily ducked behind her morbid meat-shield Marcus. Though students assumed Fran was a genius, she relied more on stealth for her success. Yes, Fran often used outside-the-box sneaking to hide in boxes and snap incriminating pictures of her teachers—pictures often with goats. Therefore, Fran's tiny size had led to a bevy of blackmail that'd shame most countries' spy bureaus.

Just then, Andy ran in with his hard drive-filled backpack that bounced enough to turn his spine into powder. His skateboard and stack of papers were also under attack, both tucked in his armpits and drenched from the physical excursion.

Andy immediately morphed into teaching mode, first trying to tell his class to sit down. But because of the jog, this command came out as some heavy panting and brief finger pointing instead. Then Andy plopped his rump onto the desk, one inch away from lodging a dozen dwarf figures up a mineshaft where they'd find no gold. No emergency proctologist needed, Andy folded the moist papers as Fran and Marcus sat back down.

"Yes! I knew you'd show up today," Emily boasted, tapping the cricket cage between her legs like bongos. "I do believe that means a certain somebody named Emily just won 10 bucks, five from each of you fools. Now pay up or feel the pain."

"Here," Marcus said, taking cash from his studded, black wallet. "I look at this dire loss of income as a chance to try fasting."

"Thank you," Emily said, taking the money. "But what about your underage lover?"

"She's 16 and way more promiscuous than me," said Marcus. "Lay off."

"Hey, Em? Can I pay you back later?" Fran asked with a grin. "I'm *short* on cash."

"Keep it!" said Emily, erupting into a snort-filled guffaw. "Your puns are priceless."

"No fair," Marcus said, back to doodling more basketball plays and decomposing pigeons on his dry-erase board. "Oh wait, it's cool. I stopped caring."

"Here you go, Mr. Gordon," Emily said, handing him an entire ream of paper with a staple through it.

"Please, Emily, call me 'Andy.' And what are you handing me right now?"

"It's the paper due next month," Emily said.

"How'd you even know what this was supposed to be about?" asked Andy, flipping through the tome. "And am I seeing Wacky Will references on every page?"

"I have my ways. And, yes, you are seeing that. But can we move on?"

"Okay, that was pretty cryptic. Anyway, good morning to the three of you today," Andy said, banging a mini battle-axe on the desk and expecting a tumbleweed to blow through his classroom. "So, all the B students left because I was late, I presume?"

"They sure did," Emily confirmed. "Does that mean that they'll miss the first quiz, drop out of high school, and wind up as underpaid sex workers?"

"I like the way you think. But I'm afraid I have some bad news, Emily."

"Oh no! The research paper sucked didn't it? Please let me rewrite it during lunch. I'll make it twice as long and three times as good! Don't make me hate myself more than I already do. I cut myself. You don't want me to cut myself more, do you?"

"No no, the paper looks like another A plus to me, but there isn't really a quiz today," Andy said, now folding his papers into airplanes. "I only sent the email threat so everyone would review last year's material and be ready to go. Plus, I was hoping the real slackers would get scared and switch to the other history teacher instead."

"What? No!" Emily said, as Marcus and Fran high-fived in the back. "I have razor blades in my desk, and I'm willing to use them."

"There's no way you got razors through security without a bribe, so I'm calling your bluff. But I do have some news that'll cheer you up. As per the school's new requirements, I will be offering bonus points to help push you through Bumble Ridge High," Andy said, then clearing his throat. "Yes, I said bonus points!"

Before Andy finished his offer, B students surged back into the room all at once. Pushing and shoving, the group now competed for bonus points like a Black Friday brawl. Some particularly desperate students even crawled in through the window.

"We're on the second floor," Andy said, raising his eyebrows. "How'd you do that?"

"There's a big pile of us on the ground out there," strained Bertha, clawing herself up and kicking away the B students below her.

Now with about half the class back and the other half injured outside, Andy zipped to his school phone near the window. After entering a sequence of verification pin codes, credit card numbers, and mothers' maiden names for his entire family tree, Andy monitored the inevitable lawsuits unfolding outside.

"Nurse Rosie, Andy here. How's the infirmary treating you today?" he asked.

"It's been a rough five minutes, but I'm still vertical and breathing," she relayed through the phone like a warzone walkie-talkie. "What can I do you for? Need some more ointment for that thigh chafing?"

"Nope, that's all taken care of, thank you. But we do have a failed human pyramid under my window at the moment. Looks pretty bad too."

"That's the third one this morning. You told them about the extra credit mandate, didn't you?"

"You bet. So they'll probably need some stitches. Oh, and when you're out there, you might want to tell the anti-science mob that you're injecting thoughts and prayers into their kids instead of medicine. Those folks look like the type who'd torch a car."

"Thanks, bud. Over and out!"

ANDY GETS CONNED

Andy hung up the phone and then inspected the future of America in front of him—his unmemorable section of B students all texting memes to each other. Such peace only lasted seconds, soon interrupted by B-Fred barreling back in the room and still clonking his clogs in a mildly offensive manner. Shockingly, he forgot his locker combination.

"I figured bonus points would get you all back here," said Andy, gliding a paper airplane to Emily. "So, with the new requirements, I've devised a fun way to shoehorn bonus points into my class. I need these paper permission slips signed and back to me A.S.A.P. for an extra credit field trip coming up. And here's how I'm spinning it: Our country's pop culture is an important part of history, so I'm taking you to a dorky convention with comic books and fantasy games. That's right, we're going to *Rejects & Reptiles* Con, everybody! Please though, if anyone asks, tell them we're all going to the Bumble Ridge smart-people museum, okay?"

"Mr. Gordon?" Emily asked, her hand in the air.

"It's Andy."

"Okay, Mr. Andy. Didn't we already use the smart-people museum excuse when we went to see all those mutant movies last year?"

"You're right. Change of plans. We'll have to go with the old Colonial Williamsburg trick then."

"Two questions, Mr. Andy! First, what if our parents ask us about what we did?"

"Then tell them you saw a bunch of sad people wearing funny hats. What's your other question?"

"Will the colonists provide razor blades, or should I just bring my own?"

"That's up to you and your anxiety, Emily. But I say bring extra to be safe."

Andy then threw another plane at student B-Fred whose mature body implied he had been failing the 12th grade under at least three different Presidencies. Theories spread that B-Fred existed long before the Bee's Needs naming trick, and that he retroactively added a B to his real name 'Fred.' Though Andy couldn't know for sure, the music blasting from B-Fred's headphones attached to a dusty boombox seemed to verify this suspicion. And B-Fred's tattoos such as 'Boo Ya,' 'Tubular,' and 'Enslave the Whales' came as close as possible to proving Andy's hypothesis—the last one a miscommunication with the tattoo artist, everyone hoped.

"Okay, so last year we covered everything from the Sumerians to the Roman Empire, focusing on their forms of entertainment. Then we compared that with modern pop culture, which seemed to keep you from burning the school down. So this year, I'd like to discuss the chunk of time starting with Rome, centered on weaponry and war tactics of our ancestors. I've already cleared my sword replicas with security and got approval to bring them in, so we can role-play now," said Andy, unloading a dagger and gladius from his backpack. "While most of these have been collected from my Renaissance Fair trips, we can still use our imagination and act like they're legit. I'll also show you real battle formations with the action figures on my desk. And fair warning: Silly voices will be used during the instruction, okay? So prepare yourselves for a semester of death, destruction, and rivers of blood—you know, some light material for once."

"I'm listening," said Marcus.

"Now please show me that I haven't let you down, and let's review Roman history a bit first," said Andy. "As we learned, the Roman Empire once had a great deal of power, but still failed anyway. What were some of the factors of its collapse?"

Fran, in awe that she had time to raise her hand before Emily beat her to the punch, hesitantly lifted her index finger. In the only way she knew how, this was her pint-size participation.

"Yes, Fran?" called Andy.

"Didn't you say that clowns were involved?" she asked, playing with the camera around her neck. "Circus clowns who ate a lot of carbohydrates and bread?"

"Um, not exactly, but close. You're thinking of the phrase 'bread and circuses,' I bet. That expression refers to all the distracting spectacles and free food Rome's government gave out that sped up the downward spiral. Want to take a stab at the question, Marcus?"

No, Marcus definitely didn't want to take a stab at anything that wasn't a deceased rat in his basement. Though after a quick hair flip, revealing his red contact lenses and black eyeliner, he managed to summon a few mumbled words.

"Did they spend too much money on their robot data plans?" asked Marcus. "I bet robot data plans were pretty brutal back then."

"Not even close," said Andy. "Your shot, B-Fred. Why'd the Roman Empire collapse?"

"Trick question. You did it!" blurted B-Fred, as Fran snapped a picture of Andy's stunned face.

"Me? I started the downfall of Rome? Okay, Emily. Should I tell them or you?"

Emily, now finished correcting some of Andy's questionable punctuation on the permission slips, fidgeted in the seat. Her caged cricket then experienced an earthquake as Emily bobbed up and down, waving her hand like an excited windshield wiper.

"I know, Mr. Andy! I know," she squealed. "The Roman Empire fell because it overextended its war efforts and became too decadent for its own good."

"Wonderful, Emily!" Andy exclaimed.

"And *that's* when the robots came and ripped out their bureaucratic spinal cords," Emily added.

"Damn," said Marcus. "I was about to say that."

"Okay, so the main topic of last year was clearly forgotten. Do any of you pay attention?" asked Andy, sinking back down and almost sending a horde of goblins into his rectal caverns. "Do any of you care?"

"I care when you talk about those zombies on your tie and your bleak social life," Marcus said, still fixated on his board. "And the robots, obviously."

"Well that's not good enough, Marcus. All the dorky parts of my lessons are supposed to help you learn the material. You're missing the point," said Andy, shifting back on his feet and pacing. "That's not what school's for. That's not why I'm here."

ANDY GETS CONNED

"Why *are* you here?" Marcus asked.

Andy froze dead in his tracks. Then his eyes opened wide, staring at the floor tiles and wishing that some type of trap door would open up and allow for immediate escape. Bottomless pit? Poisonous snake room? A chamber filled with every woman who turned him down and put him in the friend zone? He would have preferred any alternative at this point.

"Well, I. That's an excellent question, Marcus. Did everyone hear Marcus's excellent question?" asked Andy, stalling for time. "I'm in this room talking to you right now because, uh, the American dream? You know, if you don't learn from history, you're doomed to repeat it. My dad always said that to me, and now I'm saying it to you because you're the closest, goddamned things to kids I'll ever have. Oh, what's the point? I'm just preparing you for dead-end jobs like mine, working as a glorified high school babysitter. And I did this for five years? Five years? Well I'm definitely doomed if I keep repeating this stupid mistake! Doomed, Andy! Doomed!"

Andy collapsed into his chair, facing an audience armed with smartphones ready to make his breakdown go viral in the exact way he didn't want. For the first time, Andy had been speechless in front of class. For the first time, Andy's brain had pictured his inevitable future. For the first time, Andy had seen most of his students' eyes paying attention. Stationary and lifeless among a transfixed audience, Andy gazed forward with only one faint sound in the entire room—Emily's cricket with disturbingly perfect comedic timing.

"What a natural performer! There's no way that I'm losing the science fair!" proclaimed Emily, bursting from her seat. "I mean, are you okay, Andy? Uh oh. Mr. Gordon? You're really triggering my anxiety right now. I don't want to have to win over a new teacher. Mr. Gordon? Andy? Andy!"

CHAPTER 3

Deep within the confines of Andy's classroom coffin, time screeched to a halt. His mind had overloaded even more than the school's cattle separator hallways, and he slipped into a meditative state. Yes, it was here that Andy repeated his unhelpful mantra—every conceivable swear word in the history of human speech.

"Will this be on the next test?" asked B-Fred. "If it is, I'll do great on this one! My parents taught me all these words a long time ago."

"Not now, B-Fred," groaned Andy.

This was no career. This was no life. Despite his best efforts, Andy couldn't inspire the youth like his father did for him. He took all Dad's best bonding tactics like history show marathons while role-playing the fun parts, yet saw no success. His dad's accurate British accents, his educational parody songs about Presidents, his puppet plays of colonists killing natives in the Trail of Felt—nothing seemed to work with today's generation. Tragically, Andy's attempt at following in his father's footsteps had ended with a trip into a tar pit, as reality struck him like a shovel to the face.

"What am I doing here? Five years. Five damn years?" Andy muttered, slamming his head onto the fake oak desk and continuing his conversation. "None of you learned anything, did you?"

"That's not true, Mr. Gordon," said B-Fred.

Andy tilted his head back up, then shifting it sideways like a pet processing weird noises it never heard before.

"Is that so?" asked Andy.

"Yeah, your historical nutrition lesson made me big and strong," said B-Fred, as he pulled a half-unwrapped butter stick from his desk and downed it with the speed of a hot dog-eating champion. "Well, mostly just big."

Andy watched in astonishment as B-Fred plunged another stick in his yapper and swished that churned breakfast around like mouthwash. After a glance left and right, B-Fred crammed the wrapper into his mouth too. And the more he pushed it in, the more fatty liquid squirted out from his lips like a popcorn butter dispenser.

"Butter. You just ate butter," Andy said, blankly. "I'm getting paid to teach students how to eat butter. Okay, class! Andy needs a long vacation. I'm thinking a room with some padded walls and a straitjacket would do the trick. Maybe my bunkmate could show me how to make decorations with human skin. Anyway, Emily, could you do me a favor and put a sign on my door saying all my classes are cancelled?"

"Anything for you, Andy. Anything...for bonus points," said Emily with a wink.

ANDY GETS CONNED

"Enjoy your day, everyone! Enjoy your life while you still can," Andy said, loosening his zombie tie.

Andy's head, now dropping quicker than his cereal bowl did that morning, smashed directly into the dwarven desk battalion with a bruising thud. Not missing this time, one of the dwarves implanted itself right between Andy's pensive eyes. The class dispersed far faster than they had during any fire drill, and Andy observed their departure from the corner of his tortured corneas. Trailing behind, B-Fred then dashed out with the boombox in his left hand and a few butter sticks in his right. Even stranger, Andy spotted a new object strapped to B-Fred's back upon exit—a baby carrier loaded with an actual, breathing baby.

Having no clue how B-Fred hid a kid the entire time or who was willing to procreate with him in the first place, Andy continued his descent into insanity. Fortunately, only three student witnesses remained—Emily, Marcus, and Fran. The trio then tiptoed to Andy's desk. And Emily's cricket tunneled under its cardboard tube, sensing the teacher's impending derailment. After Emily rested her cricket cage on Andy's desk and the cricket carved his Last Will into the plastic, she removed a pastry box from her backpack. And like a dessert goddess from the sky, she placed a pink-frosted cupcake in the middle of Andy's dwarven manger scene on his desk.

"We come bearing gifts for our favorite teacher," said Emily. "I made this cupcake from scratch this morning. If you're going to wash it down with something though, you better not use your coffee cup. All those B letter students are really disgusting."

"I drew you as a Grim Reaper crushing the principal's skull," said Marcus, presenting his whiteboard filled with red marker blood.

"And I'm taking a picture of you getting both those gifts so you can remember the good memories," Fran said, capturing the moment with her camera. "It's the *little* things that count, right?"

"We're sorry if we drove you crazy," said Emily, as she snatched her cricket cage and backed away to the door with Marcus and Fran. "If you completely snap, please give your three favorite students a heads up. We'd like to skip school whenever you finally drive a tank through this place, okay?"

Avoiding any sudden movements, Emily shut the door and crafted a sign for the last bonus points she might ever earn from Andy Gordon. Minutes passed, then a few more. And before Andy knew it, his quiet and low-key meltdown had morphed into a much-needed nap—surprisingly without consequence. Nobody had ratted him out, nor did anyone ignore Emily's cancellation sign and bother the hibernating headcase. Yes, in another first for his career, Andy's students had managed to follow directions exactly as written.

As Andy slumbered, the stench of vanilla protein bars grew stronger than before and a man cloaked in black crept into the room. With a ski mask obscuring his face and B-Fred's baby carrier in hand, the man slinked past Andy. And he placed his drooling delivery upon a student's desk in the front row. The man then grinned, his teeth beaming through his ski mask with choppers so white that they looked like they belonged in a denture catalog. When another bell rang and the man rushed out, Andy reached up where his alarm clock would be back at home and swung downward. No snooze button to be found, Andy's palm pulverized the dwarven manger scene instead. And pink cupcake frosting splattered around the room as the bell kept ringing.

"Fourth period?" questioned Andy, raising his head and revealing a plastic, dwarven unibrow. "Was I really sleeping that long? No way!"

Andy sniffed his frosted finger and licked it off, the concept of finding unknown sugar substances on his hands not all that strange to him. Shaking off the face dwarves as the bell ended, Andy removed an anti-bacterial wipe from his desk drawer and cleaned off the drying dessert catastrophe. Seconds later, the piercing cries of what sounded like a newborn baby filled Andy's ears. His eyes then confirmed what he heard, focusing on a familiar baby carrier currently teetering in the front row.

"And *now* I see a baby. Okay, time to go," Andy said, collecting his backpack and skateboard while heading for the exit. "Hey, brain! Out of all the things you could conjure up, you made a baby mirage? Enough's enough. Tonight, I look for a new job!"

The baby's bawling worsened in severity. Though Andy knew he had a detailed imagination, this was far too real to be fake. Plus, with his warped head, any baby hallucination would have been a hell of a lot cooler; his mind would have whipped up a newborn equipped with octopus tentacles or one with weaker lungs that wouldn't spoil every movie theater experience. This had no chance of being Andy's brainchild.

"Hmm. Maybe I should check."

Andy shuffled closer to the likely-existent infant and made a cross with his fingers just in case. He then noticed a butter stick in its albino mouth, adding even more authenticity to the child. Though Andy had given up on having kids, knowing they'd break his gaming statues and inherit his mental illness, this one was kind of cute.

"Wow. This is strange. I guess butter really does make everything better, even babies."

Protection mode in full swing, Andy tucked his skateboard under an arm and leaned in to aid the triglyceride-filled crier. Quite familiar with the effects of eating too much butter at a young age, Andy had to act fast. So he picked up a pacifier near the kid's foot. And then he prepared a replacement procedure way safer than the baby's predictable double bypass.

"Who's the cutest little butter baby I know? Is it you? Yes, it's you," Andy sang, popping its pacifier back in. "There we go. No need to attract any more attention."

Possibilities filled Andy's brain as to where this kid came from. Elaborate prank? Forgetful B-Fred? Irrefutable truth that storks do, in fact, deliver babies and even they suck at their jobs? Regardless, Andy figured that few would ever believe he found a buttered, abandoned baby. So he activated his skateboard camera, recording the kid's innocent coos.

"Hello. If you're watching this, you're likely one of my friends, relatives, or potential jury members in a kidnapping trial. But here's what happened. I just found a baby next to my desk at Bumble Ridge High, and I have no idea where it came from," Andy said, tickling the baby's greasy chin. "Hey, kiddo. What are you doing here? Say 'hi' to the camera and all the people who probably think I'm doing something really illegal."

As if already trained in the 'stranger danger' process, B-Fred's baby belted out a wail. And it was so loud that it even ruined the mood for all cockroaches in the basement trying to 'get some.' Launched by such a scream, the pacifier flew like a popped wine cork at light speed. Then it ricocheted off of a Wacky Will poster promoting accordion lessons, shot straight through the windowpane, and struck a poor cat outside.

"Hey, I can't give you your butter back, but I can give you the next best thing," Andy said, fetching a spoon from the brown lunch bag in his backpack. "Here, baby, let's have a snack together."

Andy scraped some cupcake frosting from his desk with the spoon and piloted it into the baby's mouth. Appeased by sweets, the baby giggled. After swallowing and running out of its flavor distraction, however, the baby went back into full bullhorn mode immediately.

"You probably shouldn't have too much of this junk. How about some physical contact instead? Babies love physical contact, right?"

Recording with one hand, Andy scooped up the bundle of tears and rocked it with the other. Andy didn't know why this felt familiar, but this was just like Mom did to him...until her back gave out one week after birth. Yes,

Andy soothed the baby as it pressed its head into him like a form-fitting, memory foam mattress and fell asleep within seconds. Though Andy's parental instincts only emerged when raising virtual pets and leveling up video game characters, he could see why these little humans had such power over others. Its soft skin, its radiating joy, its humorously disproportionate body parts—all eased Andy's troubles as the baby latched onto his zombie tie and cuddled with his squishy bosom.

Not a second later, supersized student B-Fred tore back into the room with his intimidating clog stomps. And he slammed the door right behind him. Signaled by another ear-piercing shriek, the baby's nap was now over. This not only sent Andy into a worse panic, but also ruined the basement cockroach coitus yet again.

"So you took my baby!" fumed B-Fred somehow louder than the newborn wails. "Hey, everybody! My teacher took my baby!"

"Um, yes, I *do* have a baby in my arms, but I didn't take it. You're angry and probably don't see the nuance of that argument so I'll stop. But congratulations, B-Fred! This sucker's real cute. The resemblance and butter consumption are uncanny!" spurted Andy, searching for an acceptable excuse as to why he was recording a stolen, lubricated baby. "I understand that this probably looks bad. This looks really bad, doesn't it?"

"Yeah, it does, and you're gonna pay. Good thing that guy dressed in black out in the hallway gave me advice on how to deal with a baby taker. I say we settle this like adults, Mr. Gordon."

ANDY GETS CONNED

Outside, student Fran peeked her head from the bushes next to Bumble Ridge High's ancient air-conditioning unit, The LegionnAires 2000. Known as the best hiding spot at school after cops found three corpses there, teens came to the place to escape their educational prison. But Fran and Marcus went near this bacteria-breeding technology for a different reason. Yes, they hid here to French kiss and learn about the birds and the bees—all of the dead birds and bees stuck in the school's thorny bushes topped with barbed wire.

Then possibly teaching his students more than he had in five years, Andy gave Fran and Marcus a crash-course in physics as he plummeted from the second-story window. Setting off the school's security alarm and electronic voice telling him to comply, Andy somersaulted twice and tore through each layer of the school's suicide-prevention nets. Fran and Marcus then paused their rigorous game of tonsil hockey and fled for safety. Now out of control at free-fall speed, Andy hit the ground and decimated that bush with a seismic thump. And he left a butt-shaped, impact crater in the Earth's crust, wiping out an entire colony of ants.

"See you tomorrow, you baby taker," said B-Fred from the window.

"Cool," said Marcus, running. "We almost died."

When Andy popped his scratched face from the bushes, his skateboard camera followed the same path down and struck his bruised cranium yet again. Not one to waste such a personal tragedy without capturing it on video, Andy reached through the splintery bush and grabbed his recording skateboard camera. Then he aimed it at his face, now with bits of leaf stuck to its bloody parts.

"Well, future Andy editing this, it could have been worse. Stay positive. Stay calm. At least B-Fred didn't shoot you, right?"

Suddenly, Andy spotted a large, round object thrust in front of his mouth. After a glance and quick double-take, Andy found himself beside local reporter Gail Ellerbach. And she was shoving a microphone right in his face.

"Gail Ellerbach, reporting live from Bumble Ridge High's outdoor science fair and its breaking news. Here, history teacher Andy Gordon has been ejected from his classroom by a young student mother acting in self-defense. As described to me over the phone by an eyewitness with a dreamy voice, Gordon stole the child of student B-Fred Barner—an African American female in good academic standing and excellent health. Then Andy threatened to harm this mother if she opened her big pie-hole," Gail pushed, brushing off Andy's impact dust from her burgundy blazer and pants suit. "To make matters worse, as you just heard, Gordon expressed relief that B-Fred Barner didn't shoot him based on the color of her skin. So, what do you have to say for yourself, you damned kidnapping, prejudiced, participant in the persistent patriarchy?"

"What? B-Fred's a man! He's older and whiter than me! And I certainly didn't steal his kid!" shouted Andy. "Then I made a comment about his conflict-resolution skills—a comment that's justified because, you know, he threw me out of a freaking window."

"Our irrefutable evidence says otherwise. She only threw you out of that window because you threatened her life multiple times."

"Stop pushing this story, Gail, it's wrong. An albino man named B-Fred did this to me. It has absolutely nothing to do with race."

"Not according to our DNA results. Our crack team of experts found out that B-Fred Barner is .0027 percent African American."

"He's not a minority. If you go back far enough, a lot of us are a little black. You know, it's our lineage, our genetics, and our history!"

"You've seen it here, folks—it's a full-blown confessional. This bigot not only hates black people, but he's also preaching his Satanic religion to your kids. With his blood sacrifices and weird sex parties requiring masks, it's no wonder he riled up the protesting mob around Bumble Ridge High this morning."

"Okay, I may have ticked off that crowd, but everything else you said is incorrect. I'm guessing it's a slow news day, huh, Gail?"

"It was until this happened."

"So who's your source? I deserve to know the name of my accuser."

"As you can all see, this detestable teacher is dodging the question that he has no explanation for. And now he's making ridiculous demands."

"Why don't you go back to your captivating coverage of a high school science fair, Gail? One of those Honors kids might be able to show you how to make an intelligent argument. Of course, to you, logic's about as worthless as your online journalism degree."

"How dare you?" Gail exhaled, hurling her microphone to the ground like a lawn dart almost piercing Andy's crotch. "Damn, so close."

Though relieved he had escaped an outdoor vasectomy on TV, Andy saw his cruel reality rush back. Gail then lifted him by the shirt collar, kneeing him in the groin like a video game combo she learned in women's defense class. When he flopped downward atop a dense dandelion patch, he gasped for air. And he did it with such force that the weed's entire reserve of fluffy seeds found a new home in his lungs.

Knowing that he couldn't punch a woman even if she deserved it, Andy fled the scene as nobly as possible—a panicked crawl through prickly bushes along the school. This sharp growth, now treacherous since school landscapers abandoned it in the 1970s, tore Andy's flesh in what felt like a thousand small paper cuts. Fumbling through the thickest section and its collection of long-dead pets, Andy headed toward the light.

"I bet this is how serial killers decorate for Halloween," said Andy, passing by generations of Fidos and Fluffys. "Home, then a snack, and then a job search. No excuses. You can make it, Andy."

Seeing only one path to freedom, Andy hoofed it through the tunnel of thorns like a carwash of cat claws and dog teeth instead of brushes. As each agonized howl ejected one of the dandelion seeds he inhaled earlier, Andy charged and leapt through an opening. Flying through the air, Andy bit his lip and waited in breathless anticipation for the spongy grass to catch his fall—the reliable and spongy grass that was always there and had no reason not to be there. It wasn't there though, he discovered, as he splashed into a bubbling mud puddle the size of a pond. And, instantly, mud coated his body like a chocolate-dipped ice cream cone.

"I have to stay optimistic. It's only mud," he said, wiping his eyelids free of the substance that burned way more than mud should.

Andy reached for the tablecloth at an experiment station by his side, wrecking half a dozen baking soda and vinegar volcanoes in the process. Foam now exploded all around him. And he scraped off most of the mud from his watch, face, and hands, feeling more exfoliated than ever before. As Andy crawled up from the mud in desperate need of a Laundromat, science teacher Mr. Schmidt removed his PH reader from the water. Andy's colleague then turned to his students, all wearing white lab coats and safety glasses.

"And therefore, with the addition of a few hazardous chemicals, this once-safe dirt patch has become a dangerous mud mixture that can deteriorate the most durable objects known to man," Mr. Schmidt said monotonously, wiping off the electrode with a thick rag. "Steel, titanium, and even your grandma's fruitcake all have no chance against this extremely volatile and acidic concoction."

Mr. Schmidt's rag then disintegrated. Andy, hoping he hadn't ventured into nudist colony culture, rapidly patted his mud-coated clothes. Though its material gave off awful fumes, at least the fabric still existed.

"Oh good, you're still there. It'd take a lot of therapy to get over something like that," he said, punctuated by his two cufflinks plopping into the mud.

Andy's dismay then doubled, and a slight breeze chilled all of the areas of his body that usually receive no breeze. Then he looked down.

"Come on, I just checked a second ago!" Andy said, now only wearing his Wacky Will watch and a matching pair of tattered boxers.

Students then recorded the 'Chunky Mud Monster' with their phones, Andy getting a little more attention than he wanted. Predicting his boxers were one gust away from indecent exposure charges, Andy scanned the area for an emergency ensemble. Then he ripped two more tablecloths from the science stations beside him, wrapping both around his pear-shaped physique.

Two lumps of mud soon flew from behind the science students and splattered each of Andy's nipples. The third mud chunk struck Andy right on the nose, recoating his eyes and burning away all nostril hair. Though Andy couldn't see anything, the mud chucker pitched one last projectile at his target's groin. And then the assailant wiped his hands on a nerd's lab coat beside him, both laughing from the back row.

"I'm on your side, fellow nerds," grunted Andy. "Please stop! Disengage!"

As Andy struggled against this mucky ambush, the cheerful mud chucker elbowed his way through droves of dweebs. Monitoring his success with a set of blue eyes that could make a nun question her abstinence, hunk Nathan Hader had appeared. Not a wrinkle in sight on his clothes or face, his image could only be described as panty-throwing perfection. His chiseled cheeks met at a master craftsman-like chin, topped off with an alluring amount of goatee scruff that added mystery to the manliness. His long, shaggy hair amplified his irresistibility too, an aesthetic choice looking like a dog that chicks couldn't stop themselves from petting.

As Andy rubbed gunk from his eyes one last time, Nathan shook a ski mask and black clothes out of his lab coat into the puddle. And with one final cover-up cough, Nathan dropped Gail Ellerbach's business card into the mud as well. His evidence then corroded away as quickly as Andy's boxers, and he hid back behind Mr. Schmidt's class. After downing a vanilla protein bar from his lab coat, Nathan initiated his next attack.

"He poisoned our puddle. Get him, nerds!" rallied Nathan. "Hit him so hard that you hurt your fists!"

The science class, unleashing incalculable amounts of sexual frustration, stormed the mud puddle, hoisted Andy up, and tossed him aside. Soon landing, he rolled into the flowers outside Ms. Cartagena's Spanish class—these allowed her to teach words like 'narcisos' (tulips) and 'cardos' (thistle). Upon stopping, however, Andy learned an additional moneymaking vocabulary word that funded much of the school—'abejas' (bees).

"Oh good, bees!" Andy yelped, scrambling from the flowers onto his bare feet. "I come in peace, bees. Peace!"

Yes, Bumble Ridge High had received so many donations from Bee's Needs that the school planted loads of flowers in a symbiotic summer initiative. More bees meant more demand for beekeeping equipment, and that meant more jobs. But more bee numbers also resulted in something a little less beneficial for Andy, as he landed on an entire hive's worth outside the Spanish classroom.

Through the window, students gazed in awe that a large man could move so quickly covered in that many bees. Unfortunately for Andy, the students' awe turned to laughter. And their high pitch ridicule seemed to enrage the bees even more, leading to enough stings to take down a baby elephant. Though luckily for Ms. Cartagena, she could now teach her students three more items in Spanish today—'vencido' (defeated), 'hinchado' (swollen), and 'probable que muera solo' (likely to die alone).

Andy now running in circles and teaching the Spanish students many new swear words, his first day back after break had officially become worse than imaginable. Bee venom coursed through his body, and Andy collapsed, now looking more like a pin cushion than human.

After drifting in and out of consciousness, his eyesight waning, Andy awoke with two distorted, humanoid creatures in spacesuits above him. As these hazy creatures blasted away the bee menace with their vibrantly colored guns, Andy passed out yet again—now calmed. Whether he'd wake up as an alien test subject or zoo exhibit, at least he'd be free from his Earth bullies once and for all. At least he'd be anywhere other than here.

CHAPTER 4

Long after Andy's shocking assistance, his vision had improved from 'legally blind' to 'needs corrective lenses the size of telescopes.' Two fuzzy figures now stood above him in a blissful, white environment with some serious paranormal potential. Stinger toxins mixing with Andy's science fiction interests, he hoped that aliens had warped him to the medical bay. But then another option struck his mind—he could have died, now an active member of the afterlife. Gulping, with a 50-50 shot of responding to aliens or apparitions, he went with the more likely option.

"My name is Andy Gordon, resident of planet Earth, and I wish you no harm," he said, attempting a shaky yet respectful bow. "I am a human, a male, and not a big fan of things jammed up my anus, if you don't mind."

"Stop it, Andy! We don't have time for that. This is Nurse Rosie and the medical unit of Bumble Ridge High," she assured, ripping off her beekeeper suit and dabbing ointment on Andy's welt-covered forehead. "You were stung by a hell of a lot of bees out there."

Andy recognized the first figure's raspy voice—it was a sound that only 50 years of unfiltered cigarettes could make. Though Nurse Rosie had been hardened in the school trenches filled with mononucleosis, pubic lice, and body odor bad enough to peel paint, she hadn't seen wounds this gruesome since 'Nam. The second figure beside her remained silent as Andy felt an unwelcoming presence, thus suspecting it was a single woman his age. Still dazed and confused, Andy swayed atop the medical exam table in his school's infirmary. And Nurse Rosie added one last dot of ointment to the hundreds already adorning his numbed flesh.

"Wait, you're not aliens?" asked Andy.

"No, now stop. This is an emergency!"

"What about your cool laser guns?"

"Those were squirt guns, Andy!" Nurse Rosie said, lifting a yellow water gun from the floor. "My helper and I had to get those bees off you somehow. They're the kamikaze pilots of the bug world, you know. Now listen, you need to tell us if you're allergic to bees."

"No," Andy responded. "Nuts!"

"What? You really want a snack before you'll answer? Okay, whatever floats your boat. I'll go find you some nuts, but I still need to know if you're allergic to bees when I get back."

Nurse Rosie bolted through the swinging door as her assistant lunged at Andy. The assistant then pried Andy's mouth open with gloves that smelled like they'd been used for way grosser procedures throughout the morning. As quickly as she exited, Nurse Rosie burst back in the

ANDY GETS CONNED

room holding a canister of nuts. And then she emptied the entire container right into Andy's mouth.

"No, I meant I'm allergic to nuts!" Andy clamored in frustration, spitting nut chunks upon the assistant's face.

"In that case, you'll need this," Nurse Rosie said, jabbing an epinephrine shot deep into Andy's thigh.

Andy contorted with a yelp, certain that Nurse Rosie was reliving her war days of planting flags in enemy territory. Though the needle felt like it penetrated bone, Andy's forceful scream helped him in two ways; it not only removed the last nuts from his mouth, but it also ejected even more dandelion seeds from his lungs.

"Looks like you made it. Better lay off the dandelions though," Nurse Rosie said.

Riffling through the school infirmary's dusty drawers, she pushed aside shock therapy manuals, lobotomy pamphlets, and a bloodletting tool seemingly kept there since the 1900s.

"You're lucky too," she added. "You used the last epinephrine shot in supply."

Now able to see short distances, Andy noticed his new clothes that the medical staff had pieced together while he was unconscious. Constricting his chest was a Bumble Ridge High T-shirt four sizes too small, and a provocative cheerleading skirt barely covered his bottom. Plus, the disturbingly moist set of B-Fred clogs on his feet didn't help much either.

"Sorry, Andy. Nathan's reconnaissance mission to the Lost and Found didn't give us much to work with. You're wearing all that was left," said Nurse Rosie.

"I bet I'm gorgeous," Andy deadpanned.

"I'll go see if we have any more shots in reserve," said Nurse Rosie. "Hey, Nathan, keep an eye on Andy for a minute. I actually like this one, so make sure he stays happy and alive. If you have to choose, pick alive."

"My pleasure," Nathan said, as Nurse Rosie goose-stepped down the hallway. "More nuts, Andy?"

Andy shook his head with a little more panic than before, his vision now back to 20/20 despite sitting so close to screens throughout childhood. The manly goatee, the thick hair, the protruding abs so large they seemed to be ripping off his shirt to save women a step before intercourse—this second presence was no alien, ghost, or medical assistant at all. No, this was vanilla protein bar enthusiast Nathan Hader, winner of 'Most Likely to Get Laid' all three years in the 12th grade.

"If you don't like those nuts, I have a couple more you haven't tasted in a while," said Nathan, reaching for his zipper as his lips mischievously stretched from ear to ear. "Let's skip rubbing these on your coffee cup this time and go straight for the mouth."

"Nathan, you can't be here! I know you probably weren't paying attention when they used a big word like 'expelled', but you're not allowed in the school anymore."

"Mr. Gordon. Andy. My bitch," Nathan said, as he inched closer. "You think low grades and a year in high-security prison are enough to get rid of me?"

"Yes, I did actually."

"Nonsense. You'd be amazed at what you can do with super good looks."

"There's no way you can step foot on this property again. No damned way!"

"Principal Murray has a lot to hide here, you know. Cockroaches, asbestos, that delicious LegionnAires 2000 water fountain outside—how do you think he'd respond if a certain student threatened to leak those to the public?"

"First, that's an air-conditioning unit you're drinking from, and you probably should go to a hospital. And second, you've got to be kidding me!"

"Nope. All I have to do is help around this place for a year, and then I'll graduate. So, work pal, do you want my balls in your mouth now or after lunch?"

"This isn't possible," Andy gnarled.

"Oh, they'll fit. You'll just need to open your mouth real wide and—"

"No, you can't be back here. I know this place is barely providing an education, but there are still rules. I'm going to go give Murray a piece of my mind."

"You know you won't. I know you won't. And you know that I know that you won't because I just said that, so zip it, fatso. That's right—I'm going to get my diploma without any percussions at all."

"That's *repercussions*, Nathan," corrected Andy.

"Whatever, you damn nerd! I'm even getting paid for this right now! Every week, Murray's lining my pockets with a couple of crisp Benjamin Hitlers," said Nathan, pulling a 50-dollar bill from his pocket and waving it in front of his pearl-like teeth.

"Benjamin Hitlers? And you wonder why you didn't pass my history class," Andy scoffed and then grinned, now imagining a long-haired, manboobed Hitler flying kites in a thunderstorm.

"Yeah, yeah. I already know what you're going to say. 'Nathan, you didn't show up to class.' 'Nathan, you didn't hand in your work—'"

"Nathan, you caught the handicapped kid's wheelchair on fire!" finished Andy.

"You're overreacting."

"And then you brought a lion into the classroom," said Andy, as Nathan lunged toward the medical cabinet. "A really hungry one too!"

"That's enough blabbering, nerd!" Nathan raged, brandishing the bloodletting tool and methodically smacking it into his hand. "Do you know how hard it is to get into college or make money without a diploma?"

"Yes. I said the same exact thing when you were in class. Every year! Multiple times!"

"Yeah, *in class,* which we've already established I didn't go to, stupid. You tried to wreck my life, and now I get to do that to yours."

"You're aware there's another history teacher here you could have taken instead of me, right?"

"That's enough, nerd! The point is that it's your turn to suffer now."

"Well I'd love to see you top what happened today."

"I don't need to top today; I did today. And last time I checked, today's not even over yet."

Andy nervously shifted his weight on the exam table. Its sweat-lubed, sanitary paper sheet then slipped, sending him to a floor lined with secondhand tongue depressors.

ANDY GETS CONNED

Following, Nathan bent over and pulled back the bloodletting tool's spring mechanism like a cocked gun.

"Calm down, Andy," said Nathan. "I wouldn't want you to start crying like a...baby."

"What?"

"You know, a stolen baby."

"No, no you didn't! You kidnapped a kid to get revenge on a teacher who failed you? That's absurd."

"Kidnapped? Oh, please. I simply took a baby that wasn't mine."

"Yeah. So kidnapping, right?"

"No, kidnapping *wrong*," Nathan revised, as if communicating with a caveman. "It's a bad thing. It's why you're in trouble and B-Fred chucked you through the window. Geez, and you call me the dumb one here. Well guess what? This schmuck also tipped off the reporter. Oh, and then threw mud at your fat face, nipples, and groin in the puddle."

"Unbelievable. And I suppose you were behind the bee attack too?"

"No, that was just your normal bad luck there."

"Well I have harsh words for you, Nathan," Andy said, standing with the table's paper sheet stuck to his skirt. "And those words are this: I can't fight back because you'll sue me. And I can't tell on you because you're blackmailing Murray, but you still better not do anything else mean to me!"

Andy brushed past Nathan's shoulder, not hard enough to get sued of course, and fled to the door. Already second guessing how weak his exit line sounded,

Andy whipped up a clever quip to sneak in before he escaped—a coin of phrase that would totally put Nathan in his place. About to let out this verbal blitzkrieg, Andy pivoted back toward Nathan.

"Oh yeah, and Nathan, remember this," Andy hyped, taking a deep breath and door to the face as Nurse Rosie exploded back into the room.

"I found the mother lode in the bomb shelter," Nurse Rosie said, a large box of shots blocking her face as Andy flopped to the floor yet again. "Hey, where's Andy? And why's our new doorstop sound a lot like Andy?"

Andy awoke minutes later to Nurse Rosie and Nathan standing over him once more, his distorted vision this time from a concussion rather than bee stings. Nurse Rosie then lifted Andy's head forward, waving a cheese curl in front of his nose like smelling salts.

"Andy! Andy! I apologize for that whack to the noggin," Nurse Rosie said. "I guess I got excited. There were enough shots down there for a few months of bee attacks. But I'd be willing to shoot you up with another if you want some more nuts!"

"No, I think I'll pass!" Andy said scrambling to his feet, the tongue depressors and half-licked lollipops now fused to his hands. "Thanks for the help though."

"Just kidding, bud," she said. "I think I've done enough damage to you today. Why don't you go home and get some shuteye?"

"Thanks for saving my life," said Andy, gathering his backpack and skateboard from the ground. "I think I saw 30 years of me playing video games flash before my eyes."

ANDY GETS CONNED

"I'd be happy to give you some nuts for the road," said Nathan, wrapping his arm around Andy and leading him away. "Hey, Rosie, I'll walk the patient out and make sure he's okay."

"Sounds good," said Nurse Rosie, unloading enough needles to please every school junkie.

"I can take you to the exit if you'd like me to, sir. I really wouldn't want you to fall again," said Nathan, the doors then shutting behind him. "It'd be a pity if your wide load crushed any of your precious students. Or, to be more specific, any *two*."

"If you knew Fran and Marcus were in that bush, this is just as bad as the lion. You could have killed them! They didn't do anything to you. Leave them alone."

"They're too nice to you in class, so they're nerds as far as I'm concerned. You would've been fired if you wiped them out with your big butt, and it'd be worth it. You know, some co-literal damage."

"You mean *collateral* damage, and that's sick! You need help, Nathan!"

"Then why are you the one who's freaking out in a skirt?" asked Nathan, slamming Andy into a locker.

Every student in the hall then stopped, turning toward the lockers. And they all stared at the butch cheerleader wearing wood and lollipops from head to clog.

"If you think today was bad, then try imagining today...tomorrow," Nathan snarled. "And then today the next day after tomorrow. Hell, a whole month of todays! Maybe even 13 months of todays to make it a full year. You lose, Andy! You lose, nerd."

Now knowing the instigator of this destruction derby-like day, Andy scrammed on his skateboard while holding back a massive storm brewing in his tear ducts. Zooming as fast as possible, Andy passed crowds of students laughing at the skirt-bedecked skater. Nathan then joined in the mockery too, growing louder as the paper sheet attached to Andy's bottom waved in his wake like a half-assed surrender flag.

"Pretty quick for a fat guy," Nathan said to himself, chomping off a chunk of a vanilla protein bar. "I'm going to destroy your life more than your diet and genetics already have! A year of todays! A life of todays even! Just you wait, Andy. Just you wait...nerd."

CHAPTER 5

Making it home before the kid's size shirt exploded off his adult size body, Andy had survived his first day back to school and his first mental breakdown. Andy then changed clothes and, thanks to a technicality, completed one of his earliest dreams—taking a cheerleader's skirt off in his bedroom. After a shower washed away most of his failure, he put on some Wacky Will pajama pants and a matching T-shirt. He then began his new plan, scouring online job posts for anything even remotely relevant to his history degree. Predictably, hours later, he had only found more history teaching jobs and one opening for a tour guide at the local creationist museum.

"Okay, how about something that's *not* related to history then? Something without as many bullies. Something where I can surround myself with people who like me instead of throw me through windows," Andy said, tapping his wizard slippers on the plastic carpet protection mat by his computer. "Hmm, bartender? Nope, too many drunk people. Lumberjack? Nah, I'd rather keep my limbs connected to my body, thank you. A manager at Bee's Needs beekeeping company? No, I am not changing my name to B-Andy no matter how desperate I get, dammit! The quest goes on!"

Andy then flung a cheese curl in the air that gracefully landed on his tongue like a kid catching snowflakes. Yes, he had mastered the exact force needed to arc even the most coiled curl directly onto his taste bud runway. Only one tragedy of the night occurred when a curl broke apart in its ascent, colliding into his ceiling fan and raining cheesy particles upon the carpet. After declaring this disaster a 'manufacturing defect,' Andy applied to every high school history teacher job within a 50-mile radius just to be safe. Some of these schools seemed to have a few standards rather than Bumble Ridge High's whopping zero, after all. Now closer to changing employers, Andy sighed with relief and blasted his demented music. Then he celebrated through some upper body dancing in his chair, backed by Wacky Will's protest song "You Can Take This Ventriloquist Job and Shove It Up Your Ass."

With his wheels rolling around the plastic dance floor, Andy grabbed a sticky note and wrote 'Job Search' on it. Then he slapped that sucker above all other obligations on his wall despite throwing off the alphabetical order. When he reviewed the next sticky note from the top, however, Andy spotted a written addition that wasn't even drafted in his own handwriting.

"Fix your gorgeous mother's computer now because you love her a lot," Andy read from her flowery penmanship. "Be right there, Mom."

ANDY GETS CONNED

The chair bopping picked up pace, now documented with Andy's camera attached to a tripod on his desk. Perhaps some physical comedy could make a splash on the Internet, Andy thought; fat people dancing went viral before, so why not him? Right in the middle of boogying down from the waist up, Andy paused as somebody knocked on his bedroom door with increasing intensity.

Who could it be? Did Nathan come back for more? Did the anti-science yokels follow him home? Or maybe the pizza guy finally acquiesced to Andy's requests for bedside delivery? Expecting the worst, Andy scooted from his seat and switched to a fisticuffs stance like a boxer from the 1800s. Then he reached under the bed for his self-defense baseball bat—the inflatable, squeaky kind—and readied himself to bash whatever intruder or beast was about to enter his nerd cave.

"Andy?" Mom called through the door. "It's me. I know you're not in there with a lady, so open up."

"Hi," said Andy, opening the door as Mom greeted him with a tray of deli meats and Nielsen's Cheese Curls. "The snack fairy's here with some bribery treats. And all Andy needs to do to is fix her computer to get them."

"Let's go finish that up now. I was just on my way," said Andy, pointing to his desk. "Say 'hi' to the camera, Mom. I think I might upload this one, and that's no joke."

"One of your vlogs passed your test? What kind of odds are we talking about, dear?"

"A 99 percent chance."

"Hot damn," Mom said, waving to the camera. "That means I have to look presentable."

Mom pulled her shoulders back and pushed her chest forward, Andy mimicking her actions as a gag. The two then hammed it up for the camera, Mom making kissy faces as Andy held honey-baked ham slices to his eyes like well-glazed binoculars. With each trying to outdo the other, Mom went into a giggle fit upon seeing Andy wedge a cheese curl under his nose like a munchable mustache.

"I haven't seen this much meat since the gangbang at the steakhouse," said Andy, as Mom's guffaw spread to him like a humorous plague.

"That was too good not to put online."

"Warped minds think alike. I'll start editing the footage tomorrow. Right after I finish up your computer, of course. Let's go do that now," Andy said, interrupted by the downstairs doorbell. "If those are packages, which let's be honest they probably are, I won't open them until your computer's back to normal. I promise."

"I don't know if that will be necessary now, dear."

Zipping past Mom and her snack tray, Andy scooped up the cheese curl bowl and rotated in a circle like a retired discus thrower with a dad bod. A few curls then fell to Andy's floor, stopping on a rug of *Space Fightin's* robotic villain. Yes, the curl landed right in Droid Blitzer's mechanized, wooly mouth.

"Nice catch, Blitzer," Andy said, rushing downstairs.

"Don't say I didn't warn you, dear," said Mom.

A vibrating hum then emanated under Andy's bed. And Mom grinned, now with possible proof that her son was sexually active and owned some of the required equipment. But this optimism was conclusively squashed

ANDY GETS CONNED

when Andy's robotic vacuum R2CheeseDoodle emerged, heading toward its orange cleanup obligation.

Opening the door and peering down at the usual location of his packages, Andy saw no box-like structures at all. Instead sat a pair of women's work boots. After questioning if he did really order women's work boots in some sleep-deprived online purchase, Andy's eyes tilted upward. First Andy saw a sliver of unicorn socks peeking out around the ankle, then jeans protecting knees, thighs, and hips—you know, normal human stuff. His gaze continued past a tool-filled utility belt, buttoned flannel shirt, and long red hair while he prepared to grill her.

Just where did she put his packages? And why wasn't she more package-like herself? Nearly ready to erupt, Andy locked eyes with the mystery woman at his door. She made no sense, her face far too stunning to be a repair person and her tools far too worn to be a stripper. And then she uttered a statement that would boggle Andy's brain more than anything he had heard in his life.

"Hi," she said.

Andy gasped. Hi? What does that mean? What does she want? Is she a solicitor? A succubus? An undercover agent here to finally bust him for all those shows he pirated on the Internet? All extreme possibilities were up for consideration. Just who was this woman and where the hell were his packages? As thoughts zapped through Andy's synapses, he contemplated a number of responses that would make him look charming and suave.

"Hi," he said, then standing there for a solid eight seconds without vomiting or exchanging any other words.

Taking another shot, the woman advanced the conversation to new levels with a clarifying statement.

"Hi. I'm Tessa."

Andy jerked backward with a gasp, sending his cheese curl bowl up into the air. Then cheese curls rained down upon both him and Tessa, one landing in a patch of Andy's parted hair. As the last curl touched down upon the carpet, the rest of its snack companions had already met their formidable foe—Andy's second robotic vacuum assigned to downstairs duties.

"Hey, little guy," Tessa said, adjusting her thick-rimmed glasses and kneeling. "Does he have a name?"

"R2CheeseToodle," Andy barely peeped. "He's the sequel. His brother R2CheeseDoodle is upstairs."

"Hey, if you make a third, you could call him Three-Cheese-P-O. Okay, that was bad," Tessa said, picking up a cheese curl on the doorstep and holding it under R2CheeseToodle. "Wow, looks like you engineered the suction intake and made it stronger than the standard model. Nice work."

"Thanks," Andy cleverly replied.

"Okay then," said Tessa, now wondering where to place Andy on several spectrums based on his responses. "I better tell you who I am and why I'm here."

He knew it; it was a solicitor after all! Andy's senses reawakened as blood pumped back from body parts it had previously rushed to. And his shock turned to rage against this door-to-door wolf in dork clothing. With snarky quips, snappy retorts, and verbal abuse loaded, Andy inhaled and prepared his assault to eliminate this

ANDY GETS CONNED

non-package person from his property. There were better things to do, after all, like getting back to his *Space Fightin'* holiday specials that he did recently pirate.

Beating Andy to the punch, Tessa tried to defuse the situation with some follow-up details. Unfortunately, those details started sounding like a few preachy pitches that Andy heard at his door before.

"So," Tessa said. "I'm here to fix your—"

"My life with the word of Jesus, right?" Andy interjected. "Damn, you people don't quit!"

"Nah, actually I'm here to kill you and your loved ones," Tessa teased. "So, if you think about it, I'm less annoying than the Jesus people."

Andy chuckled, dropping his loaded insult arsenal and choosing playful banter instead. Somehow in a matter of seconds, Tessa had dismantled a defensive wall that took years to build.

"So is your family all in one spot, or will I have to hunt them down separately?" Tessa asked.

"Ah, a murderer, eh? Well in that case, come right in. I was on the market for a door-to-door slaughtering."

"I don't think I could kill anyone wearing Wacky Will pajamas though. Maybe we could pop a cap in your neighbors instead?"

"Are you real?"

"Let me start over. I'm Tessa. And I'm here to work on that pesky computer of yours."

"The name's Andy, and it's a pleasure to meet you, Tessa. But I think you have the wrong house. This must be some mistake."

"No mistake at all," Mom said, stepping over R2CheeseToodle. "Hi, Tessa. I didn't think you'd make it tonight. Your boss said you had a loaded schedule."

"Yeah, Bumble Ridge is teeming with malware these days, so we've been super swamped," said Tessa. "But my boss said you cracked jokes on the phone about giving her some bribery flowers. You made her laugh, so she bumped you up the list."

"Right, my bribery...jokes. Lovely," said Mom. "Oh, and don't mind the mess. I was trying to lure *somebody* down here with snacks to fix my computer. And that was after *somebody* had been tinkering with it for weeks—a certain *somebody* standing beside me."

"Right, the same *somebody* who gave you a place to stay when you got booted from the nursing home," Andy said, then grinning at Tessa. "She still doesn't get why strip shuffleboard tournaments are a bad idea."

"Yes, he's very caring," Mom advertised. "And a respectable high school teacher too."

"And the son of somebody who doesn't know how to be very subtle," Andy nervously laughed, his face now far redder than Tessa's hair.

"And you're both talking to a computer repair lady who's charging you by the hour," Tessa added.

"Yes, the computer's in the living room, Tessa. Come on in," Mom said, tugging Tessa inside.

Now oddly undaunted by a lack of packages, Andy could barely breathe. Did he see unicorn socks? Did Tessa just reveal she liked Wacky Will? And did Mom really hire a goddamn ringer?

ANDY GETS CONNED

"Tes-sa," Andy said to himself, plucking the cheese curl from his hair and taking a playful bite. "Tessa."

In the living room, Mom guided Tessa past a wall-sized monitor to a massive table. No regular piece of furniture, this was magical mahogany that Andy and his friends used for their medieval meandering. Atop it lied piles of dice, snacks, and reptilian figures surrounding Mom's computer like guards of an ancient obelisk.

"Thanks for coming on such short notice, dear," Mom said, flipping on the ceiling fan and light above the table. "And you look awfully familiar. Have I seen you somewhere before?"

"I hope so," said Tessa, unfolding a poster of herself from her belt and then matching its cheesy thumbs up. "I've been promoting my stand-up show all week. I think I put enough of these up to wipe out a rainforest."

"I'd love to go. Do you have any more tickets?"

"Way too many tickets," exhaled Tessa, removing a roll of them.

"We'll take two!" Andy said, rushing in with another overfilled bowl of cheese curls. "We'll pay more if you autograph them!"

"It's my treat," Mom said, reaching for her purse on the couch and pulling out a fistful of bills. "We love comedy. Here's 50 bucks, Tessa. Keep the change."

"That's so generous. Thank you," Tessa said, ripping two tickets from the roll and placing them in Andy's hand—her clammy palm grazing his. "And what a tip! Geez, are you trying to get into my pants or something, Mrs. Gordon?"

"I like you a lot, dear," Mom said. "And please, call me 'Mom.'"

"And that's not just because she's trying to arrange our marriage," said Andy, fidgeting. "She makes everyone call her 'Mom,' except for lovers."

"You're kidding," said Tessa.

"Nope, it's her legal name. Show her the goods, Mom," said Andy, as Mom reached into her cleavage and pulled out a driver's license, passport, and car title with the name 'Mom Gordon' on them.

"That's amazing!" squealed Tessa, inspecting Mom's identification. "You two made my day, you know that? You're my first sale! I'm happy that anyone wants to watch me make a fool of myself."

"And Mom's happy you didn't ask why she paid you all in ones," Andy said.

"I bet she has a bank vault's worth of ones after winning all that strip shuffleboard, right?" Tessa quipped, opening the computer and aiming a flashlight at the video card. "Let's see what's going on with this. Hmm, interesting. What do we have here?"

"Oh, you mean the video card? I gave her a beefed-up version in case she wanted to game with me," said Andy.

"No, behind that," Tessa said, reaching in and removing an object lodged between the motherboard and video card. "So, this must be the troublemaker."

"I've been working on it for weeks, going through all the diagnostics I could think of," Andy said, as Tessa holstered her flashlight and pressed the computer's power button. "I doubt you'd be able to fix this so quick—"

ANDY GETS CONNED

It worked. The wizard woman Tessa made Mom's computer work! One for the record books, Mom and a crowd of figures just witnessed Tessa serve Andy a piece of troubleshooting pie.

"There we go, all done," said Tessa.

Andy gasped again with an even more forceful flinch. Within seconds, his replacement cheese curl bowl flew straight into the ceiling fan, disintegrated upon impact, and coated the living room with loads of orange fallout.

"I bet the computer was *more* broken before I got here," said Tessa. "The video card wasn't getting enough power because the electrical charge was diverted by a foreign metallic object."

"What does that mean, dear?" Mom asked.

"There was a metal dwarf stuck in there," Tessa said, unclenching her hand and revealing one of Andy's *Rejects & Reptiles* figures. "Honestly, this PC has been upgraded and cleaned recently—I can tell. And there's better cable management in this baby than what they do at the factory. It's impressive, Andy. I'm guessing that you fixed it first, then this dwarf fell in the last time you played. Looks like you have a lot of fun here."

Tessa dropped the dwarf into Andy's other palm, Andy now never wanting to wash either of his hands again. Switching attention to the metal figure, Andy squinted at it like a stare down in a Western movie.

"Jumbo Shrimpit, how could you?" Andy pleaded, looking into the dwarf's pewter eyes.

"Jumbo's from the *Rejects & Reptiles* third edition, right?" Tessa asked. "Don't be too mad at the little guy though. I bet he was trying to level up during the night and unlock his ultimate Grave Digger combo. Plus, you'll be rich with all those rare earth minerals he probably found in your computer."

"You like *Rejects & Reptiles* too?"

"No, I love *Rejects & Reptiles*. I haven't played in a while though, so I must have missed the dwarf axe upgrades. They look like they're made from real metal now. And what's the plastic cap attached to the axe? Do those add attack buffs or something?"

"My dad and I made custom armaments for Jumbo. His axe might be tiny, but now it's sharp enough to slice a frozen pizza. The weapon's historically accurate and lethal, so my dad and I also made that snap-on cap for protection," said Andy. "Or as my immature friends and I like to call it, Jumbo's axe condom."

"I think I might get along with your friends," Tessa said, casting her eyes upward at a cheese curl fragment tucked in her hair. "Hold on. There's an intruder!"

Tessa reached at her hair, plucked out the curl, and struck it like a fish to a worm. Then a phone rang from her utility belt, playing the *Space Fightin'* musical theme.

"Yum, these are Nielsen's aren't they?" she asked, then answering her phone. "Hey, boss. What's up?"

"Yeah...the only cheese curls fit for a king," said Andy, flabbergasted.

It was official. Andy's brain was now blown more than ever before, even beating the time a psychedelic toad hopped in his mouth at summer camp. Muscles he didn't know existed locked up. And Mom's persistently jabbing elbow had no effect either as Andy remained transfixed on Tessa—the funny, adorable, smart geek who seemed to enjoy her employment.

"I can absolutely do that. I'll be right there," Tessa said, hanging up. "Well, the work of a mildly cute computer repairwoman is never over. Let me know if you have any other problems with your machine, Mrs. Gordon. Sorry! I mean, Mom! And don't worry about the bill. You gave me more than enough for the tickets to cover it. Bye, Andy! See you at the show?"

Tessa headed outside and scurried to her red station wagon for another stop in the circus freak show that is home computer repair. As Tessa cruised down the street, Mom waved her hand inches in front of Andy's dumbfounded face.

"Andy?" called Mom. "Dear? Hello?"

Andy's circuits had overloaded, and his mouth opened wider than the worm monster from *Honey I Enlarged the Annelid*. His heart pounded faster than the final chase scene in *Two Krauts on the Run: A Race Odyssey*. Tessa had spun a web and wrapped it tighter than Droid Blitzer's mechanical stranglehold in *Space Fightin'*. And her quirky words now crippled Andy more than the part in *Prehistoric Park* when the Spitsasaurus spat poison in the fat guy's face. This was a Hollywood 'meet-cute' and he knew it. Yet, all that came from his mouth was a grunt, as if Andy were a keyboard whose entire set of buttons were jammed down at the same time.

"I'm never getting grandchildren," said Mom, sitting down and then clicking on her dating profile inbox. "You go ahead and process this while I get back to the Internet, dear. Let's see how many messages I missed in a few weeks. A full inbox? Oh my! Who do we have here? Too old—delete. Too bald—delete. I'm pretty sure this is one of those 'dick pics' you told me about—we'll save that for later, but he's not dating material. And I'm sorry, Mr. plump mobility scooter man, but this lady likes to dance!"

Mom then spent three hours filtering through the sea of creeps and Nigerian princes, messaging a few acceptable suitors. Working up an appetite, she also managed to make a meatloaf and mashed potatoes from scratch as Andy stayed stuck in the same place. When complete, Mom popped up from her seat and stuck a cheese curl into Andy's open mouth.

"You'll have to feed yourself after you finish this curl, dear. I left meatloaf and mashed potatoes in the fridge. See you in the morning, okay? Momma has a date."

Mom kissed Andy's cheek and then fetched her sequined jacket from the coat rack. After locking up and heading outside, she peered through the living room window at her mannequin-like son.

"Show your mother that you're not dead again. Come on, Andy!" Mom said, knocking on the glass.

Andy complied, straining and squeezing with the effort usually reserved for opening pesky pickle jars. Now struggling like a coma patient trying to tell his family not to pull the plug, Andy executed a left-handed wave that lasted half a second.

"Love you too, dear! If you hear any loud noises coming from the garage apartment tonight, everything's

ANDY GETS CONNED

fine. And if you don't hear anything, that's even better because the guy owns a house," Mom said, hurrying for her car in the driveway.

As Mom revved the engine and headed for her romantic adventure, a small explosion filled the living room that was imperceptible from afar. Yes, she was now leaving behind not one, but two inoperative objects in the quiet house: her tongue-tied son and his R2CheeseToodle robot, the latter now ruptured after taking in too much cheese curl dust. Observing his robot's overfilled container pop to the ground, Andy sighed in a moment of reflective solitude. His sigh soon became a terrified scream, however, when the bot's filter erupted in flames...the house now seconds away from getting more scorched than a pyromaniac's campfire hotdog.

CHAPTER 6

Though the birds belted out their rude daybreak chatter yet again, Andy awoke in good spirits now with Tessa and vlogs on the brain. In fact, he had only heard the birds after a whole flock dive-bombed his window trying to eat the cheese curls lining his living room. Even after a night on his back and a floor with no lumbar support, optimism still flowed through Andy's body. And the weight seemed to lift right off his mind, then strangely concentrating on his left hand.

"If this were a heart attack, it'd be pain in my chest, not my hand," Andy said from the carpet, shifting his eyes to the cold object in his palm. "A fire extinguisher? Oh, right, I almost burned alive before bed last night."

Wham! A second set of songbirds then struck Andy's window, the worm eaters now worm food because of some deceptively clear glass. Figuring he better shut the blinds and save a few birds, Andy tried to sit up but failed. Yes, he was stuck to the floor with a paste made from cheese powder and firefighting foam. Andy then yanked both arms free from the gooey carpet and rubbed his eyes with two well-flavored fingers. When the pain diminished, Andy spotted his creepy mailman looking right back at him through the window. And the mailman then bolted away, leaving Andy's opened mail in the bushes.

"Mom's car isn't back yet. Looks like she found a keeper," Andy said, removing his phone from its designated pajama pocket.

Andy then inspected his text messages, the most recent one from Mom. Their roles now reversed with Andy relieved that she wasn't dead this time, he read the last message out loud.

"I'm having a great time, dear, and will be back in the morning. Don't forget about the meatloaf. And here's more proof that your momma still has the moves," Andy read, looking at Mom's selfie with a silver-haired, senior fox snoozing in a sleep apnea mask.

"Go Mom!" Andy said, texting back. "And thanks for wearing clothes in this one."

Hearing a rhythmic clang close by, Andy had to get up before events got any weirder. With a jerk, Andy finally ripped free from the retro shag carpet, rolled to his side, and saw the devastation: Cheese curl crumbs shrouded all of the living room furniture. More puzzling, a clear path through the cheese led from the kitchen to his feet and then outlined his body like crime scene chalk. The trail ultimately guided Andy's eyes to the little trooper who went out with a bang—his out-of-service robot vacuum R2CheeseToodle now getting repeatedly rammed by the upstairs R2CheeseDoodle.

ANDY GETS CONNED

"Get a room," Andy said to himself with a grin, fighting off an urge to make cheese curl-angels in the dust. "I live a strange life."

While there was a time his robots couldn't mingle because of the stairs, Andy and his dad constructed a ramp for their handy helpers over 20 years ago. By converting an old laundry chute into a ramp, the geeky engineers never had to manually suck up filth again. Most pets made messes, but the Gordons' companions kept their floors spotless with only two simple needs: one battery charge every month and one strict house ban on all high-powered magnets.

After mulling over these memories and doing a couple cheese curl-angels due to weak willpower, Andy rolled over and grabbed his bot's container from the ground. With an emergency surgeon's pace, he emptied the crumbs in a trash can, taped up R2CheeseToodle's container, and blew off the last particles like a dusty video game cartridge. Andy finished by slipping a battery into its vacuum base from a charger behind him, bringing the bot back to optimal functionality in seconds. His cheeks dimpling as he recorded with his camera, Andy watched R2CheeseToodle reboot and sniff R2CheeseDoodle's rear vent—an unnecessary software flourish that Andy added for his own amusement. Both robots then tag teamed the mess, sucking up snacks in circles like a pair of synchronized skaters.

"You little guys have no reservations. You know your goals, you never give up, and you don't need a treadmill to counteract all the garbage you eat. Somehow you work and play at the same time. And you don't have to put up with any mean people in the process—now that's the life," sighed Andy. "I remember when you used to be a couple of store-bought, baby automatons. Man, they grow up so fast, don't they, everybody?"

Though Andy stopped recording, his bots continued their OCD mission for motorized maid perfection. As they rounded his feet, Andy gave each bot a loving tickle, pondering their longevity. With the proper maintenance, they'd at least last most of Andy's lifetime. But what would happen if he bit the dust before them? Soon coming to a darker conclusion, Andy figured that their peaceful interactions were limited; if he croaked in the house first, those emotionless bastards would smear his liquefied guts all over the floor. It'd probably take a week for his friends to find the big pool of Andy ooze too. By then, the dead bird pile in his yard would be a two-story tower after they dive-bombed his delicious body and splattered their avian brains upon the window. And Gail Ellerbach's inaccurate news coverage of this carnage would certainly ensure Andy's psychopathic status forever.

"That's it! Today I reorder my priorities once and for all. I'll be damned if I die alone at home," Andy said, running up the stairs. "Or worse, die with all of the people I hate at work!"

Back in the bedroom, Andy bounded to his sticky goal list upon the wall. After ripping down Mom's old note about her computer, Andy pasted two more at the top beside his recent 'Job Search' addition: 'Finally Release Video' and 'Don't Repulse Tessa.' As if desiring a witness to this drastic shift, Andy placed his metal dwarf Jumbo Shrimpit onto a shelf beside the list.

"There we go. Life reboot initiated. And you were here to see it, Jumbo—you are now looking at Andy 2.0. With you as my *Rejects & Reptiles* map marker, we've taken down the deadliest dragons. But now we're about to tackle something even bigger. If I finally release some videos, who knows, maybe I could get a following and do it full time. My life and this bizarre town are interesting enough to put online. Making geeky vlogs with friends could be a career, right? Plus, if this plan works, I'll finish two goals and get to focus on Tessa!"

After drinking coffee and showering at the same time to avoid another late arrival at work, Andy downed Mom's meatloaf for breakfast and finished off a box of ginger snaps. But then he did something completely different—applying his prescription-grade sunblock for the incoming change to his daily commute. Soon lugging an even heavier backpack of extra camera batteries, Andy skipped his public avoidance shortcuts in need of better backgrounds and lighting for his next vlog. Today's wardrobe also saw a change for the camera. Rather than his teacher attire with small geek touches, Andy went all out with an unbuttoned, Hawaiian-print suit jacket over a custom-made T-shirt. The message on this shirt, fitting with Andy's mood, uplifted all nerdy onlookers with the words 'Gravity's Such a Downer: Stand Up and Fight It.'

Weaving on his skateboard through an obstacle course of dog turds dotting the sidewalk, something deep within Andy popped. It was no artery or appendix, but a mental dam of pent-up pet peeves mixed with creative mania. Years of mistreatment coming to a salty surface, Andy tilted the skateboard camera at his face with his foot. And then he finally let loose, converting this plethora of poop into comical fury.

"Okay, world, let the rants begin! This video is on behalf of all responsible citizens out there who consider how their actions affect others. Imagine if our ancestors were more considerate when they blew resources on war or weapons that compensated for their tiny wangs. If they were smarter, our society would be a lot more sci-fi than lo-fi for sure. And I'd probably be ranting from a nerdy space station full of Wacky Will holograms by now. Our actions always waft into other nostrils, and some people don't have the slightest clue that they're making the world a stinkier place. So let's stomp out these problems together, starting with an issue right at my feet," said Andy, passing a jogger on the sidewalk.

"Someone understands my struggles!" the jogger shouted, jumping over anal artifacts. "Give them hell, sir!"

"Thank you," said Andy, refocusing on his camera. "So I'm one bad skateboard pivot away from getting a face-full of number two. Yes, I know that you saw your dog make these doody dollops on the ground, or judging by the size of that one maybe it was your moose, but you still left it there for someone else to suffer through. For example, that little brown treat that I passed by in Nurse Rosie's lawn is going to haunt the side of her garage for months after her husband hits it with his lawnmower. And that sidewalk bomb ahead is going to be a big wakeup call

ANDY GETS CONNED

for any hopscotch player who lands on the last, overflowing square. So pick it up, people, because folks like me are tired of washing it off our soles and scraping the treads clean with a toothbrush. It's about time to put yourself in someone else's shoes!"

Andy's heart pumped. His mind raced. And his sweat glands went into overdrive. What a rant! What a vlog! Andy wasn't sure how he wove such an eloquent argument while dodging that much dookie, but he wanted more. He could do that again in video form; hell, he could do that for hours if people wanted to watch. His morning commute now with purpose, Andy recorded another vlog along the way. Yes, he had morphed into a modern-day, skateboarding philosopher within minutes.

Soon back at Bumble Ridge High with new priorities, Andy bounced through his workday like an irrepressible peasant. His tangible progress now saved to memory cards, nothing could stop Andy while he wielded footage he wasn't disgusted with. In fact, he finally wanted others to see his work now too.

Using his free period, Andy registered all of the social media pages he'd need to promote his future online video depository. With its application fully submitted for a government-granted trademark, the JumboAndy brand would soon be legit. And with Andy's new creative dreams, he'd make his way onto even more screens than Bumble Ridge's malware-laden pornography.

Readying his first entry, Andy finished the dance music video shot in his bedroom; and it now contained clips of him and Mom playing with lunch meat. Though his students were the same, his job blew by, now understanding the tips on 'auto-pilot mode' in the *Teacher's Sanity Manual*. Not even B-Fred's nutrition or Emily's razor blade threats could bring Andy down from this rush; when the last bell rang, he had completed over 45 minutes of content between breaks. And as Bumble Ridge High's security doors opened, Andy ran away faster than his surrounding students. Then he hopped back on his skateboard and headed even farther away from home, Andy racing toward the next step of his exciting, new day.

"Now we need some more misfit actors," said Andy, recording on his skateboard. "It's time to hit up the nerdy casting couch."

Soon downtown, Andy skated through what he referred to as the Skip Strip, a collection of well-known businesses that he had no desire of supporting financially. He first whizzed by High-End Honey, an elitist honey shop charging the equivalent of a car payment for bee spit. Next up, Andy zoomed past the Three-Fifth Chasers speakeasy and its many intolerant intoxicants. With an insistence on using pure ingredients and segregating the water fountains, billionaire Kerry K. Kirkpatrick kept his speakeasy open since the Prohibition despite its dwindling attendance. His extreme wealth as mind-boggling as his senility, Kirkpatrick seemed to keep the place operating with one goal—being on the wrong side of history.

Andy then blew by PerspirNation Gym, a popular workout spot for high school football players and steroid salesmen; this combo was coincidental, according to the bosses. Recently, the gym closed for renovations after two running backs bent a support beam with their legs thinking it was some extra-resistant equipment. With the Skip Strip now cleared, Andy had reached today's target—the set of his next spectacular vlog. This was his Mecca, his home away from home, and his only reason not to shop entirely online anymore.

"Here we are, folks. Welcome to Leo's Larping & Comics," said Andy, recording the shop's floppy cardboard sign taped to the window. "Today, I cast my actors. Wish me luck!"

CHAPTER 7

In front of Leo's Larping & Comics shop, Andy panned his camera across its thin cardboard sign written in marker. He then recorded its list of products like Costumes, Toys, and Games, stopping on the shop's scribbled slogan—The Best Role-Playing Wizards in Town. After documenting the sloppy sign, Andy rushed inside with his camera rolling; it was time for his next vlog of epic proportions. Yes, now targeting the fantasy genre, Andy took no risks of getting pigeonholed into one type of content this early in his career.

"And so I, Jumbo Shrimpit the dwarven baker, will venture inside the marketplace to reunite with my party of possible performers. Here, I will make inquiries that could affect my future. Then I'll be picking up a rare dice set—if the post office didn't lose the box, of course," Andy said in dwarf character, then ambling through shelves of comics while recording. "Wait, do my eyes deceive me? What bovine wonder! It is my human pal previously inflicted with a zombie curse. And he's still perusing comics with large-breasted women in skimpy outfits. I must capture this with my magic wizard box."

Andy aimed his camera at Ben, a man clearly reading something from the shop's adult section.

"I do not care how super you say those women are," Andy continued. "Their titanic-sized tatas are in no way aerodynamic or fit for flight at that elevation."

"You're in a goofy mood today," said Ben, still distracted with the comic.

"Yes, Jumbo Shrimpit is feeling particularly, as you say, *goofy*. It is a fine goofy, indeed. So, zombie, how can you read such implausible rubbish? You know those mountainous mammary glands would snap all those women's spines, right?"

"Me zombie. Me eat brains of Jumbo if Jumbo doesn't shut trap," Ben groaned in character, his vacant eyes morphing into a wink at the camera. "Zombie will steal Jumbo's magic wizard box and capture pics of zombie junk again if Jumbo not careful."

"A dwarf is not interested in the feelings of the dead, undead, or whatever preferred state of decay you wish to be called these days. And if you need my assistance removing your zombie curse with our robot companion, you will allow me to criticize your erotica."

Leo then peeked his face through a multicolored beaded curtain behind the checkout counter. His long, patchouli oil-coated hair soon passed through the beads as well, followed by his neck with a flowered tie attached. Fully emerging in a brown hemp suit that looked freshly ripped from an old grave, Leo held a package under one

ANDY GETS CONNED

of his arms. And he locked and popped with the other, looking like a well-lubed funky robot.

"Greetings, Jumbo," Leo droned in robotic character, spotting the camera. "Your primo-priced dice have reached their time-space destination."

Leo then raised the box as high as possible. Shining down from above, angelic light illuminated the cardboard box in all its recycled glory. With no windows on that side of the shop and the light likely coming from real angels, Ben went bug-eyed and fell to his knees.

"Please forgive me for all the dirty things I do with these weird comics when I'm alone," begged Ben.

"I'm glad you got that spotlight installed, Leo! It makes delivery day so much more epic," Andy said recording, as Leo turned off his spotlight's wall switch.

"Damn you both," Ben said. "But the light's cool!"

"Yeah, it's money in, money out, man. Mostly *out* these last few weeks though."

"The customers should be rolling in any day," said Andy, taking the box as Ben went back to his illustrated perversion. "But you should really get to work on a new sign outside. People can't see it. There aren't any graphics either. And I don't think anyone knows what this shop even is. That's a shame because it's a nerd haven in here. With that spotlight—a nerd heaven."

"We'll have to agree to disagree. My sign's just fine," Leo said. "I'd rather focus on some word-of-mouth marketing first, not some shallow aesthetics."

"Okay, we'll talk about the sign later then. But I've been thinking about your marketing too, actually. How about I whip you up a promo video with this footage I'm shooting?" Andy asked. "I'll get some shots of us role-playing around here and some of us at my place doing the same. Insert some footage of the decorations in this place, then slap on some special effects; it'll bring in the bucks for sure. Plus, I'll upload it to all my online outlets I created today for even more exposure!"

"A video?" Leo asked. "A completed Andy video released online? A completed Andy video released online that could score me some clientele and therefore afford hot water? Well that'd be swell! I'd owe you big time my entire life, man, as well as any future lifetimes!"

"Good, after I make you this video, you'll be jonesing for a savings account in no time. That's one step closer to a profitable shop!"

"One step closer to self-actualization," said Leo.

"One step closer to a shop filled with geeky girls," added Ben. "The fame, the fortune—"

"The ability to pay for 99 cent comics," said Leo, yanking the comic from Ben's hands. "Stop bogarting my inventory, dude! Especially the naughty ones—those sell."

Sensing a disturbance with his inner chi, Leo placed the comic back on its shelf and handed Ben a broom. Though no fan of the criminal justice system, Leo had to apply some consequence to Ben's frugal abuse.

"You know the deal: when cheap, you sweep. Now assume the broom," Leo said.

"I could make you a vacuum that'd give you way less sass than him," Andy smiled. "Watch your back, Ben; a robot's about to take your job."

"Don't you dare. I'm sweeping! I'm sweeping!" Ben said, picking up the pace.

"So did I hear you right, Andy? You said you established your fabulousness online?" asked Leo.

"Sure did," said Andy. "I made a video page on VoyeursSlashVanity called JumboAndy. And then I registered every social media outlet with the same name. Nothing's up there yet, but I'm making some killer content that I want the world to see."

"No way! So, what gives today, man? You're confident. You're jovial. You're, I can't believe I'm saying this, way happier."

"Oh, typical story, you know. I had a breakdown then a few breakthroughs. And after that, I exchanged words with a woman who rocked my world more than an asteroid belt. Aw, she had a belt too; there were electronic tools in it. Her name's Tessa. She likes Wacky Will and eats cheese curls. I think she likes me too. Did I mention the unicorn socks? Tessa has unicorn socks. Okay I'll stop, I'm gushing."

"Gush away, man. It's an amazing occasion to fall for somebody who likes you back. That hasn't happened to you since college, right?"

"Yeah, Helga."

"Well Tessa sounds way better and hotter than Helga ever was," added Ben.

"Hey, Helga was a lovely lady," said Andy. "You can't judge a woman just by her glandular problems."

"Well it's about time some good fortune appeared around here. So are you in pursuit of Tessa?" asked Leo.

"Yeah, I'm awful at picking up signals, but I'm pretty sure we're in each other's tractor beams."

"Way to go, Andy!" Ben cheered, sweeping the dust into a pile. "Does Tessa have a sister? Maybe a transitioning brother?"

"I'll get back to you about both of those. But if she doesn't, I'll scope out all of her female friends to assist my pals—don't worry," said Andy.

"Much appreciated," said Leo. "But find one for Ben first. I've got business on the brain."

"What are you waiting for then, Andy?" asked Ben. "Go get Tessa! For you! For us!"

"I need to sort out my life first too, which is another reason I'm here. Leo, I've had a question I've been meaning to ask you for months. How much longer before you can hire a full-time helper around here?"

"Well, I could probably swing the salary of an undocumented worker in a few years," Leo said. "But if you're talking minimum wage, that projection's more like a 15-year plan at best. Why do you ask?"

"I'm looking to switch careers."

"Hey, if things turn around here, you'll be the first to know. Never say never. Stranger things have happened in the universe."

"Yeah, like the platypus," Ben added.

"Keep sweeping," Leo sang, gleeful that his freeloader friend became free labor. "So you've mastered the teaching gig then, huh?"

"Not mastered. More like *slaved*," said Andy.

"Well, what are you looking for?"

"Sanity mostly. Some creative fulfillment. If I had a job here, we could shoot videos in between customers, you know? I made a music video today plus a few rants around the neighborhood. And they're great! I've been thinking about recalibrating this video hobby as an online career. I don't have a weird business name yet to fit in with the town's requirements, but that's not going to stop me. You're looking at Andy 2.0, guys."

"So what's this mind-shifting music video that passed your quality standards, man?" Leo asked.

"I combined footage of me dancing in a chair and shots of my mom and I playing with meat products. It'll make sense when you see it, I promise. How about we schedule a video break during our next gaming session? I can show you both then!"

"Sweet!"

"Your mom played with your meat?" asked Ben, now sweeping dirt under the carpet.

"If you don't knock it off, I intend to extend your zombie curse in *Rejects & Reptiles*," threatened Leo. "I'm the Reject Master and therefore your god on Fridays."

"No, wait!" Ben shouted, lifting the carpet and then scooping up dirt with a dustpan. "Forgive me, Reject Master. We're clean now, see?"

"Spectacular," said Leo. "Man, what a plan. We have a busy weekend ahead of us. Dice testing, video watching, promo making—it can't come soon enough."

"Actually, I don't want to wait for the weekend," said Andy. "I've rebooted. The new me wants to get started right now. Let's game and work on the promo tonight!"

"I'm in," Ben said. "I'm always in!"

"Don't you still have to motivate some minds tomorrow?" asked Leo. "I have to be here working bright and early too, you know."

"I do, but screw it," Andy said. "I can teach while tired and still be better than my inebriated colleagues. And you can take naps here during your downtime, which will be most of the time until we get that promo video done. Come on; don't make me beg."

"I dig the energy, but I'm not so sure about this."

"We're making videos for a new me, a new career, and your new advertising. How could we put that off?" Andy asked, removing the tripod from his backpack and placing the camera on top. "Let's take a risk! Let's treat life like a random roll of the dice for once."

"It's awfully hard to resist the positivity pouring from you right now. Should we?"

"Reject Master Leo, I present to you my closing argument," said Andy, then whispering in Ben's ear as they both cracked a smile.

Andy and Ben leaned in closely, wrapping one arm around the other in front of the camera. After a second, they both furrowed their brows and performed an exaggerated frowny face in unison.

"You two make a convincing argument. We'll go game after we close tonight," said Leo.

Beside the counter, Andy inserted a coin into the basketball machine shaped like a guillotine—one of the first ideas he and Leo concocted to drum up interest in the unknown shop. First rolling out from the guillotine

ANDY GETS CONNED

came Queen Marie An-twine-ette's plushy head, a rubber cranium with rooted twine poufs for hair. Palming the eye indentations like a bowling ball, Andy lined up his shot while an executioner's voice counted down from five.

"I'm beyond stoked," said Leo. "We've been hoping you'd unlock your Andy vault and let those videos free for years, man!"

"There's so much good stuff on my hard drives; there's decades of footage!" Andy said, as he tossed the head and it bounced off the edge of a mounted wicker basket. "There's video of the time your trippy toad climbed into my mouth at summer camp. And Ben's fake bar mitzvah when he tried hooking up with the rabbi's daughter. I was even recording when we brainstormed this *Alley-Oops* basketball game."

"I still say the name I proposed was better," said Ben.

"No way. *Head to Head* is the much better subtitle. Be glad we gave you that," said Andy, watching a swollen and purple noggin roll out from the guillotine. "Ah, you're up next, Alexander the Grape."

Andy then sent his second head straight at the basket. On Alexander's path, the metal cutout of a Roman emperor popped up with a parchment pardon. Yes, Andy's shot had been imperially blocked.

"Oh, come on, emperor," said Andy, facing the camera. "You could have totally *aqueduct* that one."

"Hey, history buff. Who's the new head?" asked Ben, as a third head tumbled out.

"We modeled this one after our machine repairman. Why he tried fixing the blade without us, we'll never know," Andy said, kissing the ball's forehead. "May he rest in coin-operated peace."

"The repairman's wife is a widow, and you didn't tell me? Emotionally vulnerable widows tend to be less picky than non-widows, you know," said Ben.

"You'll forget all about that after tonight," said Andy, shooting over the repairman's glum cutout family. "Swish! Nothing but wicker! Well, Jumbo's really feeling the urge for expedition. Can we close a little early? I'll show you all the footage I have. The old material needs some work, but it's time you two see it all. I want lots of feedback so I can make it even better."

"We concur, human," said robot Leo.

"Me stop sweeping now to help?" grunted zombie Ben, as Andy opened his box and removed the dice case. "That good excuse to stop thankless zombie work, right?"

"Aye, in exchange, this dwarf offers you his newly acquired dice to take down the Komodo dragon menace and help ZomBen get his human groove back. And for you, our robot guardian LSD-401K, I'll produce an unforgettable shop promo with my magical wizard box," dwarf Andy said, kneeling and holding his fancy dice case into the air. "Also, I have lots of cupcake ingredients at home, so there's that."

Leo flipped his spotlight back on and kneeled with his friends, all three now lifting the dice case while bowing their heads in embellished veneration. Just then, in such a weird looking pose to anyone lacking context, Leo's doorbell jingled. The trio twisted their heads at the new customer, still in their pious position, as a brawny man traipsed inside gripping his phone. Stopping dead in his tracks, the muscle man then lowered his sunglasses.

"This isn't the gym, is it?" he asked, as his neck arteries throbbed with confusion.

"Not in this reality," replied Leo.

"This happens sometimes. Hold on! Let me retrace my steps," said the muscle man, scratching his head. "First I saw the PerspirNation gym sign. The gym door was locked, so I tried the other PerspirNation gym door beside it. I opened that gym door and saw you here at the gym. And then I asked you if this was the gym, but you said that it wasn't the gym. Hmm, that didn't help me. I'm really confused why this isn't the gym."

"We're a separate entity than PerspirNation," said Leo. "Didn't you see my highly informative sign?"

"What sign?"

"The cardboard one."

"Don't play games with me, hippie. No business owner's dumb enough to use a cardboard sign. Look, I'm a paying customer who wants to use the gym. My phone led me here, so this has to be the damn gym."

"The hippie is right, and your phone is wrong," said Andy. "Can we help you with anything else?"

"Nope. Well, I'm going back to the phone company and getting a new one then. Later, guys," said the muscle man, then performing a number of air punches and kicks before exiting.

"I have to put him in one of our videos," Andy said, pointing to his camera. "Did you see his torso? That guy was so bulky he couldn't put his arms down. Hey, viewers,

I think we all caught a rare glimpse of the species I'd like to call 'Tyrannosaurus Flex.'"

With no way the meathead could have heard or even comprehended Andy's insult, the doorbell jingled again. Was Andy louder than he thought? Or perhaps steroids also enhanced hearing ability now? Andy winced nevertheless, expecting to receive a few toilet swirlies and a punch to at least one of his vital organs. Stomping up in her black boots, however, was a decked-out dominatrix with a shiny bullwhip.

"Your window says you're the best role-playing wizards in town. Well I'm looking for some dirty piggies who want some rough role-play with me," she said, cracking the whip.

"Wrong kind of role-play, Miss," said Andy. "We're the kind of guys who watch videos of people like you."

"I get it now, piggies. You mean the nerdy kind of role-play. I'd be more specific when you list 'costumes' and 'toys' on your sign out there."

"Yeah, really unclear, isn't it?" Andy said, nudging Leo. "Sorry about that."

"You better be," she said, cracking her whip one last time and then leaving the shop.

"I'll do it!" Ben shouted too late, as the door swung shut behind her. "I'm a piggie. I'm a dirty piggie!"

"Let's get the hell out of here before anybody else shows up," Andy said, scrambling to his feet and shutting off the shop lights.

Andy, Ben, and Leo grabbed their belongings in the dark, fumbled through the door, and locked up before

ANDY GETS CONNED

another noncustomer made them any more uncomfortable. Then tiptoeing backward away from the entrance, all three bumped their butts into one more surprise—a hooded KKK member reading the shop's sign.

"I'm tryin' to find the Grand Wizard," he said, pointing at Leo's slogan. "Y'all seen him?"

"You're at the wrong place, sir," Andy gulped. "The speakeasy's two doors down to your left. When you see the minstrel show posters, you're in the right spot."

"Thanks, brothers," the Klansman said, lurching toward the speakeasy. "See ya at the meetin'."

"So about that new sign," Andy huffed, running away with his pals.

"Yeah, I'm ordering one as soon as I get back to my pad tonight," Leo added, dashing to his van. "The universe just sent me a clear message. It's a pricey message that might make me have to consume cat food for a month, but it's a message nonetheless."

"You two crossed the line back there!" Ben grumbled. "No woman's ever going to talk to me that way again. Piggies? She was perfect for me!"

The gang loaded into Leo's van painted with flowers and rainbows, each strategically placed to conceal dents. Blasting patriotic music as a safety precaution in case the Klansman heard them, they puttered down Andy's Skip Strip. And that's when they passed three familiar characters walking into the speakeasy together—the dominatrix, the KKK member, and Tyrannosaurus Flex.

"If you look to your right, you'll see the visual representation of a joke setup that I don't want to witness the punch line to," said Andy, his camera already recording from the van. "A punch line that probably involves actual punching of minorities, sadly."

"There she is!" Ben shouted. "Stop now, dammit!"

"It's too late. She's with other men, Ben," said Leo, speeding away.

"And those men might rip off the parts that you need to have fun with a dominatrix anyway," added Andy. "Keep driving, Leo, and make haste! *Rejects & Reptiles* and cupcakes await us!"

As Andy's late-night gaming session, video shoot, and potential romance all whirled through his mind, his reboot kicked off with a phenomenal start. Now more likely to make videos with his band of merry men back together, Andy had experienced more change today than when he went through puberty. Though, like puberty, this change was just an inch of Andy's incoming growth spurt. And today's setbacks were mere zits compared to the problematic acne about to rear its ugly head.

CHAPTER 8

One *Rejects & Reptiles* quest became two, and two then 64, as Andy's group pounded those dice on the game table from every position imaginable. Acting in character, the trio had solved numerous disputes over the campaign's 18-year run; decisions made by dice rolls saw far better results than Democracy ever could. But with the extra energy from Andy's video making tonight, the trio blasted through Leo's carefully crafted reptile campaign even quicker than usual. And they were so close to reaching the elusive Komodo King that they could smell his royal cloaca.

Fueled by the buffet in Andy's living room, the reptilian games went on. After retrieving 12 detachable tails for a salamander tribe, the troop completed trade deals with a deceptive chameleon commune known for its unethical transparency. The trio then rode those chameleons into war, impaling iguanas and gutting geckos like the cold-blooded killers they were. They even scaled Mount Heat Rock, finally reaching the mighty Komodo

King's terrarium hall. But when Leo described the hall's rock waterfall and Andy's chocolate fondue fountain trickled atop the game table, creative juices weren't the only thing filling their bodies; the gang all needed a pee break. After their brief hiatus, as Ben and Leo waited with empty bladders, Andy reappeared with a snack. In his hands were now items that gave off aromas even more pleasant than newly-opened electronics bags—baked goods fresh from the oven.

"We have to keep our energy meters filled, so I whipped up some treats," Andy said in his apron, holding a tray of cupcakes on UFO saucers. "It's my goal to make you laugh out loud at least once in this Komodo King finale. We need a good ending for the promo video, so eat up. For my future rich business bud Leo, I made you two cupcakes with money symbols on them. For myself, two cupcakes with director's chairs. And I think I really outdid myself with yours, Ben."

"These are amazing!" Ben shouted.

"The sprinkles are nipple tassels," added Andy, scooping the fountain chocolate into bowls.

The gang raised their cupcakes and pressed them together like wine glasses, then dipping them in chocolate and eating them unlike wine glasses. Using appropriate bachelor etiquette by cupping a hand below their chins, they blocked all crumbs from raining upon the Komodo King's hall. Hyped up for what was about to go down, Andy attached his camera to a tripod while Ben slurped his bowl of chocolate. And Leo went back to his key role of the past 18 years—Reject Master.

ANDY GETS CONNED

"With their groovy stomachs full of enough flora and fauna to slash biodiversity across the land, Jumbo Shrimpit, ZomBen, and LSD-401K ventured into the great Komodo King's hall," announced Leo, then vanishing behind his Reject Master barrier board.

A few second later, Leo emerged from behind the board in a rubber Komodo dragon mask.

"Welcome to my cave, fearless dwarf, zombie, and fancy machine man," Leo said, now sounding like an old lizard with a lisp. "Please sheathe your weapons, for I am a pacifist Komodo dragon. May I interest you in a soy shake or perhaps direct you to my compost pile toilet?"

"You pacifist? You not fight?" asked zombie Ben.

"With this new knowledge in my brain and cupcake in my belly, I inspect the room for incense burners and hacky sacks," said dwarf Andy, rolling his newly acquired golden die. "Search roll! I got an eight."

Leo ducked behind the Reject Master board and popped out once more, now without the mask. Leading a game with Andy and Ben meant that Leo had become accustomed to such tomfoolery. It also meant he had the patience of a hostage negotiator.

"As Jumbo the dwarf rummages through the room, he sees a collection of hacky sacks and incense burners from the farthest reaches of the kingdom," Leo said. "As well as lava lamps, kombucha drinks, and posters of bra-burning Komodo dragons with hairy armpits."

"Thank you for your warm welcome, Komodo King. And may I offer my apologies for searching through your personal belongings already. I am Jumbo Shrimpit, a dwarven baker. This machine man is LSD-401K, our robot guide and sometimes ride when the horses need rest. And this is my companion ZomBen, formerly Ben, struck by a real rotten curse that he cannot seem to shake," said dwarf Andy, as Komodo Leo popped out sipping some kombucha from a pocket flask.

"I see," said Komodo King Leo. "Have you attempted a cleansing enema yet, my friends?"

"I'm afraid we have, many times," dwarf Andy smirked. "The curse is beyond our abilities and we seek remedy from your powerful scrolls. It is said that the reptiles have protected this knowledge far before feather and fur came to be. Thus, we respectfully request your ancient assistance."

"Your awareness and bravery shall be handily rewarded," Komodo King Leo said. "May I ask which adversary applied ZomBen's curse so I can ready the proper remedy?"

"Can't Komodo King fix me without questions?" asked zombie Ben.

"No, for if the incorrect scroll is applied, you could perish in unimaginable, unforgettable, excruciating torment and pain," Komodo King Leo warned.

"I take risk."

"As you wish, zombie. May you find great comfort in knowing that if you do perish, your nutrients will do wonders for my compost pile."

"I believe that I can provide a clue for this matter," said Andy, pushing his Jumbo Shrimpit metal figure toward Leo while trying to keep a straight face. "My partner ZomBen may or may not have violated a dolphin that had magical powers."

"Jumbo!" shouted zombie Ben, slamming the table. "You break pinky promise!"

"Please inform me that you are both yanking my Komodo chain. You molested the majestic Dolphin King of the Southern Coast? He's the most skilled spellcaster in all the land," said Komodo King Leo, then sipping more kombucha.

"Aye," said Andy. "An important life lesson that playing a dolphin like a trombone is never a good idea."

Caught off guard, Leo choked up his fermented drink the way most people do when first tasting kombucha. And he sprayed Ben right in the face. Andy then exploded with laughter as Ben wiped his putrid pores clean, Leo continuing as if no bodily fluids had been spread.

"I should have advised you to close your eyes before the first step of purification. Please accept my apology," said Komodo King Leo. "After I share your rare tale with the crew at the juice bar, we will send your dolphin confession into the sky by burning ancient twigs and berries. The world must hear your sins while we chant text from the scroll, and then your curse shall be removed. Man, the many followers of our smoke signals are going to get a kick out of this."

"No! I lunge across room. I bite Komodo King in his stupid Komodo King neck," zombie Ben said.

"I highly recommend not doing that, cursed human," robotic Leo said.

"Buzz off, LSD-401K! Neck wound roll, now!"

Ben picked up the golden die and rolled it with a forceful flick of the wrist so fast that Andy's camera only captured a blur. The die whizzed across the table and bounced off soda cans like a pinball machine, then stopping with the highest number possible face up. Yes, it was the rare critical 20, now flashing in a bright gold light of lethal splendor.

"ZomBen get critical 20," Ben said, completing his most idiotic move of the entire campaign.

"And the Komodo King's dead from Ben's stupid bite," harrumphed Leo, slapping the rubber mask down. "His higher consciousness escapes his third eye, and his body falls toward the floor. On his way down, he knocks the lava lamps over. And then his entire library of magical scrolls bursts into flames, especially the super cool ones. Side note, these super cool scrolls would have totally cured Ben's zombie curse and taught him Tantric sex positions as a bonus!"

"No. I regret my bad choices! I take it back," Ben screamed, as Andy whipped his head to the camera with wide-opened eyes.

"Too late, dude. You're screwed," grunted Leo.

"I want those scrolls."

"And I want allies who don't kill off main characters in a storyline that's been building for half our life."

"What you want is dumb, you junk pile!"

"You're grinding my gears, corpse boy!"

"How about we roll one more time and see who leaves this game forever?"

"That's the first smart thing you've ever said!"

ANDY GETS CONNED

"I don't think so, guys!" shouted Andy, stepping between the two. "We just shot some of our funniest footage yet. We're not splitting the band up after recording our biggest hit!"

"Hey, wait a minute! Leo broke character!" Ben realized. "Leo didn't stay in character when he insulted me! That's against house rules. That means he's kicked out for the day, right?"

"Technically, but we all broke character," said Leo.

"Robot wrong. ZomBen not break character."

"Andy, I want this brainless brain eater out of here."

"Cease your squabbling!" dwarf Andy shouted, grabbing his camera from the tripod. "I, Jumbo Shrimpit, push between my associates and distract them with my magic wizard box. Should you agree to not eliminate any party member, I will show you moments of our journeys saved by this device, as promised!"

"My anger's dissipating from irate to frustrated," said Leo. "It's a fine time for a break."

"I'll make the popcorn!" added Ben.

"Prepare to see a few things I bet you both forgot!" exclaimed Andy. "And a lot more things you'll probably wish you could."

By connecting Andy's camera to his wall-sized monitor, the trio watched years of dorky events and videos that no other person had seen before. Yes, Andy and the gang watched their entire history replay in just a few hours, seeing the video quality improve while their love handles got worse. During the screening, Andy took notes of jokes bombing or material deemed too awkward for the public. Of course, most of the notes marked times when Ben mooned the camera from a distance, now visible thanks to the large screen. After wrapping up the classics, Andy then introduced his focus group to some new material—the dance music video featuring him and Mom acting goofy.

"Divine work!" said Leo, clapping. "My ego sensed one problem with the music video though."

"What's that?" asked Andy.

"We're not in it."

"Yeah, it could use way more Ben butt too!" added Ben. "One hundred percent more Ben butt."

"We can definitely do your idea, Leo," Andy said, taking more notes. "We'll get some footage, and I'll slip you both right in there. But then we get to my agenda for the night. First, I want to run some ideas by you for my video release plan. Second, I want to involve you in all of the videos in that release plan. And third, I'd appreciate if you could help me make some of my branding too. Oh, and Ben, that's not the type of branding that your butt obviously had in the past. Seriously, how are you sitting down right now?"

First, Andy filmed his friends' disgraceful dancing for the music video. Then he described his brand to Ben and Leo while editing, both designing the graphics needed to establish their online presence. Surprisingly, Ben led the graphics initiative with skills in all the relevant computer programs; though he learned by putting himself into pictures with Popes to look cool if women came over, Ben was an image-manipulating master. And within the

ANDY GETS CONNED

hour, they uploaded the music video to their JumboAndy page—now filled with a collage of Andys in dwarf costumes and novelty T-shirts.

"The graphics look amazing! And the music video's set to 'private' so nobody can see it until the big reveal," said Andy. "I can't believe we did this so quickly!"

"Three heads are better than one," said Leo.

"Yeah, unless it's a birth defect," yawned Ben.

"I agree with both of those statements," said Andy. "Imagine what we could do with a bigger group of friends—an entire crew of comical nerds!"

"Yeah, real work is exhausting with just the three of us. We could use a couple interns," said Ben, resting his head on a bag of cheese curls like a pillow.

"Let's just release the video now," said Leo. "We can see if anyone's on our wavelength. Maybe we could attract some assistance quicker."

"Not yet," said Andy. "I want my Internet entrance to be even grander than this. It has to be an event."

"Maybe we can do a video stream from the shop to announce it!" said Ben. "Those barely need any editing or, you know, work."

"I knew we kept you around for some reason," said Andy, as Ben started snoring. "Great! So we'll stream when the JumboAndy page is ready to go. I want to make an even more memorable splash though. We need to go full-on viral cannonball here. We can do this even better!"

"How else can we enhance the plan?" asked Leo. "The music video's topnotch. The graphics are fantastic. You're too good to stay incognito."

"That's not what I mean. We have the quality, now let's go for quantity. One video's not enough! Good things come in threes, right? Movie trilogies, The Great Pyramids, us—why not use what already works? What if I spam the Internet with three videos on the same day? I figure I can combine all my rants for a second video. Then the third could be our promo for your shop with the *Rejects & Reptiles* clips. Combined with the music video, that's three pieces of content in three different styles on one day. What do you think?"

"Right on! First impressions are crucial, so let's do it. I'm positive Ben would approve too if he weren't snoozing on the food."

"Okay, so I'll get to work on the promo video while you set up the next part of our *Rejects & Reptiles* campaign. We have some Komodo dragons to deal with; I bet they're already crafting some conspiracy theories about who killed their beloved king."

"Not to be a buzzkill, but it's already 11:30—our responsible adult bedtime. Want to call it a night and reconvene over the weekend?"

Andy swabbed frosting off of a cupcake with his finger. And then he pointed into the air, pausing for dramatic effect.

"No, Leo, we're living on the edge now, dammit; tomorrow I'm taking a half day off from work. This trio's in for one enjoyable and irresponsible night," Andy said, then wrapping his lips around his finger like a calf to a frosted teat. "Right after we break some bad news to the Komodo King's wife and kids, of course!"

ANDY GETS CONNED

"Woo!" rejoiced Ben, waking up. "More game time! More snacks! More fireproof and curative sex scrolls!"

And so the gang played on, adventuring through swamps and forests and back to the swamps in search of ZomBen's lost house keys. Though Ben found the keys in his own role-playing pockets, the twilight stars quickly came and went. And, soon enough, the real-life bee swarm completed its daybreak garbage can raid. Bodies recharging, the trio slumbered for some time until their final foe approached Andy's house. Yes, it was an enemy to all late-night gamers and insomniacs—the grumpy morning garbagemen had arrived.

While the garbagemen prepared their acoustic assault, Andy's brain burrowed into a wondrous dreamscape full of hope, confidence, and Tessa. In the fantasy, Andy and Tessa frolicked down an expansive aisle of Leo's shop dressed as dwarves. Amidst the skipping, he and Tessa performed their favorite film quotes speaking like pirates. And their friends and family threw fistfuls of Nielsen's Cheese Curls in the air, showering them with snacks. To top it all off, Wacky Will Zimmerman stood at a polka-dotted podium as minister. And he pumped out an accordion ballad for their misfit matrimony, also serving as bandleader. Though right as Andy and Tessa leaned in for a kiss, Zimmerman's drummer smacked his cymbal. And then Andy heard the sound's disappointing source as he awoke—the garbagemen banging trash cans outside.

"Why's the garbage truck here so late?" Andy asked, rolling to his side on the kitchen floor. "It's not supposed to be here until morning."

With a few seconds to process, Andy sat up and peered around at the kitchen's new look. Much of the *Rejects & Reptiles* supplies had been moved under the kitchen table. And the table was now retrofitted as a fort using all of Andy's blankets, pillows, and mattresses. Worse, the fort items seemed to be bonded with hardened mortar, though Andy's brain was too foggy to contemplate midnight masonry at this point. Raising his hand from the linoleum, Andy still clenched a filled, yet unused, coffee filter; this was the result of his crawl to the coffee maker while fighting fatigue, he suspected. Behind the fort, Leo slept in a blanket hammock that was nailed, screwed, and stapled to the support beams. And Ben, between the two, snored atop the counter with another nontraditional pillow—a lumpy sack of potatoes.

"Oh well. We'll clean this up in the morning," Andy said, covering himself with a small rug on the floor. "The very far away morning."

Andy cupped his hands into a makeshift pillow and drifted back to sleep, now resting his cheek upon the filled coffee filter. After a packed day of completing video content and devising a plan to leave teaching, Andy passed out again without issue; a night of conquest and smiting his long-term fears had triumphantly tuckered him out. In a few short seconds, his brain warped him back to the wedding for its big finish. And there, Wacky Will Zimmerman returned to the podium's microphone.

"Because you all demanded an encore, here's my slightly altered version of a beloved wedding song. I call this one 'Here Comes the Groom,' and it's available at most physical stores and all online piracy sites as we speak. So shut your yappers and start clapping—here we go," said minister Wacky Will, then starting his parody:

> *Here comes the groom.*
> *The bride is doomed.*
> *She's hot, and he's not,*
> *She's blind, I presume.*
>
> *Wait, that's not true.*
> *She's smiling too?*
> *Though weird, my check cleared,*
> *So I will approve.*

Andy gazed into Tessa's eyes, seeing the reflection of Wacky Will in each pupil as a bonus. With two swift pecks to each other's cheeks and their love therefore consummated, the quirky couple pranced outside. They then rushed to their robot vacuum car and got in, dragging Nathan Hader behind them over a series of speed bumps and roadkill carcasses. Without question, Andy's dream ecstasy had gone into overdrive. And dopamine flowed through his brain even more than the time he ate one of Leo's special brownies.

"Thank you, everybody, thank you," said Wacky Will, now outside Leo's improved storefront. "I'd like to end my moderately-priced appearance with some words of wisdom to my personal pal, Andy Gordon. So listen up, my demented amigo! Here's the secret to attaining success in the comedic arts and finding your self-imposed purpose; you better remember these words and remember them well, Andy...Andy! Andy? Andy Gordon! Andy, it's time for school again! You're late, dear, wake up! Oh no, that didn't work! It always works! Is he breathing, Leo? Ben, is he alive? No mother should ever have to bury her son! Don't do this to me; don't do this to me, dammit! Wake up, Andy! Please! Wake up!"

CHAPTER 9

"Andy Gordon, you get up now or I'm calling an ambulance!" shrieked Mom, shaking Andy as his eyes popped open. "Maybe two ambulances—the fanciest ambulances I can find! You could spend a lot of money on toys instead of fancy ambulances!"

"No, I'm alive! I don't need any ambulances!" shouted Andy, taking the filled coffee filter off his cheek and placing it in the maker. "Mom? What are you doing here? What time is it?"

"It's 8:30 in the morning, dear," Mom said, pointing at the clock behind her that reinforced her claim. "You weren't answering your phone. And you didn't react to me banging on the wall from my apartment either! But you *did* scare me half to death!"

"Shhh. Please be quiet, the children are sleeping," Andy whispered, rolling to his feet and then leading Mom to the living room.

"They didn't even blink when I screamed that you were dead, so I think they're conked out. Was Leo sleeping on a hammock stapled to the walls? And did I see Ben using my sack of potatoes as a pillow?"

"Yes, you did. And it's a long story. I don't know why my phone didn't ring. Where's my phone?"

"Let me help," said Mom, removing empty milk jugs from the cushion-less couch. "Looks like you had a wild night. Were you three doing one of those milk chugging contests to see who pukes first?"

"Nah, we took down a lot of cupcakes though," Andy said, picking up a frothing glass of milk that appeared to be trembling. "Hmm, how long do you think it takes bacteria to evolve and invent vibration-based language?"

"I don't want to find out," said Mom, turning toward the glass and seeing Andy's drowned phone. "Clever, dear. Throw it away."

"Poor phone. I must have been so tired that I thought it was a giant ginger snap," Andy said, pulling his milk-logged phone from the glass. "At least she died with some super strong phone bones."

"You're late for work and joking around. What's going on here?"

"I'm really looking forward to Tessa's show. And let's just say that a certain somebody's being a bit rebellious right now. I sent an email to Principal Murray last night and asked for half a sick day even though I wasn't sick. So I figure I'll go in around lunch time."

"What fun! My boy's in love and playing half hooky! So, what'd you do other than baking last night?"

"We played *Rejects & Reptiles* for about eight hours. Then we ate too much chocolate and passed out."

ANDY GETS CONNED

"I'll take what I can get. Baby steps, dear. Baby steps."

"Wait until you hear this then," said Andy, tossing his calcium-enriched phone into the garbage can. "I may have also finished editing our music video and a promo for Leo's shop. They're both online and set to 'private,' but I can show you with a special link before they're released. I'm launching my video page and web presence as soon as I finish editing one last compilation of my rants. And that's happening today."

"Wonderful! I can't wait."

"What a night. I'm exhausted, but it was so worth it."

"Good, you enjoy your half hooky day and recover then. Who knows, maybe even more of your students will realize how great you are with a mean substitute taking your place? I hope Murray found a real son of a bitch for the morning classes."

"Eh, I bet everything's the same over there without me," said Andy, unaware of the smoke currently billowing from his classroom window. "Coffee's ready!"

Across town at the raging inferno, four fire trucks blasted water solely at Andy's classroom. And all of Andy's students, except B-Fred, now huddled under blankets outside—their hair soaked and their clothes charred. Then Nathan Hader, in his assistant nurse scrubs, swung open the front doors with student B-Fred beside him. As Nurse Rosie handed them both blankets, water gushed down their crispy clothes.

"I'm sorry, B-Fred," Nathan grinned, flossing his taint with the blanket. "I had no idea that gasoline was so flammable—no idea at all!"

"Yeah. It's okay. If you knew, you wouldn't have dared me to try it," said B-Fred, as a firefighter kicked through the doors holding B-Fred's baby.

"Who left a baby in here?" shouted the firefighter, then sniffing its head. "And why the hell does it smell so delicious? Did somebody baste this thing with butter?"

Back in Andy's kitchen, Mom put milk in her coffee while Andy added some flavor to his—two dollops of butterscotch, three cups of creamer, and four dashes of cinnamon to eliminate any hint of coffee. To go with it, Andy grabbed a fistful of ginger snaps and then returned to the living room with Mom.

"That's a lot of fire whistles out there," Mom whispered. "I hope everyone's okay."

"I bet some nut job went after the morning bee swarm with a flamethrower again," joked Andy. "Or, you know, maybe the school burned down. Cheers, Mom!"

Andy and Mom clinked their coffee mugs together and then sipped some legal drug relief. Soon after, sounds of Ben rolling off his kitchen counter bed and slamming to the floor made it to their ears. And this was immediately followed by more snoring.

"Ben always was a heavy sleeper, wasn't he?" Mom said. "Remember when Mr. Gentzel drove his car into the living room? And then crashed into Ben's sleeping bag? And Ben didn't even notice?"

"Yeah, then the horn got stuck and kept blasting. So Mr. Gentzel started screaming at Ben, but he still didn't wake up," said Andy, punctuated by a thud and Ben grunting. "There went the sack of potatoes."

"It's nice to see you smiling, dear. It's been ages. Well, I know this probably doesn't seem like good motherly advice, but screw it. Here's to a healthy dose of reckless behavior!"

"I agree, now who wants some breakfast?" asked Andy, grabbing the chocolate fountain from his gaming table with both hands.

"Not that reckless."

"Well let's see what you think about this next idea then. Gimme your phone."

"Robbing me isn't the right kind of reckless either, dear," she joked.

"Seriously, give me your phone."

"It's in my purse. One second."

Mom placed her coffee cup down, sat on the couch, and rested the purse in her lap. Then she reached in with both hands, almost diving into the endless pouch. And she rummaged through 30 years of pens, lipsticks, and enough stolen silverware to make two dinette sets. Now in elbow deep, she swirled her arm around as if artificially inseminating a cow, but then paused as her eyes lit up.

"You have a problem," said Andy.

"Almost there, dear."

Her phone still elusive, Mom pulled out a head lamp instead. Then she stretched its elastic band around her bouffant, powered it on, and went back in. After what sounded like a series of combination locks and cracked safes, she emerged from the purse with her phone—a bejeweled, rhinestone-encrusted phone that was inches thicker than the factory made it. Andy then grabbed the phone, and its heftiness nearly pulled him to the floor. Breathing heavy, he curled the phone up in a killer bicep workout, dialed it, and jammed it to his ear as it rang.

"Hello, this is Principal Murray. You're on speaker phone 'cause I'm lazy," answered Murray, his male secretary fanning him with a jungle leaf.

"Principal Murray, this is Andy Gordon."

"Who?"

"One of the history teachers."

"Oh, you're the guy with the leg braces, huh?"

"No, the *other* history teacher."

"Holy hell! I'm being haunted from beyond the grave! Gordon's disgruntled ghost just called! Secretary, fetch me my holy water!"

"I'm not following the logic of your joke, but I'm assuming you didn't get my email. I said I wouldn't be coming in until around lunch today."

"I'm a busy guy. You think I check my email so early in the month? Let me get this straight; are you trying to tell me that you did not, in fact, die in a fire today?"

"Murray, please be more principal and less insult comic for a second," Andy said, Mom giving him two thumbs up in support.

"Prove that you're Gordon or this chat ends now."

"I play the snowman at our Christmas pageant. Every year you pull my pants down and my shirt up. It's clearly harassment, especially when you jiggle my stomach and yell 'avalanche' at the same time."

"Well I'll be damned, I'm talking to Gordon all right! Why'd you go and fake your own death if you're still

ANDY GETS CONNED

alive? Insurance scam maybe? And if so, could I get in on this insurance scam?" Murray asked, then facing the secretary. "And if *you* want in on this scam too, you'll keep your mouth shut, leaf guy."

"Wait, was there really a fire at the school? You're not joking?" asked Andy.

"Huge fire, Gordon. Only in your room though. We found a large quantity of charred fat and bone near your mini-fridge and assumed the worst."

"Well, I *did* have a collection of ham hocks in there, but that's beside the point. Did anyone get hurt?"

"No people injured. Everything's fine except my wallet. Oh, and all that dorky crap on your desk."

"What?"

"All that plastic junk that you liked. It's gone."

"My action figures and toys were destroyed?"

"Yup. Not by the fire, but by us afterward. I mean, we did think you were dead."

"I can't believe this!"

"Well you'll have plenty of time to think about it when you come back today. You'll have to move to the bunker until we make some minimal repairs, of course. Are you one of those weird people who doesn't like cockroaches or mold?"

"Murray, I want to thank you for making what I'm about to do much easier," said Andy, winking at Mom. "I've only taken half a day off in the past five years. So how many do I have left?"

"Glad to see you're taking this so well. Hey, secretary, how many sick days do these suckers get a year?"

"Ten days, sir," the secretary said.

"Let's see. You get 10 days a year, Gordon. And you've been here five. Subtract the half a day and that's, uh, little help please?"

"Forty-nine and a half days," Andy answered.

"Yup, sounds about right. Hey, you want to be the math teacher too?"

"No. But starting tomorrow, I want two full weeks off. No questions asked, Murray."

"That's fine, Gordon. It means I won't have to hear you eat ham for two weeks when I walk by. How could I say 'no' to that?"

"Excuse me?"

"Oh, I was commenting on how you eat like a pig, that's all. I'll see you in two weeks, oinky."

"You know what? I change my mind. Give me *all* my days off. In a row," Andy said. "Forty-nine and a half days off with pay, or else I tell the health department about your LegionnAires 2000 air-conditioning unit. Oh, and about the mold and cockroaches you just mentioned too."

In the living room, Mom spit out her coffee in shock. And her hot liquids nearly struck R2CheeseToodle, now trying to suck up a potato that rolled there from Ben's pillow. The spray particles then dissipated, lit up by Mom's head lamp, and she reached back into her purse. After tossing a number of objects behind her, she pulled out a large roll of paper towels. And then she hastily blotted the coffee-dampened carpet.

"You got some big nads, Gordon—just like me. So I'll be straight with you. Your request seems like it shouldn't

ANDY GETS CONNED

be allowed, but there's nothing I can do to stop it," Murray said, his secretary then also doing a spit-take.

"Sir?" the secretary questioned. "There's a huge book in front of you with the exact rule explaining why he can't do that. There are plenty of ways you can stop him, and those are in the book too."

"I said there's *nothing* I can do," insisted Murray, nudging his rulebook into the trashcan. "Gordon, have a lovely vacation."

Andy hung up the phone, watching Mom double-hand yank a 30-foot magician's handkerchief from her purse. Then dropping her distractions, she pounced at Andy, hugged him with an elated squeeze, and somehow lifted him off the ground.

"Wow it worked!" Andy said, all the air escaping from his lungs. "Mom, I need oxygen, you know."

"I'm so proud of my boy!" Mom said, loosening her grip and giving Andy a series of lipstick-coated kisses. "You deserve that vacation, dear."

"This feels odd."

"What does?"

"Having a spine, pursuing dreams, not planning everything—I see why people like it."

"Yes, it is refreshing isn't it? Now this is something we need to celebrate!"

"Right. Where'd that chocolate fountain go?" Andy asked, then noticing Mom's pile of thrown purse objects touching the ceiling.

Andy gazed at the mound and its hoarded contents cascading downward like an estate sale rockslide. He first noticed every homework assignment that he completed since kindergarten. Below those rested fast-food ketchup packets spanning six decades. And then the last object that Andy spotted rolled right to his feet.

"Why do you own a bowling ball?" Andy asked, pushing it back with his foot.

When the bowling ball struck Mom's towering pile, it knocked down two more from the top. And then both of those landed on Andy's feet too.

"Scratch that!" Andy yelped. "Why do you own *three* bowling balls?"

"I think it's probably time to clean out my purse," said Mom, as Andy ladled two bowls of chocolate from the fountain and gave her one.

"Here's to a new software update for the Gordons!" Andy said, both then sucking chocolate straight from their bowls. "New outlooks, new plans, and newly discovered balls. Plus, we can make our upgraded debut at Tessa's comedy show tonight. Don't worry; I'll help you pick up some dudes there too."

"That's what I was trying to call you about," Mom said, handing him the tickets. "I have another date tonight, dear, so I can't go see Tessa. I'm sorry."

"Hmm, same guy?"

"It's baffling, but yes. I enjoy his company a lot."

"Hot damn, Mom! That's fantastic. I knew that feeble mind of yours still had a chance at love."

"And you do too tonight, dear."

"I'm hoping so! Before I go, I should research some conversation topics that'll charm her unicorn socks off,

ANDY GETS CONNED

shouldn't I?" Andy asked. "Wait, no! No, I *won't* do that research. Reckless, that's right—reckless!"

"So good luck, have fun, and don't you dare worry about me," Mom said, using her purse to scoop up her stuff like a pelican.

"Great, we'll gossip tomorrow at the flower shop, okay? Sometime in the afternoon? I can't wait to hear all about your heartthrob. And judging by the amount of birth control pills I just saw in your purse pile, I'm guessing things are going really well with you two!"

"They are, dear—he's a keeper. But those pills expired decades ago. It's really time to clean out my purse."

"See you tomorrow, Mom," said Andy, as fabric ripped in the kitchen and Leo screamed.

"I'm stuck on the staples, man! I'm stuck on my hammock staples!" shouted Leo. "Why'd I ever agree to hammock staples?"

"I'd save you, but I don't want to burn breakfast," yawned Ben. "Who wants potato pancakes?"

"And you think I have problems," laughed Mom.

"I'll yell at them after I have one potato pancake. Just one," said Andy, bolting for the kitchen as Mom dipped out. "There you go, Leo, good as new. Plus, if you make up a cool origin story for this scar, you'll score major points with the ladies."

After Andy slapped bandages on Leo's back, the trio shared a fine potato pancake breakfast and cleaned up the results of their wild, prolific night. With all objects back in place, including the mortar-connected pillows after some intense chiseling, the gang traveled their separate ways.

Leo rushed to his comic shop, researching neon sign companies with the fastest shipping options. And Ben moseyed off to the mattress store for more sleep. But as soon as they left, Andy got down to business with Tessa in mind and much lotion below to reduce friction. It was something sweaty to lessen stress and make him last longer, should tonight go well. With his cheeks glowing, blood pumping, and brain filling with endorphins, Andy was enjoying himself...outside. No, not through jail-worthy passions of the flesh in public, but through a foreign concept to Andy for most of his life—*intentional* exercise. The lotion was for his thigh-chafing.

CHAPTER 10

Energy surged through Andy's body as if jamming a fork in a toaster, now burning calories around the neighborhood and continuing his reboot. With an online presence about to launch, a student-free vacation, and Tessa's comedy show on the horizon, Andy started taking care of himself. He figured that some cardio and better health could be the next step toward Nirvana or, if he died in the process, at least Valhalla. Though he stopped frequently to lather more lotion and reduce the thigh chafing, Andy power walked with fire in his eyes. No, not even the hostile dogs or their sidewalk soft-serve could put a damper on this day.

Soon, Andy's power walk became a full sprint when two demonic Dobermans destroyed their fence and chased him into a fast food dumpster on the corner. Though surrounded by burgers, some still in their wrappers, Andy avoided noshing on any free meat scraps for his entire leftover layover. Appeasing the dogs with a dumpster's worth of dubious meats, Andy made his move and then survived a few more laps thanks to the slowing dogs. The explosive combo of exercise and lukewarm mayonnaise, however, meant the Dobermans' owners did not see such pleasant results on their carpets later.

After a shower and shopping trip for today's alterations, Andy skateboarded down the sidewalk in his *Rejects & Reptiles* themed suit jacket adorned with dwarves. Underneath, Andy wore another custom shirt emblazoned with the text 'You're History...Give It Time.' And below that sat plenty of 'courtesy sweat' napkins to soak up any nervous armpit downpours around Tessa. On his shoulders rested a backpack filled with his fruitful store scouring—the packaging for a new replacement phone, a bouquet of flowers in the water bottle pocket, and healthier snacks including actual fruit. Tapping the 'Record' button of his skateboard camera, Andy began accumulating more footage for his rant compilation video.

"Today's topic—nutrition facts that seem a lot more like nutrition fiction to me," Andy said, tilting the camera toward his face with his foot. "I've been investigating these mysterious calorie maps called food labels. And if these are right, then I'm definitely eating wrong. Did you know that the serving suggestion for butterscotch is one tablespoon and not, in fact, half a jar? I put more than that in my morning coffee. Plus, I was eating enough ginger snaps to sustain an entire African village. And for pizza? Two slices are the norm, not two whole pies with breadsticks and another slice of pizza for dessert! Who's making these suggestions? An anorexic scientist? Some bigwig with a small, stapled stomach? Or maybe there's a

ANDY GETS CONNED

darker reason for this; perhaps our government's in cahoots with food companies and all those gym lobbyists raking in the dough. With deceptively tiny suggestions that no normal person consumes, 'we the eaters' get considerably fatter. And as obesity grows, the more of us fill their gyms and pad those owners' pockets with cash—fat cash! Well I'm tossing away all of my snacks, and I hope that you do too; we can overcome this if we join together and purge the—"

Andy paused mid-sentence as he felt a vigorous shaking from his pocket. Was the government triggering an explosive chip implanted at birth? Did he drink some mutant annelids about to burst from his body and eat his face off? Or, less exciting, maybe he just had Parkinson's disease? As the vibration continued buzzing his leg, a strange series of shrill beeps and boops emanated from his pants pocket.

"Oh, it's my new phone. I haven't heard a default ringtone in years," Andy said, pulling the device from his pocket. "Hello? Hey, Leo! What's shaking, disco papa?"

"You're a modern-day alchemist, dude!" said Leo through the phone speaker. "I checked out the private link you sent me for the promo video. You transmuted our goofiness into gold! Such vision, such style, and that animated explosion of you blowing up our competitor's store was a real blast. I never knew computer-generated imagery could seem so real. Hilarious CGI, man!"

"Yes...CGI. That's what it was. Anyway, I want to finish another rant for the last video and then we're ready to launch. I'm giddy! Do I sound giddy?"

"I share the excitement, man. And thanks again for supporting the shop."

"You bet. Business is about to pick up for you soon. I'll see you later. And we'll chat about some shop promotion videos that I'm planning for the future, okay?"

"Right on. What time can I expect your arrival?"

"Now actually," said Andy, skating up to Leo's shop and waving at him through the window. "You better double check the shop's maximum occupancy because we're about to pack this place!"

"Question for you, Andy. Were you on your way when I called, or did I space out and lose all concept of time or something?"

"The first guess! I'm headed to a comedy show and have an extra ticket that you get dibs on. You win over Ben since you've treated me to, well, anything before," Andy said, squishing his tickets on the shop's window. "Ten o'clock. You interested?"

"Hold on, I definitely spaced out then. My eyes last locked on the clock around 8 p.m. But that only felt like a few seconds ago."

"Oh, it's eight all right, but the early bird catches the worm. And by 'bird' I mean 'me' and by 'worm' I mean 'less mental anxiety.' The earlier I am to the show, the fewer chances of screwing up courtship with Tessa. That makes sense, right?"

"Oh, I have to experience this then. I probably shouldn't close up the shop for too long though. Those geeky, post-work, adult crowds are my most lucrative spenders—yourself included."

"How about you shut the blinds and put up a note saying you'll be back in 30 minutes? Maybe add that you'll be returning with some new and highly exclusive trinkets. That'll spark some interest."

"I don't possess any new and highly exclusive trinkets to spark interest."

"Yes, but you *will* after you hide a couple crates of unwanted merch in the van and bring them back later. Shoppers will see the note and have to wait. Then they'll see you coming back with the boxes. And suddenly your junk is treasure. They'll basically throw money at you."

"You're my favorite investor and, between you and me, my only investor. Groovy, we'll cross paths at 10 then. And remember this advice: Keep your cool. Maintain!"

Andy hung up, did a few jumping jacks to get his blood pumping again, and then power walked to the Three-Fifth Chasers speakeasy. Having done a little research about the place, Andy's opinion had changed. Though billionaire Kerry Kirkpatrick started the business, he was recently hospitalized and sold half his shares. With his senile mind stuck in the 1800s, he only charged two nickels and a shoeshine for half the establishment. Press coverage of the purchase said that Janet, a speakeasy employee, was the buyer. And she apparently had big plans to change the place.

Janet seemed to be curbing Kirkpatrick's bigotry as co-owner too, hosting events that welcomed the previously discriminated. Yes, Lynch Mob Mondays were a thing of the past. And there'd never be another Gas Shower Happy Hour. Instead, Tessa's comedy show coincided with Janet's newest plan—a Heathens-Only night. While progress felt slower than erosion, the speakeasy at least seemed to exist in the right century with Janet's help.

Outside of the speakeasy, three homeless men sat at a burning cross. No coincidence, Janet's warm donation not only made heat for the vagrants, but also accentuated her heathen theme. The closest vagrant, in a downy coat that covered everything but his eyeballs, shivered worse than the others despite his thick protection. To his right sat a vagrant in a muumuu dress. And the third vagrant, only wearing a fanny pack, gave dog treats to his pet—a stuffed animal bee beside him. Nearing the men, Andy extracted his Wacky Will wallet from a pocket dice bag.

"My treat, guys," Andy said.

"We don't want that stupid wallet," said the downy-coated vagrant.

"No, sir, I mean these," said Andy, handing three 5-dollar bills to the downy-coated vagrant. "Here's some cash for each of you."

As Andy put his skateboard into his backpack and entered, the muumuu and fanny pack vagrants reached toward the money. But right before they had the bills within their hands, the downy-coated vagrant crumpled them into a ball.

"Well this won't make us warm either," the downy-coated vagrant said, tossing Andy's cash onto the burning cross. "What an idiot!"

"That was money!" screamed the fanny pack vagrant. "Homeless people need money! We let you join this team thinking you'd pull your weight!"

ANDY GETS CONNED

"Calm down," the muumuu vagrant said. "He's learnin'. Gotta give him time."

"At least make him wear the training badge then!"

"That's fair. We didn't wanna demoralize ya even more, but ya gotta wear this," said the muumuu vagrant, sticking an 'In Training' napkin to their novice with chewed gum.

Inside, Andy hit up the ATM, preparing for any unplanned expenses with 500 bucks of versatile 5-dollar bills. While predicting future expenses wasn't in line with his reckless behavior reboot, blowing that much cash on non-nerd activities certainly was.

"Ahh, the benefits of living a child-free, ex-wife free, paid-off mortgage life," Andy said, pocketing his bills.

Now set, Andy took a deep breath. And then he strolled up to Janet the bartender, a woman seemingly ripped from a plus-size pin-up calendar. Her short, spiked hair looked like a shiny sea urchin in the neon lights, Janet wiping the counter with a rag. This early in the night, only two other patrons kept Janet company—one close by, one far, but both way out there. First up, Andy felt the disparaging stare of a scruffy male biker fitted with an eyepatch. As the biker turned in his booth and tracked Andy, his long beard scraped off his beer's fresh foam. The other stare came from a wheelchair-bound, half-legged veteran in Civil War garb. And as he walloped a cue ball around an empty pool table, he screamed a racial slur with each strike.

"Hi, sweetie," said Janet. "Ya lookin' for the geek shop? That's two doors down the block."

"Nope, I'm in the right spot. I've never seen the inside of this place. Look at the history all over these walls...the newspaper clippings of protests...with the cops abusing a rainbow of skin colors."

"I know, it's revoltin' isn't it? Like your shirt says, we're all history in the long run. Life's too short to be hatin' people for somethin' so stupid. We're all just a pack o' colored crayons meltin' together in the same box, ya know? Anyway, this talk's too sad, and I haven't gotten ya a drink yet. So, what would ya like, sweetie?"

"Have any self-esteem on tap?" smirked Andy.

"Haven't had any o' that since I got here. There's plenty o' self-doubt if you're interested."

"How about a diet root beer then?"

"Sure thing. Ya wanna upgrade to an ice cream float?"

"No thanks. A diet root beer will hit the spot."

"Comin' right up," said Janet, sliding a root beer bottle to Andy. "Welcome to Heathens-Only night. Are ya recoverin' or a designated driver?"

"Neither, actually. I'm just a heathen supporting the agnostic arts. So, what's the comedian like tonight? Know anything about her?"

"Glad to have ya here. The comedian's a nerdy girl with a strange name—Tessa. Funny gal too. She started doin' stand-up 'round here 'bout a year ago. But she doesn't go on for another two hours. You're mighty early, ya know that?"

"Okay, I'll fess up," spewed Andy. "I didn't want any chance of missing her act, so I'm here before she is."

"Big fan, eh?"

"You could say that. I'm kinda crazy about her. Does she come across like a heathen in her act?"

"Big time. She cracked a resurrection joke on Easter. Somethin' 'bout breads only havin' the power to rise twice. That one made me slap both o' my knees."

"And she doesn't seem like a racist?"

"No, she's not, sweetie. And I'm not either. She's what we need 'round here to help this place evolve a bit."

"You've been a huge help. Thank you, Miss..."

"Janet."

"Oh, you're Janet? I've read a lot about you online!" said Andy. "Don't take that the wrong way. I mean that I've read about all your new plans for this place online. Nice to meet you, Janet! We'll talk later, but I'll go find a seat now, okay?"

"Good luck with that. The place is packed right? If ya need me, ya know where I am."

Andy bolted at the stage like a kid in the toy aisle, gleefully giggling as the few puzzled patrons watched. And then the brawny biker shifted his gaze to Janet with a dead-eyed stare.

"You never said you had floats," he grumbled.

Instead of testing all the seats for optimal eye contact, Andy plopped down in a chair in the very last row. Yes, sitting in the back was still the naughtiest action that came to his nerdy mind. While waiting, Andy edited his nutrition vlog into the rant video, uploaded it to his JumboAndy page, and scheduled all three videos to unlock at 3:27 a.m. This specific time not only celebrated the moment he was born, but also likely reached his target audience of late-night gamers. Thus, the last missing piece for his comedic launch was finally complete.

"All done and ahead of schedule too! Rest up, videos. You all go public in the morning no matter what happens!" said Andy, putting away his laptop and then squinting at the stage mic that felt miles away. "Wait, Tessa won't see me here. Time for a seating change. I can overthink this a little bit, right? I can be flexible. Flexibility's still pretty reckless compared to what I used to be! Here we go!"

Now combining an analytical perspective with his wild evening, Andy evaluated his seating options. A simple mistake like choosing the wrong chair could wipe away all his advancements, Andy assumed. But selecting the right chair could lead to Tessa and Andy living happily ever after—their minds uploaded to robots so they wouldn't get old and die. So his test went on, now in a seat in the first row. He was right in front of the microphone too, as close as he could be. When his eyes scanned upward while picturing Tessa's legs inches away, Andy jumped up from his incorrect and stupid seat selection.

"Way too weird even for me. I shouldn't be eye-level with her crotch this soon."

Since shadows made men look so cool in those old movies he watched with Dad, Andy looked for the right amount of lighting—half lit and half dark like a cinematic face paint. But the only area that provided this lighting was a small bench where pool players rested during tournaments. And this meant that Andy was very likely to be hit in the head with a pool stick.

ANDY GETS CONNED

"Hey, I could see this one working," said Andy, immediately hit in the back of the head with a pool stick.

"Die, you dirty Commie!" hollered the veteran, stabbing the cue ball and landing a powerful shot right into the jukebox.

"What war were you even in?" asked Andy, recoiling in pain and rubbing his head.

"All of 'em! Quick, help me, comrade! They're hidin' in the trenches! Grenade, corner pocket!"

"I hear these guys will surrender and come out from under the grass if you put a quarter in here," Andy said, placing a coin into the pool table and releasing its balls.

"Thanks, pal. These sand-suckers don't have a chance now. The name's Zeus," he said, arranging the balls into a skull shape on the table. "Who do I have the honor of servin' with today?"

"Andy, but you can call me pretty much anything you want as long as you don't kill me."

"Welcome to the front line, Private Pretty-Much-Anything-You-Want-As-Long-As-You-Don't-Kill-Me! You got a great last name—a bit long though. Is it German? Or maybe you're one of those Spanish chicks who marries a lot?" Zeus spouted, now wheeling backward and lining up his shot. "If I don't make it out of this alive, tell my wife and kids and my mistress and her kids that I love 'em all!"

"I'll do some reconnaissance and report back to you soon, commander!" shouted Andy, escaping.

"Burn in Hell, you dirty cabbage eaters!" Zeus yelled, racing forward with one hand and wielding the pool cue with his other like a jousting match.

Andy moved to a booth near the bathrooms, now with a grapefruit-sized head lump. And mesmerized by Andy's bad luck, the biker still watched from his booth.

"Low stalker profile. The cushions look comfy. And it's a convenient location if I have a nervous pee coming on," Andy said, squeezing into the booth that narrowed like a distorted, haunted mansion hallway.

Bones popping and blubber pinching, Andy was stuck. Wiggling didn't work, nor did his head banging or butt shaking timed perfectly with the music to mask the panic. Imagining the news coverage of a man's quest for love stymied by his oversized hiney, Andy summoned all of his strength to escape.

"I'll be damned if I let a booth get the best of me," Andy said, gripping the table with both hands. "Brute force activate, now!"

Andy repeatedly threw himself forward for Round 2 in the booth, making no progress like a gym class pull up. So he skipped to Round 3 by oscillating his entire body and preparing for potential liftoff. Left then right, Andy continually twisted and shifted. Then planting his feet, he heaved himself backward with one tremendous tug.

And that's when the wood cracked worse than the time he split a rocking chair right in half. Now out of control and lacking the proper brakes, Andy tumbled backward through the booth and flipped onto a rather precarious place. Even though he avoided piercing his patootie on a pile of splintered wood and jagged metal, Andy landed in a spot even more dangerous—directly on the bearded biker's lap.

ANDY GETS CONNED

"If you're gonna sit there, you gotta call me 'Peaches,'" the biker grinned.

"I'm so sorry, Peaches!" Andy screamed.

"Those flowers look real pretty," Peaches said, noticing the bouquet in Andy's backpack.

"Do you want them? They're all yours, Peaches! Please don't kill me."

"Peaches don't kill when he's sniffin' pretty flowers and havin' ice cream," he said, pointing at his two empty pitchers of root beer floats.

"Thank you for your kindness, Peaches. Hey, Janet? Order this guy as many floats as he wants. And put them on my tab with whatever I owe you for the booth too. Don't forget to charge extra for your troubles. You want a new eyepatch, Peaches? I can give you cash, checks, and all my credit cards. Anything you need, I'm your man!"

Andy quickly left Peaches' lap and ran to the middlemost table, skirting death yet again. Now far away from everyone, Andy cleaned the wood chips off his *Rejects & Reptiles* jacket with a lint roller. Then to be safe, he replaced his armpit napkins and removed all visible sweat with a blow dryer from his backpack.

"Ah, the perfect seat. It's the middle—the normal and completely safe middle."

After resting his arms behind his head, Andy flinched, now conditioned for another sudden strike of misfortune. Where was the clumsy waitress schlepping around spaghetti and red wine to unload on his clothes? Where was the muscle man Tyrannosaurus Flex from Leo's shop claiming that Andy stole his favorite seat? Where was the radioactive rat bound to bite his cankle and grant him the superpower of finishing sex within seconds? None of those coming to fruition, Andy gasped as a familiar hand caressed his shoulder instead.

"That's the strangest game o' musical chairs I ever saw," Janet said, holding a roll of tickets.

"Sorry. I'm scaring away customers, aren't I?"

"No, it's not your fault," said Janet. "Peaches loves ya after all those free floats. And ol' Zeus over there says he'd follow ya into war ridin' elephants any day. Just a slow night, that's all."

"Well I hope things pick up. Could you bring me another diet root beer and a water?"

"Yeah, 'bout that, sweetie. My co-owner told me to shut down early with how low the numbers were."

"But you're the co-owner. And you're improving this place. Can't you stay open anyway?"

"I would if I could, but Kirkpatrick gets final say as senior co-owner here. And if my ideas aren't pullin' in people, he stops 'em pretty quick. Ya know, I thought this Heathens-Only night would change up the atmosphere and add some color. It's too bad, but I'm gonna have to call Tessa and let her know the show's off," Janet said, presenting a roll of tickets. "I've only sold two o' these tonight, and Kirkpatrick ain't happy. He's pretty sick and old, so things like this won't be happenin' for too much longer. I hope it's soon."

"You're not cancelling this," Andy said, jumping up and saving the perfect seat with his backpack. "I'll go fix your problem right now!"

ANDY GETS CONNED

"Sweetie, you're too cute to go take out the ol' geezer. Plus, he's got guard dogs protectin' his hospital bed."

"No, not that problem. But I can get you an audience. How much time do I have?"

"I can give ya 20 minutes."

"I won't let you or Tessa down! Here's a hundred bucks for that roll," Andy said, stuffing a wad of cash into Janet's hand and taking the tickets. "Does that cover it?"

"Almost. There's a three-drink minimum too."

"Okay, put whatever the audience drinks on my tab, and I'll pay it all tonight. Now, to find an audience. I'll have this place teeming with heathens in no time!"

CHAPTER 11

Outside Three-Fifth Chasers, the two senior vagrants roasted pigeons over a fiery cross. But their trainee chose not to participate, instead resting his face atop a sewer drain. Yes, with fumes of bird entrails and charred feathers filling the streets, the downy-coated vagrant puked his guts out through a small eye slot in his coat.

"First you burned our cash and now you're wasting our food. That's pretty rude even for a homeless guy," scolded the fanny pack vagrant.

"You gotta let your gut get used to the bird germs, that's all. Keep it in there," the muumuu vagrant said, as Andy charged out of the speakeasy

"Attention, street people!" Andy shouted through his cupped hands. "This loud, fat guy's giving away money."

As if Emily's comedic science fair cricket had been busy bumping uglies since Andy's breakdown, a chorus of its relatives chirped. And Andy's offer brought no audible attention. Following up, he re-cupped his hands and added one important clarification.

"You don't have to have sex with the loud, fat guy for the money either. It's free!"

Suddenly, from the nasty nooks and corrupt crannies of the darkened street, crowds of homeless people, gang members, and prostitutes encircled Andy like a cyclone of sin. Still nibbling their pigeons, the muumuu and fanny pack vagrants sprung from their spots and joined in too. But the downy-coated vagrant took a different path yet again, sneaking inside the speakeasy unnoticed. Despite seeing a familiar dominatrix in the crowd around him, as well as a few of his former students, Andy continued with his limited-time proposal.

"All you have to do is head inside this speakeasy, drink as much alcohol as you want, and watch a comedy act on your best behavior. I'll pay you all five bucks now and another five after the show."

In their shockingly well-mannered fashion, the group filed inside as Andy handed each passing person their cash and ticket. His vlog career would more than make up for the cost, he rationalized. Andy then ran back into the jam-packed speakeasy, now ready for Tessa to blow these drunken degenerates' socks off.

Stopping by the ATM again, Andy took out enough cash to cover the crowd's second payment after the show. But when Andy saw Peaches' pyramid of root beer float pitchers, he pulled out an extra grand for his increasingly large tab. As Andy pocketed the money, two firm hands covered his eyes from behind.

"Of all the times I could have been robbed. Not tonight!" yelled Andy.

"I'm not gonna take somethin' from ya, sweetie," Janet said, spinning Andy's hips around as the two now stood inches apart. "But if ya keep charmin' me like this, I might *give* you somethin'."

"What are you doing?" asked Andy, as Janet bit her lip and unbuttoned her blouse.

"I don't know how ya did that, but you're a life saver. My Heathens-Only night's a hit! So how can I pay ya back?" Janet asked, wrapping both hands around his delectable derriere. "I have an idea how I could pay ya back, if you're too shy to tell me yourself, sexy."

"I, uh, I wish I would have met you sooner, Janet," Andy spurted. "You're very attractive, and I'm flattered. But, alas, my heart is captured by a lady in another castle."

"A man with ethics gets me goin' even more," said Janet, squishing their groins together closer still. "I appreciate the honesty, Andy. If she ever breaks your heart, ya know where to find me."

"You know what?" Andy said, as Janet pulled back. "There is one favor you could do for me."

"Oh, yeah?" Janet asked, ripping the rest of her blouse off. "Ask away."

"You are persistent, woman! But no, not that!"

Backstage, Tessa paced behind the curtain. And she now wore an elegant black dress with holes cut around the shoulders for maximum airflow. Flapping her arms like a chicken and drying some sweat, she murmured to herself.

"What if I get heckled? What if I bomb? Or worse, what if I do well and have to go through this all over again? Ugh! Stop it, brain! You can do this, Tessa!"

From behind, a finger tapped her exposed shoulder. Then a few more fingers joined in, soon becoming a squeeze. Yuck! What womanizer was hitting on her now? Was it some frat guy about to say she's funny for a chick? Some jock dropping a quarter and asking her to pick it up? Some middle-aged man crushing a can of beer on his head and then asking her to bang? Whoever it was, they were about to be pepper sprayed, kicked, and impaled on the mic stand—thrice, if necessary.

"Whoa there, Tessa," said Janet, holding a manila envelope and bottle of root beer behind the stage curtain. "Hey, sweetie. A man in the audience bought ya a drink."

"Ohh, root beer!" said Tessa, taking a sip and then pausing. "Wait, it's not from that biker who makes you call him 'Peaches,' is it?"

"I'm thinkin' your answer's in here," said Janet, presenting the manila envelope in her hand. "Ya have a pretty big fan in the crowd."

"Someone who can write?" asked Tessa, ripping the letter away. "Who is it? Who is it?"

Using her fingernail, Tessa tore open the envelope. And then she dumped its contents into her hand despite the bioweapons that could be inside. Fortunately, Tessa found something far more surprising than anthrax or substances visible via blacklight; the metal dwarf from Andy's *Rejects & Reptiles* game now sat in her palm.

"Jumbo Shrimpit!" squealed Tessa.

"Judgin' from that reaction, ya both belong together," sighed Janet. "Want me to throw away that envelope for ya? How 'bout the plastic packagin' on his axe?"

ANDY GETS CONNED

"No thanks, I'll keep the envelope for the memories and the plastic protection so I don't lop off any fingers," Tessa said, poking her head through the curtains.

Tessa shifted her eyes past Peaches slurping floats and Zeus lobbing pool balls at the jukebox like grenades. Then scanning each row of the crowd, her eyes passed a long-haired hippie in the middle of the room. Her peepers then locked on a familiar face attached to an even more familiar body in the centermost chair.

"Andy!" she called, waving.

"There she is, Leo," said Andy, nudging. "Hi, Tessa!"

Andy waved back with a half-open, toothy grin. And Leo did a double-take, now processing his friend's stunning Tessa target.

"She's outta your league and this world," said Leo.

"You haven't even seen how funny she is yet. Get ready!" exclaimed Andy.

"Good luck out there, Tessa," said Janet backstage, dimming the lights and then pushing her forward. "It's a packed house tonight—your biggest crowd yet. So knock 'em dead! Or, at least make 'em drink."

As the room fully dimmed, a bright spotlight from above beamed down in the shape of a swastika—another item Janet hoped to replace when Kirkpatrick kicked the bucket. Tessa then jogged out to the microphone and rubbed the metal dwarf in her pocket for good luck. All of her fingers still intact, it was show time.

"Hey, everybody. First off, I'd like to apologize for how bizarre it was watching me run right there. I am so awkward; I can't even go through happy events without being awkward. Here's an example: It was my birthday last week and my uncle bought me flowers. Flowers, those are happy right? Not to my brain. When he gave me those I was like, 'Yeah, uncle, nice try celebrating the beauty of life with something we both know's going to die in a week.' That's what I said to somebody giving me a gift; those words came out of my mouth. Not quite as nice as 'thank you' is it? Nope, not at all. And that's me every single day—awkward!"

The crowd chuckled and respectfully listened as Andy sighed with relief. He had risen to the occasion! He had saved the show! He had gifted Peaches the flowers that Tessa would have totally thought were stupid! And now with butts in the seats, Tessa's self-deprecating approach had managed to warm the reprobates' hearts.

"Why's anyone think flowers are good gifts? We all know they have a short shelf life. But for some reason people think it's okay? Try using that same logic with other gifts. 'Here you go, Tessa, it's chocolate. But the chocolate only stays fresh for 30 seconds, so it'll spoil by the time I finish my sentence.' Or, 'here you go, Tessa, it's a car. But the engine explodes after you drive it 10 feet.' Or, 'here you go, Tessa, it's a cute little kitty! And, oh yeah, it has leukemia too. Yup—a leukemia-ridden kitten, but it's the thought that counts, right?' Wrong!"

Such dark humor struck a chord with the tough crowd, their laughs both deranged and real. While Andy observed his skilled soulmate, all water in his mouth dribbled out like an impressed Niagara Falls. She was funny! She was smart! And she didn't run away when he was within smelling distance! Inspired by this quirky tour de force, Andy's brain then ventured back to the dream wedding with Tessa. And in his mind, both misfits started spazzing out at their Wacky Will dance party reception.

Ten minutes later, Tessa managed to mix philosophy, nerd culture, and a couple 'dead baby' jokes into her non-hack routine. Therefore, Andy was ready to storm the stage, make a move, and start banging out comedy videos together. The audience agreed, roaring in response before their inevitable return to the callous streets. As Tessa took a bow, Andy sprung from his seat and applauded louder than anyone there; if he had smacked those hands any harder, he would have clapped off his damn fingerprints. Playing up the heartening response, Tessa acted as if the jovial energy struck her like a speeding bus, bowed once more, and then pranced backstage.

"Am I biased or was that brilliant?" asked Andy.

"Marry her, Andy," Leo said, as he joined the standing ovation. "As your friend and Reject Master, I approve of her vibes! Plus, it'd be killer to have a female role in our campaign who's not played by a dude!"

"Yeah, a chick with an Adam's apple always seems to ruin the in-game romance, doesn't it? But Tessa would be great with our group. She's wonderful! She's perfect! I'm asking her out right now," Andy said, as Janet rushed over with another diet root beer.

"Ya just gave Three-Fifth Chasers the best damn business it's seen in years," Janet said, handing Andy his drink and caressing the dice bag in his pants pocket. "Are ya positive I can't weasel a date out o' ya, Andy?"

"I'm afraid I can't. If we would have met a few days ago, it'd be different; I'm locked on Tessa, and it wouldn't be fair to you at all. If things don't work with me and her, you bet your britches I'll be back to check on your single status after I recover."

"I see," Janet sighed.

"But in the time being, and I know this transition is going to sound totally forced, I'd like you to meet my best pal Leo," Andy said, pushing the two together like endangered pandas at the zoo. "Why don't you two talk? I have some business to take care of outside."

"We have toilets in here, ya know," Janet said, elbowing Leo with a smile.

"I'll be coming back to this place, without a doubt. It was a pleasure meeting you, Janet. And Leo, see you later. I think you'd both make a great couple!" said Andy, then escaping into the crowd.

"I apologize for my planetary companion," said Leo. "This is a colossal change for the big guy."

"Hey, if that saint endorsed ya, then ya can't be that bad. That scar ya have on your neck's pretty neat too. Where'd ya get it? Looks fresh."

"Oh that? I was battling eight rattlers at once and I...okay, I can't lie. I got these gnarly nicks from some hammock staples."

"Another honest man 'round here? How 'bout I buy ya a drink and ya tell me more."

"No bad energy intended, Janet, but can I take a rain check too? I have to go rejoin the 'counter' culture; I operate the comic shop down the block."

ANDY GETS CONNED

"You own Leo's Larpin' & Comics? So that's two great men offerin' two depressin' rain checks," Janet groaned. "I read ya loud and clear."

"Don't get me wrong, Janet. My job's on the rocks, and my company's woes are making me bad company," Leo said, then kissing each of Janet's knuckles. "But our energies will meet again if you're still single and ready to mingle in the future, okay?"

As Leo escaped, avoiding the monetary obligations of courtship, Janet guzzled two beers from a neighboring table. With applause showing no signs of stopping, Tessa rushed backstage and leapt in the air like a cheerleader launched via catapult.

"Yes! You did it! You are a warrior! An animal! A savage who put hundreds of hours into a set for 50 bucks," Tessa spouted, then touched again from behind. "Thanks for putting me on, Janet!"

As Tessa spun around and swung her arms open for a hug, she recoiled at the sight and smell of the downy-coated vagrant. Yes, he reeked like an overcooked pigeon...with a hint of regurgitated, vanilla protein. Unzipping his thick winter jacket and loosening its face-hiding hood, the vagrant threw his coat to the ground. His symmetrical set of sensual lips, his imposing brow, his statuesque abs—Andy's old student Nathan Hader was here as one hunky homeless guy.

"Oh, hello. I'm sorry; I thought you were somebody else," said Tessa. "Hi, I'm Tessa!"

"It's cool. I get mistaken for other people all the time, mostly male supermodels though. The name's...*Luke*," said Nathan with a smile. "Really nice job out there tonight. Boy, that sure was different."

"Thank you. So, you liked my set?"

"Oh, I really liked your *set* out there. And your set now. You have a nice set on you, you know," Nathan said.

"Okay, I should be going now. I have a friend in the audience I want to catch up with."

"Hold on. But you know what's even better than your set? Your acting. How'd you look so happy with the fake audience out there? You should be in movies!"

"Um, what do you mean by that exactly?"

"The movies where you don't need to take your clothes off. You know, the boring ones," said Nathan, as sincerely as possible. "You have the body to be in the movies where you take your clothes off, but your acting's so good that you don't need to take your clothes off."

"No, I meant the fake audience part," Tessa said, scowling. "Those were real people out there."

"I thought you were in on this. You weren't in on this at all? Are you kidding me?"

"Some specifics would really help me not freak out right now. What are you talking about?"

"I feel bad for you. Your chubby manager Andy must be trying to protect your feelings then. I'm sorry."

"You need to start this conversation again, Luke," Tessa said, clenching her fist. "Back up a second."

"All right," Nathan said, physically stepping backward. "I don't see how this helps."

"That was kinda funny, but please be serious right now. Tell me what you think is going on."

ANDY GETS CONNED

"Your manager Andy is out in the audience, right? Next to the hippie? He told us that his new client Tessa needed an audience because she has no fans. Then he paid us to act like your jokes were funny no matter how awful they were. His words, not mine."

"You sound confused, sir," Tessa said, forcing a smile. "Let's see if we can find you some help at the shelter, okay?"

"Wait, you didn't know? He said you knew. He told us you two have this scam where you buy a crowd, bribe them to laugh, and then raise your fee the next time you come back to the place. He said if we faked the laughs, your hot body would do the rest. And then you'd use that hot body to have sex with him for all his hard work later."

"No, he wouldn't do that. And I'm not letting you upset me anymore. How about we go clear this up with him right now? He's nice. I bet he'll even walk with us to the shelter."

Outside Three-Fifth Chasers, Andy leaned against the wall as his crowd exited—most still chuckling. Watching them return to their destitution, Andy doled out his second payment of 5-dollar bills.

"Thanks. Thank you. Thank you very much," Andy said, as Tessa walked out next and saw money dangling in her face. "Thank you."

"Andy? Why are you paying these people?" asked Tessa, as Nathan exited in his face-obscuring coat.

"I was, uh, oh hi, Tessa! There's a very good reason why I'm paying all these whores and drug dealers. Give me two minutes and I'll intricately describe what's going on here," Andy gushed, seeing Tessa's furious face. "Hey, you were fabulous tonight!"

"Did you really pay these people to laugh at my show? At my, supposedly, *awful* jokes?"

"What? No. That's not right. I—"

"Enough, Andy!" Nathan said, unzipping his coat. "No more lies tonight! Just stop this parade."

"What are you doing here? Get the hell away from her," Andy growled. "And you meant *charade*, you idiot!"

"Hey, my sweet ride's parked right over there," Nathan said, facing Tessa. "I'll take you home tonight. Why don't you have a seat?"

Nathan pointed at his transportation—a shopping cart parked at the curb. Inside rested a collection of aluminum cans topped with vanilla protein bar wrappers; this was the definitive homeless chick magnet.

"Way to ruin a memory! I thought this was my career-launching story! I even hoped we'd make out tonight!" Tessa said, Andy noticing the painful past tense. "You're a liar. I can't believe how wrong I was about you."

Tessa stormed off, dropping Andy's gift on the pigeon bloodied sidewalk. She then climbed into Nathan's shopping cart, displacing loads of cans like some low-budget playhouse ball pit.

"Look, Tessa. I don't know what's going on here," Andy pleaded, picking up the envelope. "Just wait a second. Can we press 'Pause' on this conversation so I can try to explain? Maybe let me spam the 'Refresh' icon a few times on our browser chat?"

"I can't," she cried, sobbing into her hands.

ANDY GETS CONNED

Traffic then stopped as a bunch of men slammed on their brakes. And they eagerly honked at the prostitutes leaving the speakeasy. With noise now closer to Tessa, Nathan turned to Andy and leaned in for the kill.

"I win again," Nathan whispered. "Have fun thinking about me...having fun with her. I've been eating lots of protein, so it'll be one big *load* of fun. Bye, nerd."

Nathan swaggered to the cart and humped its handle, but all Andy could do was stare. So Nathan left with a grin and steered through traffic, his middle fingers serving as turn signals. Peaches stumbled from the speakeasy soon after, his belly now filled to the brim with a creamery's worth of floats. Then Peaches stopped beside Andy, and both watched Nathan navigate through all the adulterers.

"Life's not fair," Peaches said, lowering his head. "Hot homeless guys always get the girls."

"That appears to be so, Peaches," Andy said, as Nathan rounded the corner. "Have any room for more dessert? I know an ice cream place that'll fill a popcorn bucket if you bring one."

"You know the way to Peaches's heart. And Peaches still owes you for the flowers, so Peaches is payin'."

The new pals peeled out on a motorcycle moments later, Andy latching onto Peaches from the rear seat. As the bike weaved through traffic and Andy screamed, Janet lumbered out from the speakeasy. Then she dabbed her eye with a bar rag, leering at their departure.

"Nobody can compete with Peaches," lamented Janet. "Psychotic, eyepatch-wearin' bikers always get the guys."

CHAPTER 12

Later that night, Peaches crashed his motorcycle through Mr. Gentzel's garbage cans and zoomed away. And Andy staggered back to his bedroom alone, now caked with gummy bears, cookie crumble, and enough chocolate syrup to take down several diabetics. The room now feeling like a high-gravity environment, Andy collapsed in his chair and powered on the PC.

Instead of looking through his lengthy list of online bookmarks, Andy only accessed one tonight—his JumboAndy video page. Though his videos were hours from their 3:27 a.m. launch, Andy belligerently clicked and unlocked all three without fanfare or fear. He then activated his web camera, starting an unplanned piece of melodramatic content. Yes, now streaming live was his next video titled...'The End of Jumbo Andy?'

"Hello, my name is Andy Gordon, and let me tell you why I suck. First, I despise my job. Second, I live in the same house I was born in. Statisticians predict I will die here as well. And third, when it comes to romance, my mom dates more than me. A fat nerd has lady problems? I know, story of the century, right? This last woman though, wow. She's the type of maiden you'd go to a Renaissance Faire with even if she didn't have a costume. The type of girl you'd pause a video game for. A woman you couldn't bear to get rid of even if she were a zombie about to slurp your brains out like a juice box. And if she thinks I'm a horrible person, then everybody else in this dreadful world probably will too. So, Tessa, if you ever see this, I'm sorry. I hope that Nathan Hader doesn't end up destroying your life as much as he did mine. He's not who you think he is, so please be careful! And to you, Internet, my fate rests in your hands. If you like these three videos, I'll make more. If not, you'll never see me again. Andy Gordon out."

As the video saved to his page, Andy growled at the top of his lungs and scared away all herbivores on the block. With a jabbing finger thrust, he powered down the monitor and then entered full decontamination mode. Andy ripped off his suit jacket with a tug, its caramelized buttons flying off and sticking to the ceiling. Then he chucked his suit away and focused on the history T-shirt underneath, trying to tear it in half. But the fabric fought back and barely stretched, defying everything Andy knew about superhero transformations.

"Damn me for investing in high-quality cotton," said Andy, fishing the metal Jumbo Shrimpit figure from his pocket. "Time to bring in the reserves!"

Andy removed the dwarf figure's plastic axe condom, its blade now exposed for tonight's slashing. With one smooth motion, the axe slit his shirt in half quicker than a laser through butter. Continuing his demolition, Andy then shook off his clothes like a wet dog, headed for the wall's organized sticky notes, and tossed his 'Finally Release Video' goal into the trash.

"Well, that's done," Andy said, also throwing out his 'Don't Repulse Tessa' goal. "And so is this!"

After a trudge to the bed, Andy collapsed face-first into his accordion pillows with a thump. And his wooden bed frame legs creaked worse than a ship hitting an iceberg. He then let out an elongated scream, kicking his feet in a tantrum as if trying to swim through the wall. Now shirtless and fatigued, Andy rolled on his back as the bed frame legs bent even more than before.

While Andy's body remained motionless, his brain's negativity seemed to outfox his positivity in a mental chess match; and the positive team only had pawns compared to the negative team's full board of menstruating queens. Yes, Andy was losing his mental progress piece by piece. And that continued until the night's ultimate checkmate—when his bed legs buckled, snapped, and slid outward like a giraffe trying to ice-skate.

"I suck so much."

At least in his dreams he could still be with Tessa, soon back at the comic shop wedding filled with family and friends. Yet as Andy slumbered, even his retreat became prison when Nathan Hader replaced Wacky Will behind the podium. A snowman costume then appeared on Andy's body and split down the middle, exposing his underpants like Murray did to him every Christmas pageant. Worse, Nathan humped a red button on the podium, opening a trap door between them. And two bins of terror now awaited Andy in the pit below: a vat of nuts on the left and a vat of bees on the right, both enclosed in plastic wrap for optimal freshness. Andy's brain still using his late-night sugar binge against him, Tessa rushed to his side…and promptly kicked him down the pit. His dream fate was now sealed, careening through the left vat's plastic wrap and deeply into the nuts.

Andy's allergies seemed to exist in the dreamworld too, his flesh instantly swelling. As his fingers looked like balloon animals and his body more like a blimp, Andy floated from his nut bath and flew above the bee vat—still unwrapped. After Tessa and Nathan slipped their beekeeping suits on, Nathan held up Andy's Jumbo Shrimpit figure and tossed it at the second vat. And when Jumbo's uncovered axe tore a hole in the plastic, bees soon swarmed around Andy's plump body like a planet's atmosphere. Their sweet target in sight, the bees landed upon Andy's nutty flesh, raised their bee butts for extra impact, and stabbed their million stingers downward. Then he popped in a glorious explosion, releasing cheese curl dust like a Nielsen-branded Big Bang. And back in his broken bed, Andy jolted awake in a cold sweat.

"I ate way too much ice cream last night," Andy said, looking down at his bloated belly. "Sleeping without a shirt on? Andy, you wild man."

Shuffling past his nightstand in wizard slippers, Andy activated the bedside coffee maker and computer monitor to start his morning rounds. His body quite cold only

ANDY GETS CONNED

wearing boxers, Andy darted to the closet and threw on a Wacky Will robe. He then grabbed his steaming coffee, opened the mini-fridge, and removed a 1-gallon glass jar of butterscotch.

"Must resist butterscotch goodness," Andy said, plunging the jar in the trash can.

Now taking a swig of his less enjoyable coffee, Andy focused on the screen.

"What was I thinking? I better delete that video stream before anyone sees it," Andy said, scrolling down. "Wait, there's one view? Somebody actually watched this and left a comment!"

Andy, after inhaling the kind of breath one would in preparation for a sneeze, read his first feedback:

"This video was the biggest waste of time ever. Except the other three videos you put up that were even worse, of course. The music video was awful. The rant video—pathetic. And the promo video makes me want to rob Leo's stupid store, not support it. You're a sad, little boy trapped inside a fat, sad man's body. So keep your face off the Internet and where it belongs—a pig trough."

As Andy read, Nathan Hader typed at his laptop back at Bumble Ridge High's infirmary. Chewing on a vanilla protein bar, he read his next comment aloud:

"If that other comment wasn't clear, I agree with what you said in your video about you sucking. You do suck, except the part of you that thinks that you suck. That part's at least right about you sucking, so it sucks less."

Nathan tapped the keyboard as his second comment appeared underneath Andy's video. Placing his legs on the exam table, Nathan nabbed a lollipop from Nurse Rosie's candy container, bit it in half, and chewed its crunchy pieces along with the stick.

"That was way too easy," Nathan said. "One more sleeve up my cards to play, and then he's done for. What a fine day's work!"

"Are you going to give me my kidney medication?" a sickly-looking girl yelped beside Nathan.

"You'll get it soon, junkie! Just shut your face until Nurse Rosie gets back."

The girl then contemplated death far too early, her lip quivering just like Andy's did back in his bedroom. Nowhere to turn but his old ways, Andy salvaged his butterscotch jar from the trash, twisted its lid off, and chugged the whole damn gallon. But as the last drop slid past Andy's uvula, a series of baffling 'ba-dums' harmonized outside. He then peeked through the blinds and spotted a barbershop quartet on his lawn, bopping up and down to their own beat.

"We see you, Andy," boomed the bass singer. "We have a message from Tessa, straight from her heart to our website to our payment-processing software to your ears. So here you go; this one's just for you."

"I don't have enough butterscotch for this," said Andy, his lip still trembling.

As Andy awaited his weird fate, the swaying singers formed a line like a vocal firing squad upon his lawn. And after a few more joyful bounces, the quartet began the next part of their suspenseful delivery—a peppy parody song of "Pop Goes the Weasel":

ANDY GETS CONNED

You're weak when you teach kids in rows.
You should be illegal.
You're somehow worse at vlog videos.
"Stop!" say the people.

Everybody online,
Thinks your content's lethal.
So they post, "Don't waste our time!"
"Stop!" say the people.

Your last contact with lady parts,
Was birth—Mom spread eagle.
You're gross and fat and bad at the arts.
"Stop!" say the people.

Everyone everywhere,
Hates Andy; it's equal.
So please ease all our despair,
"Stop!" say the people.

After Andy closed his blinds with no reaction or tip, the callous quartet took a dump on his lawn. And then it stomped off to sing its next hostile song of the day. Now grappling with this mean melody, Internet hate, and Tessa attack, Andy was about to go full-blown berserker too.

"I'm never using that website again!" Andy spewed, yanking out the power cord and the outlet with an explosion of dry wall. "Or that outlet apparently!"

Andy then free-fell backward into his leg-snapped bed like a trust-gaining exercise without the catchers. All of his electronics now off for perhaps the first time, both figurative and literal darkness filled the room. Too loaded with coffee to sleep but too filled with misery to move, Andy gazed up. And that's when he saw the glowing star stickers on his ceiling, now with a new addition—a few caramelized button asteroids as a reminder of his gluttonous, milky ways. But Andy was still back on his phone within seconds, now accessing the JumboAndy page for a different reason.

"And this'll stop me in case I have a moment of weakness," said Andy, changing his JumboAndy password by tapping in a random chain of numbers. "Try and get past that, future me!"

To further enhance his emotional security, Andy opened his phone's parental controls and blocked the JumboAndy page. And he set this password as another series of random keyboard characters. Yes, what he lacked in willpower could easily be fixed with some classic phone-assisted censorship.

Hours later, after trying to crack the passwords a few hundred times, Andy ambled downtown in a black tuxedo and bow tie with no skateboard below him. Continuing his exercise routine, Andy admired the town's worn sidewalks as he burned off the bathtub's worth of frozen dairy that he ate the night before. After moseying around Bumble Ridge and running into a couple telephone poles because he was looking down, Andy entered the town's only florist shop—Mom's Petal Peddlers.

Wearing a sunflower visor, Mom watered daisies with a spray bottle behind an ivy-decorated counter. Andy's

ANDY GETS CONNED

entrance then triggered an alert chime fitting with the store perfectly—a pedal harp's chromatic scale. Approaching Mom, Andy passed by the 'Employee of the Month' plaques hung on the wall. And this month's plaque was just like the others, featuring Andy's top student.

"Emily managed to win again, eh?" asked Andy.

"Hi, dear! She's nice, thorough, and willing to work extremely long hours for almost nothing. So she's going to keep winning this until she quits," said Mom, spraying away with a smile.

"You might want to change that to 'Indentured Servant of the Month' then."

"Good one! Now lay it on me. Tessa likes you right? How'd it go last night?"

"You don't even want to know."

"Okay, I'll be honest. I heard things from the garage apartment last night—things that you'd usually hear me doing. I heard clothes ripping and the bed breaking. Don't be modest. I want details!"

"Nope, that was all me. I was covered in ice cream and cut my clothes off with a dwarf figure. Then my fat ass broke the bed. Tessa hates my guts."

"What happened?"

"I was born."

"Let me be more specific, dear. What went wrong at the show?" Mom asked, zipping around the counter and grasping Andy's hand.

"I'm not sure. Nobody showed up, and it was about to be cancelled. So I paid some street people to be an audience for her."

"Well that's creative. You helped her and saved the show. How'd that go wrong?"

"For some reason Tessa thought I paid them to like her jokes. Remember that angry student who made me have a quarter-life crisis? Nathan? Well he's involved in this somehow and he won her over. Now Tessa pretty much control-alt-deleted me from her life."

"I'm sorry," Mom said, adjusting Andy's bow tie. "Nathan's a douchebag. Maybe if you give Tessa some time, she'll figure it out. She seemed smart."

"I wish I knew what happened and what Nathan said about me. I know I just met her, but I think we had something special going on. This blows!"

"If you think there's no chance, at least you tried, dear. And I know it doesn't help now, but all wounds heal with time. You know Mr. Gentzel suffered some pretty severe burns on his face, but even his skin grew back."

"Bring it in, Mom. Bring it in," Andy said, hugging and lifting her off the floor. "This world would suck a lot more without you around. It's probably for the best anyway that Tessa and I didn't work out. She said flowers were stupid gifts in her stand-up act."

"What?" Mom asked. "She'll get what she deserves!"

Right as Andy was in mid squeeze, the harp entrance rang again when Police Chief Chris entered the premises. Now in a standstill, his white, bushy eyebrows shot upward. And, just as quickly, his hand whipped out two guns from his hip holsters.

"Freeze, police!" Chris said, readying his guns and pointing them directly at Andy's head.

ANDY GETS CONNED

"This is my mom. She consented to this hug!" Andy shrieked, driving his arms into the air as Mom softly landed on her feet.

"Never thought I'd catch the infamous Andy Gordon," Chris said. "You're goin' away for a long time."

"Officer, I swear I didn't intentionally download every season of *Space Fightin' Confessionals* last week. Or those holiday specials. It was an accident, that's all!"

"I'll act like I didn't hear that," teased Chris, his face switching to a clown-like grin.

Surprisingly, Chris sauntered to Mom and holstered a gun on his hip. Then he aimed the other right at his face and fired. No bullet or brain splatter popped out though, as a plastic magician's flower sprang from the chamber instead. This was a total cop prop.

"Ready to tear up the dance floor tonight, Toots?" said Chris, clenching the flower stem with his teeth and shimmying in place.

"Holy shit!" Andy screamed.

"Dear, this is Chris. Chris Hill, the gentleman I've been seeing. You know, the one I found after you helped fix my computer," said Mom. "A bit of bad timing, but I told him to play a prank on you the first time you met."

"Your mom said you liked comedy," Chris said. "What's funnier than almost dyin'?"

"He went a little darker than I imagined," Mom added. "I'm sorry."

"Did you like it, Andy?" asked Chris.

"Air! I need air!" panicked Andy, burying his head in leafy shrubs and inhaling their oxygen.

"Be glad I didn't blast Emily with a bunch of fake rubber bullets like we planned," Chris said, patting his holstered weapon. "She had the blood packs strapped on and everything."

"Wow, you got me good," said Andy, popping out from the shrubs and spraying his face with a water bottle.

"I'm sorry again, dear. But it's nice that you two finally get to meet," Mom said, wrapping her arm around both Chris and Andy.

"Apologies, Andy. Pleasure to meet you," said Chris.

"Not a problem, guys," said Andy. "You found yourself a great woman here, Chris."

"Your mom's the best thing to happen to me since my second angioplasty."

"You're right, Mom. This guy does have a great sense of humor. You two seem like a nice fit."

"I've heard a lot about you, Andy."

"Depressing isn't it?"

"Want me to shoot somebody? You know, for real. Always seems to cheer me up."

"And I'll act like I didn't hear that."

"I knew you two would get along," sung Mom.

Carrying a large flower arrangement with balloons, Emily stumbled from the back in her visor. By itself, the arrangement was about the same size as a small Christmas tree. But the foil balloons increased its girth even more, as robot vacuums and ancient world leaders lined the pot's soil like a junkyard fence.

"Andy's flowers are ready!" said Emily, holding the face-obscuring plant. "Freshly cut!"

ANDY GETS CONNED

"How'd you do that, dear?" asked Mom, helping Emily lift the plant up to the counter. "I was sharpening all the shears out here. What'd you cut these flowers with?"

"I have my ways! Sometimes it's best not to know how the sausage is made or how the wrists are slit."

"What was that last part?"

"Nothing!"

"Well, thank you anyway," said Mom, as Emily moved from behind Andy's flowers and saw the store's two new visitors.

"Hello, Mr. Gordon. Hello...Officer," said Emily, winking at Chris and then scurrying to the back room.

"Well I'm off to see Dad," said Andy, hoisting up his flowers as Chris opened the door for him.

"Tell him I said 'hi,' will you?" Mom asked.

"Sure thing. Nice meeting you, Chris. You take care of my mom or I'll cut you. And, yes, I'm fully aware I just threatened a cop."

"Ten-four," Chris said, as the door shut behind Andy. "What a guy! He's like the son I never wanted."

"You two played so nicely today. Here's your reward."

Mom grabbed Chris's collar and locked her lips with his. Then she fondled the 50 years of shrapnel tucked away in his chest, followed by a gentle butt squeeze. As Chris reeled back after such a seductive smooch, his holstered gun blasted fake bullets into the floor.

"You'd be shocked how often that happens," said Chris, sharing a snuggle with Mom.

Emily then re-entered the room, her leg and pants now caked in red goop.

"Oh no, Officer. I think that real bullet that you shot at Andy grazed my femoral artery instead," Emily winced in a moment of acting that belonged in a soap opera. "Boy, I don't feel so good."

"Plan's off, Emily. Abort! Cease and desist!"

"Too late now," Emily said, ending with a dramatic fall as red liquid gushed from her shirt, pants, and visor.

"You only had two tiny blood packs. How are you gushin' so much?"

"I reverse engineered them and made my own," Emily said, the blood geyser now propelling her off the ground. "I can't stop!"

"Chris!" Mom yelled between her teeth.

"Don't worry," Chris said, wrapping his arm around her. "I'll write up a vandalism report right now. This place will look brand new in a week."

"That's fraud, isn't it?"

"You say 'fraud.' I say 'way to get new carpet and paint,' understand?" hinted Chris, as Emily blasted up through the roof. "And that'll be your new sky light!"

Andy continued to scuff his shoes until he reached a large hill on the outskirts of town. Lugging his flowers up a gravel path, as well as a family-sized bag of cheese curls, he passed through a metal gate. And after a brief stroll to the nerd section, Andy finally stopped at some weathered gravestones by his feet.

"Afternoon, fellow Gordons. Have you seen Dad? Oh, he's in his favorite spot? How unpredictable."

Andy then reclined against a gravestone marked as 'Alvin Linda Gordon.' No typical stone, this was engraved with dice, historic figures, and a naughty limerick about a man from Venus in binary ones and zeros. Guiding the bulky flower arrangement between his legs, Andy sighed and rested his head against the cold, moist marble.

"Hey, Dad. How's it going? Mom says 'hi' too. She's doing pretty well right now. It's weird, but she found a guy who has a sense of humor almost as sick as ours. I think you'd like him a lot. I met him for the first time today, and he pointed guns at me. Yes, multiple guns. As for me, well, that's a long story and I'd rather not bore you to *death* with the details."

Andy paused with an anticipating grimace, cupping his hand around his ear.

"Was that a giggle or a groan? Speak up, Dad, you sound muffled for some reason. I wish you were still here—so much happened that I know you'd want to see. Wacky Will came out with a new album last month, and you'd love it. Oh, and there's an updated *Rejects & Reptiles* rulebook that adds an intricate snack bartering system to the advanced rules. Plus, it'd be great to hear how you'd handle a pain in the ass student like Nathan Hader. You know, if either of us believed in this silly afterlife stuff, I'd ask you to pop down here and give me some help like a guardian angel. Hell, or maybe even pop out of your dirt bed and devour whatever's left of Nathan's brain. But we both know you're worm food by now, and I have to fix my own problems. So let's get to the main event, okay?"

Andy crawled up to his knees, and then feet, as if his body were taking shifts in the standing process. Balance attained, Andy opened the bag of cheese curls and inhaled its preservative gas.

"Well, it was nice seeing you again. I love what you've done with the place. Hey, at least the crickets think I'm funny. Okay, so it's the same gift I always get you since I know you'd go nuts without them. But I did get you the family-sized bag this time. Knock yourself out, Dad."

Andy emptied out the bag, raining cheesy goodness all over his father's resting place. Orange mixing with the green grass, Alvin's grave now looked like the old gelatin molds that Mom made for dessert long ago.

"Share some of these with the others around here, okay? They're looking a little *bony*."

After tucking the bag away in his tuxedo pocket, Andy took a deep breath and stretched his legs like he was about to jog. Starting the ceremony, Andy curtsied not once, but twice with each foot. And then he formed binocular-like shapes with his hands around his eyes while wiggling his fingers. Yes, Andy had begun the peace dance of Alvin's favorite portly pilot Pinnette from *Space Fightin'*—the one performed when he took down Droid Blitzer in the finale.

"Dewem, Warpem, and Howem," Andy chanted, still wiggling his fingers. "Or as we say in human English: To those who view the world askew, must warp together to pull through. Love you, Dad!"

As a bee swarm descended and consumed the ceremonial dust, Andy's tribute concluded. While Andy felt some solace, a nearby widow and grieving teen now stood in astonishment as if victims of a prank.

ANDY GETS CONNED

"Sorry you had to see that," Andy said, trekking back down the gravel path.

Though his cemetery audience was less than enthused, another person also secretly observed Andy with a completely different reaction. This adolescent viewer, on a laptop hundreds of miles away in Alaska, now watched Andy's music video in front of a frosty window. As a blizzard outside coated the evergreen landscape like confectioner's sugar on a funnel cake, the Alaskan teen posted 'lol funny' with a smile. Seeing other content Andy produced on his page, the teen clicked on the 'End of Jumbo Andy' video next—its view count now at a whopping 42 rather than its previously crushing one.

CHAPTER 13

Ignoring phone calls from Leo and Ben throughout the evening, Andy meandered around town. And more unbelievable, this was his longest break from the Internet since Dad got him hooked in preschool. He then blasted through most stages of World Wide Web withdrawal, searching for 'Help Wanted' signs at Bumble Ridge's odd businesses. After keeping his heart rate up for a few hours and submitting résumés, Andy entered familiar territory. But this was no place to be, especially when hungry; he had wandered right into Glutton Grotto—a row of unhealthy eateries between two convenient hospitals.

"I deserve a little treat. It's about time I enjoyed life with a few friends I've neglected—my taste buds."

Though Andy could have stuffed his stomach at a Southern Baptist buffet named Self-Fulfilling Prophecy, he walked right by. He instead went to the ice cream parlor that he and Peaches depleted, AbsZero, ordering a small dish rather than his usual popcorn tub. Yes, AbsZero's name not only fit with the ice cream's extremely cold temperature, but also with its clienteles' chances of seeing their own abdominal muscles.

Emerging from the parlor with a cup of butterscotch ice cream, Andy took a whiff of its freezing fumes and ginger snap crumble topping. He then plunged a bite into his mouth, but stopped with curled lips; it was as if he had eaten a rotten skunk covered with fresh kale. Rushing to a garbage can in a moment of gastronomic blasphemy, Andy spat out the treat and chucked the rest away. And as a swarm of bees now consumed his abandoned delicacy, Andy contemplated what the hell just happened.

Maybe the creamery used expired butterscotch? Maybe they goofed and gave him a sugar-free scoop? Or maybe AbsZero got a bad batch of milk from some bipolar cows? With such possibilities, Andy continued his attempts at public mastication. Next was one of Pretzel Reject's weirdly shaped soft pretzels, Andy nibbling upon what looked like a baked baby kraken. When the sea beast's formerly irresistible wasabi mustard guts didn't even hit the spot, Andy panicked. And he pitched the kraken into another trash can.

"None of this works anymore! Am I dying? I'm dying!" he screamed, as the bee swarm behind him gobbled up the kraken's kosher tentacles.

Perhaps his tongue went on strike? Did a tumor take over the flavor section of his brain? Or was this another Nathan prank where he paid off Andy's eateries to change their recipes and pack them with laxatives? Andy then darted from diner to delicatessen, erratically slamming currency on counters and shoving specialties down his

ANDY GETS CONNED

esophagus. But each attempt failed and met the same garbage can fate. No, not even the exotic meats of an endangered animal food truck tickled his fancy anymore.

In a last-ditch effort to see if cheese curls still electrified his taste world, Andy dashed toward the gas station for a small bag of edible redemption. Just outside, however, Andy froze at a telephone pole stapled with businesses flyers. Swelling orchestra music then blasted in Andy's brain. The angelic choir joined in too. It was here he saw his potential flavor salvation, his eyes locking on a flyer of a new Indian food restaurant—Fire in Da Hole.

"Hey, that might work!" exclaimed Andy, reading the flyer. "Where are they located?"

Andy's eyes excitingly shot around the flyer until reaching its address at the very bottom. Then his heart sunk, and the music stopped. What agony! What rage! What woe! First, the place was so far away that he'd need to drive to get there. And that meant he'd have to clear away years of junk blocking his car in the garage. But second, there was a cruel reminder below the address itself. Yes, Andy had spotted a column of Tessa's old comedy show posters with the same damn adorkable pose she did in his house. Frantically, Andy tore a Tessa poster from the pole, compacted it into a hushpuppy-sized ball, and plunged it into his picky pie hole.

"There, is this what you want, mouth? Does Tessa do anything for you?" Andy grumbled, chewing her marketing efforts. "Wow, she used the tough cover stock paper for these flyers. Dammit, even her stationary selection's cute."

Andy spat out the paper into one last garbage can, now with a rainbow-colored tongue and matching saliva. As a few passersby shuffled away thinking this was some avant-garde street performance, Andy pocketed their tips and inspected the other flyers.

"Food's not cutting it. I need a replacement career I'm passionate about now," Andy said, closing his eyes and waving a finger around the flyers options. "Okay, world. Time for some more of that irresponsible behavior. Let's get out of this rut. Let's find a realistic career that's not teaching history or making videos. Job search randomization, now!"

Andy poked his finger at the pole, landing on a flyer near the top. Removing the hand from his eyes, he saw his fate flapping in the breeze...his unsystematic choice almost too good to be true.

"Accordion lessons it is!" Andy said, taking the flyer.

Thanks to low demand for accordion lessons, Andy easily locked in squeezebox lessons the next day. For a job, he could do shows on the street or be an accordion tutor if he had to—that wouldn't be so bad compared to teaching history. Plus, he'd be one step closer to his idol Wacky Will Zimmerman after all. So on this abnormal Friday, Andy met an old gypsy woman named Gertrude for a night of buttons, bellows, and boiling borscht.

"'Zis 'vill only take eight hours to teach you 'ze basics," said Gertrude, strapping an accordion to Andy's chest as one already rested on hers.

"I think I've picked up a few tricks from watching Wacky Will over the years. I'm pretty much a prodigy."

ANDY GETS CONNED

"'Ze basics, Andy! You need 'ze basics! Pump 'zis soft to learn 'ze motion," Gertrude said, lightly squeezing hers.

"Nah. I got this, Gertrude," Andy said, completely ignoring her wisdom.

With too much gusto, Andy swung his arms widely and tore the accordion in half. While Gertrude had given Andy first-hand knowledge, Andy gave Gertrude her first near-death experience with an accordion. Yes, Andy walloped that geriatric gypsy right in the face. And, worse, she then flew backward into the bubbling hot borscht.

Andy wasn't about to let one injured gypsy stop his montage of job questing though. So after a long night of hearing swear words in Gertrude's native tongue at the hospital, Andy went back to the telephone pole for Saturday's flyer selection.

"Here I come, paint-based art! I can paint *Rejects & Reptiles* figures, so portraits shouldn't be hard."

Soon after, Andy headed to the art gallery for its advanced portrait class. Maybe he could paint caricatures in the park and make people laugh at 20 bucks a pop—that'd be better than school bureaucracy. Andy pondered such possibilities as he sat on his stool next to an easel for today's studio instruction. Like every easel in the circle, Andy's was as blank as his recent online search history. A robed, female model then entered behind the instructor as Andy squirted some paints on his palette. When the model disrobed, Andy recoiled and squeezed his green paint bottle with such force that he toppled backward. And then he flew to the floor like a corpse, compacting a can of paint remover with the back of his head.

"Call an ambulance!" shouted the instructor, as an earthquake-like aftershock wobbled Andy's easel.

As green paint continued streaming into the air from Andy's bottle, his easel fell to the side. His collapsing art then struck an adjacent easel, starting a chain reaction that knocked down the entire circle like priceless dominoes. When the last canvas descended toward the nude model and she attempted to flee, she slipped on the pond of green paint. And then she collapsed to the floor with the kind of crack that only a hip could make.

"Call two ambulances!" the instructor revised.

When the model became conscious at the hospital near midnight, she greeted Andy with some attempted choking. But her green-stained hands tired quickly, so Andy left and tore off Sunday's flyer on the way home. The result this time? A 'buy one, get one free' coupon for the Mallard Murder Emporium's special Weekend Waterfowl Massacre. Maybe he'd discover his flawless aim, then becoming a sharpshooter or crowdfunded vigilante—he had to try, right?

A few hours of sleep and a gallon of butterscotch-free coffee later, Andy rowed in an aluminum boat on Pollen Valley Lake. And Police Chief Chris ran the rudder behind him, both draped in enough flannel to reupholster a couch. Reaching their remote cove bordered by thick reeds, the hunters removed their duck calls and blew out a few seductive quacks. Andy and Chris then readied their guns and aimed up as a flock flew above them. And, with each alluring quack, their horny mallard mouths frothed in a race to get to the imminent duck orgy first.

ANDY GETS CONNED

"This is probably what it looks like when we hit on women," said Andy.

"Ever play that video game where you blast these sons o' bitches with a bazooka?" asked Chris.

"Yeah, I made it to the sociopath level, but these are living ducks! These are actual guns!"

"You get numb to real murder really quick. Remember, killin's okay if the target's delicious. There they are! Shoot!"

Many mallards then dove at the boat, so blinded by their duck libidos that they were willing to swing outside their own species today. With the flock overhead, Chris pulled the trigger and blasted up like shooting flying fish in an airborne barrel.

"Duck!" yelled Chris, as one deceased bird splashed down beside them.

"Good job!"

"Duck!" said Chris again, with another successful shot.

Andy then closed both of his eyes and pulled the gun's trigger. Though he couldn't make out exactly what type of bird he just struck, it sure sounded like he hit the largest target up there.

"Goose?" questioned Andy.

Andy then leaned back, awaiting a splash from the big, dead bird any second. What he got instead was the agonized wailing of a morbidly obese paraglider, now plummeting into the lake.

"Never heard of the game Duck-Duck-Homicide before, Andy," chuckled Chris.

"I hope he has good insurance," said Andy.

"Hi, I'm the guy you just shot. My name's Winslow," he gurgled. "Could you both please stop with the quips and save me?"

All hospital staff now knowing Andy on a first-name basis, he stayed with Winslow through the night. They quickly found commonalities too, bonding over similar misfortunes and needs of seatbelt extenders. After making it through the first season of *Space Fightin' Confessionals* on his phone with Winslow, Andy went back to the telephone pole. Then he fetched his next flyer-driven job investigation, this one with Janet's bartending class at Three-Fifth Chasers. He could share anecdotes of his own life and make sad people feel better about theirs for a living—all he'd have to do is learn how to make a few drinks. Soon back in his broken bed, Andy covered up with enough dinosaur blankets to reform his cocoon. And when the triceratops on his tummy seemed to growl, he patted his hungry friend.

"I know this week's been tough, Mr. Stomach. But I can only give you a few cheese curls every day," Andy said, shutting his eyes. "There's plenty of fat for you on my butt and thighs though, so get to work."

Early the next day at Three-Fifth Chasers, Janet showed Andy the ropes—the old nooses she found in storage. Then she taught him how to mix drinks. After a few lessons and a lot of flirtation, Andy arranged ingredients on the counter for his morning guinea pigs. At the counter now sat Janet, Peaches, and Winslow with casts on his left arm and leg. Though Winslow needed casts on his entire body and weeks of treatment, his

ANDY GETS CONNED

penny-a-day insurance only provided coverage for half his surface area. Thus, Andy paid for Winslow's cab fare to get here, keeping an eye on his paragliding pal's recovery.

Now set, Andy reached behind the bar, blindly choosing two boozes. The first was a 200-proof whiskey, followed by a wine so ancient that its name was etched in hieroglyphics. He then dumped half of each bottle into the blender while adding strawberries, brewed coffee, and a scoop of cheese curls. Though smelling like the sewer plant after a hot wing festival, the chunky concoction oozed nicely from the blender into three cups.

"Down the ol' hatches," Janet said, swallowing the sludge with a healthy chug. "Wow, I'll be damned!"

Janet shifted, kissing Andy on the cheek. And then Peaches took his turn—at the drink, not the kissing.

"Peaches is kinda scared," he said, the oxidized drink now blacker than his eyepatch.

Peaches then downed the drink and approved with a pleased burp. Seeing such results, Winslow gave it a try too by scooping one spoonful into his mouth. But he instantly lost consciousness and bashed his face onto the bar. Though Winslow's head fortunately missed the knives a few inches away, the sliced lemon pile pressing into his eyes was an equally painful experience. But Peaches nabbed Winslow's glass anyway and finished off the slop in seconds. Craving more, Peaches raised the whole blender to his mouth and guzzled every drop of the rice-pudding consistency drink.

"I'm startin' to feel a rumblin'," said Janet, running to the bathroom.

"Peaches also regrets his decisions," he said, following Janet as Andy dialed his phone.

"Hey, hospital? Andy Gordon again. I need an ambulance at Three-Fifth Chasers for a concussion and three stomach pumps," said Andy, as Winslow's bowels roared like a bear. "And bring some hazmat suits if you have any. Trust me on this one."

After a trip to Winslow's pad for new pants, Andy and his injured friend made it through the second season of *Space Fightin' Confessionals* in the hospital. Fortunately, the sad season finale let Winslow cry out the last lemon juice from his eyes and fall asleep. Andy then signed Winslow up for a free, yet risky, clinical trial to aid his broke and broken friend. And with his new pal partially mended, Andy left for the next arbitrarily chosen flyer.

One more paper rip and trip later, Andy soon entered the newly renovated PerspirNation Gym. Yes, his randomly generated strategy had taken him deep into bully territory. Maybe he'd lose weight and start training even more pathetic people like Winslow, Andy thought, now in a moment of mental gymnastics. Starting with his treadmill power walk, Andy panted like a hound having a heatstroke; his sweat-absorbing hoodie had to go. He then stripped down to a T-shirt branded with Wacky Will's recent album *3.14159 in the Sky*. And, unsurprisingly, he was listening to it on repeat.

"This is way better than exercising outside," Andy said to himself. "No dogs! No substances that come from dogs either! And I haven't been publicly shamed in any way yet. This is stress-free aerobic activity!"

ANDY GETS CONNED

To his right, a female gym member stepped onto a treadmill in her sports bra and shorts small enough to be a bikini. Thus, Andy glanced sideways, and she ignored him. But both kept the same pace despite their difference in waist size and likelihood to start grease fires when cremated. Her warmup already over, she spammed the speed button until sprinting. Then Andy increased his speed a few times for a mildly brisker walk. Seconds later, the familiar Tyrannosaurus Flex front-flipped onto his treadmill to Andy's left. And Flex mashed his speed button too, matching the lady's pace while winking in her direction. Now with a front-row seat to their budding romance, Andy struck his button half a dozen times to look a little less out of shape. Indeed, he was stuck in the middle of a fitness sandwich.

Grasping onto the bars with sweat streaming down his face, chest, and legs, Andy surveyed the row of treadmill enthusiasts behind him at max speed. Hell, even Zeus the veteran kept up by rolling his wheelchair on top of one. So Andy slammed his controls to the fastest possible option, galloping at a rate he had only experienced via car before. At full blast, sweat poured from Andy and soaked the treadmill belt below. And the screams of utter shock behind him encouraged him to push even harder.

"Didn't expect me to pull this off, did you, jerks?" huffed Andy.

He charged faster with a second wind, sweat soaking his treadmill as the noise behind him sounded oddly like gargling. Andy then snapped his head around, spotting the river of sweat flowing backward like a log flume ride. The back row now dry heaving and drenched, Andy made another necessary call on his sweat-resistant phone.

"Hello, I have a war veteran who might be drowning at PerspirNation Gym. Please hurry!"

After Zeus awoke in the hospital, Andy helped him equip his bedpan like a helmet. And when Zeus charmed the staff with war stories that had to be war crimes, Andy headed home to recover. Sure, today was tough. But Andy knew that tomorrow's journey would be even harder, expecting his exercise pains to escalate quickly.

He was right, of course, waking up the next day feeling like he was struck by a bus, train, and two cruise ships that fell from the sky. Andy's body in no condition to walk, he borrowed Mr. Gentzel's snowplow tractor to clear a path in the garage to his car. And he did just that, parting the nerdy collectables until spotting his ride—a yellow hatchback with the text 'lemon' painted on its doors. After one last stop at the mechanic for a new battery, Andy drove back to the telephone pole.

Following another indiscriminate flyer rip, Andy drove to the woods for his next career exploration—the perfectly safe and never perilous logging industry. Perhaps more terrifying was the flyer's less than encouraging text: 'Help Desperately Needed at the Troubled Knots Tree Cutting Company.' If Andy survived this and liked it, he figured he could live in the woods, carve dorky knickknacks, and sell them on the Internet; at least that'd be somewhat safer than posting videos online. Soon observing his lumberjack boss cut through a tree with a chainsaw, Andy stepped away to a safe distance.

ANDY GETS CONNED

"Timber!" the lumberjack hollered, as the tree fell onto its designated spot. "Now do it just like I showed you, Andy. Don't get creative."

The lumberjack handed his chainsaw off and ran 40 feet away, taking no chances with Andy's accident-prone background check. Andy's arm muscles still inflexible from yesterday's exercise, he hobbled to the tree. Then he picked up speed, hoping he'd make up for a lack of forward strength with velocity. Soon about halfway through and weakening every second, Andy slowed so much that the tree almost had time to grow its bark back.

"Push, Andy, push!" shouted the lumberjack.

Not one to be outdone by a plant, Andy removed his chainsaw from the tree and took a few steps back. He then charged at the pine like a bull with a chainsaw and made contact again. But he had so much momentum that he fully sliced through it and couldn't stop.

"Shiver me timbers!" shouted Andy.

Small sapling after sapling became toothpicks as Andy wiped out those oxygen makers like a woodchipper. With way too much speed, Andy then struck a utility pole as sawdust showered the forest floor. Though Andy toppled the pole and took out half the town's electricity in the process, he also managed to lop off one last limb after that—the poor lumberjack's arm.

"Tourniquet! I need a tourniquet!" Andy screamed.

As soon as the lumberjack's arm touched ground, a bee swarm appeared and consumed it like piranhas from the sky. So Andy acted fast, first laying a tarp in his hatchback's cargo area. Then he sprayed it with disinfectant and loaded the lumberjack inside, now practically a paramedic. But Andy provided more than emotional support or money at the hospital this time, his blood type an exact match with the lumberjack. Doctors also found cancer in the lumberjack's arm and began treatment. Therefore, Andy's career search had led to two new friends and one saved life. And after donating what felt like half his blood, Andy gulfed down some glucose through a glorious fruit salad. Yes, in one week of novelty, Andy had changed his food habits, applied to jobs, and narrowed down professions that he'd never pursue again.

Looking forward to his last day of soul-searching, Andy eyed down his two remaining options at the telephone pole: a Fire in Da Hole Indian food flyer and Tessa's old comedy show poster.

"Well, that's all of them," Andy said, extending his fingers toward the pole. "Except for you, my dear. It's time to update again. Get ready, world, Andy 3.0 is here."

CHAPTER 14

As Andy 3.0 headed for the next stage of his transformation, Nathan Hader ramped up his own plans at the efficiency apartment complex. Nathan, still in his homeless disguise, jammed a protein bar in his mouth and then stuffed its wrapper into the closest receptacle—an air vent in the wall. Pictures of Andy with red X's over his eyes lined Nathan's room, as did voodoo dolls and a huge map. On the map, Nathan added some cutout, paper flames to Bumble Ridge High with a thumbtack. And he also attached a barbershop quartet to Andy's house. He then linked each location back to his apartment with yarn, doing the same with Three-Fifth Chasers and the Tessa poster beside it. Finishing the wicked arts and crafts project, Nathan placed a target on Leo's shop with a grin.

"There we go. All updated," Nathan said, interrupted by an egg timer beeping on his desk. "No! Already? She'll be at my homeless home any second!"

Nathan chomped down another protein bar, pressed its wrapper into the vent, and picked up a tall sheet of cardboard before exiting. The cardboard featured drawings of a door's kick plate and knob that, upon getting stuck in the door frame, looked just like the real deal. After a shove through the frame, Nathan ran onto the exterior corridor that connected all apartments on the third floor—now packed with partying college students. Holding his door up with one hand and sticking the other out like a crossing guard, Nathan stiff-armed his way through throngs of sloshed Bumble Ridge scholars.

"All you idiots got accepted and I didn't? Move, losers!" grunted Nathan, barely fitting down the stairs.

Confusing the drunks with a door that was far more mobile than it should be, Nathan scuttled away to the dumpster. Once there, he rested his door in front of a makeshift hut constructed from boxes, magazines, and trash that wouldn't attract bees. Thus, in most sections, Nathan's walls were literally paper-thin. This was prime real estate for a wannabee vagrant too, conveniently located beside the bountiful dumpster. He then attached the new cardboard with duct tape so that it functioned as a hinged door. With his dilapidated home away from home now complete, he entered, collapsed, and gasped for air.

"It's done," Nathan grimaced. "And with minutes to spare too! She'll never know the difference!"

Decked out with furniture stolen from yard sales before dawn and houses after fires, Nathan's hut looked more like a nest. Artwork also scattered the walls, crudely drawn with markers to class up the joint for expected company. Sitting up on his asphalt floor, Nathan rifled through the garbage, removed his laptop, and activated its web camera. And then he downed one more protein bar, now prepared for the next part of his project. Still chewing, Nathan unfolded a Three-Fifth Chasers cocktail napkin and read from his brilliant script:

"What's up, my people? You're looking at me, Nathan, and welcome to my online show *Nathan Says*. We're in Day Eight of my 'Hate Andy Gordon' campaign, and I can feel the disdain rising. 'Disdain's' a good word, isn't it? I got it from a book called *The Saurus*. It helped me learn a bunch of new words that I can use instead of the word 'hate,' like 'disdain' for example. I used it about a week ago to write a song and learned the word 'despair' too. Disdain, despair—okay, I only looked at the D words, but so what? I'll put a link to Andy's videos in the comments so you can leave him lots of disdain. Oh, I also got a letter today I want to share with you while I open it!"

Nathan picked up a letter from the floor, quickly slicing it open with a used syringe. After trying to read the letter upside down, he corrected the mistake and went back to his riveting video content.

"Let's see what my fans at Bumble University admissions have to say about my third application," said Nathan, skimming through the letter with his finger. "We regret to inform you that—no! No, you fools, no! I bet you're all a bunch of nerds too, aren't you?"

As Nathan threw the syringe behind him and it stuck into a cat drawn on the wall, a knock began shaking his floppy cardboard door.

"That's it for *Nathan Says* today!" he yelled, hiding his laptop under some trash in the corner. "Enter!"

"Luke! It's so nice to see your place," said Tessa, barging in with two pizza boxes and hunching over in the low-ceiling hovel. "So the town lets you stay here, huh?"

"Yup. All I have to do is volunteer around Bumble Ridge. You know, help out the orphan kids and the wounded troops. Oh, and the wounded, orphan troops."

"We do recruit young around here, don't we?" said Tessa. "We might as well call it...an *infantry*."

"Why'd you deliver that like a joke?"

"I'll tell you why it's funny later. So, how are you?"

"Homeless."

"And other than that?"

"Filled with disdain," Nathan said, holding up the Bumble University letter while hiding his name with his dirty thumb. "Stupid colleges and their high school diploma requirements."

"Sorry. Did you ever think about taking the equivalency test? I'll help you study. I can divide fractions like nobody's business—except mathematicians, of course, since that *is* their business."

"Unnecessary. I made a pact with my old principal, and I'll be getting a diploma at the end of the year. I went through some real nasty stuff that the school doesn't want to leak out, so they're being pretty nice right now," said Nathan, still staring at the pizza boxes. "But that's all I can say about it! I probably told you too much. They swore me to secrecy. I'll just have to wait until the end of the school year for my diploma, I guess."

"Okay. Well, great, so all we have to do is keep those spirits up for nine months then? That's easy, Luke. And

ANDY GETS CONNED

who knows, one of those colleges might let you in before that. It only takes one 'yes,' only one person to give you a chance. We'll get you in college and then employed no matter what, don't you worry."

"Thanks. Now let's eat those two pizzas."

"I know you've had a hard life, but remember what I said about manners? You'll need those in college, so let's work on that, okay?"

"Yeah. So before I eat this pizza, I should ask you how you're doing, right?"

"Good!"

"Wait. Was that you confirming that I should ask how you're doing right now? Or are you answering me and saying that you're good?"

"Both. I'm doing well."

"Ah, so you got some sex last night. Who's this lucky Mr. Well you're doing?"

"No, Luke," Tessa laughed. "It's acceptable to say that you're 'doing well' as an answer. In fact, people expect you to say it even when you're not well. I'm in an okay state though, you know?"

"State? Now you're bringing up geography? Stop trying to trick me!" Nathan shouted, then taking a whiff of the pizza boxes. "Sorry. I get grumpy when I'm starving and there's food nearby that I'm not eating. Please answer my question about how you're doing."

"Honestly, I could be better. But my complaints are nothing compared to yours. You know, after hanging around a bunch of comedians, time with you has been nice. You're real. And honest. You're a breath of fresh air even though we're so close to that dumpster. You help me put my life into perspective."

"Yeah, I'm way worse off. But continue your feelings until you're done with your disdain."

"Thanks. I can't get Andy's lie out of my head. I felt so good after my show, but I was duped. It was all fake. It's like my brain's water-boarding me."

"Look, some of us are entertainers, and some aren't. Even if you aren't, that's okay," Nathan said, as Tessa folded her arms. "But don't forget! Andy thinks you're the worst comedian ever, not me."

"Oh, I'll never forget that. Apparently, I can't attract an audience if he had to buy me one. But what if he was just trying to fill the speakeasy so I'd have a crowd? Are you positive he was just lying to sleep with me?" Tessa asked, opening the top pizza box and taking a piece as Nathan snatched two.

"I'm positive. I heard through the homeless grapevine that he did this before too. He acts like a nice guy and then uses people for sex. I don't want him to hurt you. And if you two have sex while he's on top, that would definitely hurt you."

"But what if—"

"You need to listen to me, Tessa. I have proof of what really happened that night. I needed to know, so I snuck to the back of Three-Fifth Chasers this morning and went through the security footage. I wasn't going to show you this unless I had to, but I found something that confirms all of our prescriptions."

"*Suspicions*, Luke, but what did you find?"

"Footage of Andy grinding against another girl that night. I put the worst parts together in this clip. Watch."

Nathan pulled out his clamshell flip phone and played footage of Janet the bartender pressing her groin against Andy's. Then Tessa's eyes widened as the out-of-context yet incriminating video continued on screen:

"I don't know how ya did that, but you're a life saver. My Heathens-Only night's a hit. So how can I pay ya back?" Janet asked, wrapping both hands around Andy's delectable derriere. *"I have an idea how I could pay ya back, if you're too shy to tell me yourself, sexy."*

The footage then jumped ahead with an obvious cut.

"You know what?" Andy said. *"There is one favor you could do for me."*

"Oh, yeah?" Janet asked, ripping the rest of her blouse off. *"Ask away."*

As the footage stopped, Tessa snapped, flattening an aluminum can on the floor with her work boot.

"He *did* pay for that audience! And he *was* trying to hook up with Janet!" raged Tessa, stomping another can like a train-crushed coin. "That pig! That conniving pig!"

"He's a real jerk all right."

"Never mind. We'll get through this. You will go to college! I will get funnier! And we won't pay any more attention to that two-faced wolf in sheep's clothing!"

"More like a double-chinned manatee in triple extra-large T-shirts. And they're quadruply stupid ones too."

"Attack the person's actions, not their appearance, Luke. And even though Andy's a lying pig, he has a fabulous T-shirt collection."

"I'll keep eating this pizza while you talk more then."

"Thank you," Tessa whimpered. "But I need to eat some food too."

Tears now dripping down Tessa's face, she bit the same piece of pizza that she had been holding. And, at the same time, Nathan finished off the top box's last slice. Poor Luke must have not had hot food in years judging from his appetite. Or, even more likely, he had a colon's worth of tapeworms sucking his nutrients dry.

"Okay, enough of the past," Tessa said, dabbing her eye with a napkin from the floor. "Let's get to the present. I got you a gift. Let me show you before I dissolve your house with my tears."

Tessa placed her pizza slice back into the greasy box, instantly stolen and scarfed down by the ravenous Nathan. She then folded open the second box with a chipper pizzazz, but no pizza or grease stains were inside this one. Continuing her surprise, Tessa closed the box, flipped it over, and revealed a square hole. Then she popped out four legs on the side of the box, making a cardboard TV.

"I asked for an extra box to help you spruce up the place," Tessa said, pulling a black marker from her utility belt and drawing on the cardboard screen. "With a little imagination, you can watch some boob tube. Oh, and that term I just used is another way of saying 'television,' Luke; it's not referring to my breasts."

"I'm disappointed but learning."

"Wait a second. There's more!"

Tessa rapidly sketched Nathan's permanent program on the cardboard. Within seconds, she added a stick figure husband watching football while his stick figure wife cracked him over the head with a rolling pin.

"And voilà, now we're watching the Stick Figure Network. Or, as I like to call it, the Anorexic Channel."

"Hold on. You're telling me the second pizza box contains no pizza? And I can't change the channel? And I'm not going to see your boobs?"

Tessa crossed her arms once more with a boot stomp, driving the crushed cans three inches into the asphalt.

"Oh, manners again?" Nathan asked.

"Yup."

"I love you!"

"Take it back a notch."

"I hate you?"

"Too far the other way."

"Thank you?"

"There you go," Tessa said, as they headed for the door. "I have to make a few more computer repairs, but I'll pick you up tonight and cook us dinner at my duplex. Tonight's lesson is about eating etiquette."

"Wait, what's etiquette taste like?"

"I'll see you later," Tessa laughed, grabbing the greasy pizza box and exiting. "Let me throw this away for you."

Tessa tossed her box into the efficiency apartment dumpster and then headed off. As Tessa's boots thumped away, Nathan observed her luscious booty bounce through his cutout window.

"I'm gonna do you with my penis," Nathan said, gyrating his hips until hearing notification sounds from his laptop. "Oh! Must be my devoted fans!"

Nathan jumped back on his stained couch, bedbugs then spewing out from the cushions as if furniture could cough. Safe again in his phony home, Nathan rested the laptop on his chest, clicked a few times, and refreshed his latest video comments.

"*Nathan Says* is awful. Please die, loser," Nathan read, then closing his laptop. "Power to you, my Internet trolls! It's mean people like you who motivate mean people like me to be much meaner than you could ever be."

Nathan sprawled out on the couch and relaxed as much as someone could while coated with bedbugs. Then he gnawed away at two more protein bars, watching the new TV brought by his red-haired marionette.

"Hey, stick figures. You better close your eyes the next time Tessa's ass bounces over here. Because things are about to get even dirtier! Man, homeless people have it made. Why don't more people live like this?"

High above Nathan, a middle-aged man heaved two 39-gallon garbage bags from the complex's third-floor corridor. Though targeting the open dumpster, his first bag missed. And it dropped directly on Nathan's living room, spilling pounds of cigarette butts and skunky beer cans upon the floor. But his second bag smacked the dumpster's edge, raining glass shards and adult diapers down the first bag's hole. Frantic footsteps then approached the man from behind with increasing pace.

"Please don't kick me out or beat me up," moped the middle-aged man, lifting his hands as if being arrested. "I'll never throw my trash from here again. Give a sad and broken man a break."

"Get out of the way," yelled a female voice, the middle-aged man then pivoting.

No cop or landlord, an exterminator now barreled right at him with an active bee nest in her hands.

"Watch out!" the exterminator warned, as the middle-aged man helped lob the nest over the rail.

"Did I just make a difference in this world?"

"Yeah. Thanks, pal," said the exterminator, as the nest slammed right into Nathan's home. "Those suckers were the killer Africanized kind that I've never seen around here before. Some jerk shoved protein bar wrappers into the air-conditioning ducts, and those bees made a metropolis in there. Of course, they got even more aggressive when that new lumberjack cut down a utility pole and the power went out—those buzzers like their breeze, you know. Now that they're powered up with protein and pissed off, getting stung by even one could kill you if they don't eat you first!"

As Nathan fled, shielding himself with the cardboard door, his student neighbors laughed at the visual comeuppance unfolding before their drunken eyes. Though the students' cheers were loud, they paled in comparison to Nathan's screams now echoing through town. His vanilla protein bar breath sending the bees into a frenzy, Nathan sprinted to the closest water source as the winged hunters stung his tongue, face, and eyelids. Despite Nathan's agony that would exceed any hospital pain scale, an even more stinging situation continued online—Andy's four videos getting far more views than *Nathan Says* ever would.

Yes, at this moment, a couple of chaps now watched Andy's rant video on their smartphones in a rustic English pub. As they noshed on their plates of 'fish and chips' and 'bangers and mash,' the men fulfilled even more stereotypes with their posted comments of 'Bloody brilliant' and 'Make more videos, ya nutter!' Their laughs soon attracted a sizable crowd. And then all the pub's patrons accessed the next video with their phones, 'The End of Jumbo Andy' playing like a surround-sound system. Better yet, it was now at a whopping 2,001 views.

Meanwhile in Bumble Ridge, hairs stood up on Andy's arms when he parked his hatchback. Such terror not only came from the screams outside, but also from how close he was to his final flyer objective. He then looked up, spotting the sound's source—an out-of-breath, homeless guy swatting at bees with a cardboard door. After the poor bastard dove into Pollen Valley Lake, Andy alerted the hospital about an injury that he didn't cause for once. And then he refocused on his final goal.

"Am I really about to do this? Okay, here goes," Andy said, getting out of his hatchback as the horny ducks humped their waterlogged lover. "Whatever happens in here, my day's going to be way better than that guy's."

CHAPTER 15

The blazing sun baked Bumble Ridge as half its residents now lacked electricity, air-conditioning, and therefore patience. Most folks without power then ventured to the AbsZero ice cream parlor, a popular spot thanks to its backup generators and meat locker-like temperatures. While cooling down inside, crowds formed friendly factions and debated their favorite flavors. But the parlor became so packed that its air-conditioning couldn't keep up, and conversation quickly got heated. So the horde grew unhappy, switching to different topics like 'why the hell the goddamn power was out' and 'who's the prick yelling so much at Pollen Valley Lake?' Yes, with rising temperatures in their cool retreat, each citizen risked starting a brawl with a slight cough. And their minor annoyances now almost led them to multiple wars.

A few blocks away, Leo used this serendipitous lack of power to install his shop's new partly solar-powered sign; it was bigger, better, and guaranteed-to-blind. Though still charging in the sunlight, its deactivated neon letters featured a slight name change—the shop now operating as Leo's Larping & Comic Stash. Below the name, Leo incorporated his new logo of a robot, zombie, and dwarf holding a d20 dice set. And Leo took no chances underneath the logo either, explaining his shop with the following extremely specific text:

'We are a geek and nerd shop that sells items like video games, board games, action figures, comics, and costumes for cosplaying and larping only. While we specialize in role-playing and we enjoy wizards, this store has nothing to do with sex or clan meetings at all! We are not a gym, nor are we a comedy club just because we mentioned comics two sentences ago. Got it? Good. Now that our shop's stock and purpose are clear to anyone reading this, please come on in and enjoy our stash! And, no, we do not sell drugs here either, so stop asking.'

Giving the sign an early test with a limited charge, Leo activated his new installation. And it instantly became the brightest object in town, even outshining the sun. As its neon letters beamed through the air, and likely all layers of the atmosphere, every moth, fly, and ladybug in town bulleted straight for the sign. Their stupid brains didn't know when to stop, however, and they explosively incinerated like festive bug guts confetti. Yes, when this bug-zapping sign lit up, it blinded all insects and pilots that looked anywhere near it. Literally an eyesore even to astronauts, this was some retina-melting marketing.

With fried bug aromas filling the area, another bee swarm arrived and consumed all charred remains on the sidewalk and sign. The swarm then left and joined forces

ANDY GETS CONNED

with its friends over at Pollen Valley Lake, attacking Nathan and his duck lovers when they popped up for air. Fully expending its solar energy, Leo's sign deactivated and started charging for its next dazzling show.

Within the hour, Leo's sign was ready for another test just as crews had repaired Andy's slain utility pole in the woods. And when electricity flowed back to Bumble Ridge, all residents left AbsZero for their more exciting homes. Now switching on his sign with increased foot traffic outside, Leo had finally attracted curious customers rather than befuddled bugs.

Leo then saw more people in his shop at once than he'd usually get in a week. After ringing up several new shoppers, Leo spotted the next tiny customer in line—student Fran standing on her tippy-toes. She stretched her calf muscles and extended them as far as they could, clearly embellishing her height like short guys do on dating websites. As she struggled for extra inches, the camera around her neck dangled. And though she had placed trinkets on the counter earlier, she now strangely kept both hands hidden near her knees.

"Hi, Leo!" said Fran.

"Sorry, little lady. Have we met before?" Leo asked, rubbing his eyes.

"No, but I saw Andy's promo video of the shop online. You guys are hilarious; it was great!"

"Oh, well in that case, prepare those pockets. Your final amount gets an Andy discount."

"Your place is so cool. Not the temperature, but everything else about it."

"Thank you, earthling. It'll take some time for the air-conditioning to make it sublime in here again. That was one crazy power outage, wasn't it?" asked Leo, as he scanned merchandise of the Internet's beloved Pillow Kitty and placed it in a brown paper bag.

"Yeah, this town already looks like the apocalypse hit most days," said Fran. "When we lose power, it's worse."

"Right on. I was a bit worried myself. I figured my laissez-faire approach of paying the electric bill finally caught up with me."

"And what's that approach?"

"Not paying it," said Leo, adjusting his tie-dyed tie as Nathan's yelping continued outside. "Okay, I can't tune that out anymore. Where's all the wailing coming from?"

"It's some homeless guy getting stung by bees and humped by ducks. It's already a meme online," Fran said, lifting the object in her hands—a case of the extra-caffeinated energy drink Palpitations. "Do you accept gold coins? I have a pot filled with them at home, you know, being a *leprechaun* and all."

"I'm sorry. I know this is going to bum you out, but I shouldn't sell you this. You're a minor, and this jazzed-up juice could wreck your developing constitution."

"Don't be so crabby. Especially to a *shrimp*."

"If you chug all these, your heart could explode. They load these babies up with antioxi-depressants for those of us with adult troubles. And I can't swing the costs of any lawyer—even a bad one."

"Come on, Leo. Don't you accept the business of *gnome-o-sexuals?*"

ANDY GETS CONNED

"Your humor soothes my soul," Leo giggled, then collecting himself and lowering his voice. "Okay, here's some absolute truth for you: I'll approve this purchase if your parent or guardian's here. Are they with you today?"

"Uh, yes. Yes, they are," Fran said, pulling Marcus away from the *Alley-Oops* guillotine basketball game. "Hi, Daddy. He's my Daddy!"

"Don't ever call me that name unless we're in the bushes, baby," Marcus whispered, his clown-sized foot then stomped by Fran's.

"Daddy, tell Leo how many Palpitations I have a day."

"I said I'd rather keep our bush time a secret!"

"You both look like you're barely old enough to vote. You need to be 21 to buy these beverages," said Leo. "But my perceptions are limited, so here's a question for you: What year were you born?"

"Years are only a construct, man," Marcus said dryly, sketching basketball plays on his whiteboard. "The only time is now, you know."

"I dig you both, but I'm afraid you failed my screening process," said Leo, sliding the Palpitations energy drinks away from his register.

"How about we make a little wager?" queried Fran. "If my dad makes three shots on that *Alley-Oops* guillotine machine, you let me buy the drinks at twice the cost. Up for some risk-reward, businessman?"

"Deal," Leo said, reaching down and then shaking Fran's doll-sized hand.

"This calls for Play Number 34," Marcus said, pointing at his whiteboard and then handing it off to Fran.

Marcus limped over to the machine, dealing with Fran's aggressive toe stomp, and swiped his credit card. Then the arcade jingle blared into his hoop-stretched ears. With experience on the basketball team, as well as years of playing with decapitated heads, Marcus scooped up Marie An-twine-ette's noggin and spun the ball on his sharpened fingernail.

When customers formed around him, Marcus thrust his finger up and sent the head straight to the basket. Lining up his second shot with Alexander the Grape, Marcus bit his intentionally split tongue and focused. Then he easily lobbed it over the emperor cutout for another point. As customers cheered him on, Marcus palmed the repairman ball and leaned in the machine with his towering height. And using his crane-like arms, he dropped it directly above the wicker hoop.

"That'll be $49.95," said Leo, scanning the energy drinks. "Under one condition: I want you to take some pictures of my establishment with that snazzy camera of yours. My website needs some visual representation of the holistic design I have going on here. You just might be the half-a-woman I need for the job."

"Okay! I'll even edit some celebrities in there for you," Fran squealed, tucking the canned equivalent of caffeinated rocket fuel under her arm. "Thanks, Leo. You really keep me *on my toes,* you know that?"

"Quick query, my friend. How many of those height-related puns do you do in a day?"

"That was pretty *munchkin* my last one. Okay, I'm done, I promise."

"Don't interpret this literally, but gimme some skin," said Leo, high-fiving Fran. "You two have a groovy day."

"Hey, before we go, has Andy been here lately?" Fran asked, as Marcus wrapped his arm around her.

"I'm afraid not," said Leo. "I haven't seen the dude for over a week."

"Damn. We're some of his dismal students," said Marcus, Fran shoving his hand away and crushing his other foot. "*Former* dismal students, that is."

"Right...my 21-year-old, touchy dad had Andy during his second year of teaching," lied Fran. "And Dad adopted me soon after that. I'm a senior in high school right now. Like me climbing a stair, the math works out. See you later, Leo!"

Leo grinned as the odd couple left, not only pleased with Fran's Palpitations overpayment, but also with Marcus's five-dollar *Alley-Oops* session. Though Leo's shop wasn't booming, the trickle of success certainly picked up after Andy's promo video spread online. And as Leo's sign charged for the evening hours, he saw a slew of new customers even weirder than his usual troop.

First, he sold a full suit of armor to Principal Murray seeking innovative detention punishments. The second sale was also Murray, impulsively purchasing two pillories on his way out the door. Though students would suffer, at least Leo recuperated much of the debt brought on by his new sign, he justified. Soon after, Leo's profits soared when a Self-Fulfilling Prophecy preacher snapped up all the Droid Blitzer helmets; there was no better way to liven up a buffet sermon, Leo argued. With three big transactions, Leo was on course to recovery. And with more students buying Palpitations when the word got out, he felt rays of hope brighter than his lighthouse-like sign.

An hour later when the foot traffic slowed, Nathan's shrieks also dissipated outside. And Leo could finally focus, rifling through bills while crunching the numbers. Now glaring at every letter once again, his chill vibes ventured to other dimensions.

"Water bill—late. Heating bill—late. A letter from a lawyer asking if I know what the bright light was that caused half a billion dollars of damage—we'll file that one in the garbage can and play stupid."

Making great progress, Leo paid or repressed most of his bills. But before he finished, the lights went out again. With no wind, thunder, or blown transformers from inquisitive squirrels, Leo expected the worst.

"Please tell me the town lost electricity again," said Leo, immediately heading outside. "Nope, all other businesses are lit. It's just my disgraceful place. I might as well get some light around here then."

Leo rushed back in and turned his sign on, heat pouring out like an oven broiler. He then viewed his new sign as the sun set, his investment now lighting the shopfront. But almost immediately, a carefree duck struck the sign and vaporized upon impact. After exhaling a few feathers, Leo wiped the ashes off his face with his tie.

"You've done great today, sign, but it may be too late; you only had an hour to charge power. It'd be super helpful if you stayed on, but you might need a nap. I bet you'll bite the dust as soon as I stop talking."

ANDY GETS CONNED

The sign bit the dust as soon as he stopped talking. Then Leo ran to his fuse box using touch as guidance, flipping the master switch off and on repeatedly. His options dwindling, Leo pleaded with all possible sky gods and energies who could help from above. But nothing worked; this was some major utility futility.

"Not now! Come on, electric company! My payment's only a little late. One month is nothing in the grand timeline of the universe."

Sounds of Leo sliding open drawers and stubbing toes reverberated through the shop. But with the flick of a lighter once used for medicinal purposes, Leo's face appeared in fiery candlelight. Leo then spread the flames to more candles around him and went back to the bills...until his door jingled. Who could find Leo's shop when the sign had no shine? Who'd enter the darkened domain? As the figure advanced with a series of sneaker squeaks, Leo gulped.

"Please be a Swiss banker who wants to invest in a struggling company. Please be a Swiss banker who wants to invest in a struggling company," chanted Leo, as the steps stopped near the comic books. "How can I be of your assistance, rad traveler?"

"Me want brains," a zombie said from the darkness.

A phone's screen then lit up the lewd comic book section. As light reflected back to Leo, it revealed a sneaky snooper's face in the shop.

"My battery's gonna die if you keep being spooky," said Ben. "Nice candles."

"Why aren't you a Swiss banker?"

"Wasn't hugged enough as a kid, I suppose. So, what are you trying to do in here, a séance?"

"I blew way too much capital on the sign! So now I'm seeking two types of enlightenment," said Leo, rubbing his temples as the door jingled again. "Come on, clairvoyance! Disco papa needs a pair of Swiss bankers!"

"Please be the dominatrix. Please be the dominatrix," Ben chanted.

"It is I, Jumbo Shrimpit, bringing comestibles for the journey ahead," Andy said, galloping into the candlelight with a tray of take-out food containers. "I have fetched fine treats from the Fire in Da Hole Indian eatery. And its aromas are as legendary as the rumblings in my tummy!"

"Why aren't you a dominatrix?" asked Ben.

"I chafe easily. And I don't wear cow products—I eat them. Any other questions?" asked Andy, resting his tray on the counter. "I love the sign, Leo! Even when it's off it's amazing. And what a logo!"

"Thanks, man. Ben helped me design the sign. It's already bringing in some extra business. Your promo video did wonders too. You were a big help, you know?"

"Well I'm glad one of the videos did something good. But what's up with the power?"

"Late electric bills. It's funny though since I made the dough to pay them off today."

"Well the second part of that is great news!"

"And the first part of that makes it a lot easier to play flashlight tag in here," said Ben.

"Look, before this conversation goes any further and it becomes weird to transition back to this, I have to say

ANDY GETS CONNED

something," Andy spurted. "I'm sorry I've been blowing you both off. I needed to sort some things out in my life and reconsider some goals."

"It's all right. We figured that you were just defragging the old bone dome," said Leo.

"Yeah, you needed space. It's fine," added Ben, handing out some medieval silverware. "And you brought food, so it's double fine."

Visibility conditions now safe with a 90-year-old's birthday cake worth of candles, Andy opened the food containers. After jamming a straw into each one for their deep sauces, Andy passed them along.

"If you don't help me eat this, I won't be able to do it myself for once," said Andy.

"You know, your chin *is* looking more slim than usual. Is this intentional?" asked Leo.

"Sure is. This Indian food's going to be my cheat night, and then it's back to the diet. Dig in," said Andy, as the trio started shoveling curries into their mouths.

"So it's fine to tag team a treat like this, but not the chick at Mardi Gras who wanted all of us at once?" Ben joked. "What's the difference?"

"We know where the food's been, for one," said Leo.

"And when we eat Indian food, we don't have to see each other naked," Andy teased, his dimples finally making an appearance again. "Thanks, guys. I really needed this right now."

"This man brings us free Indian food and he's thanking us?" Ben asked, slurping. "Man, maybe you should ignore us more often."

"Keep eating. I'll talk," said Andy. "You know, I tried out more hobbies and jobs this week than I have in years. Hell, maybe a decade."

"Variety is the spice of life, man," said Leo.

"Not for the half a dozen people I almost killed in the process, but it did help me come to a conclusion," Andy said, nibbling on the stuffed naan. "Try this—there's lamb in it! So, I've been thinking a lot about the rest of my time on this planet. I've analyzed all new data from the week. And with the little downtime I've had, I was able to watch two seasons of *Space Fightin' Confessionals*. Can you guess what I finally realized?"

"That Commander Courtney's right tail is way hotter than her left one?" joked Ben.

"I agree, but that's not it. Every time a character has a major breakthrough in that show, they seem to give an emotional speech soon after. And those speeches always include some contrived comparison to something else— you know, to sound deeper than what the breakthrough actually is. Well, after installing some Andy 3.0 software, I went through something pretty profound myself. And I finally have my own speech!"

"Preach on, brother Andy," said Leo, snarfing down a cube of rice. "May your words cleanse our bodies like this extra-spicy food already is."

"Like a hose to the rectum!" added Ben, as Andy gulped down a shot of paneer.

"Cue some of that heartfelt and bittersweet music, Ben," said Andy, Ben then playing a Wacky Will accordion instrumental from his phone.

ANDY GETS CONNED

"Life's like a buffet," said Andy, gesticulating with his fork in the air. "Every day, your options are right in front of you: your meats like this tandoori chicken, your dairy like this paneer, and those always-sensational, carb-loaded samosas. So, you want to sample as many types of food as you can at the buffet. But if you try them all, you wind up on one of those shows where a crane has to lift you out of your house. Our stomach space is limited. There's not enough room to search for new flavors when you already know what works. And every time you eat something you don't love, like this weird carrot dessert that I think might be spoiled, you waste a little bit more space in your gut—space that could have been filled with the safe samosas. Well right now in my life, I don't have the energy to experiment anymore. I only want my samosas."

Andy wrapped an arm around Leo and Ben, squeezing them closer. Leo and Ben then paused their chewing as their eyes shifted toward one another.

"So there's no need for the new! I've had my samosas here all along," Andy finished, as Leo packed some black, carrot substance into his mouth and instantly regretted it. "And if that means I have to put up with the boring rice known as 'teaching' to fund our samosa festivities, so be it. I love my samosas, and that's all I need."

"First, you're right because this carrot pudding is mind-blowingly bad," said Leo. "And second, we're happy you chose the samosas, but I'm concerned about your return to teaching. We had plans for your JumboAndy channel and branding. Those videos were all wonderful too. What happened?"

"You know how the universe sent you a signal to buy a new sign? Well I was recently blasted by two messages, both equally destructive. Tessa crossed paths with that old student of mine Nathan Hader, and he must have corrupted her somehow. Then she ended up hiring a barbershop quartet to insult me via song. On top of that, the first comments on my videos were nasty even for the Internet. After I launched those videos and reached for some dreams, my life became even more unbalanced than usual. So, I want nothing to do with Tessa or a vlogging career—absolutely nothing."

"I'm so sorry, man," sighed Leo. "Can we assist?"

"Just keep treating me like you always did. And don't worry, I still plan to make some videos on the side like before. But this time, I won't hide them from you guys. Screw the other people out there. The only audience I need are you two, my mom, and maybe this new guy named Winslow I shot down from the sky; we'll get to that later. I was silly thinking I could create videos as a job. Or find love again. I'm an okay teacher who lives an okay life. I'm learning to be okay with being okay. So let's focus on the one thing in my life that's better than okay right now—spending time with my samosas."

"Hold on, I must be one step behind. I don't see any more samosas. We ate all the samosas," said Ben, sampling the carrot dessert.

"Would it help if I said that they were dwarf, robot, and zombie samosas?" asked Andy.

"Yuck. Those sound even worse than this carrot crap," Ben said, spitting into a napkin and fleeing for the restroom. "Was that even edible? The tang's still in my mouth! I need water! Water!"

"Well, Andy. I'm not grooving with your conclusion, but it sounds like you've had a bleak week. Ben and I will be happy to spend time with you until you wise up and show videos to the people," Leo smiled, as Ben slammed the bathroom door and slurped up sink water.

"This is my decision, Leo. And I'm sticking to it more than that carrot disaster does to the back of a throat."

"Samosas it is then, Andy. I guess that means you won't be joining us on our supersized surprise."

"What was the surprise?"

"An unforgettable, cosmic vacation, that's all."

"Oh, no way; I am never eating your special brownies again. Don't even try."

"No, those years are behind me. And the cosmic vacation was going to be something way more euphoric than that. It was a real vacation that lined up with your days off. It was a planned pivotal experience. It was a geeky convention road trip, and we wanted you to make funny videos about the journey," Leo said. "But we can go by ourselves. We understand, man."

"Now hold on. That'd be an excuse to spend time with my samosas. As long as the videos are just for us, it works with my new plan. It'll be the same safe samosas, but dipped in a new, scrumptious chutney. Yeah, I'm in."

"Really?" questioned Leo, pulling Andy close with his arm. "Well, Andy, prepare yourself for the sensory overload of a lifetime. There won't be one, not even two, but three large fandom conventions in a row!"

"Damn, I missed the reveal. Hold on," Ben said, jogging back and wrapping his arm around Andy. "It's a Convention Crawl! You know, like a 'bar crawl' where losers get drunk, but for dorkier losers like us."

"Holy orc tits, yes!" Andy exclaimed. "Let's do this! I'll definitely record footage for a Convention Crawl!"

"See, I knew you'd change your mind," added Leo. "What'd it take, 30 seconds? Your videos are spectacular. And the Internet's a better place with your face all over it. Let's shove your mug out there as much as we can and—"

"Hold on," interrupted Andy. "I'm serious about this safe samosa comparison. I'm joining you and making videos, but they're *not* going online. I mean it, Leo. It's just for the three of us. I'm happy to do that, but these are for our eyes only. No fame, just friends. You know, I'd be recording for the samosa memories?"

"Okay, I'm not ecstatic about that. But as long as our atoms are all loading into my van and your atoms have a camera touching them, I'm completely copacetic for now," Leo said. "Let's make some memories."

"Promise me. Nobody sees this footage," said Andy.

"It will be like us when a new video game comes out— it won't leave this room," added Ben.

"Great! When do we start?" asked Andy.

"Saturday, my man," said Leo. "Departure at 4 a.m."

"So, I only have tonight and tomorrow to pack? That's somewhat irresponsible, but I can manage," mulled Andy. "Jumbo Shrimpit whole-heartedly accepts! By the way, if you had this all planned, how'd you know we'd cross paths today and I'd agree to go?"

ANDY GETS CONNED

"We would have used any means necessary in the cosmos to get you to come," Leo said, wryly.

"We were gonna break into your house and hogtie you if we had to," said Ben.

"I'm going to hope Ben's kidding and leave before I think about how frightening that is," Andy said, wiping up the last bit of curry from a tandoori box with naan. "I'll walk off some of this food and then get the video equipment ready. Call me later so we can figure out our costumes for the conventions, all right?"

Andy sprinted away, tossing his empty container on a mound of them so large that it covered the cash register. Yes, the counter was now piled with dozens of scrunched up boxes—most that Ben and Leo didn't remember.

"Dude, there's no way his tray had that many boxes on it when he came in," said Leo. "And worse, how'd that many boxes fit *in* us?"

"We're pigs," added Ben, spooning the rest of the carrot dessert into his mouth. "Dirty, disgusting pigs."

Suddenly, Ben's beloved dominatrix kicked down the comic shop door and cracked her whip twice. Now in near cardiac arrest, Ben finally dropped the carrot dessert container from his hand. But when the black ooze splashed outward, it disintegrated Leo's rug and ate a hole right through the floor.

"Hello, my piggies," the dominatrix grunted. "I'm actually here to buy geeky stuff this time!"

Another new customer in the building, Leo strolled over to make a sale. Meanwhile Ben, losing all grip with reality, fainted backward. And then he landed right on the

Alley-Oops guillotine game, inches away from becoming its fourth ball. With Leo's shop catching on, Andy's videos had made a difference. But with his Andy 3.0 plan, he no longer pursued new careers or love. Yes, this was yet another example of software updates that took one step forward and two steps back. Such a rushed release to market, Andy 3.0 remained clueless about the glitches in his system...and the people who would hack these new vulnerabilities first.

CHAPTER 16

Following his jog and solid sleep, Andy spent the next day packing so much that he might as well have been moving to a new house. It was such a large project that Mom came over to assist as well. While reviewing three days of bot-sitter duties, they filled Andy's Convention Crawl suitcases to the brim. From instant coffee to antibiotics, every necessity was packed in triplicate; nothing could stop the samosas now.

Preparing for his early departure, Andy went to sleep at 8 p.m. with a full dose of melatonin and half a roofie from Ben. And, thanks to these substances, his dreams didn't torture him at all. Yes, Andy sprung from his legless bed eight hours later full of energy. After a few jumping jacks, he showered and applied his dwarf costume with one extra accessory—a drinking helmet with coffee travel mugs attached to each side.

Soon exceeding the recommended intake of caffeine before dawn, he loaded up his hatchback and made it to Leo's shop within the hour. He then got another workout, heaving his hefty suitcases into Leo's van all by himself. Andy's companions still nowhere in sight, the only sign of life was a tent in front of Leo's shop. So a now-winded Andy tiptoed to the tent, slowly unzipped it, and poked his dwarf head inside.

"Hey, piggy," whispered Andy. "It's me, The Dolphin Dominatrix of the Southern Coast. I saw what you did to my dad in *Rejects & Reptiles.* And now I want a turn with you. My naughty dorsal fin needs to be spanked!"

"It's about damned time! Where have you been all my life?" Ben said in his zombie outfit, bleary eyed and fondling Andy's beard. "Screw you, Andy."

"Weren't you staying at Leo's last night?"

"Yeah. But he said I was making dolphin noises in my sleep and then kicked me out. I slept here instead so I wouldn't be late."

"How nice. His van's here, you know. He must be sneaking in some work before the trip."

"Why didn't you say something?" Ben asked, as a bright light illuminated the tent. "Let's go."

"Wow, where'd you get all these paintings of the dominatrix? And is that her kindergarten picture on the wall? Look at her tiny whip!"

"No more questions!" Ben said, pushing Andy's head from the tent as Leo jingled keys behind them.

"Should I give you two some privacy?" asked Leo, taping a note inside his door.

"No, I was just leaving anyway," said Andy, then reading Leo's note. "We're away for three days to purchase more merch. But the rarest of wares will appear

ANDY GETS CONNED

right here soon. So get your groovy cabooses down to our dope re-opening this Tuesday!"

"I wouldn't have brewed that up without you," said Leo. "So are we ready for levity?"

"ZomBen want know why LSD-401K not wear outfit," groaned Ben, shoving his tent into Leo's van. "This not fair. We made pact to look stupid together."

"My costume blocks my line of sight, and I'm driving. I'll slip it on when we get there," said Leo. "Let's bounce!"

The trio then loaded in Leo's van and cruised through pre-dawn traffic, passing Palpitations-chugging truckers along the way. Their road games now as odd as their tabletop fun, they sang Wacky Will songs and displayed funny signs to other cars like 'Please Help: I'm a Hostage!' After 50 miles of travel and a couple close calls with cops about the hostage thing, the trio made it to their first Convention Crawl stop in Burgpeters—a quaint town founded by its dyslexic leader Peter.

Soon, the samosas strutted toward the convention center. And all three of their fanciful costumes blew in the Burgpeters breeze. Andy then clipped a camera to his dwarven axe with custom attachments, now recording his braided hair, prop beard, and prosthetic nose. Fully secured, Andy's costume remained intact when the breeze became a powerful gust. Ben's bloodied zombie suit wasn't affected by the wind either. But Leo's costume saw different results, the wind lifting his boxy robot outfit a few inches off of the ground.

"Calm down, Mother nature," Leo whined, clutching Ben's shoulder with his silver clamp hands.

"'Twas good aerodynamics that nearly nixed the bot," Andy quipped, still recording with his camera. "Hey, ZomBen. Can you guess what this airborne machinery's reminding Jumbo of right now?"

"Plaaanes! Plaaanes!" grunted Ben.

"LSD-401K is not amused, humans," grunted Leo. "I almost lost my cube head!"

"Jumbo would like to confirm that you both will not be sharing these magic wizard box memories with others. You both will not spread these via smoke signal accounts or any other method, correct?"

"Affirmative, human."

"ZomBen agrees," said Ben. "Get shot of me though. ZomBen want brains. Brains and busty women."

"Hello, future us!" said Andy, looking into his axe camera. "You're looking at Jumbo Shrimpit, ZomBen, and LSD-401K on their first day of the Convention Crawl. Today we set off on a gargantuan journey that will be captured with my magic wizard box. Should we succeed, we may make the geeky history books."

"Hey, Andy?" asked Ben, already breaking character while Andy focused on the shot.

"The legend—a Convention Crawl. The objective—enjoying samosas. The cost to our already faltering popularities—severely detrimental."

"Andy!" Ben cautioned.

"Nevertheless, the trio set off on its insane plan to visit three geeky fandom conventions on three different da—"

Andy's face then met wood as he rammed into a telephone pole and collapsed backward.

ANDY GETS CONNED

"Even I saw that," said Leo from his robot head.

"Are you okay?" asked Ben.

"It's all right. I come from a long line of thick-headed Gordons," Andy huffed, sitting up. "Plus, it's a classic case of revenge. You should have seen what I did to that pole's family in the woods."

Soon inside, Ben and Leo covered Andy's eyes. And they guided him through the maze-like line, shuffling behind a crowd of waiting weirdos. Minutes later, when the convention's signage and registration staff were visible, Andy's samosas removed their hands for the big reveal. Then Andy gazed forward at a room filled with mythical beasts, medieval marvels, and one woman worker with a gargantuan guest list.

"Welcome to today's nature-based destination of magic and mystical mayhem," Leo said. "Or as it's also known, today's chance to blow half-a-year's salary on material possessions!"

"I see goblins. I see centaurs," Andy hyped, piecing together his location. "I see a *Rejects & Reptiles* Convention sign that totally beat me to the punch. Wow! I was going to bring all my students here for a field trip, but this is way better!"

The trio then finished their slow shuffle, passing through a body scanner disguised as a dragon's mouth. Acing their screening, the samosas exited the dragon's digestive tract. And they proceeded with caution to today's ultimate gatekeeper—the registration table's lanyard lady. Getting into these 'cons' required more verification than voting in most states, so they had to be careful.

Maximizing their last seconds, they grilled each other about phone numbers and addresses of the past 10 years. Then they arrived, now ready for the woman who could kill their Convention Crawl with a pen. Of course, this effort became meaningless when the lady leaned over and revealed her cleavage, Ben then improvising.

"Hey, it's me, the man of your dreams. My name's Ben, but you might have me down there as Zombie Stud," he said, licking his decaying lips.

"Let's see. I don't have anyone here as Zombie Stud," she said, inspecting the list. "But I do see a Repulsive Loser. Last name McNoChance? With a phone number of 555-BACKOFF, freak-boy."

"Please tell me you were recording that sick burn," Leo said, leaning in front of Andy's axe camera.

"I sure was, LSD-401K!" responded Andy.

"BACK OFF as my phone number?" Ben asked. "Hmm, pretty close. You just need to change the B to a J. You know, jack o—"

"You have 10 seconds to give me your real name before I call the cops," the lanyard lady interrupted.

After picking up their lanyard badges, the trio made its way to a merch table near the main entrance. Beside them, a boy rooted through the bins of junk that nobody bought the year before. His head buried in discounts, all that could be seen was his fluffy hamster outfit with two pterodactyl wings on his back—an exact match of the weakest monster in *Rejects & Reptiles*. As the hamster-boy burrowed deeper into the bin behind him, Andy aimed his axe camera at his face yet again.

ANDY GETS CONNED

"*Rejects & Reptiles* Con wouldn't be complete without its overpriced playthings spanning the game's history. Getting here early will increase your odds of finding that elusive variant you've always been looking for. And remember what else your attendance here also increases your chances of—nobody ever loving you," said Andy, the hamster-boy then whimpering and running away. "Hey, come back, kid! Nobody should hear their fate that young. Wait! I, uh, got you a present! Come back and get your present!"

Andy reached into the discount bin, pulling out a brightly-colored book and waving it in the air. And when the hamster-boy cautiously returned, Andy handed him the book without looking. Relieved, Andy patted him on the head as the skittish kid began to read. But then the hamster-boy screamed in complete terror and bolted away, crying even louder than before.

"Andy, what'd you do to him?" asked Leo, he and Ben running toward the commotion.

"I just gave him some book from the discount bin, that's all," said Andy.

"You mean this book?" Ben asked, lifting it off the floor. "*Darker Truths: Extra Grim Fairy Tales of Even Grimmer Existence?*"

"They banned that book in 48 states," said Leo. "It distressed and depressed pretty much everyone who read it. No wonder the kid blew his lid."

"If he has a dad, we're dead," Andy gulped, running.

Moments later, in an area filled with life-size dungeon props and torture-based photo opportunities, Andy captured more madness with his wizard box. Attendants posed in shackles while laughing, and they took pics while sitting on Judas Cradles. Even scarier, the horseplay took place in precarious locations—between statues worth more than all the geeks' kidneys. Yes, despite the torture motif and everyone being one butt bump away from bankruptcy, this place was having fun.

"Camaraderie is key at these conventions," Andy said to his camera, as the hamster-boy played near an iron maiden. "While we fight like hell online, we make amends here. It's a place where we geeks come together and bond closer than anywhere else on the planet."

"Turn that damn camera off," yelled a voice from the crowd. "And do it now!"

Andy squinted as a grumbling, Yeti-sized man advanced toward him. Before Andy could even think about retreating, this manly mountain charged closer, elbowed the hamster-boy's iron maiden shut, and stomped up to his target. Not only did the man have no concept of personal space, but he also seemed to like drinking moonshine before noon...judging by his breath.

"Hey, are you the jerk who made my Robby cry?" grunted the drunken father. "That's my job!"

"You mean the innocent kid who you just locked in the iron maiden?"

"Yeah, of course!"

"Uh, then no, it wasn't me. It was some other guy who looked and sounded nothing like me. In fact, I think I see him over at the nacho booth," Andy said, pointing behind him at whatever poor scapegoat happened to be in line.

ANDY GETS CONNED

"That nacho-eating son of a bitch," said the drunken father, abandoning his trapped kid.

As the drunken father changed targets and approached the nacho booth, his soon-to-be victim turned around with a cheese-lathered face. Dressed in jester's red tights and a checkered cowl with cutout spots for his casts, Winslow was yet again in the wrong spot at the wrong time. Still suffering the effects of Andy's shotgun blast and brief attempt at bartending, Winslow now wore a neck brace and head bandages. Atop those bandages was one final piece to his costume—a three-pointed fool's hat adorned with jingle bells. His threatened eyes peering into the drunken father's unbalanced soul, Winslow bit one last nacho before the father helped him chew with two well-placed uppercuts. Andy, Ben, and Leo now winced from a distance as the father violently jingled Winslow's bells and decked him down the hall. Though not quite Christmas music, it was about to become a slaying song.

"No, that's not him! It was some skinny twerp!" shouted Andy, heading for Winslow. "He must have gone somewhere else. Go check the salad booth!"

"Fine," grumbled the drunken father, dropping Winslow and storming off to find somebody healthier. "Come here, salad man!"

"Hey, Winslow. I know your eyes are swollen shut, but it's your pal, Andy. I'll take you to a doctor, okay?"

"You're my hero," cried Winslow.

Andy then loaded Winslow into the van and rushed him to a Burgpeters hospital, his ill-fated friend soon resting with two black eyes and a broken nose. With such easy fixes and a lot of ice, Winslow was released within the hour. But then he slipped on that ice and cracked his coccyx on the way out, forced to stay overnight in the hospital yet again.

When Winslow conked out with the free drugs from his next clinical trial, Andy drove back to the convention. And he was soon with his samosas in the comic book section, hoping that some capitalism could put them back on track. Surrounded by long tables of sleeved comics, Andy recorded his pals rifling through each box. Though many of the books were new, others were as old and xenophobic as their grandparents. Leo then squeezed a stack of marked-down comics under his arm, perusing the rest for discounts and pricing errors too good to refuse.

"What a stash! I think I found every low-cost comic in the joint," Leo said. "These classics will pad out my inventory for a few weeks."

"And here we are—the comic book section," Andy said, recording. "Most people make their pilgrimage here for the well-known fantasy and manga, but they're totally missing out on lost treasures like *Nazi Babies* and *Dolphin Cop: Maverick from the Sea*."

Leo held up a *Dolphin Cop* comic from the box, its protagonist blasting pistols with his flippers. Yes, the main character was a dolphin in full riot gear with extra clips stowed in his blowhole. Pushing this comic at the camera, Leo tapped a squiggly signature on the dolphin's belly.

"Now *this* is a score!" Leo exclaimed. "Hollywood adapted *Dolphin Cop* into an atrociously bad, female-empowerment film a few years ago. And if I'm perceiving

ANDY GETS CONNED

this signature right, it looks like the dolphin lady of the sea signed this herself with a waterproof pen."

"Yes, that looks like the late, great Barb Adolfini's autograph to me," said Andy. "Your career can't be tarnished by one film, Barb, no matter how pandering it was. Rest in seaweed, Miss Adolfini."

"What the hell?" asked Ben, seizing *Dolphin Cop* from Leo. "What kind of friends are you two? Neither of you ever told me about *Dolphin Cop!*"

Suddenly, a hickory walking stick whacked Leo twice, the first stabbing a hole in his robot head and the second knocking it to the floor. As Leo's eyes adjusted to the light, a salesman came into focus with a clenched jaw.

"You touch, you buy!" shouted the salesman.

"But I touched a ton of these, man," said Leo. "My digits tickled hundreds of them."

"You touch, you buy!" repeated the salesman, drawing a revolver from his pants and clicking back its hammer.

"Hi, Mr. Gentzel! Those facial burns are healing up nicely," Andy said, recording scar tissue worthy of a horror movie. "Guys, this is Mr. Gentzel. He's my very pleasant and super balanced neighbor. He's the guy who politely calls the cops on us when our *Rejects & Reptiles* games get too loud. You probably don't recognize him; the explosion made him a lot more handsome."

"Hi, Andy!" Gentzel said, his revolver still aimed at Leo. "Nice to kinda see you again. You know, my eyes aren't what they used to be after the face-melting fire."

"Wait," interrupted Ben. "You mean that's not a mask? He's not in a costume?"

"Zip it," said Andy, nudging Ben. "So, neighbor. How about you lower the weapon? That robot's no threat."

"That's right, no threat at all with what I'm packing," said Gentzel, removing a blunderbuss from his suspender-supported pants. "You touch, you buy!"

As Mr. Gentzel pointed his revolver and blunderbuss, a mass of well-armed citizens withdrew their arsenal and targeted the comic-groping hippie. Within seconds, hundreds of red laser sight dots then danced around Leo's face like shifting robotic acne.

"Did everyone bring a gun?" asked Leo, his question confirmed when Robby skipped by with a double-barreled shotgun. "Okay, I buy! I buy!"

After storing Leo's comics in lockers at gunpoint, the trio continued their *Rejects & Reptiles* Convention antics. And before they knew it, they had captured hours of vlog bonding and Ben failing to pick up every woman in the place. But such a nonstop day led to exhaustion, the trio voting to retire early and skip all nerd parties at the hotel. Entering the room first, Leo toted his robot cube head—now overflowing with Mr. Gentzel's forced purchases.

"Man, the universe can be one unstable cradle sometimes," Leo said, holding down the lofty stack with his chin. "This went from super fun to surplus real quick."

"I'll forge autographs on them if it'll help," Ben said, following with two small comic stacks under his arms.

The weight now too much for Leo's bohemian back, cascades of plastic-protected comics dropped to the floor. Sweaty and frustrated, he shook off his robot suit and then leapt onto one of the beds. Ben dropped his light load and fell to the floor next, worming into a sleeping bag while still in his zombie garb. There, he picked up another *Dolphin Cop* and immersed himself in tales of aquatic anti-heroes who shoot first and squeal questions later. And that's when Andy entered, wheeling in two luggage carts overloaded with comic-filled crates.

"You sure fondled a lot of these," Andy said, as Leo curled into a fetal position on his bed. "Stop worrying. We can sell these and make a profit in no time."

As Andy disconnected his dwarf beard and stripped down to Wacky Will pajamas, Leo rubbed his temples.

"I'm sensing another new decoration outside my shop in the near future," said Leo. "An eviction notice."

"Guys, do you think it's possible for a male dolphin to love a human man?" Ben asked, as Andy climbed in bed.

"Owning a dolphin is a serious responsibility, Ben," said Andy, grabbing the dice bag from his costume. "And mating with one's a felony."

Andy opened the dice bag and removed his wallet, yanking out cash in his several-step financial extraction. Aided by a couple of fake coughs, he rolled and tucked money under Leo's sulking elbow.

"Here's the rest of my Convention Crawl cash," said Andy. "I don't need to buy anything else except some healthy snacks, so it's all yours."

"I appreciate the gesture, but I can't take your gracious donation, man," said Leo.

"Okay then, you won't be taking it from me. Hey, Ben, hit me with an issue of *Nazi Babies*."

"You got it," said Ben, rummaging.

Ben then picked up an issue of *Nazi Babies*, a perplexingly progressive publication that made its content accessible through Braille hate speech. With a flick of his wrist, Ben sent that caustic comic through the air. After catching his new reading material, Andy displayed its controversial cover—eight blond-haired, blue-eyed babies on a quest for racial purity and pureed bananas.

"I'm buying this then," Andy said, gripping the repugnant publication. "I hear it's rare and worth the exact amount that I tucked under your elbow."

"I'll reimburse you with interest once this bad mojo runs its course," said Leo, opening his laptop and updating his expense report. "Thanks for the assistance."

"And thank you for your video production skills today," Ben added. "Oh, and for helping me discover *Dolphin Cop* too!"

"You're both welcome," said Andy. "I think this is some of our best vlog work yet."

"So maybe we should rip up that little contract you coerced us to sign?" asked Leo. "There's no need to legally forbid any online releases since the videos are so good, right?"

"The Samosa Clause exists for a reason. I'll never be an Internet video maker; I have to let the idea die. That pipe dream was a pipe bomb."

"I think it's time to blow Andy's mind, don't you Ben?" asked Leo.

"I'm ready," said Ben, excitedly kicking his legs in the sleeping bag. "But are you ready, Andy?"

"What are you guys talking about?" asked Andy.

ANDY GETS CONNED

"We need to show you the truth, dude. Your dream's attainable. Your fans are demanding another Andy fix right now," said Leo, passing his laptop to Andy. "Look."

"My fans? Guys, this isn't funny. I don't have any fans, and I don't want to see my site ever again. I haven't checked it since I ripped the outlet from my wall."

"We know, which is why you've been missing out on all this," said Leo, pointing at the screen.

"Just check the view count and stop distracting me," Ben said, intensely gazing at his comic book. "I don't even care that you're a dude, Dolphin Cop. You're irresistible! That's one fine piece of tail if I've ever seen one."

As Andy's eyes hadn't seen the website for over a week, they locked upon view numbers now much higher than before. Unbelievably, the screen displayed his 'End of Jumbo Andy' video with over 10,000 views and hundreds of positive comments. Would Leo and Ben have spent this much time faking a cruel joke? Was the extreme heat of wearing dwarf prosthetics all day now making him hallucinate? And did Ben just admit that he wanted to bang a dolphin? With too much to process, Andy's peepers protruded rapidly as if about to blast outward from his own head.

"Ten thousand views? Ten thousand!" Andy screamed. "I haven't talked to 10,000 people in my life."

"It's official, dude. You have an audience," said Leo.

"You better get used to having more fans than just the two of us and your mom," added Ben.

"Most of these comments are supportive," said Andy, scrolling with the touch pad. "All of the other videos have over 10,000 views too. Wait, you both knew and didn't tell me about this?"

"We tried! And you ignored our calls for a week. By the time you came to the shop, we already worked this reveal into the Conventional Crawl plan."

"Yeah, we staged something, and I even kept it a secret," bragged Ben.

"That you did! And what a way to kick this Convention Crawl off! Well, the Internet has spoken. I won't go crazy though; I can still teach and make videos at the same time until the JumboAndy page catches on. Then I can tell Principal Murray to shove it. So we'll call this version of me 'Andy 3.5.' Are you ready? This Conventional Crawl vlog's gonna make me and my samosas Internet famous."

"Glad to see you back in a full-circle revolution," said Leo. "So, about those contracts?"

"Burn those suckers in the street like your hippie forefathers!" exclaimed Andy. "The Samosa Clause is formally terminated!"

"Yes!" cheered Ben.

"Now, I need some instant coffee from my suitcase and your laptop, Leo. There's work to do!" said Andy, rolling out of bed and heading for the closet.

"Coffee at this time? You better be talking decaf, man," said Leo.

"Afraid not. Ideas are bursting from my brain. It's like a creative explosion in there," said Andy, opening the closet and grabbing his camera. "Which is also what the closet looks like now too."

Andy then recorded the aftermath of a double-stuffed suitcase eruption. The closet, now loaded from top to bottom with emergency supplies, looked like a messy survivalist's bunker.

"Those backup hard drives fit just fine, but the 14 extra pairs of underpants must have been a bit too much for my suitcase," Andy added, snatching some instant coffee packets from the pile.

"No deal, Andy. It's sleep time. My brain and back need rest, and so do you," said Leo. "Any conscientious objectors better become unconscious objectors unless they want to see me blow a fuse. We'll work fresh tomorrow. Convention Number Two awaits us soon, travelers. We rise at dawn!"

As Andy rushed back to bed, Leo closed his laptop and switched off the light. A few seconds later, Andy's face lit up from Leo's laptop while he dumped coffee packets into his mouth. Words then spewed from Andy's fingers like a madman writing his manifesto. And he clacked those keys loud enough to drown out all nerd parties down the hallway.

"Not tired yet," Andy said. "Can't sleep."

"Me neither," added Ben, activating the light on his phone, still reading *Dolphin Cop.*

"Go to sleep!" Leo yelled. "Go the hell to sleep now!"

Instantly, the laptop and phone went black. And Andy productively plotted while Ben freakishly fantasized within the confines of their own minds. Andy and friends then popped in earplugs with sleeping masks over their eyes, allowing slumber despite all the activity around them. Yes, even with the hotel parties and acrobatic couple next door on their honeymoon, the trio snoozed undisturbed.

Now with all noise muted by their earplugs, the trio let loose a cacophony of snores and gas expulsions from all possible orifices. And when Ben's dream-inspired dolphin squeals mixed in, the trio's slumber had ended their day in Burgpeters as oddly as it started. Of course, the honeymoon couples' audible boinking also ended at the same time. Apparently, with their noses full of methane and ears full of Ben's bestiality, the love birds decided to check out early.

Though Andy, Ben, and Leo had ruined the honeymooner's weekend, they made great headway with theirs. Andy's creative plan had rebounded while Leo found more support from a Jumbo backer. And Ben had discovered desires while his freaky fetishes flourished. Now like time travelers awaiting breakfast, the trio re-energized for Convention Crawl Day Two—an impending sequel that hopefully didn't suck.

CHAPTER 17

Just before sunrise, Andy worked at Leo's laptop while his samosas slept. And he gulped coffee from a cup, one of the hundreds in the room, with eyes so bloodshot that he looked like he took two allergen pies to the face. Leo awoke soon after and stretched on his bed, followed by Ben cramming a bunch of *Dolphin Cop* comics into his luggage. Andy then finished another coffee and stacked his paper cup on top of the others, completing the last piece of his Recyclable Colosseum construction.

"No fair," Ben said. "I slept too late. I wanted to read a few more comics before we left."

"Did you get any rest, Andy?" asked Leo, performing a downward dog yoga pose on his bed. "Your mind's not gonna be open if you didn't get any shuteye."

"I'm sleeping right now," said Andy, increasing his typing speed that'd rival a hacker. "Can't you tell?"

"Call me crazy, but it looks like you tuned out when I told you to sleep. Judging by the size of that cup structure, I'd guess you hit up every coffee shop on the block."

"And every muffin place too," added Ben, yoinking two blueberry muffins from Andy's bed.

"Hey, I'll have you know that I extended my coffee search to three blocks," said Andy. "I've been productive thanks to these coffee runs. I even did some physical running every time I went out for more. And I bought those two muffins for you guys; I had an apple instead."

"You're just saying that to make me feel bad, right?" Ben asked with a mouth full of muffin.

"Nope. You inhaled Leo's breakfast. It's okay though; we can pick up something healthier during the trip anyway. You know, my stomach feels a lot better when I don't load it up with butterscotch and ginger snaps."

"That's a lesson in digestion if I've ever heard one. But what about your mind?" asked Leo, now contorted in a pretzel-like pose. "You didn't sleep at all?"

"My brain only let me snooze a few minutes, but I edited another promo video for your shop when I woke up. Then came the coffee. I may have also finished a dozen old videos from our back catalogue that are all ready to upload now."

"If sleep deprivation means you're making videos and some of those are for my shop, I can't be mad."

"Good! I crafted the exact rebrand that your shop needs. And it's gonna stuff your place more than Ben's mouth is with muffins. Or Ben's luggage is with dolphin smut, for that matter. Here, take a look while I get ready!"

Andy headed to the bathroom while Ben, still in his zombie costume, belly flopped beside Leo. Each listening through an earbud connected to the laptop, they played

Andy's video and gazed as vibrant colors flashed onto their astonished faces. Fireworks then lit a path to Leo's shop in the video, and hordes of animated dwarves ran toward it holding moneybags. Factions of robots and zombies rushed in next, then joined by werewolves, wizards, goblins, pirates, and Dolphin Cop hopping on his tail. And as they all funneled into Leo's Larping & Comic Stash, the deep-voiced narration kicked in:

"In a world where geek anticipation and unreliable release-day delivery from online retailers collide, Leo's Larping & Comic Stash emerges as your savior. We've got tabletop and video game supplies, plus full-blown costumes for fandom conventions and Renaissance Fairs! Our shop also contains the world's only Alley Oops basketball game using human heads throughout history. With that alone, this place is bound to become one of the wonders of the modern world, if you ask me. So come on over to Leo's Larping & Comic Stash, a place where everybody knows your screen name. Whether you're looking for material goods or like-minded misfits, we've got it all at Leo's. Dash on down to the stash today!"

Now inside Leo's shop on screen, all animated factions assembled and drank mead as they watched the main event—dwarf women grinding on stripper poles. As their thick-haired, dwarf legs scratched off the poles' polish, dice rained from above until the video ended with one magnificent volcanic eruption.

"Where in the biosphere did you find a professional announcer so early in the morning?" asked Leo. "And a staff of great animators?"

"Penniless freelancers in different time zones, my friend," Andy answered from the bathroom.

"This is, without a doubt, the finest video you've ever completed. Upload this baby now!"

"Yeah!" Ben shouted. "I need to see that Dolphin Cop cameo whenever I want. Put it online!"

"I already tried," Andy said, emerging in a towel that obscured his naughty bits. "I forgot that I set a random password on the JumboAndy account to block myself from logging in."

"Can't you reset the password?" asked Ben, licking the muffin wrapper.

"When I try to reset my JumboAndy account password, I'm having a bit of a problem. The video website sends my phone a URL where I'd normally swipe my thumbprint and do a retina scan to verify it's me. Unfortunately, I also blocked the website on my phone with parental controls using another random password. So I basically locked myself out. But it's okay."

"You're not bummed about this?" asked Leo.

"Hell no. I already have my mom's boyfriend cracking that sucker. He's the Bumble Ridge police chief and has access to a wide range of privacy-invading technology," said Andy, reapplying his dwarf costume. "All he had to do was pull his staff away from a few murder cases—now it's just a matter of time."

"Those people are dead already, so the website's more important," said Ben.

"Exactly. As soon as they reset my password, I'll upload the promo and a few of our old videos too. Let's

ANDY GETS CONNED

keep this Convention Crawl moving and crank out more content. You two better hit the showers!"

"At the same time?" asked Ben, wheeling his luggage into the bathroom.

"Hurry up!" insisted Andy. "And if we hear you reading *Dolphin Cop* in there, we're breaking down the door, recording whatever's happening, and emailing the footage to your friends and family."

"Loud and clear," Ben said, pushing his luggage back out of the bathroom and grabbing his clothes.

"We need to make a quick stop along the way," Andy said. "It's time to expand our party."

After they scrubbed off their joyful funk and burdened the van's shocks with Leo's comic archive, the trio continued its Convention Crawl. Their first exciting stop? The hospital, of course. As Leo and Ben waited in the van, Andy rushed in for the surprise guest. And moments later, Andy emerged pushing their fourth party member in a wheelchair—his new buddy Winslow with a cast on every appendage.

"Guys, this is Winslow," said Andy, loading him into the van. "And Winslow, the hippie driver is Leo. The zombie's Ben. Don't worry; they're both geeks like us."

"Hi, Leo and Ben!" exclaimed Winslow. "You guys are my best friends, you know that?"

"Our pleasure," said Leo. "So how are you doing?"

"Nobody ever asked me that before," said Winslow. "Boy, where do I start?"

Such a normally innocent question, Leo's words opened up a can of worms with the man who had been a laughingstock his entire life. Somebody in Winslow's proximity now showing some compassion, he then shared enough stories of bullying and harassment to last the entire 3-hour trip. Yes, even when entering Ohio under its new 'Travel Rights are Wrong' policy, Winslow still managed to captivate the van. Before the quartet knew it, Leo's van sputtered into a packed parking garage. Andy then led the group's slow-motion swagger down the sidewalk, dressed as a dwarf pushing his wheelchair companion with one hand. And beside them, zombie Ben and robot Leo now strutted in slightly different costumes.

"Did I miss the memo about leaving our heads exposed today?" asked Andy. "ZomBen, your bloody hair and brain matter are missing. And LSD-401K's cube head is gone too. What's going on?"

"The rest of our getups have yet to be revealed," said Leo, as they approached the convention center full of flashing lights and laser sound effects.

"Either aliens are invading, or this is a science fiction convention," Andy said, recording with his other hand.

"Getting warmer," said Leo, then bringing back his robotic voice. "Please add some specificity to your search terms...Mr. Pinnette."

"Pinnette? That's from *Space Fightin'!* This is the *Space Fightin'* Convention isn't it? You two really outdid yourselves! But I have so many space outfits back at home. I wish you would have told me so I didn't come as a dwarf. I really look out of place here."

"No worries, man. It's all taken care of," Leo said, opening his robot chest hinge and handing out three

ANDY GETS CONNED

astronaut helmets hidden within. "This will help my companions adapt to alien environments. Plus, I'll be able to see and breathe this time compared to my old head. Sorry, Winslow, we didn't expect another guest today, so we had to find yours at the last second."

"I'm honored to be a part of anything," said Winslow, as Leo placed a pointed birthday party hat on his head. "I love it! Thank you!"

"Well I'm suffocating!" Ben shouted in his space helmet, its visor still closed.

"Press this button on the side for some air, dude," instructed Leo, using his robot clamp.

"It's a sci-fi sauna in here," Andy said, smashing his helmet button and gasping for air.

"Try not to make these helmets too groady, guys. I have to sell them as 'new' when we get back to the shop. They have to be in mint condition."

"Already covered," said Ben, flipping up his visor and pulling out a gooey material. "I got spearmint gum all over mine, so we're good."

"No, I meant 'mint condition' as in quality. You know, keep them cherry," said Leo.

"I don't have any cherry-flavored gum. Stop being so picky about this."

"You're a major pain in my first and seventh chakras, Ben. And a contributing factor of me needing to know two chapters of bankruptcy. Clean that gum off!"

"I will as soon as we add the last part of our costumes," Ben said, swinging open Leo's torso box hinge and reaching inside. "Prepare to feel even cooler!"

"There's more?" asked Andy.

"Yeah. I present to you—space capes!" Ben said with a yank, accompanied by a ripping cloth sound.

"Those weren't space capes, man!" lamented Leo, now looking at his tattered pair of peace-sign boxer-briefs in Ben's hands.

"I can fix those up in a jiffy," said Winslow. "I've gotten pretty good at repairing ripped underpants from all the wedgies over the years. Anybody have a stapler?"

"Maybe there's one in here with the capes," Ben said, reaching for Leo's box again.

"No, lay off, guys!" Leo said, slapping Ben's hand away and reaching in. "I have enough staple scars already. Here, these are the capes!"

"Now I'm prepared to make one small step for dwarf kind!" said Andy, tying on the cape.

"Space capes!" Ben shouted. "Here's yours, Winslow. I only brought three, so this is the best I can do."

Ben then affixed a lobster bib around one of Winslow's chins, securing it above his neck brace.

"You all know how to make someone feel special," said Winslow, gazing at a convention hall of *Space Fightin'* cosplayers and creatures.

"*Space Fightin'* Con, the second frontier," Andy said recording, stretching his Adam's apple to the deepest recesses of his throat. "These are the voyages of four social misfits. Its three-day mission: to explore pedantic worlds; to meet other life-forms craving futuristic utopia; to boldly go where nobody ever really goes unless they have to—Southeastern Ohio."

ANDY GETS CONNED

"Convention Crawl Day Two is here!" Ben added.

"Right on!" Leo cheered.

"I am being accepted socially!" Winslow celebrated, as Ben grabbed the wheelchair from Andy and pushed.

"Thanks, Ben," said Andy. "Now to make our next video. Let's interview some people for the vlog. Whose likeness should we capture for eternity first?"

The group examined their surroundings, sweeping the crowd for their initial dweeb contact. And right between two gelatinous mutants at the video game demo booths, the quartet locked onto a divine slice of cosplayer pie. As mutants undulated past, they revealed the toned, peachy shoulders of Commander Courtney—the deadly yet seductive feline Commander from *Space Fightin'*.

"Her! Let's talk to her," Andy and his three friends proclaimed in unison. "Boy, that was weird. Actually, it's still weird that we're continuing this unison in such a perfectly timed way. I say we walk toward the beautiful lady that none of us have a chance with. And then we never speak of this freaky unison accident again. Great, I'm glad that we agree about this. Now let's go."

Joining the demo line, the group sidled up behind Commander Courtney's two puffy tails. And they all caught a whiff of her cheese scented hair, now lost in her flowing locks topped with pointy cat ears. At least from behind, her attention to detail was quite clear; she perfectly recreated a character's backside that the quartet had studied since childhood. Beyond intimidated by a lady with those looks in that outfit standing in line to play video games, the quartet whispered in each other's ears.

"We have to introduce ourselves without scaring her," Andy said, as Ben stopped listening and went in solo.

"Hey, Commander Courtney. Wanna be on camera with four dudes at the same time?" Ben asked.

"How about I give you a pepper spray facial instead?" asked the woman, turning.

As she pivoted, her sturdy tails whipped Winslow right in the face. And the guys now gawked at the hundreds of military pins upon her furry chest. But then they looked up at her whiskers, Andy seeing something even more jaw-dropping. That lustrous red hair, those endearing dimples, her deadpan delivery—Andy only had one word come to mind.

"Tessa?" Andy winced, then morphing into attack mode. "Look, if you and some barbershop singers are about rip my heart out via song again, I'll declaw you right now. Leave me the hell alone."

"I have no idea what you're talking about!" Tessa yelled with rising intonation. "You've lost your mind!"

"Don't play coy with me, cat lady. I know you hired that barbershop group to tell me I was fat and gross and bad at the arts. Drop the act."

"Wait, this is Tessa?" Ben blurted. "You mean that imbalanced woman who you had a huge—"

"Hey, Ben!" Leo interjected, pointing into the distance. "I think me and Winslow see a wet T-shirt contest over there. Looks pretty dynamite!"

"Less talking, more getting the hell over there," said Ben, whisking Leo and Winslow away from the tense conversation. "Don't stop now, baby. Shake those flukes!"

ANDY GETS CONNED

"So you had nothing to do with that barbershop song?" questioned Andy.

"No. Maybe it was one of the women you lied to and hooked up with," Tessa said, clenching her fists.

"What are you talking about?"

"I saw security footage of you and Janet at the speakeasy with your groins jammed together. It sounded like you packed the place with an audience so you could screw her that night and me later," Tessa grumbled, facing away from Andy. "Actually, I'll revise that. I bet you were going to try to get a three-way going instead."

"No! Janet was throwing herself at me. I turned her down because, well, let's just say my mind was elsewhere."

"I find this very hard to believe."

"Hold on," Andy said, scratching his dwarf beard. "We're nerds, right? We like evidence. Call Janet. Call her right now. She has no reason to lie about this."

"Fine. But just in case you had this planned, here's a different idea. You call Janet instead and act like I'm not listening. Then I'll hear the truth directly from her."

"Yes, even better! So what's Three-Fifth Chasers' phone number?"

"Like you don't know."

"I don't! What is it?"

"It's KKK-KKK-KKKK. All fives," said Tessa.

"Get ready to hear my innocence," said Andy dialing, then activating speaker phone.

"Hi there, ya' reached Three-Fifth Chasers. This is Janet speakin'. How ya' doin?" she asked.

"Janet, it's Andy."

"Hi, sweetie. What can I do ya for?"

"I have some good news: I'm thinking about making you a commercial for your speakeasy. You know, to help show Bumble Ridge that you're not racist."

"That's mighty excitin'. Can I help ya?"

"You can, actually. I'd like to share stories about the place—you know, testimonials from satisfied customers like me. My brain's a bit foggy after Zeus smacked me with all those pool sticks though. Could you tell me your version of how we met so I can work it into the video?"

"Sure. Ya came in here lookin' forward to seein' Tessa. Pretty endearin' if ya ask me. My co-owner told me to close for the night since numbers were low. And then ya helped get me a crowd so the place could stay open."

"Oh, that's right! Then you pressed our genitals together and asked if I wanted anything in return?"

"Embarassin', but yes," Janet said, as Tessa's eyes lit up. "I put the moves on ya pretty hard too. I don't know how ya resisted me. But ya let me down easy, and I still have hope you'll come around."

"Thanks, Janet! I'm sorry if that opened any old wounds, but I'm going to make you a great commercial."

"You're the best, ya cutey patootie."

"Hey, thanks again for the info. I'll send you a link to the video for some feedback when it's done, okay?"

"Sounds good. Bye, Andy!"

"Take care," said Andy, hanging up with a grin.

"So you aren't interested in her?" asked Tessa, unclenching her fists. "And you don't have a phone full of other women's numbers?"

ANDY GETS CONNED

"No! She's attractive and very forward, but I chase one woman at a time. And I'll give you even more proof. Look at all my contacts," Andy said, giving Tessa his phone. "See how few there are? They're numbered in order of appearance in my life—one to 78, here goes. Number 1 is Mom. You already met her. Number 2 is Leo, and Number 3 is Ben. They're the robot and zombie who just ran away."

"Okay, and numbers 4 through 10 seem to be the local hospitals? Wait a minute! That could be for all the women you're impregnating who need to give birth. Birth happens at hospitals, you know!"

"I'm clumsy and accident-prone so quick hospital contacts are literally life savers. Come on, I know you want to believe me."

"Fine, but why's your next contact skip to 76?"

"The missing ones were all the restaurants in Bumble Ridge that delivered. And I deleted all those when I started my diet."

"That's logical, I suppose. So, Number 76 is...Helga? Number 77...Chris? And Number 78 is Winslow? Those could all be women's names!" scolded Tessa. "Did you really think I'd stop looking after the first few?"

"No, let's go in reverse order. Winslow was the guy in the wheelchair with Ben and Leo," Andy said, moving beside Tessa. "If you're worried that he's a woman, look at this text referencing a particular protuberance of his that I spilled coffee on at the hospital."

"Oh, god. Winslow's definitely a man. Is he okay?"

"Never. I don't know why he even leaves his house."

"Okay, so how about Chris then?"

"He's my mom's boyfriend. You'll see half of his texts are pictures of him and my mom making out around town," said Andy, scrolling. "And the other half tease me for shooting Winslow out of the sky on a duck hunt."

"All right, but I bet you saved the most incriminating for last. Who's Helga?"

"She was my long-term lady friend from college—my one and only real romantic relationship."

"I need more details."

"Her name was Helga. She had a glandular problem. We met in History 101 and dated for four years until we split on good terms. The night before graduation, we binged on strudel, gazed at stars, and made up our own X-rated constellations. Then she went back to Belgium so she could take over her dad's blimp company."

"Yeah, yeah. I've heard that one before."

"Look at the texts," Andy said, as Tessa read the messages. "We're still friendly. See?"

"Hold on and be quiet. I'm analyzing."

For 10 silent minutes, Tessa scoured Andy's entire texting history with Helga. No manipulation, no nude pics, and no bad blood at all between them—this was a healthy, former relationship.

"You two text with proper punctuation and grammar," Tessa said, misty-eyed. "That's so cute. Dammit, you're right. The rumors about you must have been wrong."

"Rumors?"

"Yeah. About paying the speakeasy crowd to laugh. About making me happy just to get in my pants."

ANDY GETS CONNED

"Wait, so you thought—I get it now. You thought I was a playa...that'd I'd hit it and quit it. And you had the video evidence to prove it. No wonder you didn't want to talk to me. Hell, I wouldn't blame you if you did send hateful singers to my house when you thought that."

"I'm so sorry!" Tessa exclaimed, giving Andy's phone back. "You were trying to tell me when I stormed away after my show."

"I was! But hey, no need to dwell on this. We're in the same room and talking again. How about an olive branch? I still want you to have this," Andy said, taking his metal dwarf from his dice bag and placing it in her hand.

"Olive branch accepted. Hey, his little axe condom stays on pretty well doesn't it?"

"It sure does. Jumbo's axe is sharper than any kitchen knife I own. That plastic cap needs to remain attached at all times, okay?"

"Got it. And in exchange for your dwarf..."

Tessa shifted to her toes and kissed Andy's cheek, her lips now penetrating his opened helmet visor.

"Humina!" Andy celebrated.

"Did you just say 'humina?' I've never heard that in person—just cartoons."

"Me too, which is even weirder."

"So, how have you been, Andy?" Tessa asked, her eyes following the beard up to his face. "Or should I say, Jumbo Shrimpit."

"I hit a bit of a rough patch, but I'm better now. I started intentionally jogging and I'm making videos again, so all's back on track."

"Life sure is an emotional roller coaster, isn't it? And everyone has to ride."

"Yeah, even if they're too short. Or pregnant. Or have a heart condition," laughed Andy.

"You're bound to see puking kids along the ride," chuckled Tessa. "Plus, we're all one mistake away from derailing at any moment."

"And then requiring serious medical attention like this," Andy said, rolling his eyes into the back of his head. "Oh no, I died on the life rollercoaster. I am so dead!"

Tessa lifted her cat tails up and pressed them upon Andy's chest like defibrillators.

"Clear! Don't die on us now, Andy's heart!" she continued, fake zapping. "Clear! Are you better now?"

"Yes! Nurse, we need two injections of Reconnection Serum, stat!"

"I missed this," said Tessa.

"Me too. So, how's the stand-up going?"

"I've been meaning to perform again, but the speakeasy incident set me back a bit. Plus, the computer repair job's been nonstop, and the tips are hard to pass up. So, I haven't had time for much else."

"Except making that intricate cat costume, right? You know, the custom one that isn't purchasable in any store?"

"Hey, a lady has needs, you know? And since my landlord doesn't allow pets, I had to figure out a way to be the crazy cat lady."

"It's official, Tessa."

"What?"

"You're funny."

ANDY GETS CONNED

"Stop," said Tessa, smiling.

"Nope, you can't make me. We're going to keep talking, and you're getting back on stage. Hey, I hope this isn't too forward, but would you like to join us? We could use a Commander Courtney in the group. We're recording videos, and it'd be a great way to get yourself out there until your next set."

"Oh, cool! I'd love to tag along, but I—"

"Don't worry, you'll fit right in with us. And we're shooting comedy videos, not porn like Ben led you to believe. Come with us."

"That's not what I was going to say," Tessa said. "Though I did get so many porn offers today that I'm almost out of pepper spray. So, I was saying that I'm here with my friend, Luke. Do you mind if he comes too?"

Andy froze yet again. Luke? Was Tessa dating another man? Was he just a friend? Or was Luke the name of another nasty barbershop quartet about to regale him with more degrading melodies? Andy's brain zapped with probable outcomes, many leading to heartbreak. But he wasn't about to let Tessa slip away again so easily.

"Sounds good to me!" Andy shouted, snapping out of it. "The more the merrier. Bring on Luke! Where is he?"

CHAPTER 18

"Ben! Leo! Winslow! Get over here! You too, Luke!" shouted Andy, waving his arms like an air traffic controller. "Hey, Tessa, when we add our friends together, I think we officially reach gang status."

"Yeah, and we didn't even have to shank any narcs to get there," said Tessa. "Luke's in the bathroom, so he'll be out in a second."

"Great. We'll be a sextet then. Just don't say that word to Ben otherwise he won't stop repeating it."

Pushing Winslow, Leo trotted back from the wet T-shirt contest in his robot costume. Then Ben sulked behind them, shambling over in his space zombie outfit. Though a soaking-wet T-shirt dripped in Ben's hands, it dragged on the floor like a disheartened janitor's mop.

"False alarm," said Leo, winking at Andy. "What looked like a wet T-shirt contest from afar was just a dork's clammy manboobs up close."

"He was so plump that I couldn't tell until it was too late," Ben said, letting go of the quilt-sized, soggy shirt.

"You guys are hilarious," said Winslow. "I'll never forget your face when he gave you that lap dance, Ben!"

"Now that's the spirit," Andy said. "Thanks for getting back so fast. I just found out Tessa's coming with us."

"Sweet. Estrogen has joined our party," said Leo.

"Humina!" exhaled Ben.

"Is 'humina' some type of inside joke with you guys or something?" asked Tessa.

"No, I swear that was unplanned," Andy said.

"Hold on, there he is. Luke. Luke! Over here!" Tessa said, then touching Andy's back. "Oh, I bet he can't hear me through his costume. I'll go get him."

Tessa ran to the bathroom greeting her friend Luke—Nathan Hader's homeless persona. Though this time, Nathan wore a mechanized suit and robot helmet masking his entire head. A flowing black cape and matching leotard also covered his bulging legs. Yes, Andy's arch nemesis Nathan Hader was here as a homeless Luke dressed as Droid Blitzer in a truly multilayered con job. Marching out as the *Space Fightin'* villain, Nathan clenched a stuffed, black garbage bag in one hand and a paper toilet seat cover in the other. With shiny gears lining his metallic cranial frame, Nathan tied the toilet seat protector around his technological neck.

"Luke! I ran into Andy while you were in there," said Tessa. "Everything you told me about him at the speakeasy was wrong. He's laughing at my jokes, he's a nice guy, and he let me snoop through his entire phone as proof. He's completely clean, and my woman senses were right the first time."

"I don't like this," said Nathan, disguised through his voice synthesizer that matched the villain's voice perfectly. "I swear that he said he was your manager! He told us with his own two stupid lips! I know he was trying to bone you, Tessa. Listen to me."

"I'm going with my gut on this one. Did you mistake Andy for somebody else? Maybe you misheard him?"

"No!"

"Then maybe you were lying because you saw Andy and I getting closer. If I'm right about that, you need to stop it now, okay? You shouldn't be jealous at all; I still want you in my life so we can help each other out. You're a special person, and that's not just a joke about you wearing a helmet."

"There's no way I can convince you about this then?"

"No."

"Fine, I think you're going to regret this. But let's go," grumbled Nathan, hoisting the garbage bag over his shoulder. "I'm keeping an eye on him though."

"Thank you for understanding," Tessa said, pulling Nathan across the room to Andy and his pals.

"Nice bib!" shouted Winslow, pointing at Nathan's toilet seat cover and then his own lobster bib with a nod.

"Yeah, that's a great outfit, Luke!" said Ben.

"Thank you, Captain Obvious," said Nathan.

"I'm not a captain—I'm a zombie. Are you dumb?"

"No. I'm Droid Blitzer. Are you blind?"

"Guys, this could go on forever," interrupted Andy, shoving himself between the two. "Welcome aboard, Luke. Now let's rock this *Space Fightin'* Con!"

"Not yet," Nathan said, adjusting the paper toilet seat cover around his neck. "I found this bib in the bathroom, so now it's food time. I'm heading over to the breakfast burrito booth. You can start without me."

"But we're bib brothers!" Winslow said. "Bib brothers binge together, not alone."

"He's right, Luke. Groups don't split at cons," said Andy. "We can accommodate your request. Let's pick up some breakfast burritos, digest for a few minutes, and then rock this *Space Fightin'* Con!"

Andy's gang quickly consumed their burritos, washing them down with coffee and Palpitation energy drinks. They then headed to their first event at the auditorium, plopping into front-row seats for a speaking panel. With Winslow beside them in the aisle, Andy and friends viewed a barely-surviving cast of the original *Space Fightin'* films. Then, in the most distracting way possible, Nathan loaded his overfilled trash bag into a seat and removed two vanilla protein bars. And he shoved them right through the mouth hole of his Droid Blitzer helmet.

"Geez, is everybody eating those things these days?" asked Andy, recording with his camera. "Please blow your vanilla protein bar breath in the other direction, Luke. That aroma brings back some bad memories."

Up on stage, the actors who played Pinnette, Commander Courtney, and Droid Blitzer were joined by two writers of the first *Space Fightin'* trilogy. Though Courtney and Blitzer wore civilian clothes to distance themselves from the franchise, Pinnette's actor sported his film attire without even being asked. Not exactly designed

ANDY GETS CONNED

for an 80-year-old body, Pinnette's all-leather pilot jumpsuit was adorned with lit-up spikes down the shoulders. And the sun design on his stomach not only exaggerated Pinnette's bulbous alien belly, but also matched his yellow, triple-lens sunglasses.

"The best science fiction is grounded in real science, carefully crafted by creative and out-of-the-box thinkers ahead of their time," Andy said, whipping around his camera and zooming in on the black-draped writers. "And you're about to see these two depressed writers get zero credit or questions over the next hour."

"Writers are even more disrespected than me," Winslow laughed.

"No way, I bet they'll get at least one question," Tessa said, then jokingly twirling her hair and chewing fake gum. "So, like, what was it was like to work with such amazing actors all the time and stuff?"

A stagehand then passed Blitzer's helmet to his actor, the audience roaring with excitement. Because Blitzer hadn't held his helmet since pursuing more important projects—like failed sitcom pilots and infomercials—this was kind of a big deal. Snugly squeezing the helmet on, Blitzer's actor strutted around stage while the crowd cheered. And now seeing another person in the room dressed just like him, Nathan launched from his seat and pointed at his android twin.

"How dare you steal my costume idea, nerd?" Nathan screamed, met immediately with a wave of hatred from the audience. "See, they agree with me too, you impostor. Boo, we say! Boo!"

"Time to go, buddy," shouted a security guard, promptly dragging Nathan and his garbage bag away.

"I like you, Luke. But these actors are pretty old, and this panel might be the last chance I have to see them alive," shouted Tessa. "But I'll meet you in the hallway when it's over!"

"She's right, you know!" said Pinnette, now tossing autographed head shots to the audience.

"What a guy," Andy sighed, catching a picture. "Hey, Pinnette, can I have another one for backup purposes?"

With the distraction now gone, actors answered questions about their life motivations, top breakfast foods, and entire bowel movement histories. But the writers collected dust, as expected. Continuing, audience members lapped up stories of Commander Courtney's method acting—eating only tuna fish and anchovies during the entire trilogy. Attendants also appreciated Pinnette's weight loss secret, a botched gastric bypass surgery, dropping 30 pounds when the docs amputated his arm by mistake. The audience didn't respond well when their heroes became cowards, however, as Nathan shouted bomb threats from the nearby hallway.

"Bombs! Lots of big bombs are about to blow up right now and kill everybody!" Nathan screamed through a crack in the doors. "Leave all of your expensive objects behind, especially the helmet on stage; because that's where the biggest bomb is!"

Crowd members then fled to the exits, security even deserting their posts to avoid getting trampled to death. The auditorium now free of any potential witnesses,

Nathan slipped back inside toward the actors' chairs. And he tossed all abandoned phones, tablets, and emotional support animals into his garbage bag along the way. Now on stage, Nathan nipped the auditorium's most precious piece by far—the original Droid Blitzer helmet prop.

"Step one, check!" said Nathan. "When I'm done crushing Andy with this tonight, I can sell it for boatloads of cash to bother even more nerds. Think of all the Benjamin Hitlers I can get for this junk!"

Thirty minutes later, after security swept the place and the closest thing found to a bomb was a stuffed colostomy bag, Nathan rejoined the Convention Crawl. Deep within a windowless room, Andy's group danced in the corner wearing their space attire lit by glow sticks. And they boogied around a leg-locked Nathan, still unenthused that Tessa signed him up for this nonsense. Even Winslow moved more than him, swaying to the beat with glow sticks lining his casts and lobster bib. Unlike most glow sticks, these were shaped like laser swords, laser guns, and laser turkey rotisseries—the latter demanded by Blitzer's actor to promote his latest infomercial product. Behind Andy's gang, droves of rhythmically-challenged attendees partied to video game music. And as everyone locked and popped like robots around Nathan, Andy whipped out the camera for another comedic vlog.

"Like all social gatherings, the most interesting people tend to congregate in corners," Andy said, recording himself and the gang. "Our corner's particularly cool. Here, we don't just tear apart the dance floor, but we do so using proper parliamentary procedure. Yes, though these rules of order started long ago in deliberative assemblies, they still work!"

"In our last session, we spoke of the unreal possibility of forming a spontaneous conga line," said Leo, pulling a stack of papers from his robot chest while shimmying. "Here are minutes from the last meeting. Are there any pressing corrections? Lay them on me."

"In Section 1, you listed the proposed conga line as going clockwise," Andy said, gyrating his dwarven hips. "But I believe we voted for a counterclockwise direction because we're rebels."

"I hear you. Is there any objection to making this correction?" Leo asked, pointing his silver clamp hand up and down diagonally.

Everyone shook their heads to the beat.

"Stellar!" said Leo. "Any additional changes?"

"There's an error in Section 12," said Tessa, whipping her tails in circles. "I'm scaling up onto Andy's shoulders at the *start* of this, not the end."

"No problemo," said Leo, moonwalking in his robot box suit. "Anything else?"

Andy leapfrogged over Tessa and Ben, all shaking their heads again.

"All right!" shouted Leo. "The minutes are approved as corrected! Is there any new business?"

"Yes, I'd like to motion that we perform the conga line right now instead of dragging this out any longer," Andy said, fist-pumping into the air. "Let's just go straight to the vote! Who's with me?"

"I second that motion!" Tessa shouted.

ANDY GETS CONNED

"I wasn't paying attention when you told me the rules!" Ben exclaimed. "But let's do it!"

"Any nonconformist discussion?" asked Leo with no response. "Good! The impatient 'Ayes' have it!"

"Conga line time!" said Andy, hoisting Tessa up as his samosas followed behind with Winslow.

Just as planned, they headed in a counterclockwise direction and attracted a trickle of dancers. Mutants and aliens joined in too, soon voting to keep the conga line going for exactly 365.256 seconds—the same number of days it takes Earth to orbit the Sun. Ending about six minutes later, Andy's group lost their next vote when the conga line set a new goal of 365.256 minutes—about six hours of dangerous dancing ahead of them. Indeed, their creation was out of control. So Andy quickly picked new conga line leaders, and the samosas escaped the dehydration death march before it was too late.

Needing a break from the crowds, Ben created VIP stamps for the gang's badges—VIP stamps that would normally cost a few months' rent. Such stamps not only looked cool, but they also allowed access to special areas protected by velvet ropes. Entering their elite swag area, they first visited the LungLube booth—a vaping company with infused flavors that the competition wouldn't touch. Its newest flavor, Chloroform Caramel, scared most VIP members away with such risqué efforts. Nathan, however, showed great interest in the product as Andy's gang headed to the next booth.

"Step two, check!" Nathan said, slipping a few Chloroform Caramel bottles into his garbage bag.

Their next stop, a booth operated by the Palpitations energy drink company, featured samples of its new, potent product. Yes, this was the long-awaited iProcrastinated drink—a mix of coffee, tea, and ADHD medication for people with poor time management skills. After each of Andy's gang took a thimble-sized shot, and then a couple laps around the room, they eventually rested at the Nielsen's Cheese Curls display. Here, a human-sized, Plexiglas cube housed a space-age snack that was previously unseen by the public.

"One of cool perks of these pricey passes is that they give you as much high-tier swag as you can fit in your arms," Andy said. "You also get to be the lab rat for a bunch of products that haven't been widely tested yet."

"Yeah, man. We're the audacious risk takers of the world!" added Leo.

"The trailblazing trail blazers!" said Ben

"And those voted most likely to need a stomach pumped!" joked Tessa, rubbing her tummy.

"I'm very familiar with that last one," cheered Winslow. "Somehow poison ends up in my mouth a lot."

"So what's the product, cheese lady?" asked Andy, placing his camera on a tripod and aiming it at the cube. "I'm hoping Nielsen's makes a healthy cheese curl soon."

"Everyone has to get inside to find out," the spokeswoman said, guiding Andy's gang into the Plexiglas cube and latching it shut. "Prepare your taste buds for a food that's even more fun to eat than Nielsen's Cheese Curls. Today's remarkable product is a squirting silly string that's edible and delicious. It's much more fun than

ANDY GETS CONNED

your usual spray cheese and much less toxic than your usual silly string."

"Really?" asked Andy, soon spurting a small squirt into his mouth. "Hey, this tastes identical to your curls! It's safe, everyone. Tessa, try some!"

As if fulfilling another one of his dreams that dare not be mentioned, Andy ejected cheese string all over Tessa's face with glee. The stream soon coiling on her head like a unicorn horn, Tessa wielded her cans of cheese for some pungent revenge.

"Geez, Tessa. You're not supposed to eat with your forehead," Andy joked, facing his camera and spraying. "Mouth, Tessa, mouth. That's where food goes! Mo—"

As Andy extended his teasing, Tessa lifted his space helmet off and sprayed back with both cans. Cheese going in every direction, Leo ducked behind a non-participatory Nathan while Ben shielded himself with Winslow. Still not satisfied with her assault, Tessa then nabbed Nathan's unclaimed snack and blew Andy away with three fire hose-like canisters at once.

"Then explain why you seem to be using yours as a hair product instead of putting it in *your* mouth," quipped Tessa, topping Andy's dwarven locks in the orangey concoction. "Lather, rinse, die, dwarf!"

Ben and Leo winked at one another behind their human protection, readied their cans, and unloaded into the ongoing Battle of Cheddarsburg. All onlookers then murmured as every square inch of the cube had been lathered with cheese product. And no signs of life emerged from the unpromising Plexiglas coffin.

"There's nothing to see here, people," asserted the spokeswoman.

As the spokeswoman unfolded a large blanket to envelop her cube, Andy's hand smacked into the cheese wall and left a ghastly imprint. Hands of Leo, Ben, and Tessa then wiped cheese from the Plexiglas door too, revealing no cheese anywhere on their clothes.

"I am astonishingly clean," Andy said to his camera.

"Us too," added Ben.

"Far out," said Leo. "If these helmets woulda stunk like cheese funk, nobody'd buy them."

"Hey, Luke. Can you believe this?" Tessa asked, glancing where Luke once was.

Their uncooperative companion could barely be seen, now encompassed by a cheese pile so big that only his android arms stuck out.

"It looks like all the cheese hit Luke. How'd you luck out, Winslow?" asked Andy, twisting toward an even larger cheese mound in the cube. "Oh no!"

"Don't worry, guys," said Winslow, then slurping his cheese pile. "I'm having a blast! And dinner!"

"Maybe we should nibble Luke out of his too," Tessa laughed. "We could be his, you know... *Jaws* of Life."

"Not funny," Nathan said, still beneath Cheese Mountain. "Stop talking and start helping!"

"Thank god," mumbled the spokeswoman. "Let's give a round of applause to our undeniably alive helpers!"

"I'm so glad I was recording this," said Andy.

"I can see again," said Winslow, poking his head from the cheese like a curious gopher. "Hold on, bib brother!"

Winslow shook off the rest of his cheese, rolled to Nathan, and began dining on his bib brother's restrictive orange dune. As the others exited and signed waivers that they wouldn't sue Nielsen's, Winslow excavated Nathan's helmet and torso. And Nathan slipped a few cans of cheese string into his leotards.

"Step three, check!" Nathan said.

"Step three of what?" asked Winslow.

"Uh...step three of bonding with my bib brother, of course," Nathan grumbled. "Now get my legs out of this damned cheese!"

After Winslow freed Nathan from his dairy-based straitjacket, the gang left with a liberal supply of cheese spray and vlog footage. Then Andy's group withdrew from the VIP area, immediately met by security guards.

"Please exit to your left," said a guard, directing everyone to the door. "Thanks for coming."

"Wait, it's over?" asked Winslow. "We just started."

"Look at the clock, buddy," said Andy, pointing. "Time flies when you're somewhat respected, doesn't it? The convention's over. Or, should I say, it's *supposed* to be over. Let's enter the password; take it away, Leo."

"Excuse us, groovy guards," said Leo, approaching. "Etlay usyay inyay."

"You got it," said the guard, letting them pass.

"What just happened?" asked Winslow. "This keeps getting cooler every second!"

Andy's group then headed for the back stairs with only five minutes of official convention remaining. While clueless attendants departed, the night's unsanctioned attraction had yet to begin. Yes, one significant secret was about to ramp up in the basement. When the clock struck six and the conga line left with their daring dance goals of 365.256 days, a few hundred folks had already snuck to the basement. It was now time for an attendant's shot at everlasting glory, for enduring respect, and for quickly expendable gift cards—the elaborate robot races had begun. Though the owners and authorities would never approve of such underground secrets, security guards turned a blind eye for a cut of the profit. By making more than a year's salary in one hour of dorky robot racing, this was a fireable offense worth risking.

"Perhaps the most guarded activity going on at *Space Fightin'* Con is the robot races," said Andy, recording as they took their seats in the bleachers. "Even though there's an abundance of gambling and alcohol, most people sin responsibly here. So it's a family affair too. My dad brought me to the races when I was a kid, and those are memories I'll never forget or admit to my mother. So bring your spawn down to the next *Space Fightin'* Con basement for some furtive fun. Unless you're the feds and, in that case, this is all green screen special effects right now. You can't raid a green screen, feds!"

"And you know what's even more topnotch than watching these little metal dudes cruise around the track?" Leo asked, reaching in his boxy chest and pulling out a large object from the back. "Using these!"

Upon reveal, Leo jerked back from the object he had removed—Robby the hamster-boy wheezing for air.

"Help," Robby gasped.

"You are sick, Leo!" Andy said. "And that's way too illegal even for the robot races."

"How'd you get in there, little man?" panicked Leo, seeing Robby's blue face and lowering him to the floor.

"I like to hide in things when Dad gets drunk," cried Robby. "Thank you for saving me, robot. Is the *Rejects & Reptiles* Convention over yet?"

"That was yesterday, kid," said Leo, pulling out two canisters of cheese curl spray and placing them in Robby's hands. "But here's some cheese until we get you some real food, okay?"

"I'll help him," said Winslow, wheeling to Robby. "I spent a lot of time with child protective services as a kid."

"I think that's a great idea," said Andy, as Robby hopped on Winslow's lap.

"Wow, your tummy's like a pillow," said Robby. "And you smell like cheese. I like you, Mister!"

"I'll be back later, samosas!" said Winslow, putting his party hat on Robby and wheeling away.

"Let me try that reveal again," said Leo, reaching back into his chest and pulling out the intended large object. "And you know what's even more topnotch than watching these little metal dudes cruise around the track?"

"R2CheeseDoodle!" blurted Andy, scooping the bot from Leo's hands. "I'm gonna sweep the track clean with this guy—literally. And then win too!"

"I hear there's some fierce competition today though," Tessa said, removing another item from Leo's robot box—her bronze catapult bot with an attached feline figurine. "Like me! I'm your competition."

"You're on. I bet you named the bot something witty, right? 'Cat-a-pult' would be too easy. So who does R2CheeseDoodle have the pleasure of outpacing today?"

"Andy, meet your worst nightmare, the future winner, and an artificial intelligence opponent that will always be on your tail. Miss Treb-Mew-Chet is here! And she'll claw a bed on your corpse."

"When did you have the time to stuff that thing in Leo's chest?"

"Remember when Leo and I went to the bathroom at the same time while Ben distracted you?" asked Tessa, putting her arms around Andy's samosas.

"Wait, you were in on this too, Ben?" asked Andy. "I knew you really didn't forget how to breathe!"

"No way, my acting was brilliant," nodded Ben. "You had no idea. Admit it."

"Okay, you're right! I'll be back after I kick her butt," flirted Andy, pulling Tessa toward the racing gates. "If you keep getting along with my friends, I'll start thinking you like me or something."

While Andy and Tessa departed for their showdown, Leo removed binoculars from his chest and scoped out this year's track. Inventing his own binoculars, Ben took two iProcrastinated paper cups from his pocket, poked holes in each, and then mimicked Leo.

"Those new traps sure look wild," said Leo.

"Yeah. I think I see a snake pit," said Ben, peering through his cups.

"Get real. You can't see with those, and there's definitely no snake pit."

ANDY GETS CONNED

"I sure can. And there *is* a snake pit," said Ben. "Maybe your cheap binoculars are broken. Wanna switch so you can get a glimpse?"

"Stop yanking my chain. And get those cups off your eyes or you'll go blind, dude. The residual energy droplets are gonna go straight to your corneas."

"Uh oh. I think it already did," Ben shivered, lowering the cups from his bloodshot eyes with retinas the size of ping pong balls. "But I still saw the snake pit before this happened. I swear!"

"Enough, you two," interrupted Nathan, getting up. "I'm talking now! Man, my stomach's going crazy after power loading all those protein bars and cheese spray cans. I need to go drain both ends of the bathroom donkey, if you know what I mean."

Nathan hoisted up his garbage bag, now filled with enough stuff for a hundred counts of petty theft. As his bag's objects collided, a metallic clank rang through the air and triggered several pacemakers of aging dorks. Forcing another protein bar through his Blitzer helmet, Nathan hustled off in the opposite direction of Andy and Tessa.

"That guy's disgusting," Ben said. "And coming from me, that's bad!"

"Yeah, but don't sweat it. Other than me almost going broke, this Convention Crawl went better than expected," said Leo. "Andy's using it like a launch pad and heading for the next creative level. He's even more energetic than the time he chased down Wacky Will in a parking lot."

"Yup, and now that he's talking to Tessa, we couldn't stop this if we wanted to," Ben said.

"That's for sure. We did good, Ben. We did good."

Leo looked back through his binoculars, watching the space dwarf and cat lady disappear behind hanging tarps.

"They're probably sucking face by now, aren't they?" asked Ben, his retinas still expanding.

"I'd deduce they're not smooching behind the tarps. That zone's loaded with pros; it's a place full of racers."

Still watching with binoculars, Leo panned across the track and saw Nathan's departure. Yes, the Droid Blitzer clone now plowed through crowds like a train with a cow pusher. And then Leo gasped, spotting something even more shocking than that—one preposterous track hazard.

"I can't believe it," Leo said, slowly turning to Ben. "You were right."

"You see the snake pit now, don't you?" Ben asked, smugly. "I told you so! These cups work!"

CHAPTER 19

Now behind a tarp wall hung from the ceiling, Andy and Tessa filed into a line of waiting racers. Though filled to capacity, this area jammed together as many people as possible with a single-file, zigzagging system. Wisely, planners placed vending machines and Palpitations fountains every 10 feet to keep the herd happy. However, beside each fountain was a danger that racers faced even before their bots touched the track—a row of portable toilets every 12 feet. Needless to say, the gas mask rental stations right before each toilet could not be ignored. But Andy and Tessa took no pitstops, passing half of their challengers within the hour. Yes, the duo had not only annoyed its competition with their developing romance, but also with their incredibly big bladders.

"The line gets even more interesting at the halfway point," Andy said, recording. "Here, it splits into four paths like a pitchfork. And the design works pretty well, decreasing disputes over who gets which starting gate. Thus, it also reduces the number of nerdy slap fights."

"He's right!" Tessa said to the camera. "Another advantage of the 4-way split is that it adds strategy; each participant can count ahead of them and figure out who their competition will be. And we all know what that means, don't we Andy?"

"No, what?"

"That I'm getting in the line beside you to kick your dwarf butt," Tessa laughed, veering to the right. "It's time to establish my nerd dominance once and for all."

Andy and Tessa then inched forward, getting in all their face-to-face flirtation before splitting up in the starting gates. To protect the racers from gamblers who lost bets on them, planners constructed layers of tarps to hide their identity. Built out of tarps and trash cans like four huts without doors, the starting gates provided complete anonymity on all sides; racers couldn't even see each other when competing. Sure, this setup looked like a roving gang's garbage base in a post-apocalyptic world, but it granted privacy to each racer. By not knowing who controlled each bot, it also provided the spoiler-free entertainment that many dorks demanded. Using this last opportunity to investigate their opponents, Andy and Tessa scoped out a rival beside them—a dumpy looking man in a top hat whose beard grew mostly on his neck.

"Tessa, look at the neckbeard beside us," whispered Andy, aiming his camera at Tessa and the opponent. "He needs to be in the video."

"Good, I can feel his eyes undressing me as we speak," Tessa said softly, leaning out of the shot. "I'd say there's a 90 percent chance he slaughters whoever beats

ANDY GETS CONNED

him. But I'll talk to him so we can capture the perp on camera; that'll help authorities locate him later."

"He's probably packing a dagger in that neck bush. Be careful," whispered Andy, as Tessa reached for the neckbeard's satellite bot veiled by his black cape.

"Hey, nice satellite there," she said, lifting his cape slightly. "How are you doing, sleepy fella?"

"Don't talk to my satellite before his race!" screeched the neckbeard. "He doesn't like to communicate! And he definitely doesn't like to be spied on!"

"That's weird, isn't it? You know, coming from a satellite," added Tessa.

"Good luck out there," said Andy, zooming in for the mug shot. "Her bot's a catapult, and mine survived several cheese curl explosions. It'll be one tough race."

"You're both irrational. I and my twin brother in the next line will defeat you," said the neckbeard, rotating.

Now facing away, the neckbeard fist-bumped his adjacent twin—the muscled Tyrannosaurus Flex. Though only wearing sweatpants and his half-unzipped hoodie, Flex displayed first-place ribbons won at *Space Fightin'* Con's costume competition. Whether the awards were stolen or given based on his good looks, justice certainly didn't exist in this world. As the twins now made kissy faces, Flex pumped each pectoral muscle in rapid succession. And his bikini-wearing supermodel assistant rubbed oil on his exposed chest.

"He's your twin?" Andy asked. "I'm sorry!"

"Yeah, he got the short end of the stick as far as I'm concerned," said the neckbeard, completely serious. "But his unpleasant appearance motivated him to be a brilliantly dirty racer."

"Hey, dwarf," grunted Flex. "Don't we know each other from somewhere?"

"We do. I'm Andy," he said. "You came into my friend's comic shop and thought it was a gym."

"Yeah, that's right. Then you came into my gym and flooded the entire back row of treadmills with your sweat. You better not try any of that funny business here, got it?"

"I got it all right. May the best meathead win," Andy said, then turning to the neckbeard. "You're right. You have a way better personality than him. Your twin doesn't really belong here, does he?"

"Shut your mouth," groaned the neckbeard. "We're going to beat you so hard."

"Hey, dwarf, get a shot of my bot with your camera," said Flex, then snapping his fingers twice at the supermodel. "Check it out."

In a flash, the supermodel tugged a sheet from Flex's robot with the embellished zest of a magician's assistant. Underneath was his phallic-shaped torpedo bot with two circular buzz saws at the shaft, its sexual innuendo potential through the roof.

"Sorry to bother you both," Tessa said, advancing in line as the next race completed. "We're going to go back to standing here and not talking to you if that's all right."

As the neckbeard and his gorgeous twin glared to their left, Andy and Tessa warmed up for the big event. Preparing, Tessa played catch with Treb-Mew-Chet while Andy sparred with R2CheeseDoodle using boxing mitts

ANDY GETS CONNED

on his feet. And with his camera on a tripod, Andy was recording R2CheeseDoodle's training montage for the vlog. In their seconds of prep time left, racers waxed their bots for less wind resistance, replaced batteries on their manual controllers, and added items to their online shopping carts should they win those glorious gift cards.

"Attention, everybody," spouted the announcer. "Our next race will start in three minutes. Make sure to visit our betting booth and check out the bots' profiles that our crack team of wannabe writers whipped up. Now, are you ready for our next set of mechanical contenders? In Gate 1, we've got the badass butler-bot capable of creating F-5 category wind suction with its intake, R2CheeseDoodle. In Gate 2, it's the processing puma bot Treb-Mew-Chet equipped to hurl traps from its innards far deadlier than the household hairball. Gate 3 is some satellite thing whose owner berated our writing staff so much that they came up with this generic description. And in Gate 4, it's perhaps the most macho machine to ever grace the track, the carnal Casanova itself—DongBot69,000."

In Tyrannosaurus Flex's gate, using the privacy provided by four tarp walls, he and his supermodel helper passed third base. Their journey to home plate became a bit too weird for them, however, when a third party joined in too—the Droid Blitzer-dressed, imitation Luke known as Nathan Hader. Crawling under the rightmost gate tarp, Nathan not only brought his garbage bag, but also another object that'd make the race a little more controversial.

"Chloroform, party of two!" Nathan shouted, headbutting Flex and the model. "It's time to win me a race!"

As Nathan's abrupt greeting sent both targets to the floor, he shoved two dripping-wet chloroform rags at their faces. Yes, Nathan used the chloroform vaping liquid in a way the company never intended. Flex and the supermodel now fully sedated, their half-naked bodies drifted into a soundless slumber. Nathan then reached into his garbage bag, removing the spare Droid Blitzer helmet and his bottle of Chloroform Caramel. After generously dumping half the bottle in his second helmet, Nathan slipped it onto Flex's head with a twist.

"That should keep you out for a while," said Nathan, resting the half-filled chloroform bottle near the sleeping model's face. "And one for the lady."

With the vaping liquid's fumes in full effect, Nathan rummaged through his bag, clutched two cheese curl spray canisters, and vigorously shook them like unwanted children. Using those snacks like a fermented graffiti artist, Nathan layered spray cheese on the soles of the couple's shoes. And then he ended with a squirt into his helmet's mouth hole.

"Cheese feet!" Nathan shouted, winging a canister directly into each of his conked-out victims' foreheads.

As Tessa loaded projectiles into her catapult, Andy analyzed this year's track through monitors on folding chairs; with such technology, all racers could view every inch of the track from their enclosed starting gates. Plus, racers got to stare at multiple screens while barely burning any calories, making the track feel more like home.

"Hey, Tessa!" Andy shouted through their shared tarp wall. "Check out Monitor 2. It looks like a new hazard."

ANDY GETS CONNED

"Is that a snake pit?" Tessa asked. "A snake pit with...drunk people throwing up in it?"

"That's what I see," said Andy. "It looks like the snakes are throwing up in there too. That's a lot of puke."

"Yeah. And look at the trap's name on the monitor. It's pretty brilliant."

"Barfboa Basin? These races get better every year," said Andy. "But I think we should treat that shortcut over the basin like women did to me in high school—a gut-churning last resort."

"Stop," said Tessa, laughing. "Let's race!"

"Attention again, ladies and gentlemen," shouted the announcer. "You have exactly 15 seconds to place your bets. And that's not very accurate anymore because, by the time I finish this sentence to hype you up, you only have about five seconds left!"

At his betting booth, the bookie began flipping a sign around with the text 'No More Bets for the Bots' on the back. Milliseconds before bets closed, Winslow plopped down a stack of cash with his cast-covered hand. Now with Robby on his lap still inhaling cheese spray, Winslow confidently connected eyes with the bookie.

"I'd like to put my life savings on the satellite, please!" Winslow huffed, as the bookie counted his bet.

"Your life savings is 158 bucks?" queried the bookie. "That's sad enough to make me ask if you're sure about this. So, here's the only decent question I've ever asked somebody: Are you sure about this?"

"Yes, I am, sir! That satellite's the biggest and fattest bot here. Therefore, it'll win. This is my moment. It's my redemption story! It's time for the biggest and fattest thing to finally prevail! And, to be honest, this is the only way I can pay my medical bills."

As synthesized trumpets squealed, three of the four bots shot underneath their anonymous starting gate tarps—DongBot69,000 nowhere to be seen. Nathan had failed to perform with his bot's phallic entrance, jamming the control stick forward yet gaining no ground. Now burning rubber, DongBot spun its wheels so much that it covered the chloroformed couple with a thin layer of dirt.

In R2CheeseDoodle's slipstream, Treb-Mew-Chet picked up speed while loading its first potassium projectile. But as they took their first corner around the oil spill hazard, Andy drove R2CheeseDoodle straight through. More surprisingly, he then slowed down and stopped like an otter drenched in the 'black gold' goop.

"What are you doing, Andy?" shouted Tessa, pulling ahead with Treb-Mew-Chet as Andy's bot sucked up oil.

"This might come in handy later. You'll see," Andy said, then looking into his camera on the tripod. "And you'll see too. Hey, Tessa. Keep first place warm for me."

As the neckbeard zoomed his bot around the corner, flames exploded from its rule-breaking, turbo boosters hidden under a solar panel. These boosters then set the track's oil on fire, and Andy jammed his stick forward in time for R2CheeseDoodle to escape the blazing puddle. With speeds only a crash-test dummy would understand, the satellite boosted ahead of Treb-Mew-Chet in seconds.

The satellite's lead growing, Andy made up for lost time as the three bots rammed through Ball Pit Canyon,

ANDY GETS CONNED

climbed Card Sleeve Hill, and ventured under bleachers nicknamed Bone Alley by convention teens. Emerging first from the alley with a G-string dangling on its catapult, Treb-Mew-Chet hurtled its garmented banana peel ahead. And it was right on target, landing in front of the neckbeard's high-speed bot. With no room to brake and no grasp of what fruit was, the neckbeard drove his bot into the biodegradable booby-trap. Then the satellite spun in circles, crashing straight into a hay bale.

"Nice shot," said Andy, blasting his bot past the satellite. "How many bananas do you have in there?"

"A whole *bunch*," she responded, giggling. "But if you really want a non-pun answer, I have 12 more!"

"Your sappy interaction disgusts me," yelled the neckbeard, activating his boosters again.

"This isn't fair!" shouted Tessa.

"Tessa, get closer to the tarp wall so we can have some privacy," Andy said, Tessa putting her ear upon it. "The neckbeard's clearly cheating, and he'll catch up in no time if we let him get away with this. How about we work together and take his satellite out?"

"I agree," said Tessa. "Maybe we could get so far ahead that he'd have to take the Barfboa Basin shortcut? And if he screws that up, we have a chance."

"That's not a bad idea since the bridge looks impossible to cross—impassably impossible. Only an idiot would try to take that."

Nathan, as if answering the call, finally figured out how to deactivate his stolen bot's brakes—pressing its unmissable 'Deactivate Brakes' button. Now under

Nathan's control, DongBot69,000 drove under its starting gate tarp and took a sharp left in the opposite direction. Then he penetrated the final stretch tunnel, backed out, and repeated that process in a moment of penile showmanship. Next, he drove to Barfboa Basin's shortcut, the risky bridge over a dip in the basement floor that held boa constrictors upon a tarp. Made with interlocked hay bales lubed with oil, this trap's unscalable walls contained an even more repulsive component—barf from everyone who drank too much at the nearby booze tent.

"These nerds won't know what hit them," Nathan murmured to himself. "Until DongBot hits them, of course. Ramming speed, now!"

His timing off yet again, Nathan triggered the bot's turbo boost down a bridge made of rickety two-by-fours that zigzagged over the basin. DongBot's wheels then screeched around each twist and turn, Nathan soon losing control on the track's only portion without rails. Passing many signs on the perilous shortcut that warned racers to reduce speeds, Nathan continued boosting until his bot's tires slipped off the edge and tumbled downward. Yes, in only a few seconds, Nathan had plunged DongBot's torpedo right into the rank pond of puke.

"Rigged! This game is rigged!" cried Nathan through his helmet's voice synthesizer.

"Hey, stop playing with my DongBot!" shouted Flex, sitting up with a head bump larger than his calf muscles. "I smell chloroform. Did you try to knock us out with chloroform? I'm in a frat, so my body's pretty much immune to anything I can huff."

Adrenaline coursing through Flex's body, he rocked to his feet. But Flex's strength stood no chance against the cheese product Nathan had applied to his shoes, his feet flying up and his head slamming to the ground. His attempts now foiled, Flex's unconscious body flopped onto his still sedated girlfriend—an act he was also quite familiar with as a frat guy.

"Time for the backup plan!" yelled Nathan, ripping off Flex's sweatpants and quickly slipping them over his Droid Blitzer leotard.

"Well that was easy," said Andy, watching DongBot sink into the puke. "And disgusting. Way more disgusting than it was easy."

"What's your plan for the neckbeard?" asked Tessa.

"Okay, you take the safe route around the basin. It's longer but trust me! This is going to make a great end for the vlog, and we're going to win!"

Though Tessa raced ahead in second place, the neckbeard's satellite continued scorching the ground like a high-speed flamethrower. As Tessa kept her word and shot past the risky shortcut over the basin, Andy didn't. Indeed, the inconsistent space dwarf now drove right onto Barfboa Basin's bridge.

"What are you doing?" asked Tessa, as Andy hit the brakes. "Just let the neckbeard win! Don't get greedy."

"Here comes the big reveal," Andy said to his camera with a wink. "Watch this."

Now parking on the bridge shortcut, Andy pressed R2CheeseDoodle's manual release button and evacuated all oil that it sucked up earlier. The two-by-fours now slippery, Andy reversed R2CheeseDoodle and escaped just as the satellite entered this ecological disaster shortcut.

"I'm racing with a bunch of amateurs," said the neckbeard. "See you at the finish line, trash!"

The satellite whizzed onto Barfboa Basin's two-by-fours and struck Andy's oil, spinning like a top along the bridge. Then the wipeout worsened as its fiery boosters ignited everything nearby—even its own slick tires. Now having no traction, the neckbeard's bot violently rolled and flipped like a 2-year-old taking a driver's test, flew off of the bridge, and splashed into its partially-digested grave.

"No!" screeched the neckbeard, dashing out of his starting gate. "Not my satellite!"

"Noo!" wept Winslow from the betting booth, smashing his casts against the floor as Robby watched. "Not my life savings! I have nothing!"

"Nooo!" shouted Nathan, zipping up Flex's hoodie over his Blitzer torso and dashing away. "They can't win!"

As R2CheeseDoodle trailed Treb-Mew-Chet in the final stretch, Tessa slowed her catapult. And the bots soon rolled side by side with no other contenders left. Both bots now racing at the same speed, the announcer grew even louder than before, whipped out a thesaurus, and shouted every synonym for 'dead heat' that he could find.

"You deserve to win," said Tessa, through the tarp.

"I'm pretty sure you earned it," said Andy. "But we could piss everyone off with a tie."

"Now *that's* the kind of trolling I can respect."

Andy flopped to the ground and crawled under their shared tarp wall, not requiring an oxygen mask after

ANDY GETS CONNED

aerobic activity for once. Now in Tessa's starting gate, Andy popped to his feet while still steering.

"Fancy seeing you here," joked Andy.

"I wasn't expecting company," said Tessa. "You're lucky I'm wearing pants!"

The convention basement swelled with cheers as Andy and Tessa drove closer to their co-victory, now 10 feet away from the finish line. Ten feet became seven, then four, and then one, until millimeters away from the race's end. But that's when two more unforeseen feet suddenly appeared—Nathan Hader's feet—right upon the two bots after jumping from the sidelines. Yes, a triple-cloaked Nathan now stomped R2CheeseDoodle and Miss Treb-Mew-Chet to pieces...their gears flying through the air in one traumatic machine massacre.

CHAPTER 20

Andy and Tessa fell to their knees while Droid Blitzer's robot carnage continued on the monitors. And, once on the ground, both let out a string of curse words that managed to make Tourette syndrome look tame. Outside of the gates, Nathan continued his destructive hopping in his helmet. But he was now concealed with an extra layer of protection—Tyrannosaurus Flex's zippered hoodie and sweatpants. After wrecking both bots with his orthopedic blitz, Nathan bowed at the hissing crowd and sprinted back to his starting gate. He then rolled under the tarp, unzipped his hoodie, and yanked off his sweatpants, now back in a Droid Blitzer cape and leotard.

As angered fans stampeded to the gate, Nathan zipped the hoodie back onto Flex and placed his sweatpants around the muscle man's cheesy feet. Seeing the criminal's hiding spot on their monitors, Andy and Tessa dove under the neckbeard's tarp wall, army crawled across the floor, and pushed under the last shared barrier; it was time to butcher this brutal Blitzer bastard! Their rage quickly switched to confusion, however, spotting two Droid Blitzers in the starting gate. Yes, a disguised Nathan Blitzer now rubbed his fist above an unconscious Blitzer with his pants down.

"Way to be late to the crime scene, guys," said Nathan through his helmet's voice synthesizer. "I had to handle the sleazeball myself. I think he was going to blame me for breaking your bots or something. Can you believe that?"

"Luke! How did you get down here?" asked Andy.

"I had to drain the old donkey, so I was in the bathroom. Then I heard this model crying for help," said Nathan. "It looks like the buff guy chloroformed her."

"That's depraved! That's disturbing!" said Andy. "Who the hell calls going to the bathroom 'draining the donkey?' Oh, and the chloroform's not cool either. Thanks for stopping him. What a scumbag."

"I hope he rots in jail. You're one of the reasons the world can't have nice things. You hear me, pervert?" Tessa yelled, kicking Tyrannosaurus Flex in the abdomen and looking down. "Well I guess we don't need to torture him too much. With what he's packing in those tighty-whities, life already punished him enough."

"Wow, that's medically possible?" asked Andy, shaking Nathan's hand. "Anyway, great job, Luke."

"Yeah, thanks for taking care of this," Tessa said, hugging Nathan.

"My pleasure," said Nathan. "It's too bad he destroyed your bots though. I guess we'll have to leave now and quit the Convention Crawl and head our separate ways. You know, never see each other again."

ANDY GETS CONNED

"No way," Andy said. "These bots aren't completely busted. I can have R2CheeseDoodle running again in a few days. And it'll be fun if Commander Courtney's repairing Treb-Mew-Chet by my side."

"I'll bring the coffee!" said Tessa, shaking Andy's hand. "We'll need lots of coffee; whole-beans-directly-in-the-mouth marathon coffee, to be specific."

"You mean you two aren't giving up?" asked Nathan. "I'd probably go back to the way things were if this happened to me. It's safer."

"I bet we'll be able to make our bots even better together," said Andy. "I'm not giving up."

"Me neither. Now, let's finish this race," said Tessa, she and Andy pulling Nathan's Blitzer hands forward.

"The Convention Crawl lives on!" Andy cheered.

Andy and Tessa then dashed from the starting gate, Nathan's robot gloves popping off like a tug of war at a leper colony. His scheme ending as a disappointing dud, Nathan fell to his knees. And then he screamed long enough to need several breaks to breathe. As the roaring crowd drowned out Nathan, the neckbeard also displayed desperation by diving into Barfboa Basin and swimming at the satellite bot. After submerging and then surfacing with the satellite at his chest, the neckbeard gazed at large screens displaying Andy and Tessa. When they hoisted their dented bots above their heads and walked across the finish line, the neckbeard matched their movements.

"You cheaters!" cried the neckbeard, pumping his satellite up as vomit and hotdog pieces gushed from its boosters. "That should be my victory, not yours!"

As puke poured onto his face like a wretched waterfall of chicken nugget chunks and jalapeño popper paste, the neckbeard splashed back into the alcoholic sludge. The basin's boa constrictors, now with lowered inhibitions from all the booze, congregated on 'Neckbeard Island' in one undulating snake orgy. This reptilian gangbang then sent him deeper, now fully submerged in the regurgitated quagmire. And, seconds later, only his top hat surfaced.

"What a race!" screamed the announcer, bounding from the sidelines with his wireless microphone. "Finishing in perhaps the slowest time ever recorded on this track is Tessa's Treb-Mew-Chet and Andy's R2CheeseDoodle. And since so many geeks bet on the damned DongBot, we made more than enough to fund next year's races and put the security guards' kids through private college. Hell, maybe even grad school! So we'd like to present you both with your $1,000 gift cards plus a little extra. From the bottom of our gambling hearts, here's a bonus 2,000 bucks for each of you. We want you to rebuild those babies and bring them back next year!"

Andy and Tessa then seized their cash prizes and hugged the announcer, finally stopping him from talking. Exiting the hug but not their skepticism, the two counted their cash while crowds surged around them.

"I'm your biggest fan!" shouted Winslow, wheeling up with Robby on his shoulders. "Sign my casts please. All of them. I'm probably going to wear these the rest of my life, so make them pretty."

"You bet," said Andy, signing and then handing over half of his cash prize. "Here, buddy. Take a grand for your medical bills too. I know it won't do much, but maybe it'll ease some pain."

"Aw," sighed Tessa.

"Hot damn! That's way more than my life savings! Thank you!" squealed Winslow. "Come on, Robby. Let's go get some medicine for my broken body. And then we'll get you some social workers who can finally find you a new home, okay?"

After signing autographs for a few hours and recording vlogs at the same time, Andy and Tessa escaped for an even more exciting location—Andy's hotel room. Yes, the duo scrambled to Andy's door and stripped off their stinky costumes, now prepared for some incoming amusement. Leo and Ben then barged in with Winslow too, everyone now peeling off their filthy apparel together. And Nathan sulked in behind them, looking like Droid Blitzer needed a new battery.

"What a remarkable nerd group!" shouted Winslow. "What an amazing day! We had fun! We got cash! And we even helped little Robby get away from his abusive, alcoholic father! This is the kind of day that makes up for an awful life! Thanks for inviting me, guys!"

"Us too!" said Tessa. "We had a way better time than we would have by ourselves. Didn't we, Luke?"

"Yes, such...joy," Nathan said.

"You can break character now," said Tessa, grabbing Nathan's helmet. "Take that thing off."

Tessa disconnected the Droid Blitzer helmet, showing a flash of Nathan's flesh and gorgeous, shaggy hair. After slapping her hand away and saving his covert operation yet again, Nathan secured the helmet back on with an entire roll of duct tape.

"The costume cost 600 bucks," said Nathan. "I'm wearing this thing until I die."

"I like this guy a lot," Andy said, ripping off his dwarven prosthetics. "You know what? I think you and Luke should finish the Convention Crawl with us. And you too, Winslow!"

"Without a doubt," Leo said. "We're slamming three different fandom conventions on three different days. The last one's tomorrow."

"Yup, and only I know what it is," Ben said, peeling off his zombie face paint. "It's a complete curveball too!"

"I don't need any more information—count me in!" Tessa said, jumping on Andy's bed.

"I get to spend even more time with you?" gasped Winslow, snapping his arm casts in half while grabbing his chest. "That just made me have a slight heart attack. I'm not kidding about the heart attack, but I'm still coming!"

"It's my turn to be dramatic now," Ben said, switching off the lamp. "We rise at noon!"

"Ben, it's 8 o'clock and still light outside," said Andy, opening the curtains to an orange sun.

"Tessa and Luke have their own room too," said Leo.

"And if we all don't shower soon, our smells might mix together and make a bioweapon," said Tessa.

"Yeah, there are lots of problems with your proposal, Ben," said Andy, switching the lamp back on.

"Whatever, freaks, but I'm going to bed now," said Ben, slipping into his sleeping bag on the floor. "Leo,

ANDY GETS CONNED

could we set your phone alarm for noon if you aren't too busy being irresponsible?"

"No problemo," said Leo, tossing his phone to Ben from the bathroom. "Time to drench my stench."

"Thanks," huffed Ben, covering his head with the sleeping bag and zipping up. "You all better get some sleep. You'll need it tomorrow."

Ben rolled over in a fuss as Tessa and Winslow helped Andy unload *Rejects & Reptiles* figures from his luggage. While Leo used his hemp-based soaps and Nathan raided the mini fridge, Andy and his new pals searched through tubs of organized plastic pieces.

"Keep it down, dammit!" Ben said, plunging earplugs into his canals. "And nobody better draw DongBots all over my face when I'm sleeping because I said that."

"It's time for the after-party!" shouted Andy. "Ever play *Rejects & Reptiles*, Winslow? How about you, Luke? Here, let's make you both a character sheet!"

"I want to be a mythical hippopotamus in a wheelchair!" gushed Winslow. "It's a second chance for the biggest, fattest thing to prevail!"

As the gang played on and drew as many penises on Ben's face as possible, *Rejects & Reptiles* went way smoother without a neck-gnawing zombie on the team. Nathan tapped out about 10 minutes in after emptying the fridge, so he didn't get in the way either. Then Winslow was next to exit the game, nodding off an hour later as his cocktail of antibiotics and painkillers kicked in. Despite losing three members quicker than a sick family on the Oregon trail, Andy's new trio moved *Rejects & Reptiles* to the balcony. There, they could get some fresh air and stay alert. As an added bonus, they now had opera box seats to the hillbilly brawls in the hotel pool below. Temporarily pausing their game, Andy recorded from the balcony as a group of yokels invaded some hillbillies' aquatic turf. And, in an instant, both groups started marking their pool territory with lots of their own pee.

After shooting an hour's worth of Podunk pool fights while narrating like a nature documentary, Andy and Tessa blasted through Leo's *Rejects & Reptiles* campaign. Yes, without ZomBen around, they had patched up their peace treaties with the Komodo dragons in a few hours. Now finished with their imaginary diplomacy and real-life video making, Tessa and Leo passed out as Andy pointed the camera at his face.

"Hello, everyone. We're officially in Day 3 of our Convention Crawl, and I never want it to end. I've spent my entire life with a small group of friends, but there are so many other cool people I've missed out there like Winslow, Tessa, and Luke. I'm making some great content with my five samosas. But imagine what could be done if more of us joined forces. What if we created our own convention just for us? It'd be a place for all JumboAndy fans to come together and be creative with the Samosas Studios crew. I know it'd be tiny at first, but it'd be incredible to meet you all and make some videos as a massive troupe. You could be one of our writers or actors or help out on set. Or if you want to come down here and make your own content, we'll be in yours too! It would kinda be like a cult, but we'd make funny stuff instead of killing ourselves—a full-blown comedy collective! What do you think? I'm going to get back to planning this now because there's a lot to do. But let me know in the comment section and share some thoughts. Seriously, pause me and get those fingers moving!"

After placing this shot in his vlog, Andy saved the files to his memory card and continued plotting on Leo's laptop until sunrise. His plans extensive, Andy had crafted a con of comical proportions; there'd be vlogging video testimonial booths scattered around the main hall and multiple film sets for different genres. There was also a main stage for improvisational comedy, writer's rooms, and even video editing stations. His brain now productively fried, Andy conked out upon one of his favorite pillows of all time—Tessa's shoulder.

While Andy, Tessa, and Leo snored on the balcony, the aquatic hicks finally fought off their land yokel challengers. And the hotel was peaceful once more, as the hicks rested upon a flotilla of Styrofoam coolers and camouflage pool noodles. Yet, as all was quiet in Southeastern Ohio, another person was wide awake chuckling at Andy—not at him sleeping, but at his online content. From a kauri tree forest in New Zealand, an elderly woman watched the 'End of Jumbo Andy'. And, even weirder, the video now had over 20,000 views. The Kiwi woman then left a message in the comment section, typing 'Good on ya, mate! Where there is life, there is hope...and most likely porn. Stay funny!'

Hours later in Ohio, Andy's samosas still slept when Leo's phone alarm sirens blared at 11:50 a.m. The alarm only lasted seconds, however, until stopped by Ben. Yes, the zombie had arisen 30 minutes early, eager to keep his third Convention Crawl day on track before waking his reckless friends. In no rush, Ben had showered, re-applied his zombie makeup, and explored the hotel's supply of complimentary muffins and non-complimentary coffee pots with Winslow. As Winslow went back for more food and tripped face-first into the waffle maker, Ben headed for his snoozing friends. Ben then tiptoed to the balcony with his feast and hunched over the trio, all vulnerable to his undead ambush.

"Zombies! It's a zombie attack!" warned Ben. "They're everywhere! One's coming right for you too!"

Andy, Tessa, and Leo then jolted awake, their brains groggy enough to fall for Ben's trick. And as Leo guarded himself with the Reject Master board, Andy jabbed a tiki torch at the muffin-munching zombie.

"I knew this day would come!" Andy hollered.

"Pepper spray powers activate!" grunted Tessa, readying her can and aiming over Andy's shoulder.

"Take a chill pill, people!" said Leo. "It's just Ben."

Andy and Tessa stopped their defenses, Ben much closer to losing his life than he'd ever realize. Now documented by Andy's camera, Ben presented the sleepyheads with a free breakfast and prepared punchline.

"ZomBen bring bran muffins. Braaan! Braaan!" he said, holding the tray of muffins and coffee pots as shotguns cocked below.

"Y'all better watch out up there!" warned a hillbilly from the pool. "That's a zombie. And if y'all is dumb

ANDY GETS CONNED

enough to take food from that there zombie, y'all deserve to die a damn dumb death."

"Thanks for the help, but we're fine!" Andy panicked, recording. "Ben's our friend—our *alive* human friend."

"Y'all sure 'bout that? We got lots o' ammo in these coolers. We make a mighty fine Molotov cocktail too."

"We're okay, really!" said Tessa. "But watch out! I think I see some minorities over there trying to take your guns, jobs, and the few chromosomes you have left."

"Chromosomes? Thems sound fancy," said the hillbilly, rowing his cooler. "Paddle hard, boys! We don't want no peckerheads takin' nothin' from us!"

"Let's scat before they come back," said Leo, pouring coffee. "We don't want to miss the next con."

"Take your time, everyone," said Ben. "Eat up and spray your costumes with air freshener; the next convention's downstairs. That's right, I picked a con that's only two minutes away, so there's no need to hurry. Plus, I can see that the hicks just got trapped in the revolving door in the lobby. And we don't want to be down there when they start shooting their way out."

After filling their bellies and showering again, the crew reequipped their gear—this time without any genre-specific accessories, per Ben's guidance. While Tessa retrieved Nathan from his hotel room, Ben and Andy spent the entire time trying to shove R2CheeseDoodle back into Leo's chest with the space helmets. But no angle seemed to work, so the two started jumping on Leo's chest to force its latch shut. And assisting at Leo's sides, Tessa and Nathan armed themselves with one last madcap solution.

"Okay, lube up R2CheeseDoodle with the spray cheese now!" shouted Andy, as Tessa and Nathan doused both sides of the bot. "If we don't fit this in there, we'll have to put it in the van and lose precious time that we could have been looking for Winslow."

"This is stupid," said Nathan, tossing the cheese into his garbage bag. "How about I take all this back to the van myself? I need to pick up some more protein bars from Tessa's car, so I'll be down there anyway. I could use some air after sleeping in my helmet too."

"Great idea!" exclaimed Andy, hopping off Leo. "We can put some of this junk in your garbage bag."

"Load it up," said Nathan.

"I bet the bag isn't big enough," said Leo, his chest contents pouring out like a dump truck and quickly filling it to the brim. "Thought so. You can transport the rest of our possessions with my robot box head."

"So, you're sticking with the space helmet again then, huh?" asked Andy, pushing Leo's cardboard cranium under the stream of stuff.

"Yeah, that'll be my primary means of protecting LSD-401K's central processing unit," said Leo. "I didn't overheat in that yesterday at all."

"Then I guess you could say that your *hotboxing* days are done?" joked Tessa.

"I didn't *trip* in the helmet either, so your quip works on multiple levels," said Leo, handing his keys to Nathan.

"Please be careful with R2CheeseDoodle, Luke," said Andy, placing his bot into the box. "After you load all that in the van, we'll meet you downstairs."

"Don't you worry," said Nathan, lugging away his bag and box. "I'll take good care of him."

"Now to reassemble our party," said Andy. "We really need to find Winslow."

"I'll listen for weeping," said Ben.

"And I'll keep my kitty eyes open for any blood trails," said Tessa.

"And I'll smell the hell out of this place for his fermented scent," added Leo.

"Great!" Andy said. "But we have to take the stairs."

"Why? That's harder," said Ben.

"It'll be good exercise. Plus, we won't die if there's an elevator fire. Those hicks might try to burn their way out of that revolving door, you know. They did say they had Molotov cocktails."

After unsuccessful scans of every floor, the group made it to the lobby and verified Andy's arson hunch. Yes, smoke poured from the shattered, revolving door that the hicks had clearly defeated. As Andy turned to the breakfast area, he finally spotted Winslow—still stuck in the functioning waffle maker. The samosas then applied a gallon of ointment to Winslow's face and a mummy's worth of bandages from Andy's luggage. And when Nathan returned a few minutes later, the sextet headed off for ZomBen's big convention reveal.

Promenading in front, Ben led the group while dwarven Andy, space kitten Tessa, and robot Leo yawned after their long night. Winslow, now back with his friends and licking batter off of his casts, wept with joy as Andy pushed him. And behind them all, Droid Blitzer Nathan shoved protein bars through his helmet mouth as Ben administered one more accessory to each member.

"Here you are," Ben said, handing out red ties to the group. "I got an eight pack of these, so there's extra."

"What geek convention needs a tie?" asked Andy, as everyone slipped the crimson cloth around their necks.

"We have to wear these to get in for some reason," Ben said. "It's a ritual that gives these pretentious nerds power. I did the research; trust me."

And trust Ben they did, as the gang approached a small conference area in a separate wing of the hotel—no dragons, no lasers, and no entertainment to be seen. Instead, small crowds of proper people in black suits and red ties filled the hallway. Their heads then whipped at the strange posse entering their professional retreat, witnessing a wheelchair-bound Winslow with a dwarf, zombie, robot, cat, and android all in cheap ties.

"So, what is this place?" Andy asked, looking into the sea of judgmental eyes.

"Prepare yourselves, bitches," hyped Ben. "It's the one and only Southeastern Ohio Future Leaders Convention! That's right, a futuristic business con!"

Then, in another moment of unplanned unison, Andy and his samosas smacked their foreheads at Ben's flawed convention selection. When Winslow's cast-covered wrist struck his head, he knocked himself out yet again. But when Leo's robot clamp hit his space helmet, it added a bongo-like tone and attracted even more attention.

"You're welcome, everybody," bragged Ben.

"So why are we here exactly?" asked Tessa.

ANDY GETS CONNED

"I second that question," said Leo.

"You wouldn't be confused if you slept like I told you to," Ben said, picking up a pamphlet. "It's a Future Leaders Convention. It's about the future! And the leaders of that future! Come on, smile! It's a convention about time travel and world domination! Get it?"

"Ben!" grunted Leo, ripping the pamphlet from his hand and folding it open. "This convention's for big business reps from the oil industry, banking, and politics."

"Yeah, the future!" insisted Ben.

"No, it's a recruitment tool for all things corrupt and evil. It's about capitalism, greed, and The Man's desire for more money and power—you know, not geeky stuff."

"I'm an idiot," Ben said, hanging his head in shame.

"Money and power?" asked Nathan, yanking the pamphlet from Leo and reading it.

"Now hold on," said Andy, stopping Winslow's nosebleed with his tie. "We only need a few more shots to finish this Convention Crawl video. I'm sure we can riff on something here and make that fun. You might be able to pick up some business tips too, Leo."

"I need to go drain the old bathroom donkey again," Nathan said. "I'll be right back."

Nathan sprinted away, navigating with the pamphlet map and evading CEOs like they do taxes. As Nathan approached Room 4A in the distance, businesspeople widened their stares at Andy's gang.

"Let's bounce," said Leo.

"No, Andy's right," said Tessa. "We can make this fun somehow. What's your idea?"

"We have to fix this right now," Andy said. "This place needs a jolt of geek energy, and I think I know how to lighten the mood for our last shot. We can do this, everybody! And I'll fill you all in as soon as we make sure Winslow's not dead again. He just hit himself pretty damned hard with that cast."

CHAPTER 21

After the gang performed CPR on Winslow and confused the businesspeople even more, Andy huddled with his samosas. Sounds of a vibrating phone then interrupted, and everyone patted their pockets to see if it was theirs. Finally finding the culprit in his dwarven satchel, Andy answered with a smile.

"Hi, Chris!" said Andy, activating speakerphone. "Do you have good news for me?"

"Sure do. We got your VoyeursSlashVanity account all reset for you," said Chris. "Put in your last known password and you should be able to upload videos again."

"Thanks so much. I'll get right on that. Tell Mom I'll have about a dozen videos up there tonight."

"As long as you promise me somethin' first."

"Anything."

"If you're plannin' on shootin' any more paragliders, get the proper permits first."

"Absolutely," laughed Andy. "As soon as you stop using the substances you confiscate."

"No deal," chuckled Chris. "Your Mom and I look forward to seein' what you came up with. Over and out."

"Thanks again!" said Andy, hanging up. "Okay, gang, the JumboAndy page is ready for new content. Perfect timing for what we're about to do too. So, here's how we'll make this place a little less stuffy. Bring it in!"

Now on the loose by himself, Nathan inspected Room 4A's sign—'How to Be an Evil Corporate Bastard: The Seminar.' Nathan then tossed the pamphlet away and peeped under the door, watching a presenter with a Kaiser mustache pace in front of a dozing audience.

"Let's get started, non-plebeians, with our training session in How to Be an Evil Corporate Bastard," the presenter said, articulating each syllable. "Upon completion of today's pre-certification, you may enroll in my 10-hour masterclass where you'll get the real certification. The masterclass costs far more than today's seminar, of course. And the price of the test to complete your certification is even more expensive. Yes, I should have told you this before you paid for the seminar, but you are all learning an evil lesson right now, aren't you?"

Nathan then kicked through the double doors and head-butted the droning presenter with his Droid Blitzer helmet. And when the presenter collapsed to the floor, all attendants placed their scotch glasses down for the first time that morning.

"Oh, the helmet guy's good," said a wrinkly businessman, nudging the businesswoman beside him.

"Silence!" Nathan screamed. "Here's how you can be an evil bastard in just two minutes. We're going to wipe

ANDY GETS CONNED

out one nerd today and then every other nerd on the planet later. Evil bastard school begins right now!"

Down the hallway, a wall of Tessa, Leo, Ben, and Winslow formed around Andy typing on a laptop. Finishing, Andy emailed this document to the group and placed his camera upon Winslow's snapped casts. The samosas then lined up as Winslow recorded, now ready for their final shot of the Convention Crawl video—an elaborate, parody song-and-dance number.

"Attention, businesspeople!" shouted Andy. "We're about to sing a little ditty for you all. It requires no monetary transactions now and has no hidden fees later. Yes, it's completely free! Samosas Studios song-and-dance number, take one!"

Andy, Tessa, Leo, and Ben proceeded to kick while locking arms, Ben doing so in the opposite direction from everyone else. While clomping loud enough to annoy janitors in the basement still cleaning up Barfboa Basin, the gang took a deep breath. And then they belted out their quickly-penned "Pop Goes the Weasel" parody:

> *We came to a lame business con,*
> *It's more painful than needles.*
> *We're lost geeks and we're not seeking yawns,*
> *Please! Be more gleeful!*

> *A dwarf, bot, corpse, and cat came today,*
> *To pitch to you rich people:*
> *Since you rinse with gold bidets,*
> *Please! Be more gleeful!*

We bet if the market would crash,
You'd flee the upheaval.
Amidst this, you'd sell your kids for cash,
Please! Be more gleeful!

Your islands, yachts, and augmented breasts,
Should make you say, "We're regal!"
Yet you still get so depressed,
Please! Be more gleeful!

As Andy and his samosas ended their dance with one final kick, a small segment of the inebriated audience politely golf-clapped. The glistening performers, now pumping out more hot air than businesspeople do at board meetings, took a bow.

"That's all the footage we need," Andy exhaled, dashing to Winslow and double checking the footage. "These people are rough, but we look funny—we nailed it on the first take. Nice touch kicking the wrong way, Ben! This is great. Let's get out of here!"

Looking up, Andy recorded his friends' jaws dropping as a horde of businesspeople rushed from Room 4A's doors behind him. And as Andy stared, he snapped his fingers near his friends' faces.

"Okay, you can stop now," said Andy, unaware of the impending doom to his rear. "I'm not falling for any more pranks after Ben's zombie wakeup call this morning."

"No, man. This is not a joke," said Leo.

"Okay, then I have a follow-up question," Andy said. "Did Winslow die behind me in some gruesome way?"

ANDY GETS CONNED

The group then shook their heads, leading Andy to the next logical question.

"Then are *we* about to die in some gruesome way?" Andy revised, his friends then confirming with a nod.

"Hey, you!" seethed the wrinkly businessman from the horde. "You're that fat guy we saw on the Internet!"

"I'm guessing he isn't a fan," Andy said, handing the camera back to Winslow. "Hey, buddy. I'll do my best to protect you. Just record whatever happens in case it's funny or possible evidence, okay?"

"You got it," Winslow said.

"Be quiet!" continued the wrinkly businessman. "Your videos are terrible. They're a public nuisance!"

"It's time that you hear the truth," said a businesswoman with football equipment-sized shoulder pads under her blouse. "We personally wanted to share our grievances and condemn your repulsive presence before it spreads."

"And we reckon it's a swell time to do just that," said a plump businessman in a cowboy hat, revving his mobility scooter. "So don't be takin' this the wrong way, but—"

"Your videos have no redeeming qualities!" the group yelled. "They are trash. They are unnecessary."

"And we heard you were cranking out another video for some boring Convention Crawl," the wrinkly man said. "But we have a recommendation for that—"

"Don't!" advised the crowd.

"You have no charisma," said the businesswoman. "No talent either! And you certainly have no right wasting everyone's time with your—"

"Nauseatingly awful and poorly made videos," they continued, as Nathan crawled behind them and hid around the corner.

"So, in review," stated the wrinkly man.

"You suck!" concluded the crowd.

"Seriously, boy, your videos make as much sense as tits on a bull," pestered the mobility scooter man. "If you had an original idea, it'd die of loneliness. I'd rather butter my balls and serve 'em up as biscuits at my pappy's weddin' to another man than watch your crap. And to drive this point home, we present you with this!"

As the crowd parted, one man emerged from the back with a recognizable object—Andy's R2CheeseDoodle robot. He then chucked it to the shoulder-padded businesswoman like a lateral pass. And with a predatory sneer, she gently placed the bot down, patted it with a tender tap, and stood back up. As if taking place in slow motion, the entire crowd then raised their alligator leather shoes and stomped the hell out of Andy's beloved bot. The demolition ramped up as their hostile heels pulverized Andy's pet and the plump man rammed the robot with his mobility scooter. Yes, Andy's gobsmacked face now matched his friends' expressions. Then Nathan sidled against the wall behind them in his Blitzer disguise, far more winded than the dorks after their performance.

Andy's lip trembled as if milliseconds away from hypothermia, now captured by Winslow's recording camera. Like a one-two punch, Andy then saw confirmation of what he suspected yesterday—Luke with his arm around Tessa's waist. After spotting the evidence

ANDY GETS CONNED

that Luke was definitely dating Tessa, Andy bolted to Winslow, grabbed his camera, and headed for the exit. Passing by the hotel's continental breakfast in a moment of weakness, Andy nabbed an Italian businessman's heaping plate of sausages, pancakes, powdered eggs, and lots more sausages.

"Very funny, kid!" yelled the Italian. "I get the joke too! You're doin' to me what I do to the destitute every day. If I weren't so swept up with how poetic your symbolic action is right now, I'd choke ya!"

"What a bunch of evil bastards!" yelled Tessa, then making eye contact with the two businesswomen. "And bitches. You're both bitches too."

"Hurray!" the group of businesspeople cheered with triumphant, upward fists.

"How'd they get R2CheeseDoodle?" asked Ben.

"They stole it from me earlier," said Nathan. "I've been mugged. I'm the victim here, really, not Andy."

"Get bent," shouted Leo.

"I don't think we can be bib brothers anymore," pouted Winslow, as Ben and Leo pushed him away.

"Come on, let's go," said Tessa, trailing them.

Not following the gang, Nathan now humped the air as his costume espionage finally paid off; indeed, he had turned Andy's meteoric rise into a doomsday descent like a flock of geese to a jet engine. Nathan's thrusts then morphed into a fake stretch, however, when Tessa popped back beside him and grabbed his arm.

"Move those legs, Luke. We're running now," Tessa said, dragging Nathan away.

"Come back!" the businesswoman shouted.

"We have much to learn," said the wrinkly man.

"We'll be bluer than a suffocatin' baby in a bowl of chili without you," moped the mobility scooter man.

Half a block down the street, Andy rocked on a park bench with both hands cupped over his face. And his camera now rested to his right with his foodless breakfast plate to his left. By murmuring as a dwarf in public, Andy managed to collect another audience this time—citizens refilling his breakfast plate with heaps of cash. Amused kids and their concerned parents now watched a dwarf's downfall, events getting even weirder when a zombie and robot arrived with their handicapped cargo.

"Show's over, folks," Ben said, obstructing Andy. "Get away from here, or I'll eat all your brains."

"Let the man cry in public, you freaks!" shouted Winslow. "Leave our friend alone!"

"Andy, it's all right, man," said Leo. "That mob's not on our wavelength. It can't judge your art without a heart. Don't fret about it—forget about it."

"No, they're right," Andy said. "Those businesspeople gave me the evaluation I've always needed. Drastic, yes. Debilitating, double yes. But wrong? I don't think so. It's time to do something I should have a long time ago."

"And what's that?" asked Leo.

"You might want to close your eyes," said Andy, grabbing his camera and climbing onto the bench. "This could get gross."

"You can't kill yourself from there," said Ben. "You're a foot off the ground. Stop it."

ANDY GETS CONNED

"No, don't do it, Andy!" shouted Winslow. "Life occasionally gets better!"

"This ends now!" Andy declared.

Andy then raised his camera in the sky, accidentally bumping his beard and sending breakfast crumbs to the sidewalk. And flocks of Ohioan pigeons surrounded him within seconds. Yes, the birds had to act fast before their new insect enemy showed up, Bumble Ridge's ravenous bees now impacting adjacent states. After shouting like a kung fu master who failed to crack a brick with his forehead, Andy chucked the camera downward. His magic wizard box then slammed into the sidewalk, shattering into streams of plastic and glass fragments.

"I won't be making any more appearances on the Internet," Andy said, hopping down on his camera near the unflappable pigeons. "I defied my Samosa Clause and look what happened! It's time to make the clause a lot stricter! No more videos. No more *Rejects & Reptiles!* And no more comic shop distractions either, including my samosas. I need to grow up with one last version of myself; this is the age of Andy 4.0."

Andy ripped off his dwarven prosthetics and ditched them on top of the cracked camera. Spotting a few pieces of sausage in Andy's costume, the pigeons then consumed all matter upon the sidewalk—including the synthetic beard and poisonous camera parts.

"Chill out," said Leo. "We are one. We are Samosas Studios. You can't bail on us like that."

"Thank you all for trying to help me," said Andy. "But I'm quitting this dorky game of life. Delete my save file, wipe my hard drive, and crumple up my character sheet. I'm done."

Tessa then hustled down the sidewalk past a series of choking pigeons, Nathan following in his Blitzer helmet. With Andy now distracted, Leo bent over and picked up an important item near his feet—the camera's memory card that survived like the black box of an airplane.

"Andy, are you okay?" Tessa asked, out of breath. "I would not be okay after what just happened."

"I'm sorry I ruined the Convention Crawl," huffed Andy. "I'm sorry you all had to see this too. I'm a downer. And I humiliated everybody. So here comes my true metamorphosis from man-child to adult."

Nathan, now with an opportune moment for his exposé, made a move that'd been building for days. Yes, after a twist, he finally slid off his long-worn Droid Blitzer helmet. And his white teeth sparkled like polished elephant ivory. Shaking off bedbugs still in his hair after obviously not showering, Nathan went in for the kill.

"Don't talk like that," Nathan said, his bare mouth widening like a devious sock puppet. "We are *so* worried about you."

"Nathan? Nathan's Luke? Nathan is your friend!" Andy scowled, charging up to Tessa. "He was with us the whole damned time?"

"Excuse me?" asked Tessa.

"Holy shit! This was a trap!" shouted Andy. "You were working together, weren't you? You two deserve an award. No, two awards: one for best acting and the other for Backstabbers of the Year!"

"Andy, it's happening again. I think this is another misunderstanding between us," Tessa said. "I have a couple of questions—"

"Well I'm not taking any questions!" Andy wailed. "So, the kiss on the cheek at *Space Fightin'* Con, the rekindling of our romance—it was just a bunch of lies to trick me and get revenge!"

"Andy, talk to me please. I'm not following."

"Game over, Tessa. I expected this from an asshat like Nathan, but not you! We're done forever!" yelled Andy, then sprinting away from his friends, the hotel, and a few bloated pigeons no longer able to fly.

"Traitors!" Leo scoffed, pushing Winslow away.

"And to think that I called you my bib brother!" yelled Winslow.

"You two watch your backs. And your necks!" shouted zombie Ben, then bolting away.

Tessa collapsed onto the park bench, crying into her hands just as Andy had done seconds ago. Surprisingly, Nathan then sat down and put his arm around her, offering his cape as a tissue.

"Forget about him," Nathan said, summoning all the platitudes he could think of. "You're better off without that jerk. You deserve more. It's his loss, not yours. There are lots of other fish in the sea. You go girl?"

"Thank you, Luke," Tessa said, smiling through her sobs. "I just don't understand. It was going so well. What did I do? And why does he think your name's Nathan?"

"You didn't do anything at all. Andy's crazy. He's mental, and you can't trust crazy-mental. Even if I was wrong and he's not a complete womanizer, I still have to step in now. Isn't he making your life worse? Isn't he toying with your emotions?"

"Well, yeah. He is, but I still feel like I should figure out what's going on here. I hate to ask, but your name's not really Nathan, is it?"

"Are you going to believe a nutcase over me, your best friend Luke? Don't be silly. Do yourself a favor and cut this unbalanced tub of turds from your life. We've made so much progress together—don't go backward with him. Even if Andy's stable 80 percent of the time, he's going to keep going off the rails the other 60 percent. You're lucky you met me. And I'm lucky I met you."

"Thank you for being here," said Tessa. "I'm tired. Will you walk me to the hotel? We'll review how percentages work on the way back."

Tessa and Nathan then strolled past a line of pigeons, all dazed from a lethal blend of metal, plastic, and dehydrated eggs from the hotel.

"Hey, will you promise me something?" Tessa asked, taking Nathan's hand and placing it around her waist. "Please don't play with my heart like Andy, okay?"

"You got it," Nathan smiled.

"And do you think we should call pest control to put these pigeons out of their misery?"

"I think the Bumble Ridge bees will take care of them when they get here," Nathan said. "It's the sickle of life, you know?"

"*Circle*, Luke," Tessa laughed. "You really do know how to make me smile."

CHAPTER 22

One week after the Convention Crawl, Andy slept so much that it could have been called hibernation. Yes, he steered clear of all junk food, geeky games, and his samosas for seven straight days. Though not emotionally healthy, his body also saw great changes; Andy's new rut helped him lose four pounds, sustaining himself with only black coffee and Mom's extreme fiber cereal.

Not even halfway through his vacation from Bumble Ridge High, Andy spent most days slumped on the couch watching history documentaries—ones he already knew well enough to recite word for word. Tonight, however, Andy let Mom and Chris cook a romantic meal in his kitchen; Mom's garage apartment hotplates and card tables could only go so far. As the love birds dined and a commercial break broke Andy's trance, he whipped his unshaven face at a bag of cheese curls. And then he spoke to it like a castaway in need of companionship.

"Isn't it nice that we can spend time together without me tearing you apart?" asked Andy, smiling. "We're good friends, aren't we? Of course, you do have an expiration date, and there are starving people in this world. So let's get wild. How about we go for it tonight, baby?"

Andy zipped to the kitchen, catching Mom doing things with her tongue to Chris's mouth that no son should ever see. He then reentered the living room with two bowls, his favorite punch bowl for cereal and a tiny soup bowl that hadn't been used since his infancy. As he plopped down, Andy placed both bowls beside the cheese curl bag like kitchenware bookends.

"This is going to hurt you as much as it hurts me," Andy said, ripping the bag open. "But now it's time for a bit of adult portion control."

Andy then emptied the entire bag's contents into his large punch bowl.

"I'd usually wolf down all this bowl by myself," he said, placing a handful of cheese curls from the punch bowl into the smaller one. "So here's a portion of those that I'll eat instead. I'm an adult, see?"

Andy lifted the small bowl to his nostrils, sucking in its cheesy air with a paint huffer's euphoria. After a whiff, he dumped the small bowl's meager serving back into the bag and placed them aside. Then grasping the punch bowl like a steering wheel, he plunged his face right in and chewed without restraint.

"That's as much control as I'm gonna have tonight."

Andy crunched with glee, now flipping through TV channels and giving them a half-second chance. After a few hundred judgmental button presses, a bright orange frame flashed before his eyes. Was the sudden influx of

ANDY GETS CONNED

cheese preservatives making him hallucinate? Did Nielsen's recently switch to a nut-based oil that set off Andy's allergies? Or maybe he sent himself into an epileptic fit by flipping the channels so quickly? Curious, Andy flipped back a few channels. Now mesmerized in reverence at the orange hues pouring from his wall-sized screen, Andy stared at reporter Gail Ellerbach in front of Nielsen's Cheese Curl factory.

"This is the one and only time where watching Gail is acceptable," said Andy. "Please don't let there be an outbreak of Salmonella at the cheese curl factory!"

On screen, CEO Lamar Nielsen leaned toward Gail, both wearing orange suits and top hats. With rows of cheese curl bag pyramids behind him, the CEO wiped sweat from his forehead.

"And that's why all the scientists are dumb and super wrong, Gail," he said.

"So, the allegations that your company genetically modifies corn to make your consumers mouth-breathing, welfare-abusing automatons have no validity at all?" asked Gail, rehearsed.

"No, Gail. And for the record, that was a confident, conclusive 'no,' wasn't it?"

"Absolutely. Well, I have no further questions."

"And in wake of these rumors, Nielsen's Cheese Curls wants to squash this negativity by reminding everyone about our ongoing campaign. So listen up, all you respected customers and investigative wings of the government! Each time you open a bag of our fine and non-toxic Nielsen's Cheese Curls, you have a chance of finding The Artificially Colored Orange Ticket," said Nielsen, reaching into his suit and removing an orange, glowing ticket shaped like a crown. "One lucky winner will receive an exclusive tour of our cheesy facilities, a whopping five hundred thousand dollars, a job on our respected food tasting team, and a lifetime supply of our perfectly harmless product. Winners can also take the cash equivalent if they don't want a job or don't think they can pass a drug test. It's options like these that make Nielsen's Cheese Curls fit for a king!"

"What a marketing scam," Andy said, muting the propaganda. "Orange ticket? There's probably a higher chance of Wacky Will showing up at my door right after I end this sentence."

Andy shifted his eyes to the front entrance with no Wacky Will to be seen, then focusing back on the pile of crumbs in his large bowl. As he sized up the mound, he fidgeted his foot. The anxiety! The wanting to know! The unlikely deus ex machina that could swoop in and solve most of his problems!

"There's no ticket here," he said, whirling his finger around the punch bowl's dust. "But maybe I should cut myself open in case I ate it? No, Andy, no! You would have felt a ticket going down your esophagus; that thing looked laminated."

Andy placed aside the big bowl, revealing an orange object upon his stomach. Predictably, it was no ticket—it was the last cheese curl of his allotted portion.

"Sorry, boy, but there comes a time in every snack's life when it has to face the food chain," Andy said,

ANDY GETS CONNED

pinching the over-baked curl like a coin-operated crane game. "Hmm, stubborn, are you? Let's see how you do against my lethal saliva storm then."

Andy cast the curl upward and caught it with his front teeth, biting so hard that it sent shivers down his orthodontist's spine. But its hydrogenated armor still resisted. For his next attempt, Andy swished the curl around his saliva moat with no signs of sogginess either. Then flicking it backward, he detained the curl with his molars and clenched down like a vice grip, growling.

"To the dungeon you go. Dinner, get served!"

Tilting his head, Andy swallowed and froze as wide-eyed panic filled his bluing face. Then he massaged his throat quickly, jiggling his double chin, as thousands of hours of video game marathons flashed before his eyes. An opposite atmosphere building in the kitchen, Mom scattered flower petals upon the table. And Chris poured her a glass of wine so large that he might as well have given her the whole bottle.

"Thanks for doing this here tonight," Mom said, lifting the glass to her face with both hands. "Andy needed some company."

"Roger that," said Chris, as Mom gulfed down her glass. "I'll spend time with you whenever I can. Wherever that cute, little keister goes, I go too."

"And my keister goes wherever those manly police hands of yours go. Are you up for a pat-down, officer? Maybe you could bring out the handcuffs later?"

"You're perfect. Since we met, you shot a jolt through these old bones like two stun guns to the nipples."

"Here's to four weeks!" Mom said, polishing off her second glass. "This is the longest I've been with one man since, well...Alvin passed away. I'm sorry, I killed the mood, didn't I?"

"Don't you worry. A day doesn't go by where I'm not thinkin' about my dear Kathryn either. But I'm hopin' both our deceased loves are up there foolin' around together. It'd be a fair swap, right?"

"Swingers on both sides of the grave? I like it. You nail her good up there, Alvin, you hear me?" said Mom, smiling. "Let's drink more."

After clinking their glasses, Mom and Chris gulped away and uncorked two more bottles of wine. As they chugged straight from their bottles, faint sounds of Andy tipping over furniture made it to the kitchen.

"Is he okay out there?" asked Chris, wine dripping down his chin. "Sounds like he's chokin'. Well, chokin' or redecoratin' maybe."

"I bet he's trying to get us back with a prank. He owes us for the flower shop joke, you know. Keep drinking."

Back in the living room, Andy slugged his sternum with both fists like an asphyxiating gorilla. His windpipe still clogged, Andy scanned the room for something better to smash himself into and regain aspiration. A skateboard? Too flimsy. A monitor? Too expensive. A coffee table verified unbreakable by three engineering teams according to the commercial? Just right.

Andy swayed backward and then heaved his chest atop the coffee table, demolishing it instantly. And then R2CheeseToodle, now in a metallic veil and mourning its

ANDY GETS CONNED

brother's demise, zoomed toward the table's sawdust particles. Andy palmed himself up using the wall and then threw his weight against the couch next, its padded arm splitting off just as smoothly as the lumberjack's had.

"He's dedicated to this prank," Chris shouted, as the panicked coughs and robotic vacuuming grew louder in the living room.

"Yes, he is," Mom said, followed by a thud and then serene quietness. "Okay, he's definitely choking!"

As Mom and Chris sprung into the living room with their wine bottles, they caught Andy in an act that no parent should see—Andy jamming R2CheeseToodle over his mouth while it sucked at max velocity. Chris then handed his bottle to Mom, hoisted Andy up, and pumped that nerd's abdomen hard with his cop-baton-callused hands. On Chris's last forceful compression, the cheese curl blasted from Andy's mouth into the window, shattered the glass, and pierced through all of Mr. Gentzel's garbage cans next door.

"Where are you, you hooligans? You touch, you buy!" screamed Mr. Gentzel from his home.

"Are you all right, dear?" asked Mom.

"Barely," said Andy. "Especially if Mr. Gentzel figures out I just wrecked his cans. Thanks for the help though."

"Creative use of that vacuum cleaner," added Chris.

"Let's be honest, that was probably the most pathetic thing you've both ever seen," Andy said. "I can't sit around here anymore and wallow. I've got to move on."

"We'll help any way that we can," said Mom, patting Andy's head.

"Thank you, but I know what I need to do. I'm going back to work. That's at least a slower death than this."

"No, you need to relax and get back to the job search, dear. You should enjoy the rest of your vacation."

"I have to be realistic, Mom," Andy grumbled, heading for the stairs. "Most adults despise their jobs these days, right? I'll be okay."

"You were my job for years, and I never despised one second of it," Mom said. "Not even the baby poop parts."

"Right. And what a fine man-child I became. A cheese curl almost killed me," said Andy, shuffling upstairs. "I'm going to bed. You two have a nice night though. I'll wear my noise-cancelling headphones, so be as loud as you want. Go crazy, lovebirds."

"I'm here if you need to talk," shouted Mom, as Andy slammed the door. "Good night, dear. I love you."

"Yell if you need my help too. Yesterday I talked down a couple of bridge jumpers, so this is nothin'," said Chris, as Mom chugged both wine bottles. "Sorry, I'm not great with kids."

Early the next morning, Andy lumbered into the kitchen with a winery's worth of empty bottles lining the countertops. Fortunately, Mom and Chris were fully clothed, dozing on the floor. After covering the couple with a blanket, Andy placed a goodbye note in Mom's bouffant, trudged to his hiking backpack, and dumped out all the video equipment. He then loaded the bag with Revolutionary War pistols, marched to his hatchback in the garage, and sped to Bumble Ridge High...now with a drastically different motive.

ANDY GETS CONNED

Blissfully unaware of the gun-toting curveball about to hit him, Principal Murray slurped a pink cocktail at his desk in a Hawaiian shirt and sun straw hat. Behind him remained the crispy wall shared with Andy's classroom from the fire, and its giant hole was covered with Andy's melted projector screen. After Murray took a few more gulps, his secretary barged in wheeling a 70-quart cooler behind him; loaded with adult beverages confiscated from the 12th-grade lockers, this was a 'team lift' cooler.

"Andy Gordon is here to see you, sir," huffed the secretary, placing down the cooler.

"You wear the gift I gave you, or I'm not responding."

"But it's degrading. It's unprofessional—"

"It's mandatory," Murray said.

Without moving his sullen face, the secretary flung open the filing cabinet, fetched a straw beachcomber's hat, and jammed the tropical prop onto his head.

"Andy Gordon's here to see you," said the secretary.

"Much better. Now which one is he?"

"He's a history teacher. Rides a skateboard."

"Not ringing a bell."

"He's been working here five years. He called you on the phone about 20 days ago, and you let him take all his vacation at once. You torched his prized possessions after you thought he died in the fire."

"Oh yeah, the fat guy. Wait a minute, he's supposed to be on vacation still, right?" Murray said, sitting up straight. "He's probably going to blow my brains out. Did you give him a cavity search?"

"Twice as requested."

"Good. And did you find anything?"

"Ten minutes into the first one, I thought he was packing a grenade up in there, but it turned out to be a long-neglected hemorrhoid instead."

"Sounds like a problem to me. So what's he want?"

"He looks troubled. He said it was an emergency."

"Of course he's troubled; he's got a bleeding butthole. What the hell am I supposed to do to help his ass wounds? I make ass wounds, not fix them."

"No, sir. It's a *work* emergency that doesn't involve his hemorrhoids."

"Right. Well tell him to go away. I'm a busy man and not in the mood to die this morning."

"Sir, he did tell me to mention this was a work emergency that you could profit from."

"Why didn't you say that sooner? Send that sad, droopy anus man in here!"

As the secretary swung the door open, Andy entered and panned his head between the two men with respectable titles wearing non-respectable hats. After snapping his fingers twice, Murray pointed at the cooler and then to Andy.

"You're not dumping ice on me, Murray," said Andy. "You've embarrassed me as a snowman too many times."

"Stop. You misinterpreted my snapping, Gordon," Murray said, as the secretary reached in the cooler and handed Andy a bottle of rum.

Murray snapped again and pointed at the door, his secretary sagging his head. And the secretary's hat slid off as he exited, descending just like his self-esteem.

ANDY GETS CONNED

"Sit down," Murray said.

"No! No," Andy flinched, holding his butt. "That's not a good idea after all those cavity searches."

"All right, you can stand. But tell me about your profitable emergency."

"I lied about that. I knew you wouldn't see me unless I lied, but I figured you'd respect that."

"Dammit, I do respect that. You don't get the rum though," Murray said, jerking it away from Andy and leaning back in his chair.

Murray then kicked his feet up on the desk one at a time, flicking absurd amounts of sand into the air.

"Did you just get back from the beach or do you have a tub of sand down there?" asked Andy.

"A magician never spoils his tricks. Now talk."

"I made a big mistake. And it's time to fix it once and for all," Andy said, pulling two pistols from his backpack.

"Whoa there! I'll give you whatever you want!"

"No, I—"

"Spare me, and we'll work together! I'll double your wages. I'll make you my new secretary so you don't have to deal with these teenage cretins!" Murray pleaded, covering both guns with his straw hat. "Somebody smart enough to get guns through security here and threaten my life is my kinda business partner."

"No, I'm not here to shoot you. These are both nonfunctional replicas," Andy said, pulling their triggers.

Andy's guns then ejected two small flags upon poles, each containing the text 'History Rules' on their red cloth.

"Oh thank god!" Murray shouted.

"They're part of my next history lesson. I want to come back and teach again," Andy said, reloading the flags. "And I mean right now."

"I should fire you for that, Gordon," Murray said, putting his hat back on. "But on account of all the blackmail you have on me, let's start fresh. Acceptable?"

"You have my word, Murray. I won't rat you out. So can I come back now?"

"That's gonna be tough with such short notice. Your substitute has been doing phenomenal work. Peek through the hole behind me and take a look."

"I see the maintenance around here hasn't changed," Andy said, spying between his projector screen's backside and the charred wall.

In Andy's old classroom, a monkey wearing a tie jumped around a crowd of captivated students—no phone distractions or disrespect to be seen. Emily, Fran, Marcus, B-Fred, and all others nodded their heads, following the monkey's trajectory like a set of bobblehead dolls.

"A monkey?" Andy asked. "This has to be a joke."

"No joke at all. After one day with her, your students could find the United States on a map. That monkey's a miracle worker."

"You're playing hard ball? Fine. I take back what I said. I *will* rat you out for all the health code violations and the extra credit mandate. I also know you worked out a deal with Nathan to give him a diploma at the end of the year even though he didn't earn it. And now we can throw this monkey into the mix. I'm friends with a cop near retirement who has a hankering to maim. But I won't tell

ANDY GETS CONNED

him you have an unsupervised, deadly animal in the classroom if you give me my job back now."

"Can I keep the monkey?"

"Yes, I don't care, but I do have some demands."

"Demands? Oh, this is precious. Anything you want as long as it doesn't rape my wallet too much—hit me."

"One: Do something about this fire damage. Two: I want newer history books published way after the 1400s. And you're really not going to like three: I never have to play the snowman at a Christmas pageant again."

"I'll see what I can do, but you start tomorrow," Murray said, snapping his fingers again. "Hey, secretary, where are you?"

The secretary then burst back into the room and, upon seeing Andy's pistols, pounced.

"Oh no you don't!" screamed the secretary, tackling Andy and yanking the guns away. "I've been waiting to blow this guy's brains out for years. He's my kill!"

"Get off the damn floor, you two! Those guns are fake!" Murray scolded, as he placed a sleeping mask over his eyes. "Gordon's coming back tomorrow morning. So go fill the paperwork out to make that happen. And give him your parking spot too. Now, if you don't mind, Gordon, please leave. A man needs his beauty rest."

"More like a beauty coma," Andy mumbled, getting off of the floor.

"What was that?"

"Enjoy the monkey, Murray!" Andy said, slamming the door behind him.

"Sir, about what happened," said the secretary.

"Let's not go there; it's water under the bridge. Now, could you move the sandbox onto my desk for me? My feet need sand to sleep."

"I'd be happy to," said the secretary, relocating Murray's tub of sand to his desk. "There we go. Thank you for understanding, sir."

"Put my feet in the sand before you leave," demanded Murray, the secretary complying and then resting Murray's heels into the granules.

"I'll get started on Andy's paperwork right away," the secretary said, as Murray pushed his feet deeper into the sand and suddenly stopped.

"Wait, I need some new sand first!" yelled Murray. "I'm pretty sure the monkey used this as a litter box."

CHAPTER 23

Sprawled out on beanbag chairs at the comic shop, Ben and Leo played video games with expressionless faces. With sales dwindling again, the two raced electronic go-karts and blasted zombie prostitutes in one genre-blending gem of gaming history. Yet they both sunk deeper into their beanbag depressions as each race ended, their hangout now far deader than the zombie hookers.

"Game night's a total drag without Andy," said Leo.

"I know," Ben moped, changing to his zombie voice. "ZomBen think we not work as couple. ZomBen need third person in relationship to make things fun again."

"You're bumming and grossing me out, man. Stop. So how long do you think Andy can sustain his brain without human contact or the Internet?"

"I thought he'd go postal by now," Ben said, engulfed by his beanbag chair so much that only his legs stuck out. "Help! Save me! Save me!"

"Wait, what did you say? Save? Yes, of course, *save!* That's how we can get out of this funk."

"I can't breathe," whimpered Ben, fully submerged.

"Save! Why didn't I think of this sooner?" Leo said, springing from his chair to the cash register. "You're a genius, Ben. What a bolt out of the blue."

After grabbing an object from the cash register, Leo doubled back to Ben and muscled him out with a tremendous tug. And when Ben exited his cushiony prison, a thunderous pop emanated from the chair as if cracking open a sealed tube of biscuit dough. Ben then flew from the chair and a fountain of loose change exploded from its beany crevice.

"Why exactly am I a genius?" asked Ben, gasping.

"You said 'saving,' man. Saving!" Leo exclaimed, presenting the object from his hand in front of Ben's face. "It's the memory card from Andy's camera. When he slaughtered it on the sidewalk, guess who secretly snatched this baby up?"

"It's not like we can reload our life from it though. Who cares?"

"You're correct, but we *can* score a healthy dose of the big guy while he's away," said Leo, picking up his laptop and inserting the memory card.

Totally invading Andy's privacy, Leo scrolled through hundreds of videos as Ben observed over the shoulder like a parrot sidekick. After Leo double clicked one of the files, footage then played of their stroll in front of *Rejects & Reptiles* Con:

"Nevertheless," said dwarf Andy. "The trio set off on its insane plan to visit three geeky, fandom conventions on three different da—"

ANDY GETS CONNED

From the camera's perspective, Leo and Ben now watched Andy ram into a pole and collapse. Finding these events funnier in retrospect, Leo paused the file.

"So, you wanna veg out and watch all these videos in a row?" asked Leo.

"I'll make the popcorn!" Ben said, scampering off.

"Stop popping my stock, man!"

"A viewing party's not a party without the popcorn."

"I hate to destroy the joy, but we need to talk about this right now."

"I'll pay you for it, I promise. What's up?"

"If you keep acting this way, somebody's gonna blow. You try to kill your partners in *Rejects & Reptiles*. You bum money from us. And you eat all our treats. This was kind of endearing when we were in high school, but we figured you'd grow out of it by now."

"Look, I know I can be oblivious sometimes. And I'm not as sophisticated as you and Andy," said Ben, rushing back to the beanbag chairs with popcorn. "But I don't want to be the annoying guy in the group. I thought you both liked my antics."

"It's funny sometimes, but it's a bit much these days. I don't want to end the friendship, but could you tone it down? If you start pulling your weight around here and displaying some empathy, we're simpatico, okay?"

"You're right. Well, you'll see a new me from now on. In fact, here's five dollars for this popcorn."

"I can't believe it was that easy. But thank you."

"Now are you done being a vagina so we can watch Andy's videos or not?"

"Ben!"

"I'm kidding," Ben smiled. "I'll work on myself, and you'll see a difference soon. Are we cool?"

"We're cool. Thanks for listening. Now let's watch!"

Hours later, with empty popcorn bags piled around them, Ben and Leo binged on buffoonery until reaching their song-and-dance number at the business convention. Before the vlog's sad ending wrecked their positive mojo, Ben paused the video.

"I can't watch how this ends again," said Ben. "Want to check out that other folder on the card instead?"

"Without a doubt," said Leo, clicking. "Holy free-range cow! We found the treasure trove!"

"Are my eyes seeing what my brain thinks my eyes are seeing right now?"

"Yeah! These look like every video Andy finished but didn't have a chance to upload."

"Hold on, I'll make some more popcorn so we can watch them all!" Ben said, sitting up and clearing off the collection of empty bags on his chest. "Here, take another 10 bucks. I owe you."

"First, I pity your colon with all of that fiber. Second, I'm totally tapped out of cash. And I don't want you to run out too."

"Well, let's fix both our problems then," Ben said, sliding the laptop in front of him.

"Dude, what are you doing?"

"Andy still owes you a second shop promo, doesn't he? I bet the animated one's on here somewhere," Ben said, scrolling through the card's files. "Let's look at the

ANDY GETS CONNED

letter L videos for Leo. Hmm, lampreys, lasers, leetspeak, and hey, there it is! Leo's Promo: The Sequel!"

"I miss the big guy and his anal archive system."

"Me too. He tried to upload this at the hotel, but couldn't, right? So let's upload it for him."

"Well, it would fulfill our verbal contract and get more of his work out there, so that's a win-win, right? Upload it before my conscience kicks in!"

"On it!" shouted Ben, typing.

"How do we get into his JumboAndy page though?"

"Chris reset the password, remember? So all we have to do is guess the old password that Andy had before."

"Let's have a little powwow. What means a lot to Andy? What gives him an out-of-body experience? What word should we try first?" asked Leo, he and Ben then shifting their gaze and locking eyes.

"Boobs!" Ben answered, prematurely.

"How about you try 'Wacky Will' instead?"

"Yours is better," Ben said, typing and entering the guess. "Nope. It says that 'Wacky Will' was an older password changed recently. Hmm..."

"What else could it be that's newer?"

Ben then took a breath and raised his index finger, his mouth quickly blocked by Leo's hand.

"It's not any other synonym for boobs either, Ben," stated Leo. "Get on his level."

"I got nothing."

"I'll start then. Type in 'Tessa.'"

Ben clicked and then typed in Leo's second non-mammary conjecture.

"It worked! We're in the Andy matrix," Ben said, as a repetitive bang on the shop's door punctuated his sentence. "Uh oh."

"What in the world was that?" asked Leo.

Before Leo rotated, Ben grabbed his head with both palms, twisted it back, and stared him right in the eyes.

"Shhh. Hackers don't look back. We're in this together no matter what!"

"I acknowledge your thoughts and accept the aftermath," said Leo, leaning toward the laptop. "Hey, check out those view counts. Each video's over five thousand now. Hold on. No, that's fifty thousand! Andy's gonna be stoked when he sees this! And I will be too if even one percent of these people come to the shop."

"Let's see what they think of this then," Ben said, clicking and dragging clips from the memory card onto Andy's page. "Let's see how the Internet handles our entire video backlog. Uploading now!"

"Including all the raw footage?"

"Of course!"

"Even the dolphin parts?"

"I forgot about that, but yes—it's time to come out of the dolphin-loving closet. The upload goes on!"

The faint pounding behind them grew louder, now with furious shouts in the mix. Leo then turned around, spotting the cause of such commotion. And, in response, Ben stuffed more cash into his best bud's pants pocket.

"I'm sorry in advance. Here's 10 more bucks," Ben said, waving at the zombie-like crowd squishing their faces on the door. "I'll let them in now."

ANDY GETS CONNED

"Why's the door locked?"

"We were watching videos. It was *our* time," said Ben, opening the door as customers poured in. "And for the record, I locked this door before I agreed to be a better person. I'm a work in progress. But here's another five dollars for my sins."

While Samosas Studios' content uploaded, Andy focused on something far less exciting across town. Yes, he now explored the adult hobby known as home repair. Wearing a yellow safety helmet, Andy squirted wood glue on the coffee table and attached its leg with a hand-held vise. Mom then emerged from the basement in her matching helmet, shuffling up with a dusty toolbox.

"Here's your dad's toolset, dear," said Mom. "I figured it was still down there."

"You know, I feel manly trying to fix something other than robots around here. Do you like the new window?"

"Yes, your dad would be proud that you fixed it. And mocking you a little bit for breaking it, but mostly proud."

"Thanks for finding this for me," Andy said, taking his helmet off, putting it down, and wiping his sweaty brow. "You and Chris have fun. I have a wild night ahead of me. If I can fix the couch, my bed, and the outlet upstairs, this vacation wasn't a total waste."

"Nonsense, dear. Chris and I can help. Then we'll all go out to dinner together. You could use some company."

Andy rested his glue on a Wacky Will coaster, and the bottle tipped over...unnoticed. A few droplets then dripped on the table's surface—also unnoticed—as Andy blew the dust off his dad's alphabetized tools.

"I planned on having some time to myself tonight. Don't baby me," Andy said, kicking his helmet away. "You two can have dinner without me."

"Are you okay? I don't want to leave you like this."

"I'll be fine, Mom. I'll fix this place up and finish my lesson plans tonight. There's always something to do."

"Okay. There are phone numbers on the fridge for the restaurant we'll be at. And then the three bars we'll be at after that. I set the paramedics on speed dial too."

"Mom," grumbled Andy.

"And I left dinner in the fridge. It's all puréed so you won't choke."

"Mom! You have to stop treating me like a kid or Andy 4.0 won't work," Andy griped, a car outside then playfully honking. "You and Chris have a great time tonight, okay? I'll see you later."

"Hold on. I'll tell him I can't go."

"No, you're going. Your future is out there, not here."

"Don't say that. It's not true."

"Just have some fun and forget about me tonight. Please. I'm not going to ruin your romance too."

"Chris will understand, dear. We can order takeout and play that video game where you shoot ducks."

"Are you going to make me sumo wrestle you out that door? Go, Mom! Enjoy your life."

"All right, if you insist, dear. I love you. We'll talk about this later when you're not so upset, okay?"

"We're dragging each other down. Admit it. I think we should talk later. And I mean way later—how's Thanksgiving sound to you?"

ANDY GETS CONNED

"But that's months from now."

"It sure is. It's about time we act like a normal family and only see each other for funerals and holidays. And I mean major holidays."

"But what about our Flag Day cake?"

"Not even for Flag Day cake. I love you, Mom, but you need to leave the nest. Fly! Be free!"

"Don't do this to me, Andy."

"It's for our own good. Let's grow up a bit, okay?"

"If that's what you want," Mom cried, escaping before eyeliner dripped down her wrinkles. "You better at least video chat with me."

As Mom skedaddled outside, Andy flopped to the floor and slammed his forehead on the table. A cold goo then filled the expression lines on his skin.

"I hope that's maple syrup," Andy said, lifting his head and the table along with it. "Uh oh."

Andy latched onto the table, all his fingers instantly sticking to the glue as well. Reacting, Andy hopped up and whirled in a rapid circle like an ice skater. And the coffee table quickly ripped free, leaving a small, red patch on his flesh and a sizeable hole in the new window. A cat outside then screeched as the table demolished Mr. Gentzel's trash cans, took out a traffic light, and shattered a glass pane carried by two window repairmen blocks away.

"I break way too much furniture," said Andy, as sounds of vehicle crashes now intruded his living room.

Andy finished his repairs and then went to bed. With his earplugs blocking out Bumble Ridge's largest car pileup in history, he slept for eight peaceful hours.

Though he had doused his head with nail polish remover to clear the glue, his dinosaur blankets and accordion pillows still rose out of bed with him in the morning. Looking like a poor person's Halloween costume, Andy spun his attachments off again, fetched black coffee from his bedroom barista, and shuffled down the hallway in some boring, brown slippers.

Minutes later, Andy zoomed in his hatchback to Bumble Ridge High. It was time for a few more decades of helping the youth sleep in history class. After passing all armed tollbooths in the parking lot and paying the mandatory meter, Andy hopped out. And then he stared down the dorky emblems lining his hatchback's windshield—decals of Darwin fish, robot vacuum cleaners, and *Space Fightin's* Pinnette.

"I'm coming for you with an ice scraper after work," Andy said. "You've been warned!"

When the bell rang, Andy strutted in front of the class like a Catholic nun. And he smacked each student's desk with a ruler as he passed by. As Emily, Fran, Marcus, and B-Fred gazed forward, Andy sat at a barren desk near his charred wall. Though Principal Murray had clearly not fixed the fire damage, he did perform the cheapest repair possible by painting the other walls black so they all matched. Without fail, Murray's frugality then came rushing back over Andy like a broken septic tank.

"Okay, we have a lot to do today," said Andy. "Though I heard you learned how to find our country on a map, I bet you've missed quite a bit of material since I've been gone."

ANDY GETS CONNED

"No more lies, baby stealer," said B-Fred. "You weren't gone!"

"It's 'Mr. Gordon' now," Andy said. "And what are you talking about?"

"It's nice to see you, Mr. Gordon," Emily said, lifting her cricket cage. "Mr. Cricket hasn't had the same comedic timing without you."

"Thank you, Emily."

"And there's a lot less of you to see, may I add. Have you been working out?"

"A little, yes. But let's get started—"

"You're all dumb," injected B-Fred. "I'm telling you—Andy wasn't gone!"

"I said you have to call me 'Mr. Gordon,' B-Fred!" Andy demanded. "And how could you not notice any difference between me and a female monkey?"

"I noticed," said Emily. "For example, the substitute's climbing ability was much better than yours."

"And it ate bananas instead of cheese curls," added Marcus, opening a Nielsen's bag with his fingernail.

"It was hurling slightly more poop than usual too," said Fran, nibbling one of Marcus's cheese curls.

"I don't believe your monkey evidence!" shouted B-Fred, as Fran looked in Marcus's bag.

"Whatever, B-Fred," Fran said. "Hey, Andy, how was your break? Did you hear about Nielsen's Artificially Colored Orange Ticket? There's prize money if you find it! And a food taster job too!"

"Call me 'Mr. Gordon!'" huffed Andy. "And, yes, I did hear about that. But it's not relevant, so drop it."

"That ticket is mine," Marcus said, lifting his whiteboard and drawing another basketball play. "Once my lanky legs give out on the court and my body deteriorates, I'll need a backup career."

"I'll find it first!" B-Fred said, opening several family-sized bags of cheese curls on his desk.

"Everybody knock off this nonsense," Andy shouted, smacking a hole in his crispy desk with the ruler. "And put away that whiteboard, Marcus."

"But the coach wants a playbook for next week," said Marcus, drawing. "Don't make me even more morose."

"Put it away. And if I hear one more word about cheese curls, I'll send you to the principal's office."

"We broke him already," said Fran.

"Wait, are you seriously serious?" asked B-Fred.

"Yes, I am. Isn't that right, Principal Murray?" asked Andy, cracking his ruler against the projector screen.

"Sure is," Murray said behind the screen. "Welcome back, Gordon. You're doing great. Keep putting your foot down on those dimwits."

The students then sat up straight with folded hands, now awaiting their authoritarian tutelage. As Andy started up the coal-powered projector, B-Fred whispered to Fran so loud that the basement cockroaches could hear him.

"He's just fussy because he didn't get bananas yet today," said B-Fred, removing the fruit from his desk and tossing them at Andy's head.

"Were those bananas?" Murray blurted. "My monkey's going crazy! If she doesn't get one, she might bite my freaking face off!

ANDY GETS CONNED

"Was that you, B-Fred?" spouted Andy. "You take those bananas next door, now! There will be no more outbursts or airborne bananas in my classroom, got it? I demand your respect."

"Mr. Gordon? Please go on with the lesson," said Emily, as B-Fred left. "We are eager to learn and not die. I will also provide more placating cupcakes, if necessary."

"Thank you, Emily, though cupcakes aren't allowed in here now," said Andy, advancing his text-based slides. "Let's get started. I'd like to skip ahead about a thousand years from where we left off and jump to the American Revolution. It was a battle of independence and a fight for our rights to party without tea taxes."

"Your slides are totally desolate," said Marcus. "Where's all the memes?"

"Yeah, and the pop culture?" added Fran.

"Well, those might work for you two, but they're not effective with everyone. Those were unprofessional teaching tactics and I can't use them anymore," Andy said.

"Could you be more ominous?" asked Marcus.

"Yes, I could," Andy said. "Easily. You want me to?"

"Mr. Gordon," Emily said, raising her hand. "On behalf of the class, could you please remove the large stick from your rectum?"

"Excuse me?" asked Andy.

"I meant, please be nice to us?" revised Emily.

"Yeah, or we'll tell Murray you're abusing us," added Marcus. "That's pretty grim, right?"

"I really don't think he'll believe you. Or care," Andy said, flipping a switch and sending his screen upward.

With the wall's hole now exposed, students stared at Murray and his monkey in pajamas. Both jumped up and down on Murray's desk, nibbling bananas with glee. And B-Fred pelted the perky pair with fruit from his pockets.

"Hey, Gordon. I put those new books under your desk," said Murray, still jumping.

"I appreciate that," said Andy, pressing a button and covering the hole back up. "And get back over here, B-Fred. As you can see, I have full support in keeping the stick firmly lodged between my cheeks. Any questions?"

The class cowered in silence.

"Good. Now today's all about getting back to the basics of our country, so I'll be reading from our new textbook with simple slides behind me. And then comes a special treat for us after that."

"Special treat?" Emily hyped. "I knew you were trying to fake us out. Bring on the dork references! Bring on the memes and bonus points!"

"Nope, I think you'll like this treat even more than that. Every time we come across a word in the book that you don't know, I'll read its definition from the dictionary," said Andy, sitting on his chair and plopping two epic tomes upon his lap. "Please come get your new textbook for the year—these ones actually go up to the 1990s. Then I need you to open to page 135 so we can cover a fun little bunch of terrorists known as the Founding Fathers."

After dispersing the books, Andy read its updated pages aloud. And B-Fred bumbled back in the room, immediately lobbing a banana at Andy's forehead.

ANDY GETS CONNED

"Who threw that?" Andy asked, looking up at a class all avoiding eye contact. "Okay, who threw that with the understanding that I'll fail everyone if nobody fesses up?"

The entire class then pointed at B-Fred as he looked forward, unaware of the tattletales. And when B-Fred noticed all of the fingers aimed at him seconds later, he saw only one option—hesitantly pointing to Emily and her cricket. With awkward chirps filling the room, Andy then prepared three words that he had only used once when Nathan Hader brought a lion to class.

"Principal's office. Now!" he said, removing a Revolutionary War gun replica from his desk. "If anybody tries anything else, they're expelled. And that includes your damned cricket, Emily. Now listen up!"

CHAPTER 24

At the efficiency apartment complex, a pregnant woman tossed garbage bags from her third-floor window. And when they missed the dumpster, they demolished Nathan's cardboard roof yet again. With trash full of pregnancy cravings now pounding the pavement, juicy pickle jar shards and eel carcasses spread across the floor. But Nathan typed at his laptop despite the waste, as Tessa worked on her own project beside him in a welding helmet. Bonding metal to her Treb-Mew-Chet bot, Tessa continued her repairs until one more eel body plunged downward and splattered her headgear.

"Break time," Tessa said, flipping up the helmet and revealing two plugs in her nostrils. "Are those eels?"

"Probably," Nathan said, typing on the couch.

"I can't believe you found that laptop in the trash," said Tessa, sitting beside Nathan. "It looks brand new. Who threw that away?"

"It was in Kirkpatrick's gold-plated dumpster. That billionaire tosses out lots of good crap."

"Good for you. I could use a new computer too. Where's he live? Can you show me?"

"No more questions. So, we're both on a break. Wanna make out?"

"Not yet," Tessa said, placing her head on Nathan's shoulder. "How's your high school work going, by the way? I know you said you were sworn to secrecy, but are they still giving you your diploma at the end of the year?"

"You remembered that?"

"Yes, I like you. People who like each other remember things and ask questions, Luke."

"Well I better be honest with you then," Nathan said, caressing Tessa's helmet. "I still have an agreement with the principal, but it's a little more complicated than I led you to believe."

"Why?"

"Please don't be mad at me, but I have to tell you the truth. Andy *was* my history teacher. He's the one who screwed me over and stopped me from graduating."

"What? Why didn't you tell me?"

"Well, do you remember when I came to your comedy show? When I thought I heard Andy say he was your manager and he was trying to get in your pants?"

"Yes, which I discovered probably wasn't true."

"Right. But when I thought he was trying to bone you, imagine how I would've looked if I told you everything," Nathan said, chewing a protein bar. "I would've said that he killed my dreams. And you probably would've thought I made up the rumor to get you to hate him."

"Okay, that makes sense. But it's not made up, right?"

ANDY GETS CONNED

"Don't be silly. I had to hide what Andy did to me, or you might have been boned in two ways. Based on the info I had, I was trying to save you."

"Valid point. So why'd he fail you?"

"He shoved his nerdy hobbies down our throats. And it made learning unbearable for those of us who weren't nerds. Plus, um, he yelled at my class every day and even brought a lion into school one time. After that, I had enough and confronted him. Then he failed me."

"My god, he should be in jail if that's true!"

"Yeah, but don't worry about it. The school's on my side, and they know he's a problem. They're about to fire him in a few weeks but told me to keep quiet. Now they let me work in the nurse's office, and I'm getting credit for it. You have to keep this a secret though because if it leaks out, I won't get my diploma."

"This is a lot of information to take in right now," Tessa said, wiping eel guts off her helmet with a protein bar wrapper. "Wait a minute, that means you spent time with us at the Convention Crawl even though Andy did this to you? That must have been hell."

"It was. But you insisted that we join them, so I played along. I figured we could give him another chance anyway until he went nuts on us again."

"And that's why you didn't take off your costume the whole time? You wanted to stay hidden? You didn't want Andy to know it was you?"

"Exactly."

"Your secret is safe with me. Thanks for sharing that, Luke. Things are starting to make a lot more sense. But can we talk about something else? Like, anything else? How's your script coming along? Can I see it?"

"Wait, what?" Nathan asked, tensing up even more. "Uh, yeah, we can do that."

"Thanks! I've been dying to look at it."

"Here you go," Nathan said, placing the computer on Tessa's lap. "But before you start, I have to tell you something else so the script title makes sense."

"Okay. I'm all ears."

"What about your lady parts? Those aren't ears. Could we stay focused?" Nathan said, straight-faced.

"Was that a joke or should I be mad?"

"Uh, joke. So here goes. Remember how Andy kept calling me Nathan instead of my real name Luke?"

"I said I didn't want to talk about him anymore."

"No, this is related. I've been thinking about that name ever since. 'Nathan'—I like how it sounds."

"Oh, you don't like the name 'Luke?'"

"I think people might respect me more as a Nathan. Maybe they'd see my true awesomeness and boyfriend potential too. It'd be a fresh start, you know?"

"I think that's a great idea. You can put the past behind you and move on to a new chapter with a name change. Plus, it's way cheaper than a witness protection program, right?" Tessa said, forcing a smile.

"There's another bonus. If Andy calls me 'Nathan' again and my name really is Nathan, we can tell him he's right. Then he might calm down and leave us alone."

"That'd probably be good for both of us. So, what's the title of your script then?"

"I'm calling it *Nathan (the Homeless Guy You Should Date) Says*. I'll record with my laptop and share my street smarts. I'll get lots of pity donations. Great idea, right?"

"I like most of that idea. How about we come up with a catchier title? Something to get you more views? Maybe *Vagabond Vlogs*? Or a name with a little more kick like *The Drifter Diaries*?"

"I don't think we can top mine."

"Well, I tried. So, what do you have here?" asked Tessa, skimming his kindergarten-worthy paragraph. "A vlog about maggots? This is hilarious."

"No, it's serious," Nathan said, ripping the laptop from Tessa's hands. "My fans will get it. You'll see."

"It's not bad. If you want to make it less funny, I should be able to help. I seem to be pretty good at that."

"I'd rather keep our work separate," Nathan said, as Tessa hunched over with a sigh. "See, I knew it! You're sad again aren't you? You're drooping your shoulders a lot, and that means you're sad! I'm seeing you in a very sad moment right now, aren't I?"

"Yeah, Nathan. I'm a bit down, but I'll be fine."

"No! This stops now! Andy's still messing this up—*us* up! You never got any closure. You never gave him a piece of your mind. Well I say we finally get you over this. And there's only one possible solution."

"Us making out isn't going to help right now," Tessa said, scooching away.

"No, something even better than that," said Nathan, shimmying toward her. "Revenge!"

"What are you talking about?"

"You need to get angry. You can't be sad when you're angry. Now that I'm seeing how much he's upsetting you, I want him to pay even more. We both need to get Andy back! It's time for revenge!"

"Nathan, I—"

"Trust me," he said, pulling a carcass from the couch. "Now let's roast some of these eels and plan an attack."

While Nathan whispered tactics into Tessa's ears, Leo ramped up his marketing a few blocks away at the shop. But this time, Leo sold his geeky goods outside to draw even more attention. His Sidewalk Sale was off to a strong start too, now profiting from pedestrian impulse buys of bright toys and Palpitations pitchers. Though Leo only offered overpriced drinks and common comics from the Convention Crawl, Bumble Ridge didn't know any better.

"We're really attracting the masses out here," said Leo, organizing change at the register. "If we keep this sale going a few more weeks, my comic surplus will be outta sight, outta mind."

"Before anyone snaps these up, I'm making a legitimate purchase," Ben said, dropping a box of comics at the register. "I want all your *Dolphin Cops*."

Ben then placed a 100-dollar bill in Leo's palm. Upon seeing cash that wasn't forged or taken from one of the board games inside, Leo gasped.

"Thanks, man," said Leo, inspecting the money. "Where'd you get this much moolah?"

"I'm no longer cheap. Let's leave it at that."

"Answer my question. How'd you amass the cash?"

"I'd rather not say."

"Tell me, or I make you pay back your entire tab."

"Well, here's what I owe you for the tab, plus interest," said Ben, removing a wad of cash from his pants. "That's right, I paid! And to show you how different I am, I'll still tell you where I got the money."

"Stop stalling. What's the secret?"

"I found out that males can donate a certain substance and get paid for it. You know, a certain substance that women can't donate."

"Say what?"

"Liquid substances that are worth more when you say you have a doctoral degree. Substances that shoot up in value when you claim your family has good genes. Substances that pay off your student loans after wearing stilts to the clinic because they like tall fathers."

"You're playing with people's futures here. How much have you donated? Spill the beans!"

"Oh, I do spill the beans. Several times a day. At different locations too."

"This is inexcusable. It's enough to pay off your student loans! Enough to settle your tab!"

"And enough to be your next investor," Ben said, slapping a stack of bills on the table.

"Charitable to me, but awful to others?" mulled Leo. "Sounds like an improvement if I've ever heard one. Bless those balls, Ben!"

"I'm glad we agree. And after I devour these *Dolphin Cops*, I'll make my money back at the clinic in no time anyway—probably tonight! I've struck gold here, Leo. Glorious, white gold!"

"Stop talking now. Your debts are repaid despite your questionable donations. I won't reject your good gesture."

"Thanks, pal."

Breaking the awkward silence, a flower delivery van pulled up beside them. And it parked inches away from Leo, blocking two handicapped spots and a fire hydrant. Mom then hopped out from the van's rear doors holding two baskets of red, white, and blue snacks.

"Hey, boys. I brought you some goodies," Mom said, scampering over and then handing Leo and Ben two overstuffed gift baskets.

"You probably shouldn't park there, Mamma Gordon," said Leo. "The meter maids are major buzz kills around here."

"Parkin' won't be a problem," said Chris, getting out from the driver's seat. "I'm a cop. We do way worse and get away with it!"

"I'm sorry, officer!"

"Don't sweat it. I know most of us suck."

"Boys, that's Chris, my man friend," said Mom. "And Chris, these are Andy's best friends."

"Is Andy okay?" Leo asked. "He's ducking our calls. He's snubbing our texts."

"Even the notes I attached to bricks and chucked through his window didn't work," said Ben.

"I didn't hear that," Chris smiled.

"Good. Because I don't break windows anymore!" added Ben. "But why's Andy ignoring me and Leo?"

"No, boys, it's not only you," said Mom. "He's not talking to me either. He's sworn off almost everything that

ANDY GETS CONNED

he loves. No more video games, no more midnight film screenings, no more me. He even passed up Flag Day cake and the goodie baskets I gave you."

"This is way heavier than I thought," said Leo.

"Yeah," said Ben, lifting his basket like a bicep curl. "Did you put some chocolate-covered bowling balls in here or something?"

"Shush," said Mom. "Now if you two want more treats, I have Andy's entire supply with me. He banished all unhealthy munchies and confections from the house, so I loaded everything in the van. Except his two-ton Nielsen's Cheese Curl reserve in the basement, of course; I'll need a few movers to get rid of that. But, worse, he didn't even deliver this snack ban in a dorky way—old Andy would have dressed up like a dwarf and recited his demands from a scroll. Now my son's a miserable adult!"

"We share your concerns," said Leo. "Can we help?"

"That's why I'm here," Mom said, opening the van's rear doors. "Hop in the back so we can chat in secret."

"Don't you worry about your little Sidewalk Sale either," Chris said, heading to the cash register and gulping down a pitcher of Palpitations. "I'll detain any crooks or hagglers on the spot."

"I'm not so positive about this proposal," said Leo. "Let me at least show you the pricing chart, officer."

"Back away into the van," said Chris, readying his gun.

"I'm cooperating!" gushed Leo, backing away.

Ben and Leo then climbed into the van, navigating through walls of flowers, vines, and lush vegetation encompassing its interior. Mom wasted no space here, the van's floor even coated with soil and ferns for her Last-Minute Landscaper special.

"I dig the plants," Leo said, in between sounds of squawking toucans, screeching monkeys, and boa constrictors crunching both previously-mentioned species.

"This is one roomy van," said Ben.

Mom then swung the rear plant-lined doors shut, her interior now looking like a rectangular jungle. Squinting her eyes at Ben, she hobbled up behind him and ripped the phone from his hand.

"Knock off the sound effects," said Mom, shaking Ben's phone as animal noises emerged from its speakers.

"They added realism in here, admit it!" said Ben, muting his phone. "Hey, is that a TV on the vines? Can you grow those now?"

Ben then pointed to a small, portable television in the corner. And Mom swiftly yanked down a screen-like vine curtain, concealing it.

"Please focus, and I'll reward you with snacks," Mom said, removing a tub of ginger snaps from the ferns and sliding it to Ben. "Now, I watched all the Convention Crawl footage on Andy's web page. I'm assuming you boys put that up there?"

"We sure did," said Leo. "Fun stuff, right?"

"Wait, you saw all the content we put up there?" asked Ben, pausing between munches.

"Yes, dear. Everything," said Mom.

"Even the dolphin parts?"

"Everything, Ben. And don't you ever be ashamed of your fetishes, okay? Anyway, after watching Andy and

ANDY GETS CONNED

R2CheeseDoodle get crushed, I'd like to do something nice for him—something he was already planning. And that's why I formed this cloak-and-dagger van gathering today. A council, if you will."

"Are you trying to be epic right now?" asked Ben.

"I sure am. Momma needs to set a dorky tone again. Andy stands upon the brink of destruction of which few could escape alone. He needs assistance and some allies to help flank his inner enemies."

"Okay, this is where you play some background music, Ben," said Leo. "Hit us with something heroic."

"On it!" said Ben, tapping and swiping his phone until orchestral music blasted from it.

"So, do you remember what Andy was working on after the *Space Fightin'* Convention?" asked Mom. "Can you conjure up the dreams he discussed on the balcony? Can you recall the idea brought forth from the ether?"

"No," said Ben.

"We watched so much footage in a row that it felt like we were on ether," said Leo.

"Then let me refresh your minds as a mother who took notes," Mom bellowed, as Ben waved his phone in the air. "Andy went into a creative frenzy during the Convention Crawl. He was enjoying himself outside of the house with friends. And then, in one of his last shots, he spoke about a big idea that could combine all of those; he was going to create his own convention. He was starting a comedy community for weirdos around the world to come together, remember?"

"Oh, that's right!" Leo exclaimed.

"Well I'll be honest with you both, but you can't ever tell Andy this. I snooped in his room when he was on a jog and found all the plans he concocted that night," Mom said, holding up her discovery.

"That's a 3-ring binder with about two feet of sheets," said Leo, flipping through its plastic sleeves. "And are these receipts?"

"Yes, they are. He rented a hotel banquet room, got some vendors, and made all of the arrangements—it's small scale, but all here."

"I bet he cancelled these payments by now."

"He did, but his smooth-talking momma called everyone back and worked magic with her checkbook. That's right, boys, I say we take his idea and run with it. He already did the work. We can have a little party with some friends and a few fans. I'm calling it The Andy Gordon Convention: Samosas Studios Strike Back!"

"Can you be my mom?" Ben asked.

"I looked at the banquet room Andy reserved, and it can fit about 50 people," Mom said. "I know we won't get that many, but we could pull in a dozen or so, right? Can you boys make us some flyers?"

"I think we can facilitate," Leo said, bowing at his leader. "I can offer you my smarts."

"And my graphic design skills," Ben said, kneeling.

"One convention to rule them all," said Mom, now backed by cheerful mariachi music from Ben's phone.

"Sorry, that was next in the playlist!" Ben said, pausing the inappropriate tune. "You want to try that line again with better music?"

ANDY GETS CONNED

"No time," said Mom. "Andy's in a rut, so he won't see any flyers as long as you avoid his new routes around town. Here's a map I made. And before you ask, yes, I tracked my son like an animal."

"Great," said Leo, inspecting the map as Mom opened the rear doors. "So, Andy travels from his house to the school to Alvin's grave and back. That's it?"

"Home then work then death," Ben said. "Got it."

Ben and Leo then poured from Mom's van like a SWAT team, their eyes blinded by the natural sunlight outside. When their vision returned, they spotted Chris folding up card tables on the sidewalk with no merchandise in sight.

"Well, I sold it all," said Chris, lifting up a cardboard box. "Except Ben's *Dolphin Cops*, of course."

"We were only in there for a minute," Leo said, as Chris opened the stuffed cash register. "What'd you do?"

"Maybe I said these profits would improve the police force, maybe I didn't. It's crazy what people will give up when they think it'll make 'em safer!"

"I'm at a loss for words, man."

"Just wait till you see the wheelbarrow full of jewelry I put in the shop," Chris said, jingling fistfuls of keys. "Hell, a few people even gave me their cars! That should keep you goin' for a while, right?"

While Leo rooted through Chris's haul, Ben created funny flyers for the upcoming convention. Capturing screen shots from Andy's video archive, Ben quickly concocted an eye-catching collage. In it, he placed two Andys staring at each other with different looks; for the first picture, Ben used an image from the 'End of Jumbo Andy' vlog. And the second image was Andy dressed as a dwarf in mid-kick from the business convention video. After placing an arrow pointing from the sad Andy to dwarf Andy, Ben added a transformational tagline at the bottom—'Andy Gets Conned.'

Working into the night, Leo restocked shelves with his last inventory from the back. And with profits like today's, Leo had the confidence to invest even more in his shop. So he logically ordered three more heads for the *Alley-Oops* guillotine game—one for each director of the recent *Space Fightin'* sequels that shat upon the original trilogy. While Andy's absence meant that the head selection wasn't quite as historically significant, Leo pandered the best he could without him.

In eco-friendly mode, Leo spammed every Internet board and comment section with an electronic link to the 'Andy Gets Conned' flyer. Ben went the traditional deforestation method, however, making 100 high-quality copies to spread around Bumble Ridge. As Leo and Ben leaned against the copier awaiting their flyers, they both fell asleep to the machine's relaxing hum. After the copier printed flyers throughout the night, Ben and Leo jolted awake from their carpet catnap. Leo's phone alarm sirens now blared, and atop them sat the night's layered accumulation—an unforeseen paper storm that left inches of pulp-based publicity.

"Fire!" Ben panicked, rolling on the floor. "Wake up, Leo! Help me put it out! Stop, drop, and roll!"

"Don't be a spaz. It's my alarm," said Leo.

"Now's no time to argue. I'm firefighting!"

"If that floor were fire, you'd be even more disfigured than Mr. Gentzel right now, dude."

"You're right," Ben said, climbing up the copier. "Well, the flyers are done."

"That's way more than a hundred pieces of paper."

"Yeah, um...add a zero to that."

"You made a *thousand* copies?"

"I did, but it was an accident, I swear!" Ben said, placing more cash into Leo's hand. "And before you say anything, here's money for more ink and paper. See, I'm different now! Come on, we have a lot of flyers to put up today. Let's go paper this toilet town!"

CHAPTER 25

The shop looking like a gerbil cage lined with paper, Leo and Ben scooped flyers into comic boxes. Then they went on their way to barrage the town with America's favorite decoration—shameless advertising. As Andy vaulted over homeless sleepers on his exercise route, Leo and Ben split up to begin the convention's clandestine hype. Ben chose the easy targets first, affixing flyers to old people shuffling down the block. But Leo chose a more dangerous path, entering Three-Fifth Chasers instead.

Leo tiptoed through the speakeasy, disregarding a hundred years of anti-Semitic 'No Solicitors' signs along the way. He then passed biker Peaches slurping down dozens of root beer floats in what had clearly become a problem. Still unnoticed, Leo placed his box of flyers on the bar as Janet toiled away on her next rebranding attraction. Dumping ingredients into her new soft serve ice cream machine, Janet prepared cones, dishes, and sugary toppings at a station on the bar.

"Excuse me, groovy lady," said Leo.

"Shhh," whispered Janet, blocking Leo's mouth with her finger and pointing to the stage.

Across the room, a group of hooded Klansmen now shouted in tongues on stage. And they all held snakes in their hands while convulsing on the floor. The congregation then entered its trance as their leader trickled buckets of pigs' blood on them and pounded the containers like a crime scene drum kit. Monitoring the group from behind a pool table, Zeus the veteran smeared blue cue chalk on his face like war paint, aimed his stick at them, and lined up the perfect attack shot.

Ignoring the confrontation that Zeus was about to start, Leo locked eyes with Janet. And they both smiled despite the lunacy around them. Leo then ran around the bar counter and they hugged, sharing a warm embrace until Janet's relaxed face morphed into neck-flexing terror. Yes, Janet had noticed another shocking squeeze going on at the booth behind them—a boa constrictor now snugly secured around Peaches' neck and face.

"Peaches can't breathe," coughed Peaches, softly.

Leo and Janet rushed to the food chain reversal in motion, both tugging the snake and trying to remove Peaches' restrictive reptilian ski mask. With his comrades in peril, Zeus then zoomed over in his wheelchair and put his pool cue between Peaches' neck and the snake—nearly making a multi-species meat kebab. Everyone now yanking the snake at full power, Peaches converted to all religions in case he asphyxiated. And then he finally broke free with a backward jerk, demolishing another booth just as Andy had done before.

As blood and oxygen flowed normally through Peaches' body, the snake also barely skirted death by soaring inches below an active ceiling fan. But after the snake spiraled through the air and plunged into the churning ice cream machine, it died anyway—quite gruesomely. The four then froze as sounds of garbage disposal-like liquification filled the speakeasy. With an entire clan now snapping out of their trance and glaring at the ruckus, Leo wracked his brain for the most expedient way to smooth over this grumpy group.

"White power?" Leo shrugged, followed by an extra-gritty grinding from the ice cream machine as snake blood splattered the wall.

"Is what we're callin' the ice cream tonight! White Power Vanilla Bean!" Janet exclaimed, wincing and pointing back at the ornamental snake guts. "With a touch o' strawberry sauce. Come and get it!"

"You'll never take me alive!" Zeus screamed, using his leg stumps as battering rams through the speakeasy doors.

"We're missin' a snake," said the bloodied cult leader. "And this ain't no normal snake neither—it's one of our elder gods. Have y'all seen our boa buddy?"

"I can't say that we have," gulped Leo.

"Don't worry, brother. We'll have some o' that there strawberry ice cream till he shows back up."

Janet and Leo then slinked behind the bar, cultists now demanding samples of Janet's tangy ice cream. As Janet served up some snake-flavored burial cones, Leo tended the register until every racist in the place had serpent brain freeze. Fortunately, the cold-blooded snake-cream was such a striking success that the hillbilly cult soon passed out in a communal sugar coma.

"Let's try this again," said Leo. "Long time no see, Janet. Are you still intrigued by this freaky, disco chicken? Or did I lose my chance to dance? Sock it to me."

"I thought ya were blowin' me off last time with the rain check. Ya actually interested in me?"

"I sure am. Business is picking up at my shop, so I have more time for a tryst. I'm in a much better place and mental state too; being further away from bankruptcy's done wonders to the psyche."

"We have a lot to talk 'bout then, sweetie. Not too often I meet an entrepreneurial neighbor 'round here. I'd like to pick your brain 'bout some ideas I have for this place on our first date."

"Quick query, deary. You own this racist place?"

"Sure do."

"Wait, I thought the eccentric, billionaire bigot Kirkpatrick ruled this speakeasy with an iron fist?"

"Well, I don't like to mention that name much anymore. He only runs half o' the establishment with an iron fist. But he's doin' it from an iron lung, so it's only a matter o' time till I get full control."

"Rad, maybe we could converse about some mutually beneficial activities later...for both business and pleasure."

"I'm thinkin' we can arrange that," Janet said, polishing the beer tap that needed no polishing. "So how 'bout tonight then?"

"I'm booked with some off-the-hook obligations."

"Ya have to stop playin' with a lady's heart like that."

"You didn't let me get the rest out. I have obligations, and I want *you* to be a part of them," Leo said, removing a flyer from the box. "Me and my companions are planning this tonight. You should tag along and help us."

"Andy Gets Conned, huh? Is this one o' those geek parties they have over at the convention center?"

"Yeah, but a heck of a lot smaller. This one's in a tiny hotel, and it's all about Andy. If you're up for it, we'd like you to dispense refreshments at the event; we'll pay for everything you need, plus your time. And I'm not just pitching you this idea because we want you to post these flyers in here, either."

"I don't know if I can handle bein' around the big guy again when he's with Tessa. She'll be suckin' his neck wattle, caressin' those irresistible jowls. It'll be pure hell. I'm not even close to over him."

"Let me purify those thoughts. Tessa and Andy aren't talking, so you won't be seeing any public displays of affection," Leo said, embracing Janet's hand with his. "Except from me, of course."

"Sure, sweetie. I'd love to help ya out."

"Great. I'll pick you up here later then. Now let's drag the clan outside. They're unconscious and covered in ice cream, so maybe the killer bees will eat them."

While Leo and Janet worked on Andy's convention plan, Andy continued his path to miserable maturity. Near his upstairs action figures in the hallway, Andy dropped cardboard boxes to the floor and took a deep breath; it was time to expunge. After scribbling the word 'Donate' on each box with a black Nielsen's marker, he sniffed its cheesy aroma. And, in the process, he accidentally gave himself a Hitler ink mustache.

"Today we donate the duplicates," Andy said, picking up a worn Wacky Will action figure. "Time to go, Will."

Andy then placed the figure into one of the cardboard donation boxes, followed by a few more backup copies of the entire Wacky Will line. As his figures rested in their corrugated coffins, Andy shoveled two loads of plastic toy bricks on top of them like a burial site.

"Plastic to plastic, plush to plush," wept Andy. "I'll be back for more of you later."

Soon in the bathroom, Andy paused and raised an eyebrow upon looking in the mirror. His reflection then revealed the repercussions of his toy disloyalty—an unintentional German mustache made via ink.

"Why'd I have to use a permanent marker?"

As Andy went back to the boxes, Ben continued his convention advertising at a mom-and-pop-and-mom-and-mom-and-mom polygamist gas station. And learning from Leo's forced comic purchases at *Space Fightin'* Con, Ben slid the flyers into magazines using hotdog tongs rather than his own fingers.

"Here's one for you, Mr. video game magazine. You too, Mr. model train magazine," Ben said, inserting flyers with the precision of a sleep-deprived surgeon. "And here's one for you, Mrs. bra and panties catalogue that I'm not looking through because I need to help Andy."

"Are you talking to the magazines again?" yelled a gas station attendant, poking her head around the corner. "And what the hell are you doing with my hotdog tongs?"

ANDY GETS CONNED

"It's for a good cause so it's okay!" Ben shouted, running past the clerk and throwing money at her. "But here's five bucks. Please don't report me!"

After Ben rushed to the Fire in Da Hole Indian restaurant and picked up lunch, he and Leo consumed food with their faces at a pneumatic tube's pace. With their stomachs soon full and their curry containers licked clean, the merry misfits began their next method of marketing in front of Leo's shop.

"Are you fueled up for a live video?" asked Leo.

"Sure am," said Ben, streaming from his phone.

"Greetings, Andy Gordon fans. I'm the collection of cells known as Leo, and this collection beside me is Ben. You might recognize us from the videos we've been bombarding Andy's page with. Andy did such a good job with those videos didn't he? Well, in one week from today, we're throwing a party that we think you'll all be interested in. It's a get-together for geeks like us. We're calling it 'The Andy Gordon Convention: Samosas Studios Strike Back!' We'll be there, Andy will too, and best of all...it's free for everybody!"

"One convention to rule them all!" Ben yelled, right as Robby the winged hamster-boy happened to pass by.

"Please don't hurt me!" shouted Robby, sprinting away and bawling his weirdly-dressed brains out.

"Sorry!" shouted Ben.

"Okay, Andy fans, we're going to go help that kid out now," said Leo. "But in the time being, treat this like a pre-order and put Andy's convention on your electronic calendars! See you there!"

Smelling an odd breeze, Ben and Leo looked to their left. And inches away from them, Robby's drunken father blew booze fumes right in their faces.

"Where'd that brat go?" asked Robby's drunken dad.

"No Robby here," said Ben. "How about you leave him alone and let him enjoy his new family in peace?"

"New family?" hiccupped the father. "You think the Bumble Ridge court system actually works? Ha! So, are you guys going to help me beat my kid or what?"

"No, we will not help you beat your kid."

"I'll find him myself then. And I'll hit him extra hard because you both made me mad."

"Hold on, man," said Leo, wrapping his arm around the father. "We're having a rad party with free alcohol. Want to hear about it?"

"Okay, but as soon as you stop talking about the free alcohol, I'm not interested anymore."

As Leo, Ben, and Robby's father continued streaming to VoyeursSlashVanity, Andy scrubbed off his marker mustache with an electric toothbrush and bleach. His flesh could easily grow back, of course, compared to his dignity. Then he changed into plain teacher clothes and headed to his donation boxes once more. With a squeeze, Andy hovered his dad's favorite Pinnette toy above the box...his hand now trembling.

"I'm sorry, Dad. I'm sorry, Pinnette," he cried, dropping it and instantly experiencing separation anxiety.

Andy's whole body then convulsed to the floor, shaking his house's foundation and most of the neighborhood. His geeky hobbies! His connection to

Dad! His mortgage-loan-sized investment in collectables! With unfaithfulness now rippling through Andy like the earthquake shockwaves around his block, he jumped to his feet and took a stand.

"Screw this! I'm keeping the toys!" he shouted, dumping each box out, crushing two, and then tossing both into the last donation box. "Adults can have toys too, dammit! And not just the sex ones either. I've gone too far with my nerd purge! What have I done? I'm cutting out all the wrong things!"

As Andy headed to school, Leo and Ben ramped up the convention's publicity with new recruits. And soon enough, the entire crew spread word around town like a contagious disease. Mom and Emily started first, doling out flyers at the florist shop. Chris joined in next, attaching flyers to all the speeding tickets and violations he gave out. Then Nurse Rosie jumped aboard the hype train too, taping flyers to lollipops for every student who aced their lice exam. And Janet finished up by pimping out the event to every non-prejudice patron who entered the speakeasy. With such teamwork, a small crew left more documents around town than the time the paper mill exploded.

Using cash acquired from today's busted drug deals, Chris finished his rounds by wrapping food items in flyers and giving them to the homeless. Sure, it was a last-ditch effort to prevent single-digit attendance, but it also fed the less fortunate. Thus, it was the least corrupt action Chris performed this shift. Targeting the dire section of town, Chris stopped his cruiser at an alley beside the efficiency apartment complex. With a large crowd now cramming around the cop car, a dark figure lurked behind them. And then it interrupted the frenzy by smashing together garbage can lids like a trash percussionist.

"Disperse, scum!" the figure yelled, still clanging. "There's a soup kitchen down the street giving away better food. I hear they have free sleeping bags, booze, and scratch-off lottery tickets too!"

As the mob abandoned Chris's offerings, the figure dropped his lids and advanced forward in a cowboy-like strut. Stepping into the light that beamed from Leo's sign 14 blocks away, Nathan Hader approached the cop car in his homeless disguise.

"Didn't know there was a soup kitchen in this neighborhood," Chris said. "Where is it again?"

"It's one block that way," Nathan said, pointing ahead.

"My station's on that block. No soup kitchen there."

"That's because I meant this other way," Nathan said, now motioning to his right.

"You're pointin' at Pollen Valley Lake."

"Well then it's this third *different* direction that I'm pointing, officer."

"That's another lake, son."

"And *this* way?"

"That's the last lake you could possibly point to."

"Give me a break. I'm homeless!"

"Okay, well this might brighten your day," Chris said, handing Nathan a brown paper bag. "Best damned peanut butter and honey sandwich you'll ever taste."

"Can I have a few extra?" Nathan said, ripping open the bag and devouring its contents. "I'm eating for 20 right now. I have to regurgitate these to my maggot babies when I get home tonight."

"Take the rest then," Chris smiled, handing over a few bags and pointing at Nathan's wrapper. "You might also be interested in a little event we're havin' on this flyer."

"You're having an event *on* a flyer? That'll be pretty cramped, won't it?"

"No, the event's at a hotel. It's a geek party with free Indian food, so think about comin'. Eat enough spices and you just might flush out all those street parasites you've got in your guts. The info's all on the flyer. Take care now, and best of luck with your maggots."

His good deed now done, Chris peeled away as Nathan inspected the flyer. And then Nathan dashed to his cardboard hut, chewing the gloppy mound of nut paste and bee spit. Soon inside and surrounded by rotten trash, Nathan entered the flyer's web address on his laptop. Leo and Ben's streaming video then played on screen as Nathan hocked up sandwich onto his garbage pets.

"Here you go, maggots. Yummy yummy! I need you big enough to ride into battle soon, so eat up! And while you're scarfing down, look at these nerdy people on Daddy's laptop—they are your enemies," said Nathan, then focusing on the video:

"So, there you have it, freaky folks," Leo said in his robot head, now reenacting the business con kick line with Ben in a dolphin mask. "All your sensory organs have been packed with particulars regarding the Andy Gordon Convention. Wanna watch Samosas Studios strike back? Then be there and embrace your square roots."

"One convention to rule them all!" Ben howled, sending his fists into the air.

"And we couldn't have paid for all these electrifying activities by ourselves. Let's give a big shout out to all the convention sponsors like Mom's Petal Peddlers, Fire in Da Hole restaurant, and Ben's lucrative testicles."

"I highly recommend all three of those," Ben added, quickly correcting himself. "I mean all three sponsors, not my three balls. I do not have three balls."

"How could you not come to a convention with folks as funny as us? Oh, and if you're watching this, Winslow, please respond to our texts. We don't know where you live, and we want you to come too."

"Yeah, please be alive."

Nathan now grinned in his cardboard hut. Then he muted the video stream and closed his laptop, nearly squishing one of his adventurous maggots.

"How perfect," Nathan said, stroking his wormy pets. "This'll be easier than taking a baby from a candy factory. Sweet dreams, maggots. Daddy has some work to do to."

CHAPTER 26

Across town at Bumble Ridge High, Andy dispersed quizzes as thick as bricks. And his students gave him no sass in return, starting their quizzes with a smile. Yes, his stricter policies had paid off, stopping the little bastards from lowering his standards anymore. Even though each cheap desk soon buckled from Andy's heavy-weighted exam, no student made a peep. Such quietness would have lasted the entire class too...if it weren't for B-Fred's quiz falling off the desk and breaking his toes. Despite his orthopedic agony, B-Fred quietly pressed on until Emily made the loudest comment of the morning.

"Shhh," Emily whispered, as B-Fred's hand went up.

"Yes, B-Fred. You can go to the nurse," said Andy.

"No way, Mr. Gordon. I'm not trying to get out of this quiz," said B-Fred, covering his answers. "I wanted to ask you something else. Can we all scatter around the room so people won't cheat off me?"

"What?" asked Andy, as his cheek quivered. "You're kidding, right?"

"No. I studied hard for this quiz. I don't want these lowlifes looking at my answers."

"Wow, okay then. That's an excellent idea, B-Fred. Go ahead and separate yourselves, everybody."

"I don't think we have enough questions on this quiz," said Marcus, scooching his desk to a corner. "And I'm not being snarky either. Will you add a few more questions?"

"I certainly can," said Andy, as both of his cheeks now nervously twitched. "I'll put a few extra on the projector screen for you right now."

"To clarify, these are *not* bonus questions, right?" asked Emily. "We don't want good grades unless we earn it. We want our diplomas to mean something."

"I have to say that you're all kicking some serious butt since I came back," said Andy, his face spasming more than when he almost donated Dad's Pinnette toy.

"I have one more request, Mr. Gordon," Fran said. "Please don't *look down* at me for asking this, but could you make the extra questions all *short* answer instead of multiple choice? I know you might think I'm just making more jokes about my height, but I'm serious."

"Okay I will, but no more talking," gushed Andy, typing questions on the computer while his face contorted like a seizure. "You have 60 minutes to complete this."

Though given the full hour, each student placed their completed quiz on Andy's desk within 15 minutes. More surprising, they also put their phones on his desk to reduce any distractions. His red pen getting no use at all, Andy trembled while grading the stack of quizzes. And his hand shook more with each correct answer. As students

ANDY GETS CONNED

quietly monitored their well-respected teacher, Andy scanned each quiz without marking one single answer wrong for 20 minutes.

"Mr. Gordon?" Emily called out. "How much longer until we get our quiz grades back? I really need to see my quiz grade immediately."

"I'm finishing the last one right now," Andy said, crossing off the final answer and wiping sweat from his brow. "Well I'll be damned."

"What? If I missed one, I'll hang myself."

"Please shut up, Emily. You got them all right. You too, Marcus and Fran. And so did all the forgettable students who never seem to speak in here. Even B-Fred only missed one. I can't believe it...god dammit!"

"I'm trying, Mr. Gordon!" shouted B-Fred.

As if history repeated itself, Andy collapsed into his chair. But now he stared at a room full of engaged, good students. For the second time, Andy was speechless in class. For the second time, Andy's brain imagined his inevitable future—now with perfect pupils. He had improved his class and fulfilled every teacher's desire, yet Andy's facial tics continued to worsen.

"Attention, everyone!" Andy huffed. "You've all complied to my demands. You're learning. We're ahead of schedule. And guess what? I still can't take it! This is still awful! Teaching history is awful!"

Andy's facial spasms then stopped. And his toothy smile raised both cheeks enough to almost block his eyes.

"It's horrible," laughed Andy. "Teaching history is absolutely horrible."

"Oh god, it's another breakdown," said Emily.

"No, my snapping days are done," said Andy, launching from his seat. "I'd like to pay you all back for your hard work though. History's more than papers and quizzes, so it's time for one final assignment under my reign. I'd like you to record a video with your phone about any historical place in town and teach us about it. You know, vlog style. And you can be as funny or weird as you want; make this your own."

"You're kidding," said Marcus.

"Mr. Gordon, please stop playing with our already unstable emotions!" whined Emily.

"No, I'm serious. It's time to use your history knowledge in a practical way," said Andy, the students then shrugging their shoulders.

"We'll take it!" said Emily. "Should we tie it back to *Rejects & Reptiles* or robots or anything like that?"

"No, I'm not forcing my dorky interests on you anymore. Tie the assignment back to your own passions, whatever they are. And before I throw in the towel, I'll give you one last lesson. I've picked up a lot of videomaking wisdom over the years that will help you suck less. So listen up, everybody, here goes!"

"Bittersweet," said Marcus. "You're the one teacher we learn from here. Most just show us how to drink vodka from their thermos."

Andy tossed his history book and dictionary aside. And then he started today's unplanned performance—one lively lecture on video lighting, cameras, and ways to deal with demoralizing feedback online. Interjecting only to

ANDY GETS CONNED

ask relevant questions, Andy's students willingly stayed as his next class crammed into the room too. And before lunch, half the school had grouped together for Mr. Gordon's video lesson while blowing off their other classes. Yes, for the first time at Bumble Ridge High, students had fun. For the first time, student apathy had no chance against Andy's magnificent metamorphosis.

"You're even better at teaching video production than history," said Fran. "And that's no *small* compliment."

"I couldn't agree with you more," said Andy. "Now I better hear the pitter-patter of your teensy feet getting out of here and doing something creative. Don't get stuck like I did for all those years! Good luck out there, everyone! And I don't know if the monkey will be here when you get back or not, but I sure won't. Consider this my mic drop; I'm done teaching forever!"

As students rushed from school and began scouting locations around town, Andy barreled down the hallway with an important delivery—his resignation letter. After leaving the note on Murray's desk, as well as another unmentionable parting gift, Andy bolted for his exit. The school security system then counted down from 10 and he rolled under the titanium security gate that slammed to the ground; Andy had escaped Bumble Ridge High seconds before its nightly lockdown. As the school buzzed with weaponized drones and dark storm clouds blew toward town, Andy headed for the parking lot before his day could get any more dramatic.

Andy now clear of the lethal school shrubberies, its leaves rustled and swayed as another mysterious organism wiggled inside for dear life. Emerging with a rip, the animal appeared—it was no dead bird or lost pet this time, but instead Tessa. She then burst from the bushes and her blouse conveniently converted into a chic sleeveless shirt. Glancing at her pale shoulders translucent enough to display her vein-laden circulatory system, Tessa ran across the street and hopped into her station wagon.

"Dammit," Tessa said. "Where'd he go?"

Now racing to the armed tollbooth, Andy jumped over parking spikes that popped up all around the paved perimeter. And then he pathetically pressed his face against the tollbooth window.

"Hello? I know I'm a few seconds late, but can I get my car out?" Andy pleaded.

"Nope. No way, no how," said a security guard, exiting the booth in a raincoat.

"Please!"

"I'd help you out, but Murray puts a security drone in each booth at six sharp, see?" said the guard, as a drone hovered inside wearing sunglasses, a cop badge, and a bushy mustache. "You'll have to come back tomorrow."

"Okay, well, can you give me a ride then? I have an important meeting to get to."

"You think Murray pays us enough to own a car? I'm afraid I can't help you. You'll want an umbrella if you're walking home though; there's a real bad storm coming."

With the sky darkening and 12-inch death spikes surrounding the lot, Andy rushed to his hatchback and threw his backpack inside. Then the rain came down fast like a lake from the sky. Fetching a tarp from the trunk,

ANDY GETS CONNED

Andy wrapped the lumberjack-bloodied protection around him like a poncho and grabbed an umbrella from the backseat. If four wheels wouldn't be able to get him to his urgent meeting, his feet had to suffice. Yes, Andy ran away through the rainstorm on foot, seeming to step in every mud puddle in his path.

While Andy ventured off in stormy weather, Ben and Leo sought shelter in the hippie van. Leo then revved the engine as Ben cranked up tunes, and the two cruised for about 10 feet until picking up Janet down the block. Though much like Andy's videos online, the van was also being watched from afar. As Leo's van zoomed away, Nathan Hader crept around the corner in a black beanie and matching clothes covered with protein bar crumbs. Nathan then tiptoed to the comic shop's door, pulled back his bare fist, swung it in a circle as if charging up power, and punched straight through the glass.

"Disdain!" Nathan shouted, then pulling a glove from his pocket and slipping it over his bloody hand. "There, that should help."

His throbbing injury now protected by a thick glove, Nathan reached through the broken door and unlocked it with his wounded hand. Unfortunately, Leo's investment in security stickers rather than a security system left the crime scene silent. Before his blood even started to clot, Nathan slipped in undetected. Then he barreled through the shop and annihilated all products in his path, unable to find any of Leo's light switches. After a few knee bangs, stubbed toes, and enough slams to the junk to make him sterile, Nathan plunged into the shop's beaded curtain.

"Bees! Those nerds set a bee trap!" he yelled, ripping the curtain down and stomping their impenetrable, round thoraxes. "It feels like I can't crush you! But you're not moving now, so I must have crushed you. Stupid bees!"

Nathan fondled the wall and flipped on Leo's angelic light, hoping to see the results of his bee obliteration. Instead, the light's beam illuminated Leo's stuffed cash register and counter.

"This is way easier than I expected," Nathan said, slipping off his black beanie and loading all the shop's cash into it, even the coins.

After Nathan placed the beanie back on his head, the collection of change banged his cranium with a metallic jangle. Readjusting his balance from the extra pounds of legal tender, Nathan picked up one of Ben's *Dolphin Cop* comics on the counter. And this revealed an even rarer find underneath—Andy's memory card. Andy's anal qualities coming back to bite him in the ass, Nathan scanned the card's custom label containing the text 'Andy Gordon Video Footage' in several languages.

"Holy crap!" he shouted. "Thank you, gods! I was just going to bankrupt these bozos, but this is even better!"

Nathan's eyebrows jutted up, shifting the cash on his head and shooting quarters from his beanie like a slot machine. He then lifted his bloodied hand in celebration, the hemoglobin gushing just as much as the cash still pouring from his beanie.

"I should probably use some of this to see a doctor," said Nathan, spinning around and spotting the wheelbarrow full of Chris's Sidewalk Sale jewelry. "And this cash too! But now it's time to beat these nerds at their own game. Then maybe I'll see a doctor."

Torrential downpour now struck Bumble Ridge as Andy plodded up the cemetery's hill against winds that could lift cows. His umbrella, flipping inside out seconds after leaving school, had already collected enough water to serve as a portable pond for two horny ducks. But the weather got worse when his umbrella canvas split down the middle, sending gallons of duck-dirtied water to his face like a fowl money shot. The two ducks then attempted flight, made difficult with their genitalia still stuck together, while Andy lifted the tarp poncho over his head. Now peering through the neck hole, Andy reached his father's gravestone while looking like a headless Halloween costume. And then he leaned against it as thick fog rolled in around him, now unable to see more than a few inches on all sides.

"Dad, I have something to tell you, and I hope this doesn't make you hate me. Or haunt me for that matter. I love you...but teaching history sucks!" Andy screamed. "I followed in your footsteps for so long that I made a rut deep enough to be my grave. How'd you do this for decades and make it out sane? And fulfilled? And so damned happy? I had the best day of my teaching career this afternoon and it still did nothing for me. I don't regret the time we spent watching documentaries or correcting the tour guides at museums...but without you around, it's no fun. I miss you, Dad, but history's not for me."

Andy reached into his tarp poncho, removed Dad's replica pistols, and placed them on the grave. With such an admission, all the hair on Andy's arms stood up as if hearing a Wacky Will song for the first time.

"I like making videos! And today made that clearer than ever, so I'm sure as hell not venturing down the safe path anymore. I'm getting out of teaching. I'm making videos again! And I'm going all in this time! I'll be telling my own stories, not reciting ones from the past. And, hey, I'll tell you what, Dad—if you want to star in one of my videos, I'll dig you out of there and we'll get you in somehow. With video budgets as low as mine, I'm quite comfortable working with *skeleton* crews, you know. Did you just roll your eyes or roll in your grave at that joke? Okay, enough wasting this brilliance when cameras aren't rolling. Get ready, Dad. And get ready, Bumble Ridge. Andy 5.0 is here, and nothing's going to get in my way!"

Andy poked his head from the poncho as crunching gravel grew louder. And a red station wagon drove out from the dense fog. As it parked, Andy shielded his eyes from the high beams like a vampire seeing the sun. With lights now brightening the fog, a figure came into view. Yes, Tessa had cornered Andy in one of the worst storms of the season. And she ran right at him, her outfit just as muddied as their current status.

CHAPTER 27

Halfway through her run, Tessa abandoned the gravel path and hit a slick patch of mud. Then her unicorn rain boots acted like skis as she slid to Andy and his rotten Gordon reunion. Forming a finger cross in front of his face, Andy scooted away from the yellow raincoat succubus and hid in a thick wall of fog.

"Be gone, demon!" shouted Andy.

"That's not going to work," panted Tessa. "Let's talk."

"Hello, you've reached the office of Andy Gordon. Andy's not available to speak to any backstabbers at the moment. If you leave your name and number, Andy will totally ignore it and block you forever. So give up now, you damned fraud!"

"No, I won't accept that, Andy. I have questions for you. And these are direct questions that will clear all of this up. We need to talk."

"Actually, we don't *need* to do that," Andy grumbled. "Eating, breathing, sleeping—we *need* to do those, but talking to each other again? Unnecessary. I'd be up for acting like you don't exist the rest of my life though. How's that sound?"

"I don't understand why you're angry at me for being nice to a homeless guy," said Tessa, kneeling beside Andy and patting his poncho. "Are these bloodstains?"

"I'm not falling for your scam again, Tessa."

"No, this is definitely blood. Are you bleeding?"

"I almost killed a lumberjack, but that's irrelevant. You and Nathan fooled me twice, and we aren't going to make this a trilogy."

"I don't think we're on the same page here. We might not even be in the same book. Or library. Nathan and I aren't going to hurt you! He tried to, but—"

"Ah ha! You finally slipped up. You called him 'Nathan!' I heard it!"

"Yeah, well he *is* going by 'Nathan' now. It used to be 'Luke,' but he changed it recently. Give me a minute—this will all make sense."

"Your lies are getting worse by the second," Andy said, pushing Tessa's hand away and curling into the fetal position. "I'm done now. Have a nice life."

Hobbling over the hill in his homeless outfit, Nathan limped up to Tessa and Andy with no downy coat or Droid Blitzer helmet obscuring his dreamy skin. Thus, his face was exposed to the outside world just as much as his unwrapped, infected hand.

"Tessa, there you are," Nathan said, out of breath. "What are you doing with the bridge troll?"

"You know, I'm wondering that too," said Tessa.

"Good! Let's beat him up then!"

ANDY GETS CONNED

"Oh, speak of the devil," Andy said. "Cease fire, Nathan. I just quit my job, so call off whatever attack you two planned. I won't be making any more students miserable like I did to you. Your days of stealing babies and luring carnivorous animals into the class are over. And my days as Mr. Gordon the history teacher are over too. You can both lay off now!"

"Let's go, Nathan," Tessa said, heading for her station wagon. "Andy just answered all my questions. You're right. He's nuts."

"Let's go party at the shelter," said Nathan. "I'll take you to the one where you get two bowls of soup if you look pathetic enough."

"It's a date," said Tessa, kissing Nathan's cheek.

"A date? You said 'date,' right? Victory!" Nathan exclaimed. "And a kiss! You've made me one of the happiest guys in the whole—"

"Cemetery," Andy finished. "Hey look, all the dead people don't give a damn."

"I don't know why I bothered," said Tessa, sulking into the station wagon.

"Well, well, well," Nathan said, approaching Andy. "Your life is ruined, your career is over, and I got the nerdy girl of your dreams. Was it worth it? All you had to do was give me a D in history class instead of an F. And now I'll be giving Tessa lots of D during one long F tonight. Hell, I bet we'll do something sexual involving all 84 letters of the alphabet!"

After a wink, Nathan slid to Tessa's car and got in. As the downpour washed away dirt and exposed all shallow graves in the bargain burial section, Tessa hit the gas. And then she reversed in a semi-circle, knocking down a cheap tombstone that fractured into a thousand pieces. Tessa's rear tires now peeling out on the gravel and shooting stones at Andy, he retreated back into his tarp poncho like a frightened turtle.

"There's only 26 letters in the alphabet, you moron!" Andy shouted through the poncho hole.

A blood curdling howl then emanated from the bargain burial area. So Andy heaved himself up, fanning away fog and revealing a bloated body upon the ground— Winslow on his knees and shouting at the sky. As rain washed away the tombstone particles and a few balsa wood coffins down the hill, Winslow gasped at his lord and savior appearing on the mount.

"Andy! Thank god you're here," shouted Winslow, climbing onto his wheelchair behind him. "That station wagon just swiped the last evidence I had of my family! It sounded like Tessa. Was that Tessa?"

"Good ear. I'm afraid it was."

"That witch desecrated my mom's grave!"

"I'm sorry, Winslow. If you want to take her and Nathan to court, I'll be your witness."

"Thank you! Let's get out of here. I came to pay my respects, not become a lightning rod."

"I'll take my chances. You heard what I said to my Dad—after admitting something like that, I need to spend more time with him. But you should definitely go. There's a groundskeeper shed at the bottom of the hill; that's probably your best shot at surviving with your luck."

"I won't forget this!" Winslow said, kissing Andy's hand. "And thank you, Alvin. Your son is my favorite person in this crappy world. Goodbye, guys!"

Now spooked by thunder, Winslow rolled down the hill in his wheelchair hastily enough to pass Tessa's station wagon. The darkest clouds now above, everyone except Andy fled for shelter; without a doubt, Bumble Ridge's weather patterns were just as unpredictable as its residents. But as wind picked up downtown, Mom still met with the convention planning council—Leo, Ben, and Janet all comfortably seated in her flower delivery van.

"I'm glad that you could all make it," said Mom. "And you must be Janet. Nice to meet you, dear."

"It's my pleasure, sweetie," said Janet.

"Do you call everyone 'sweetie,' dear?"

"I do, sweetie. And do ya call everyone 'dear?'"

"Yes, dear," Mom smiled. "Oh, this is going to be fun. Welcome to the council!"

Chris then climbed inside as cascades of rain struck the metallic van like tiny gun shots.

"Sorry I'm late," said Chris, shutting the doors. "Just finished arrestin' the meteorologist for sayin' there's a zero percent chance of rain today."

"Serves him right," said Mom. "Okay, there's only one more day until The Andy Gordon Convention kicks off. How are we doing? I want a status update from each of you. You first, lover."

"I notified everybody I saw today," said Chris. "The pimp daddies, the hoes, myself in the mirror—everybody!"

"And we plastered flyers everywhere," Ben added.

"Includin' the speakeasy," said Janet. "I got RSVPs from Andy's two best pals there. Peaches and Zeus are definitely attendin' the convention."

"There's a paradigm shift coming, and I can sense it," said Leo. "We'll have no problem passing single-digit attendance now. How many people can the hotel banquet room fit again?"

"About 50, but I'm hoping we can get around half that," said Mom, as the rain became hail. "Gee, it's really coming down out there. That's not your sound effects again, is it Ben?"

"Not at all," he responded.

"That hail's really poundin' the van," said Chris with a grin. "It's like music to these old ears. Reminds me of my days on the battlefield!"

"Vietnam?" asked Ben.

"Nah, I meant my first job drivin' one of those carts around that collects golf balls! Got fired my first day after I rigged up a couple baseball pitchin' machines and shot back at those pricks."

"No matter how low the numbers are, we'll make it work," said Mom, as brick-sized ice now pelted the van. "Don't worry, Janet. Even if it's a small crowd, we'll still need your help distracting people with drinks."

"I'll be there for ya bright and early," said Janet.

"Wonderful," Mom said, then facing Ben and Leo. "Chris and I have one last kink to work out, but all you two need to do is get Andy to that hotel tomorrow. Ben, stop giggling that I said 'kink.' And, Leo, please don't let Ben screw this up."

ANDY GETS CONNED

"Don't sweat it," said Leo. "Ben's strictly responsible for travel snacks and the sing-along harmonies when we deliver Andy. He can't screw this up."

Back at the cemetery, Andy writhed in pain and squirmed as absurdly-sized hail bombarded his body. And a frigid collection formed atop his tarp poncho the size of well-fed cats and small dogs. The frozen precipitation then buried him, Andy protecting his face like all those years of gym class dodgeball that he worked so hard to repress.

"Must resist cold chunks of pain," he said, as ice coated Andy like a long-lost fish stick in the freezer. "We'll brave this storm together until it's over, Dad!"

Though the council's van meeting concluded, Andy's transformation into permafrost continued until the storm subsided around midnight. Marcus, Fran, and a few Goth teens then flocked back to their hill hangout, far away from all the other bothersome breathing people. But when the ice pile upon Alvin Gordon's grave jostled, it startled them more than their unplanned pregnancies would later. Yes, teens flinched as Andy emerged from his frozen mound, now looking like the festive snowman that Principal Murray forced him to be many times before.

After dashing home, taking a hot bath, and asking a few questions on the 'Does This Look Frostbitten to You?' forum, Andy passed out. Warmed and reassured, he then drifted to sleep. A little after sunrise, however, his life again became complicated when two intruders entered his home. Just as Andy's bedside coffee maker started its morning brew, Leo and Ben tiptoed toward him, pulled out air horns meant for large sea vessels, and belligerently blasted Andy with one wicked wakeup call in his snoring face. Andy then jerked up, knocking both air horns down to the floor. And both broke with their buttons stuck in, causing two continuously strident tones that made three grown men shriek like little kids.

"Dammit, guys!" yelled Andy. "What do you want?"

"We demand that you grace us with your presence," Leo said, ending the air horns with a stomp.

"Yeah. We have needs," added Ben.

"This isn't a good time," said Andy, rolling on his stomach. "Please don't talk to me until I have coffee."

"No can do, big guy," said Leo.

"Give me a few minutes until the coffee's done," said Andy, covering up with the dinosaur blankets. "I'm tired. I had a wild time at the cemetery last night."

"That's disgusting even for me," added Ben.

"Shut up."

"Come on, let's hang out," Leo said.

"Few things will get me out of this bed until the coffee's ready," Andy grumbled.

"We found something at the grocery store that you have to see to believe. Your Mom said you're still eating healthy. And it must be true because those pajamas look a little loose in the caboose. We think we're about to rock your world. Nielsen's just came out with some cheese curls that are baked, organic, and mostly vegetable based."

"Yeah," added Ben, scooping out a bag of cheese curls from his snack backpack and seductively crinkling the plastic. "We repeat: We have healthy cheese curls that won't make you fat."

ANDY GETS CONNED

As if Ben had triggered a Pavlovian response by scrunching plastic, Andy heaved up from bed again and nabbed the cheese curl bag.

"Well that's *one* of the things that'll get me up!" Andy said, opening it and tasting a curl. "Hey, these aren't bad!"

"I bet they'll go well with coffee too," said Ben, handing Andy a cup from the coffeemaker.

"I'm glad you guys are here," said Andy, dunking a cheese curl into the coffee. "I figured out my life yesterday. And I think you're both going to like it. I quit two big things that were really bad for me."

"Both rocky and road?" laughed Ben.

"Funny, but no. I quit teaching and Tessa. I kept giving them a chance while they kept kneeing me in the emotional nads. But now they're completely out of my life. I'm finished with both forever!"

"Good! Tessa's so evil that I don't even care that she's hot," said Ben.

"Holy cow!" Leo exclaimed. "Andy banned his abuse, and Ben grew as a human? I think both of my samosas just leveled up!"

"I'm as shocked as you are," said Andy.

"You quit teaching? You really quit?"

"Sure did, and I couldn't feel better. I left my resignation letter on Murray's desk yesterday. He should be finding it about now too."

Over at Bumble Ridge High, Principal Murray entered his office. And then he paused, now staring at a gift box upon his desk. After placing his ear to it and making sure it wasn't ticking, Murray tore the gift open.

"Wait, why's my straw hat in here?" Murray asked, lifting it from the box.

Today his hat happened to be much heavier than usual, filled with the clumpy contents from his pet monkey's litter box. On top of that heap of digested bananas was a Bumble Ridge holiday card with Andy as the school snowman on it. But this time Andy flipped Murray off with both frosty middle fingers. Murray then pinched his nostrils shut, snatching the card and reading its personalized message:

"Hi, Murray. You can shove that corncob pipe up your ass because I quit!" he read. "And I hope you enjoy the enhancements I made to your hat. If you think the monkey poop stinks a little more than usual, it does—human poop's in there too. *My* human poop. Oh, and I stapled a bunch of dead birds from the bushes to your ceiling. You think that's dirty? There's more! Because if you don't fix your school and replace the LegionnAires 2000 air-conditioning in one week, I'm calling the cops, the feds, and a bunch of hippie groups that hate monkey slavery. Got it?"

Slowly tilting his head up, Murray gazed at the hundreds of decaying blue jays and rotting robins attached to the ceiling. As bird intestines dangled above like avian party streamers, Murray ground his teeth. And when he saw that the guts were arranged to spell the words 'Fuck You,' he cracked a couple molars.

"That frosty son of a bitch!" Murray fumed, picking up his phone. "Secretary, I need a new air-conditioning unit pronto. I don't care how much it costs. Do it now!"

ANDY GETS CONNED

Back at Andy's house, all three samosas now sipped coffee upon the bed.

"I don't even have another source of income yet," said Andy, plunging his hand into the cheese curl bag. "And I feel great! I'm finally free!"

"Well this is excellent timing then," said Leo. "Chris helped sell a lot of inventory during a Sidewalk Sale and got me a wheelbarrow full of cool jewelry. I counted up the amount it was worth yesterday, and there's enough to invest in lots of stuff. Since I'm back on track to success, I could probably hire you part time around the shop now."

"Thank you, but I'll pass. I'm back to making videos again. No more half-assing this and doing it as a hobby—I'm all in. And my samosas are going to help every step of the way. You're looking at Andy 5.0, gentlemen!"

"You were already fixed before we got here? What a waste of gas and air horn money," said Ben, Leo promptly twisting Ben's arm behind his back. "I mean, we'll take all the Andy time we can get."

"Holy orc tits! I don't believe it!" yelled Andy, his eyes widening as an orange glow emanated from the curl bag.

"Don't question our visit!" Ben pushed, wincing.

"No, not that. I think it's the Artificially Colored Orange Ticket!" blurted Andy, whipping off his covers. "I won the contest! I won! Look!"

Andy pinched himself more than relatives did to his chubby cheeks throughout childhood. Then he removed a nonedible, orange object from the unbelievable bag. Soon accompanied by Ben playing angelic music from his phone, Andy raised the long-sought object above his head.

Affixed with one wonky LED light taped to an orange piece of cheap wood, the life-changing ticket looked nothing like the crown-shaped one shown on television.

"Things never look as good in person as the commercial, do they?" asked Ben.

"Congratulations, man!" Leo said. "Talk about life changing! This is wonderful, but you probably don't want the curl-tasting job, right?"

"Not a chance! I'm focusing on videos now. Nothing's distracting me from that. Plus, the food job would really wreck my new diet. Even if they let me spit the curls out, it'd be too tempting; I might relapse. And these things leave an awful aftertaste with whatever they coat them with," said Andy, inspecting the ingredients. "Yup, I thought so—embalming fluid. Let's go redeem the cash equivalent prize instead though!"

"To the factory!" shouted Ben. "There's even more good news. We packed the van with healthy snacks to lure you out of your house. So we have road snacks now too!"

"Hey, that's great! Things are really looking up again," said Andy. "And don't you worry, I'm not letting the prize money go to my head. You'll both get a lump sum for your support over the years. I'll help fund the shop way more than I could before, Leo. And, Ben, we'll get you a complete collection of *Dolphin Cop* comics—maybe an entire warehouse full of them. Oh, and I can finally get Winslow good health insurance too."

"Is he still alive?" asked Leo.

"Yeah, and his worst years are behind him once he gets this cash. I need to shower quick, then we'll head to

ANDY GETS CONNED

the factory," Andy said, vanishing to the bathroom and continuing the conversation. "We'll shoot some funny videos there too if they let us! People love watching other people go through pivotal moments like this. I'll meet you down at the van, samosas!"

"He's already planning out what to do with all the money," whispered Leo. "This is dangerous, dude. I don't think we thought this through."

"We're in too deep! It's the point of no return," pushed Ben. "Great, Andy! We'll see you at the van!"

CHAPTER 28

As Leo and Ben hurried downstairs, Andy's singing shot through the house at an opera star's volume without any of the skill. They both then rushed back to Leo's hippie van and loaded inside, one step closer to delivering today's oblivious guest of honor.

"Apparently Andy reincarnated overnight," Leo said from the driver's seat. "He respawned before dawn."

"Yeah, he didn't need our help at all," Ben added, sliding open the door behind him. "Here he comes."

"Act as normal as you can."

Andy bolted over and then crammed in the backseat between treats still in their bulk food dispensers from the supermarket. Weirder, some floor tiles were stuck to the bottom of each one. Tossing his skateboard and backpack beside him, Andy straddled a sack of apples on the floor as if mounting a red horse.

"Welcome back, man," said Leo, starting the van. "Have a seat and a treat!"

"Where'd you get all these dispensers?" asked Andy.

"If you throw enough cash at a manager, you can buy anything at the grocery store," Ben said. "Anything."

"And where'd you get the money to do that?"

"You don't wanna know, dude," said Leo.

"Okay, fair enough," Andy said, pulling one of the dispenser levers. "Oh, dried chickpeas? And you got the nut-free factory ones so I won't die. Thanks, guys!"

"You're welcome," said Ben, biting his lip. "Also, did you notice how I didn't laugh when you said the words 'chickpeas' or 'nut-free?'"

"That's commendable, Ben! But I'm ready for the car to move now! Let's talk and drive at the same time."

"Right," added Ben, leaning forward.

Ben then opened Leo's glove compartment, removing three pairs of sunglasses behind a bunch of recycled napkins and kombucha bottles. After Ben handed Leo and Andy their pairs, all three dramatically whipped the sunglasses onto their faces. And for the last badass action, Andy took a bottle of sunblock from his backpack and squirted a dollop into everyone's hands.

"Hit it!" shouted Andy.

Leo revved the van's engine and zoomed down the driveway, sideswiping Mr. Gentzel's garbage cans.

"I can't see!" Leo screamed, swerving onto the street.

"Ditch the glasses. Ditch the glasses!" Andy advised, smacking the sunglasses off Leo's face.

"Hey!" screamed Mr. Gentzel from his yard. "So you're the thugs who keep wrecking my cans!"

"Sorry, Mr. Gentzel! I'll get you new garbage cans when we come back—I promise. Please don't shoot us!"

ANDY GETS CONNED

"If I don't see new garbage cans here soon, I'll shoot your house with this rocket launcher. You touch, you buy!" demanded Mr. Gentzel, extracting a rocket launcher from his bushes and then shooting it into the sky. "Uh oh. The safety was off!"

"Hit it faster!" Andy shouted, slapping Leo on the shoulder. "Now! Faster, Leo!"

"I already gave you one acceleration," said Leo. "I'm not wasting gas and suffocating nature with two."

"If we blow up, all your gas is gone. That's not fuel efficient! Floor it now or we die!"

Leo complied, racing away from a neighbor who clearly hadn't had that much weapons training. From the rearview mirror, the trio tracked a small object plummet back down to its origin and land in a fiery explosion.

"Poor Mr. Gentzel," Andy sighed, munching some chickpeas. "Those old facial scars were finally starting to fade. Maybe I can give him some of my money for anger management classes and help him out."

"He'll need cash for new skin grafts too," Leo said.

"I'll call an ambulance, but don't stop this van until we hit an electronics store. I need to make a minor purchase before we get to the Nielsen's factory."

Minutes later, Leo and Ben slurped fountain drinks in front of a plaza while awaiting Andy's return. Ben then twisted his head toward Harry's Hardwarriors—the town's disturbingly hawkish hardware store.

"Hey, it looks like Harry got another Killer Bee Defense shipment in today," Ben said, as a stream of customers exited with bug zappers and flamethrowers.

"We should invest in some protection too," said Leo. "There's tons of those fuzzy buzzers around here now."

"Should we stock up then? My treat!"

"Don't sweat it yet just yet. Andy should be back soon. I wonder what he's up to in there. I thought he was making a minor purchase."

Andy then emerged from the electronics store, now carrying two stuffed shopping bags.

"He has no job and thinks he won money! We screwed up big time," said Leo.

"I'm hoping for one of those cheesy moments where he realizes friends are more important than money so he's not pissed at us," Ben said, as Andy flung open the door and belly-flopped inside.

"Hey, big guy. What capitalistic, conglomerate pig dogs did you support today?" asked Leo.

"None," said Andy. "I know this is a bad way to break the news to you, but you're both accomplices in theft right now! Go go go!"

"Are you joking?" Leo asked, shifting and heading in reverse. "I'm bookin' it in case you're not joking!"

"Does it look like I'm joking? Get us out of here!"

"Obey the crazy man!" Ben panicked. "He must have crashed and rebooted in pirate mode."

"Would you do me a solid and tell me what the hell you stole?" questioned Leo, blowing through a red light onto the highway. "Why would you do this today?"

"I may or may not have exaggerated to get you to go faster," Andy smirked. "To be fair, the prices were so low in there that it did feel like I was stealing."

ANDY GETS CONNED

"Not cool!" shouted Ben. "When there are sales like that, you tell your friends first, dammit!"

"He fibbed, dude," said Leo, slowing to a crawl. "Economical cruise control it is."

"Whatever," said Ben. "Are you going to show us what's in those bags or do I have to look myself?"

"I got us a little something to celebrate," said Andy, removing a box from the bag. "A new, top-of-the-line, super-ultra-high-definition video camera with attachable telephoto and wide-angle lenses. There's a tripod, a shoulder rig, and even a button to stream video directly to the abandoned social media outlet of your choice."

"Then what's in the other bag?" asked Ben.

"Their entire stock of batteries," Andy said, dumping them into his backpack.

"How'd you swing the cost of that?" asked Leo.

"I emptied out my retirement account. Who needs a few grand when you have half a million coming?"

"What? You better keep those receipts in case you need to take anything back, man. You know, to be safe," said Leo, exiting the highway as his unassertive GPS advised him to take a right if he felt like it.

"Receipts are for wimps. I'm all in, remember? Wait a minute; you took the wrong exit. The cheese curl factory is a few miles ahead."

"Sorry, I could have sworn the factory was here," Leo said, driving into a hotel parking lot. "How about you pop on out and ask the staff where the factory is?"

"I know where the factory is. I've been detained by its staff for trespassing on multiple occasions. And I'd rather not go into the hotel if you don't mind; I booked this place when I was trying to start a comedy convention for us. They aren't too happy that I cancelled."

"Stop talking and look, Andy!" shouted Ben.

Leo stopped as Ben reached behind him and slid open Andy's door for the big reveal. A large banner on the hotel displayed the text 'Geek Convention Moved to the Zimmerman Event Center,' as Andy peered outside.

"There's another convention over at the Zimmerman Center today?" Andy asked. "We should check that out after we shoot some vlogs and get the cheese curl cash."

"Uh, yeah," said Leo, locking eyes with Ben and clearing his throat. "We'll swing by on the way back."

"Why aren't you moving? Move!"

"Well, Andy. We better tell you the truth," said Leo.

"There's no time for the truth!" interrupted Ben. "How about we play a game first?"

"Yes, a game to distract me from whatever you two are being weird about today," Andy said. "Sounds good."

"I'll describe something I see while you guys guess with your eyes closed," Ben said, hindering Leo's vision with a hand to the face.

"Leo needs to drive, so I think he should do the describing part," Andy said. "My eyes are closed! Go!"

"I spy with my third eye," Leo teased. "A metal object in the sky decorated with symmetrical, flashing lights."

"It's a flying saucer!" Andy guessed.

"Not quite," said Leo, as Ben rooted through his snack bag. "It's a helpful dude who intervenes from above to stop human disasters."

ANDY GETS CONNED

As Andy opened his mouth about to reiterate the UFO answer, Ben removed a jar of beef jerky and fished out a wooden tube from it. Like a passenger seat ninja, Ben aimed the tube at Andy and blew. Then a dart shot into Andy's neck, knocking him out and sending his face straight into the apples.

"You want to take a guess while you're bobbing for apples, big guy?" asked Leo. "No? How about you, Ben?"

"I wasn't listening," said Ben. "I was too busy fixing our problem."

"Problem? We don't have any problems. So...nobody has a guess then? I spotted a traffic light. Get it, guys?"

"It's okay, Leo. He's out," Ben said, presenting his blowgun as Andy snored.

"Dude, what did you do?"

"You put me in charge of the snacks. So I fixed our problem with snacks."

"If he's dead, it's your fault. And you'll have to deal with his mom's wrath, not me!"

Reaching the Zimmerman Center minutes later, Leo inched his van through traffic thicker than rush hour construction during an asteroid evacuation. With Ben blasting Wacky Will music and waving chickpeas under Andy's nose like smelling salts, the dart sedatives soon wore off. Then regaining consciousness, Andy shook his head, stretched with a yawn, and filled a bowl with healthy cereal from one of the food dispensers.

"Hey, big guy. You enjoy your nap?" asked Leo.

"Where are we? How long was I out? And why is there a bandage on my neck?" Andy asked, inspecting the cars around them while taking a bite. "Wait, we're even farther from the cheese curl factory now. Do you *not* want me to be rich and share money with you? I need to be at the cheese curl factory to do that!"

"We have some good karma news and some bad karma news," said Leo.

"Give me the bad first."

"You didn't really find the orange ticket," Ben said.

"We figured that was the only way to get you out of your rut," added Leo. "We didn't know you'd evolve and fix yourself first."

"We were only trying to help," said Ben. "The good karma news is better though."

"But I *did* win! What's this ticket if I didn't win?" Andy panicked, balancing his cereal on the apples. "There's undeniable evidence right here!"

Andy rummaged through his backpack and raised the orange ticket into the air. Its crudely attached LED light then plopped into the cereal, splashing milk upon the ticket. With the ticket's paint now softening, Andy scratched some off with his fingernails and revealed the real object underneath—a car's air freshener.

"You tried to help me by making me think I was rich when I wasn't really rich? I'm failing to see the logic here," grumbled Andy.

"That brings us to the good news," said Ben, sliding open Andy's door again at their new location.

Andy peered out, his eyes locking on pictures of himself far bigger than he had ever seen. Beneath the images, an even larger banner flapped in the breeze. And this banner contained some rather unexpected text—'The Andy Gordon Convention: Samosas Studios Strike Back'—printed in a glorious eight billion size font.

"That's right," shouted Ben and Leo. "The Andy Gordon Convention!"

"The...*me* convention?" Andy asked, softly.

"That's right, man," said Leo. "You got conned. Your videos have been blowing up all over the Internet since you last looked."

"So we threw you a party and invited some of those fans," said Ben. "Please be too happy to strangle us."

"You did it. You guys pulled off my convention idea?" Andy said, spastically shaking in the back seat enough to wear out the van's shocks. "I kinda regret emptying my retirement account now. Oh well—we can make that money back after we crank out more video content, right? Let's go shoot some vlogs, boys! Who needs money when you have friends like this?"

"I knew he'd say that," whispered Ben.

"Woo!" Andy shouted.

As the van seesawed left and right, Leo and Ben held onto the dashboard. And they both barely stopped themselves from getting launched through the windows. The conservative parents in a car behind them had a slightly less joyful moment, however, shielding their kids' eyes from such unholy van rocking in public. When Leo parked the van and three men emerged, the virtuous car parents grew even more uncomfortable. And the parents started praying as loud as possible, hoping that their honks would bring on the rapture.

As Andy rushed ahead with his camera and the parents looked up all nearby baptism locations, Ben and Leo jogged after their friend to the entrance. With their plans unknowingly changed, the two shrugged their shoulders at one another mid run. And they were filled with even more questions than the conservative kids stuck in traffic. How did Mom pull this off with so little time? Why was their convention moved to the Zimmerman Event Center? And perhaps even more importantly...just who was waiting inside?

CHAPTER 29

Andy swung open the convention doors and came to a standstill, now greeted by crowds of creatures in geeky garb from a century's worth of wedgie-inducing fiction. Though, this time, most attendants sported a new outfit—the one and only dwarven baker Jumbo Shrimpit. Yes, each Jumbo man, woman, and child now bonded in their braided, beaded, and well-burnished beards. Adding their own flair, each attendant also accessorized based on Samosas Studios' video catalog; some sported red ties and space helmets while others wore Andy's teacher clothes. A few ladies even came as cleavage-exposed, sexy variants of Andy in short skirts, likely confusing all teenage boys and their sexual orientations for years to come.

"I thought you said this was a small party, guys!" shouted Andy. "There are enough dwarfs in here to start a mining operation."

"We had no clue, dude," Leo said. "We're surprised by the size too."

"Seriously?"

"Yeah, he's not lying," said Ben, wearing his snack bag like a backpack. "I don't know what shocks me more—that so many people came today *or* that these chicks look so damned good with beards."

Moving aside, the fans snapped pictures of their favorite Internet trio while Andy streamed to the JumboAndy video page. Andy then panned his camera across the room as two fans rushed toward him. The first fan, a blonde-haired supermodel, sprung forward with her long runway legs. And following the model, a rotund hunchback woman swiftly waddled behind like a handicapped camel.

"Hurry up. Andy's here," said the supermodel. "I need you to stand beside me and make me look hotter."

"Not if I get to him first," grumbled the hunchback.

"There he is! Andy! Andy Gordon! Look at me!" badgered the supermodel, as Ben and Leo shielded him like secret service agents.

With the supermodel stopped at Andy's defensive line, the hunchback ran around Leo and Ben. And then she latched onto Andy with her hairy, muscular arms.

"I can't believe it. It's the best vlogger of all time," confessed the hunchback, squeezing Andy with the strength of a gorilla.

"Thank you," grunted Andy, still recording as all air left his lungs. "God, you're strong."

"No way!" the hunchback cried, as she released Andy and inspected her hands. "I'm drenched in Andy's sweat!"

"You are! You are!" squealed the supermodel.

"Help," eeped Andy.

ANDY GETS CONNED

"Andy's off the market, ladies," said Ben.

"Okay, then. We'll just go sniff his sweat in the hotel room instead," sighed the supermodel.

"If you're interested, I'm looking for a relationship right now," offered Ben.

"Gross," said the supermodel.

"Excuse me, I was talking to your more desirable friend," Ben corrected, putting his arm around the hunchback. "She's quick and clever. Plus, it looks like there's no sofa she couldn't lift herself."

"No thanks," added the hunchback. "Maybe some other time when we're more desperate."

"Ben rejected the beauty, but got burned by the beast," Andy said, hugging Ben with one arm and still streaming. "That's a good ending for this video. Some lady's bound to give you a sympathy date if they see it. Do you mind if I keep it up on the website, Ben?"

"You can leave it up there," sulked Ben. "If it helps me find my soul mate, I'll deal."

"And done!" said Andy, pressing buttons on his camera. "The first video's up for everyone to see! No editing for us today; let's upload so much embarrassing footage that we'll never be employable anywhere else!"

"We have tons of fun lined up for you today," said Leo, B-Fred then tapping Andy's shoulder while dressed as Pinnette from *Space Fightin'*. "But we might not get to show you anything if these people keep interrupting us."

"Are you kidding? This is spectacular," said Andy. "I'm going to hug you both harder than the hunchback just did to me."

"Will you be in our vlog?" asked Fran, popping out from behind B-Fred with Marcus.

"And sign my whiteboard?" queried Marcus, hoisting up a whiteboard with the text 'We Knew Andy Gordon Before He Was Cool.'

"Then you'll hold my baby, right?" begged B-Fred, lifting his bearded baby to Andy's face. "He won't be any trouble. He just had a nap and another coat of butter."

"My pleasure," Andy said, signing Marcus's whiteboard while cradling B-Fred's baby. "Great costumes! Especially you, B-Fred. You know Pinnette's my favorite character."

B-Fred twirled in his traditional Pinnette attire, an all-leather pilot's jumpsuit with light-up spikes down the shoulders used in the original trilogy. A cloth supernova sun stretched over B-Fred's sumo stomach as well, with an extra buttery set of three-lensed sunglasses on his face.

"Well geez. I never would have thrown you through the window if I knew that," said B-Fred.

"So what's the vlog?" asked Andy.

"We're doing a video for the history substitute about your teaching career," said Fran. "We're saying it counts as history since you don't do it anymore."

"Plus, we learned that the Zimmerman Event Center was built on a Native American burial ground," said Marcus. "Applicable yet ominous, right?"

"You're all weird and I love it!" shouted Andy. "I never expected to see you here."

"Oh yeah, half the school took a sick day so they could come see you," said B-Fred. "Some teachers even

ANDY GETS CONNED

showed up. Mr. Schmidt and Ms. Cartagena brought all their students here for a field trip."

"Are you ready for our vlog?" reminded Fran.

"Sure am. Let's make some magic," said Andy, as Fran applied makeup to his face.

"I'll be back in a few," said Leo, pulling Andy's 3-ringed convention binder from the snack bag and inspecting it. "I need to go check the rest of these sets and make sure all the lights are right for the shoot."

"Sets and lights for video content? This sounds awfully similar to my plan," said Andy, snatching the binder. "And this binder *is* mine. You pulled off *all* of my old arrangements?"

"We were just helpers," said Ben.

"Yeah, your mom had everything covered," Leo said. "But she took the binder from your room, not us."

"And then she told us about your plan in an epic speech that belonged in a movie," added Ben. "We can reenact it on the fantasy set later if you want."

"This is too good to be true, but I'll see you soon," said Andy. "Hey, Fran! I'm ready for your vlog; I don't think I can smile any wider."

"Have fun, big guy," said Leo. "I'll meet you both in the auditorium later."

Nearby, a small group of Andy fans packed inside a photobooth equipped with video cameras to capture fan testimonials—one of many booths around the hall. Jetlagged after her long flight, the old Kiwi woman who had supported Andy from afar now squeezed between the two English fans like a can of international sardines. As she handed them two bottles of ale, the chaps shimmied sideways and squished Andy's Alaskan teen devotee against the booth wall. And, conveniently, his face activated the 'Record' button.

"We traveled the farthest, so we must like you most, Andy," the teen groaned.

"We're knackered after our flight, yes we are," said one of the chaps, toasting his ale. "But we're tickled to bits to be 'ere even 'round this ankle biter, ain't we?"

"Things are 'bout to get real cheeky wit all 'ese anoraks and alcohol 'ere," said the other chap.

"I took a tiki tour from the wop-wops to get here, so I trounce all these munters with my Andy fandom," said the Kiwi woman with a grin.

"I don't know if it's my age or the concussion, but I have no idea what you three are saying," laughed the Alaskan teen, toasting his diet root beer. "To Andy!"

In another video testimonial booth beside them, Robby the hamster-dressed boy tiptoed up to the camera. After pressing 'Record' in his booth, he began whispering a rather unconventional testimonial for Andy.

"If anyone sees this, please save me from my dad," Robby sobbed. "Every time the courts take me away, he gets me back somehow. Bumble Ridge is a hell I can't escape. Help me, Andy. You're my only hope."

"Hey, are you ratting me out?" said Robby's drunken father, stumbling into the booth.

"No, Dad. You're a great dad. Please don't kill me."

"Don't make me hit you and hurt my hand again. Now scram! I gotta take a leak before we leave."

ANDY GETS CONNED

Robby fled as his drunken dad unbuckled his belt and unzipped his pants. Then the father put his hand on the wall, ready to make this particular booth unbearable for the rest of the day. Patting down the seat, he shifted his eyes to a blinking red light on the booth's camera.

"Where's the toilet hole in this thing? Hmm, what's this red light?" asked the drunken father, then reading the sign. "Share some words about Andy Gordon for a convention video? Is this how I activate the toilet hole? Okay then, I'll do my best. So, when I met Andy, I wanted to punch his face in. But then I saw his videos, and he became the kinda guy you want to have a beer with. Then a few shots with. And then maybe a couple crates of moonshine with. Okay, so I have a drinking problem, but you get the point. Andy's great, and I really need to go to the bathroom. So open up!"

Not far from the main hall, Janet the bartender wiped down a table of Andy-themed merchandise with a rag. The Andy bobbleheads now clean and jiggling, Janet activated a neon sign of dwarven Andy above her. And then she immediately became the center of attention, all nearby fans flocking to the new, shiny object in the room.

"T-shirts, toy robots, bobbleheads to watch ya while ya sleep. It's a one-stop shop for all things Andy," Janet said. "I got snacks and booze too!"

"Excuse me, Miss," laughed Andy, emerging from the crowd with Ben. "We saw you rubbing the bobbleheads' nether regions. Right in front of kids too. Pretty creepy."

"Howdy, guys!" said Janet. "Welcome! Would ya like some Andy-branded cheese curls?"

"Would I?" exclaimed Ben, taking a bag from Janet's hands and giving her a 50-dollar bill. "Keep the change."

"Wow, thank ya, Ben," Janet said. "Ya' interested in any curls, Andy?"

"No thanks," said Andy, pointing the camera at his stomach. "I've lost a Thanksgiving turkey's worth of weight, and I'd like to keep it that way."

"You're lookin' great. Don't lose all o' that neck wattle though—it looks good on ya. How 'bout a diet root beer on the house then?"

"Make it two," replied Andy.

"And put it on *my* tab," said Ben.

"Would ya like it in a bottle?" asked Janet.

"No," replied Andy.

"A mug?"

"Not that either."

"Then how would ya like it?" asked Janet, popping open two bottles.

"How about I slurp it straight from your navel instead?" suggested Andy, wiggling his eyebrows.

Janet gasped, accidentally jerking the root beer bottles backward and sending foamy streams into the air.

"I thought ya'd never ask," she sighed, handing Andy and Ben a new bottle. "I'll think 'bout that navel drinkin' proposition though. Okay, sweetie?"

"Great. And I will too," said Andy with a wink. "A lot! Catch you later."

Andy grabbed Ben's arm and the two strutted away. As Andy pushed on, Ben peered back at the spiky-haired female biting her horny lip with her hornier teeth.

"I've never had a woman look at me like that," said Ben. "I'm glad you're back in the game!"

"Yeah, it'll be tough to trust any estrogen after what Tessa did. But Janet's always been nice to me and she's cute, so I'm finally going for it," said Andy, squeezing Ben closely. "And that means we're finding you a lady in our next video stream; I'll be your wingman. Ready?"

"I'm game. Lights, camera, action! And I mean both types of action!"

Andy and Ben guzzled their diet root beers as Robby's drunken father staggered between them holding his beverage—a jug of moonshine with multiple X's etched on the side. Playing along, Andy and Ben wrapped their arms around him as they all chugged.

"You're a good drinking buddy," disclosed the drunken father. "You make me forget about my little hamster-boy accident."

"We need to talk about that," Andy said, passing his camera to Ben and pressing his face into the drunken father's. "We just recorded you, and you're clearly drunk before noon. That's damning enough to make you lose Robby even in Bumble Ridge's broken court system. So if you want to avoid jail, here's how you're going to put him up for adoption the right way—now listen!"

As Andy and Ben worked on ending Robby's scarring childhood, Mom exited the Tinkering Wizards computer fix-it shop miles away from the convention. After rushing to the flower delivery van, Mom hopped in the passenger's seat and shooed bees out of the window as Chris lowered his magnum revolver.

"Hittin' those bee bastards is harder than you'd think," said Chris, unloading the gun. "Any luck inside?"

"They don't know when she'll be back."

"Damn. I'll get the whole force on this search if I have to. Maybe even break out the old coon dogs. Hold the phone, is that her?" Chris asked, pointing ahead of them.

Mom peered forward, spotting Andy's friend Winslow on crutches now gimping down the sidewalk. Seeing Mom and Chris, Winslow quickly heaved his cast-wrapped and burlap sack-surfaced body toward the van.

"My goodness, no," said Mom. "That's Winslow."

"I meant *behind* that thing," Chris said, pointing.

Now closer to the van, Winslow grinned and waved at Chris's misinterpreted signal. Without any attempt to let a man down easy, Mom and Chris vigorously shook their heads and pointed in an upward arc around him. Then passing behind Winslow, Tessa paused and squinted at all of the nonverbal communication now in view. After processing her likelihood of being kidnapped, Tessa waved back with a forced grin.

"Get ready to drive like hell and break some laws," said Mom, buckling her seatbelt.

"Copy that!"

Chris revved the van and accelerated toward Tessa as the persistent bee swarm trailed behind in pursuit of flowers and Flag Day snacks. When Chris slammed the brakes seconds later, every bee splatted into the van's rear doors and liquefied instantly before Mom hopped out.

"Hi there," said Tessa, as Mom pushed her to the van's rear doors and opened them.

ANDY GETS CONNED

"No time for small talk. Get in the van."

"Geez, you sound like my uncle," said Tessa, teasing.

"That's disturbing. Now get in the van. There's a surprise party for Andy and—"

"No, I...I can't go. I'm sorry."

"I'm afraid you cut me off too soon about why we're here. It's an Andy party. It's a place for friends, family, and fans to be happy. And we don't want you anywhere near the damn place, got it? In exchange, we'll drive you to the spa, pay for it, and even throw in some extra hush money so we never hear from you again."

"What?" questioned Tessa, as Winslow approached behind her.

"Move, you big bully!" shouted Winslow, heaving himself closer. "Can I go to the con? Please let me go!"

"Sure, dear. We're headed there after we drop Tessa off," Mom said, as Winslow loaded himself in the van like a nesting sea turtle at the beach. "Hurry it up, Tessa! Get in. It's an offer you can't refuse."

"Mom!" Tessa huffed, pulling a white handkerchief from her utility belt.

"No, I'm not your Mom anymore—it's Mrs. Gordon."

"I won't go to Andy's party. I swear! If you see me anywhere near the place, you can lock me up forever. Or better yet, you and your cop friend can wipe me out like you just did to all those bees," Tessa sobbed into her handkerchief, then bolting away.

"Don't ever mess with a pissed off mother," Mom snarled, climbing into the van with Winslow. "And don't you ever go near my son again!"

"Fine! Whatever you say!" Tessa cried, fleeing.

"I'm watching you, you red haired ginger witch! Keep running! Keep running!"

With a group of mothers at the nearby park applauding Mom's retaliation, Tessa waved her white handkerchief in the air from a distance and escaped to her duplex. Mom then leaned outside the van and pounded its rear door twice with her fist, spraying some of the smashed bee guts across her face.

"Hey, Chris, change of plans!" Mom shouted, removing paper towels from her bra and wiping her face. "Head straight for the convention instead. I think Tessa got the message."

"Hold on to that tushy, Toots. We'll be there in no time!" Chris said, peeling away as Mom shut the doors.

"Wow, there's so much room in here," Winslow said. "And there's a TV! Can I live here? The plants make me forget about the nightmare that is my existence."

"What's with the burlap sack shirt, dear?"

"I bet on a stupid robot and lost my life savings," Winslow sighed. "So most of my wardrobe had to be repurposed as boat sails to help pay the rent. And that's why I have these second-hand crutches too."

"I'll buy you some new clothes at the convention. You should be in a wheelchair too. You look too hurt to be on crutches—cheap crutches, at that."

"Oh, I had a wheelchair. My insurance company only covered it for a few days though, then they got me these crutches instead. Tomorrow they're downgrading me to a bubble wrap suit."

ANDY GETS CONNED

"That is so sad. But we'll be at the convention in no time. While you wait, here's some of Andy's snacks to help you heal."

"No way! Is this Flag Day cake?" Winslow munched, as the van barreled down the bike lane and over a couple of its occupants.

Back in one of the convention center's testimonial booths, Bumble Ridge's art instructor held a large painting draped with cloth. Removing the fabric, she then revealed an oil painting of Andy getting crucified with mounds of cheese curls around him.

"Andy's such a positive influence on the world. He's loving. He's kind. This man even knocked over my students' work so they had to buy more overpriced supplies from me. What a godsend!" she said, as the one-armed lumberjack barged into the booth.

"Yeah, when the big guy hacked off my arm, I was angry. When my stump got infected and I almost died of gangrene, I was damned near irate. But when I got an endless supply of painkillers, all that hatred left my body quicker than my arm did," gushed the lumberjack. "Plus, the docs found cancer they wouldn't have seen without Andy's accident, so he saved my life. You think he'd cut off my other arm so I can see what's hiding in there too?"

"No, you are aesthetic perfection," said the art instructor. "I must paint you."

Just then at the registration table, another unexpected guest had arrived. Yes, as if throwing a wrench into the gears of a wrench factory, Nathan Hader plowed through crowds in his Droid Blitzer helmet, cape, and matching leotard. Likely to change the day's events quicker than a bomb threat, Nathan forcefully advanced his cart topped with a dusty, blue tarp.

"Move, nerds. I'm a veteran," Nathan said through his helmet's voice synthesizer, nudging past eager fans.

"Peaches don't like cutters. You just made Peaches mad," shouted biker Peaches in line, fully ripping off Nathan's helmet.

"Well I didn't like cutters either when I was tortured. In the war," said Nathan, forcing his helmet back on. "I can cut because you owe me, you draft-dodging coward."

"Peaches remembers you from the speakeasy. You flipped off Peaches and his friend Andy," he said, squeezing his fists so tight that all his knuckles popped at once. "Peaches will contain his rage...for now."

"That doesn't surprise me that you know him. You're both weak. Now shut up; I'm next," Nathan said, turning to student Emily at the registration table. "Let me in now."

Before Emily could speak, she gagged at an overpowering stench wafting from the cart. Pinching her nose, she handed Nathan a folder with Andy's dwarven face printed all over it.

"Welcome to the first ever Andy Gordon Convention, Droid Blitzer," coughed Emily. "I don't remember your intergalactic shopping cart from the movies at all."

"It was in a deleted scene. Now let me in. I'm a vendor with goods to sell to these nerds."

"Okay, so let's see. You're selling...dead fish apparently?" Emily asked, looking at his cart and then her list. "I don't see 'dead fish' on here."

"It's sushi," Nathan said, peeling back the tarp and revealing lifeless fish. "People love sushi, especially the real pungent stuff these days. Check your list for 'sushi.'"

"Let's see, sushi sellers. Oh, Mr. Nakamura?"

"That's me."

"Can I see some identification?"

"I lost that in the war. Now hurry; I need to plug my cart's refrigeration in before the sushi spoils and these maggots get too excited. Wanna see them?"

"No, no! That's all right," Emily said, covering the cart's rotting contents back up and directing Nathan through the line. "Take a table close to the bathrooms please—right under the ventilation fan!"

"My pleasure."

Nathan hustled away and passed lines of nerds all sniffing their armpits, his cart's cargo making them question the effectiveness of their deodorant that day. With Emily falling for his plan hook, line, and sinker, Nathan slipped into the bathroom with bated breath. After one of his cart's mackerels smacked against a tile corner and maggoty eggs splattered outward like chum, Nathan had officially spawned the bathroom's most putrid payload all morning. Now accurate in two ways, Nathan was up to something...fishy.

CHAPTER 30

Now safe at her duplex and far away from the wrath of any more militant moms, Tessa lounged on the couch in her onesie Wacky Will pajamas. Computer parts surrounded her on the floor, as did a fresh collection of used tissues. Playing a tech news podcast on her laptop and animal videos on her phone, Tessa distracted herself with an overload of multispecies multitasking. When the podcast discussed a new processor that *dwarfed* all competitor's products at the same time her phone displayed baby *reptiles*, Tessa's body went limp. And then she collapsed into her cat-shaped couch pillows, sniffling.

"Dwarves? Reptiles? Everything reminds me of Andy, dammit!" pouted Tessa.

Scanning the tissues strewn about the living room, Tessa grabbed a box from the floor.

"Empty? Oh, wonderful," she grunted, lifting the whole tissue box to her face and then pausing. "No, Tessa, you are *not* blowing your nose into a tissue box. Have some respect."

Tessa reached at the table beside her, blindly feeling junk mail flyers of Bumble Ridge's weird eateries and seasonal bee zapper sales. After pressing a flyer to her nostrils and blowing like a mucous-filled musical instrument, Tessa pulled it away and froze. Yes, she was now making eye contact with Andy's snotty peepers.

"This must be the party," she sobbed, unraveling Andy's convention flyer. "There's a URL? Geez, what kind of get-together is this?"

Tessa entered the hyperlink on her phone, Andy's video page then tormenting her brain and data plan with its happy, high-resolution pictures. As she flung the flyer at her trash can currently filled with tissues piled to the ceiling, a video of Ben and Leo auto-played:

"This is our last outcast update before the mind-expanding Andy convention," Leo said at the camera. *"Which means it's also the last chance for us to guilt or trick you into coming!"*

"Hey, at least we're honest," added Ben.

"So come on down, or up, or even over, depending upon your space-time location's relation to us at the moment," said Leo. *"It's one convention to rule them all! In the time being, you can check out our other funny work below like the Convention Crawl content. Or if you wanna see a real tearjerker, click the 'End of Jumbo Andy' video where he lets loose about this reprehensible con artist named Tessa."*

"What's Andy telling these people?" shouted Tessa, tossing one of her cat pillows and knocking down the snot tissue tower. "I'm sorry, Pillow Kitty! Andy's friends made

ANDY GETS CONNED

me throw you. And now they're making me watch this stupid video that'll make me even madder!"

Tessa then found the video and hit play, nearly piercing a hole through her phone with an aggressive finger jab. And like an electronic time capsule, Andy's depressive confession began playing in her palms:

"Hello, my name is Andy Gordon, and let me tell you why I suck. First, I despise my job. Second, I live in the same house I was born in. Statisticians predict I will die here as well. And third, when it comes to romance, my mom dates more than me. A fat nerd has lady problems? I know, story of the century, right? This last woman though, wow. She's the type of maiden you'd go to a Renaissance Faire with even if she didn't have a costume. The type of girl you'd pause a video game for. A woman you couldn't bear to get rid of even if she were a zombie about to slurp your brains out like a juice box. And if she thinks I'm a horrible person, then everybody else in this dreadful world probably will too. So, Tessa, if you ever see this, I'm sorry. I hope that Nathan Hader doesn't end up destroying your life as much as he did mine. He's not who you think he is, so please be careful!"

Two vertical lines appeared over Andy's face in the video, now paused. And a tear dripped down Tessa's cheek, striking the letter F on her phone's keyboard. The next two tears then hit the letters U and C. But before her face leak became a rain of profanity, Tessa screamed and slammed another pillow into her face like an airbag.

"I am so confused!" Tessa growled through the pillow before chucking it. "Andy looks devastated. Nathan's last name is Hader? And he's screwing with Andy's life? This sounds like a good time for an ice cream-fueled Internet search if I've ever heard one!"

Back at the Zimmerman Center, Nathan plowed his cart into a women's bathroom. And then he removed its tarp, revealing a putrefied sheet of fish in various states of decomposition. Using a windshield squeegee, he pushed off the top fish carcasses for his true load underneath—red gasoline containers filled to the brim. Nathan then grabbed two of them and splashed gas around the stalls, missing toilets only slightly more than your average public bathroom user. Now acting like a flammable lawn sprinkler, Nathan spun in a circle as gasoline doused every square inch of the bathroom.

"Excuse me!" screamed Janet from one of the stalls.

"Uh, sorry. My water broke," Nathan said, as Janet opened her stall door, drenched.

"How dare ya go and do somethin' so revoltin'?" Janet asked, exiting. "Grossed out lady comin' through!"

In the vendor area, Janet dry heaved to the merch booth and scrubbed off the toxic pre-birth with some Andy-themed hand sanitizer. Minutes later, after Janet had decontaminated and changed into Andy-branded clothing, Nathan dumped the last gas into a sink clogged with dead fish. He then loaded more protein bars into his Droid Blitzer mouth, interrupted by the wrinkly businessman and shoulder-padded businesswoman opening the door. And trailing behind, the plump businessman on a mobility scooter followed while smoking his cigar. His brakes ineffective on such slippery

ANDY GETS CONNED

gas, the mobility scooter man skidded and screeched to a halt inches away from Nathan.

"Sorry 'bout that," said the mobility scooter man, reversing as loud beeps emanated from his scooter.

"Every bathroom's coated now, boss," said the businesswoman, yanking away the mobility scooter man's cigar and soaking it with the faucet. "Let's prevent a premature incineration. Okay, partner?"

"Excellent work, bastards. Excellent," Nathan said. "I'm glad to hear some good news after my maggots didn't live up to the hype."

"You weren't seriously trying to ride those were you? We thought that was a joke," said the businesswoman.

"Yeah, a joke..." Nathan said, pushing a pile of crushed maggots under the sink with his foot. "Big joke."

"What'd this Andy fella do to you if you don't mind me askin', boss?" queried the mobility scooter man, jerking back and catching a new cigar that fell from his cowboy hat. "He screw you in a business deal or somethin'? Maybe bang your wife?"

"Worse. He failed me in history class," Nathan said, his statement immediately met with a cacophony of laughter. "Hey, he failed me multiple times!"

"Fine, boss. You probably don't want to say somethin' too incriminatin'—we get it," chuckled the mobility scooter man. "History class? What a hoot!"

"I totally understand why you all think this is funny," Nathan lied through his teeth. "Boy, am I funny or what?"

Nathan joined in their amusement, each howl of the mobility scooter man sending another cigar from his hat to the slick tile. Dozens of cigars soon on the floor, Emily then popped open the bathroom door as everyone froze and avoided eye contact.

"This is mighty uncomfortable right now," said the mobility scooter man, breaking the silence and puttering past their new visitor.

"We women sure do make a mess of the bathroom, don't we?" said Nathan, shoving the businesswoman out the door sideways so her shoulder pads would fit through. "We'll go get a janitor."

"I hate people so much," said Emily.

Nathan and his minions skittered from the restroom, crept into a video testimonial booth, and closed the curtains behind them with a not-so-innocent whistle. Nathan then removed his Droid Blitzer helmet for some air, unleashing a rank bouquet of gas, dead fish, and vanilla protein bar breath that had collected inside.

"We almost blew it back there," said Nathan. "Did anyone follow us?"

"Let me check," added the businesswoman, peeking her head through the curtain. "Nope, nobody's out there."

As the curtain shut, Emily leaned from behind the booth and waved Janet over. The two then reenacted humanity's first version of invasive surveillance—cupping their hands to their ears—and snooped in on the ongoing booth conspiracy inside.

"Okay, bastards, it's your time to shine. Andy should be on stage by now, so we need to work fast," Nathan said. "Go wait in each bathroom on the main floor. When you hear the signal, torch the place."

ANDY GETS CONNED

As Nathan's group flung open the curtain yet again, Emily dove around the booth and escaped undetected. Greeting the gang's faces, however, was a dumbfounded Janet cupping her hand. And worse, she was now in a fresh Andy T-shirt and themed jeans. Though caught off guard, Janet faked a yawn while reaching for her pocket.

"Boy that big guy on stage is as dull as a rusty doorknob, I tell ya," Janet said, removing lipstick from her pocket and crossing out Andy's face on her shirt. "My friends are never draggin' me here again. Let me in there so I can take a nap."

"Our pleasure," said Nathan, marching away with his business minions.

On stage in the convention center's auditorium, Andy skated in a figure eight. And with the video camera attached to his skateboard, he was now streaming without any technical or biological hiccups; this was a non-fumbled, freewheeling performance. Cheered on by the devoted crowd, Andy broke out his mouthed engine sound effects again—this time into a wireless microphone.

"Is everyone having fun?" Andy asked, doing an ollie.

"Yeah!" yelled a majority of the crowd.

"And to those who didn't respond, I'm guessing you're just a little indecisive, right?"

"Perhaps!" the rest of them whimpered.

"Congratulations, everyone!" Andy cheered, pressing a button on his camera. "We just finished my 14th streamed video of the day. Number 15's coming right up after the break, so sit tight. While you wait, here's some footage of us trying to dance at *Space Fightin'* Con. Feel free to join in because, remember, you can't look any dumber than we already do! Take it away, Peaches!"

At the stage control panel in the wings, Peaches dimmed the lights, cranked up video game music, and lowered a large screen. As Peaches bobbed his head and his Andy-branded eyepatch flopped to the beat, he hit one more button. And video played on screen of the samosas dancing around Nathan at *Space Fightin'* Con. A community dance then erupted in the auditorium as Andy skated to Ben and Leo, all three pulling off the same moves as the ones on screen.

"What a natural!" Leo said, executing his sprinkler dance. "How'd you learn to work a crowd like that, you social shaman?"

"You know, all those years of trying to keep bored kids awake are paying off," said Andy, shaking his hips while disabling his wireless mic. "I'm making videos, I'm spending time with my samosas, and my show's going well even though I didn't plan this part. I think I'm finally nailing my life."

"Good! Now could we please focus on landing me one of those fangirls out there?" Ben asked. "One should have low enough standards to date me, right?"

"You know it, Ben! I'll bring you on stage next and we'll do a dating show so you can find your soul mate. This couldn't be going any better. I know I'm probably setting us up for disappointment, but this is fantastic!" Andy smiled, as Janet hustled up to the trio.

"I have terrible news, sweetie," said Janet.

"I spoke too soon," Andy said. "What's going on?"

ANDY GETS CONNED

"Bring it in, guys," Janet said. "Peaches, come on over here too please!"

As the group huddled on stage, Mom and Chris boogied toward them in the dancing crowd. Despite their age, they pulled off the smoothest moves amidst a sea of flailing arms and uncoordinated spasms.

"What a turnout!" Mom said, shaking her booty.

"Looks like more than a few dozen people to me," said Chris, enthusiastically raising the roof. "Unless I'm way worse at math than I thought."

Mom and Chris then grooved to the stage wing, bumping fannies until reaching Andy's gang in a circle. With a presence approaching behind, Peaches spun around, growled like a grizzly bear, and shielded his cubs from the geriatric invaders.

"You want Peaches to kill these people?" he asked.

"Stand down, Peaches," said Andy. "That's my mom and her boyfriend."

"Hi, dear," said Mom, with a nervous smile.

"You're...Mom?" Peaches gasped, breaking from the group and giving her a massive hug. "Peaches heard a lot about you from Andy. So Peaches is a big fan. You raised a remarkable son; he opened up a world of root beer floats for Peaches that changed Peaches' life forever."

"Mom, Chris, get on in here too," Andy said. "I'm sorry for going full hermit on you. We'll catch up over some Flag Day cake later, okay? Or, if you wouldn't mind, maybe some Flag Day apples instead?"

"Don't even think twice about it, dear," exhaled Mom, as Peaches lowered her to the floor.

"Okay, so a gang of thugs wants to end the convention and embarrass me in the process. I'm pretty sure I know who their leader is too," said Andy.

"I can radio dispatch for some backup," Chris said. "They're all over at Leo's shop figurin' out who broke in and trashed the place. Wouldn't take long to get here."

"Wait, what?" asked Leo.

"You didn't get a call from the station?"

"No," Leo pushed.

"Sorry. Most of my employees are incompetent. But don't you worry; the thief left hemoglobin all over the place like a stuck pig on blood thinners. We'll know who it is pretty soon."

"Somebody stole my stock and stained my store?"

"Affirmative. But we'll be makin' the perp regret it big time. Maybe with a little taste of the electric chair."

"I'll pull the lethal lever myself!"

"I'm sorry, Leo," said Andy. "And I'll help fund whatever you need once the video cash starts coming in."

"Me too," said Ben, slapping cash into Leo's hand.

"But I'm afraid we don't have 10 minutes to wait for backup," said Andy, pulling the group closer. "We need to act fast. So listen up, everyone, I have a plan: It's time we all did a little...role-playing."

CHAPTER 31

Inspired by the dance video, Andy's convention audience formed a conga line and bunny hopped around the auditorium like a rhythmic centipede. Andy then summoned his inner gym coach, blowing a whistle until his role-playing posse broke from their huddle on stage.

"Where'd you get the whistle, dear?" Mom asked.

"No time for questions," Andy smirked. "So let's move, people! Move!"

Andy's gang then rushed in different directions. Peaches, reaching his stage control panel first, faded the lights back up and blasted *Space Fightin's* soundtrack for the battle about to go down. As Andy jogged in place on the side stage and hyped himself up, a large figure appeared in the shadows beside him.

"Can I help?" asked B-Fred, his baby tucked into his Pinnette costume jumpsuit.

"You don't realize how perfect this is—yes, you can help! Here's 100 bucks. Now take off your clothes," Andy said, B-Fred's eyes exploding open. "Let me back up. I gave you money to borrow your costume for a few minutes. Go hit up the merch booth and get some new clothes first, then leave your Pinnette costume right here when you get back."

"You got it," said B-Fred, taking the cash.

"I'll be on stage when you drop your costume off. So good luck out there, pilot Pinnette!"

B-Fred dashed away in clogs as Andy cracked his neck and readied the skateboard for the first part of his role-playing plan. While most of his audience took their seats, as well as their heart medications after all that conga line cardio, Andy skated back on stage lit via spotlight.

"Hey, everybody! You stared at me long enough, so *you* get to be on screen now. Get ready to see yourselves in a little segment I'm calling *15 Seconds in Frame*," Andy said, tightening the camera onto his skateboard. "Get it?"

Like two team-based superheroes activating their powers at the same time, Andy and Peaches synched the camera and projector with the press of a button. Live footage of Andy's crowd then played on screen as Andy rolled toward his randomly selected front-row guest—the one and only Winslow dressed in Andy garb from the merch booth. Unfortunately, the close up also showed Winslow's bulky body squished into a small seat; and his blubbery rolls encompassed both seats beside him like expanding pizza dough.

"Hey, everyone, look! It's Winslow!" Andy said, as his cast-covered image displayed on screen. "I shot this guy and almost poisoned him when I briefly tried bartending, but he still showed up! Take a bow, my friend."

ANDY GETS CONNED

"This is my moment!" yelled Winslow.

Winslow then grabbed the crutch beside him, attempting to heave himself upward. And that's when the audience got a glimpse of Winslow failing once again, stopped by his body's airtight seal with the seat.

"Well, I guess not. I'm destined to be miserable."

Despite an entire room of laughter directed at Winslow, a voice even louder and more scornful stood out among the rest—Robby's drunken father standing behind the back row.

"Hilarious!" the father mocked. "The fat guy's stuck because he's fat!"

"Please stop laughing, everybody," said Andy. "This is not a bit. I repeat—not a bit!"

While Andy continued his crowd work, Mom and Chris headed through the audience to Fran. Though too small to sit in her own seat, she balanced atop Marcus's gangly shoulders like a pirate ship's lookout. After Mom and Chris whispered into their ears, Marcus jumped to his feet and ran for the exit with Fran. Fortunately for Robby seated behind them, he could now finally see the stage. Of course, his drunken father then stole the open seat, sipping from a car-sized keg strapped to his head and obscuring Robby's view even more. As Robby sobbed, he could now only hear Andy's interaction with the next peculiar member of the front row.

"Have I seen you before?" Andy asked, aiming the skateboard at his beady-eyed, creepy mailman.

"Yeah, and I've seen *a lot* of you," the mailman said.

"Wait, aren't you my mailman?"

"Yeah."

"And haven't you been opening my mail?"

"Double yeah!"

"You really need to stop that," smiled Andy. "Hey, everyone, are there any restraining orders in the house?"

With crowd members chuckling and the creepy mailman letting out a high-pitched squeal, Ben and Leo fist bumped fans as they hurried down the rightmost aisle. Stopping at Nurse Rosie, Ben whispered in her ear and she promptly smacked him in the face.

"Never propose to a stranger," she barked.

"Ben sent the wrong message," said Leo, then leaning in and delivering his soft-spoken secret.

"Now *you* know how to talk to a lady," Nurse Rosie said, standing and then pushing them toward the exit. "Mush, boys! Mush!"

Going two for two with humorous interactions, Andy aimed the skateboard camera at his next participant who managed to be even more disturbing than the high-pitched mailman. The room gasped and Andy paused as his next guest removed the Droid Blitzer helmet from his head. Yes, now on screen, Nathan Hader shook his hair like a shampoo commercial and then glared forward.

"Brave enough to show your face today, huh, Nathan?" Andy growled into the microphone headset. "Why don't you leave and make this a lot less dramatic?"

"Not a chance!" Nathan yelled, grabbing his helmet and then climbing on stage.

Leaving no time for retaliation, Nathan ripped the headset off Andy's face and attached it to his. Now

ANDY GETS CONNED

equipped with a way to be heard without blowing out his vocal cords, Nathan put his helmet back on.

"I'm louder than you now," bragged Nathan. "And protected too. Try and stop me."

"We have plenty of microphones around here," said Andy, pulling another wireless headset from his rear pocket and slipping it on. "Did you really think I'd be on stage without a backup?"

"Fine," Nathan said, facing the crowd. "You should all be ashamed for showing up today and supporting this loser. Andy's a bad teacher who tried to end a good student's life. And he's even worse at comedy. Well, I'm here to finish this nerd off once and for all today. Let's end his baboonery."

"Quick question for you first, Nathan. Ever get your ass kicked by a nerd in front of a crowd of other nerds?"

"I'll ask the questions around here."

Nathan leapt, landing a double-handed shove into Andy's chest as if mixing martial arts and CPR. With the wind knocked out of him as well as one last dandelion seed, Andy fell to the floor with a thud.

"Your 15 seconds of fame are foiled," said Nathan. "Your plan's been dusted. You finally bit the last chapter."

"None of those phrases made sense," Andy said, crawling back up on his feet. "And none of them were questions either!"

In his skillfully nuanced manner of dealing with a heckler, Andy charged at Nathan at full speed. Stopping him almost instantly, the wrinkly businessman and shoulder-padded businesswoman popped out from the curtain. And both latched on Andy like a squad of squid trying to take down a rhino.

Audience members then stared slack-jawed as the mobility scooter man zoomed on stage and swung a lasso above his mascot-sized cowboy hat. With a flick, his rope flew through the air, wrapped around Andy, and prevented movement with its binding bondage. As the mobility scooter man drove closer with smoke fuming from his cigar like a steam locomotive, the two businesspeople forced Andy into a chair and tied him to it with various extension cords.

"I can't tell if this is real or part of the show," Winslow said, turning to veteran Zeus in the aisle.

"If it's real and Andy needs help, I'm packin' heat," said Zeus, wearing a necklace of snake bones and pool balls from the speakeasy. "But if it's fake and the finale sucks, I'm packin' grenades."

"Please don't kill anybody."

"You two in the front! Zip it!" screamed Nathan, then refocusing on Andy. "Face it, fatso. I'm better than you in every way. You have no chance. Look, even your friends are against you now."

Nathan squeezed Andy's face between his maggot-slimed hands and twisted it like a rushed chiropractor. Now in Andy's view, Leo and Ben struggled in their extension cord jails. And Peaches squirmed beside them in his restraints, duct taped to the control panel. As they wiggled, three signs on their chests jostled containing the text 'Andy sucks,' 'Feel our disdain,' and 'Peaches concurs' in Comic Sans font. Such written claims proved to be indefensible thanks to more tape adhered to their lips. Nathan then flipped the skateboard into his hands and aimed its camera at Andy.

"I'm way smarter than you and definitely prettier," Nathan said, lurching closer. "So, I want to thank you for the audience today, tubbo. I deserve all this fame and attention, not you."

"Just like you deserved a passing grade in history even though you wrote that Dr. Benjamin Hitler discovered electricity?" Andy growled.

"Silence! Tape him!" demanded Nathan, as the mobility scooter man yanked open a roll of duct tape and coiled a few layers around Andy's mouth. "Everyone, if you will, please direct your attention to the screen for a world premiere I whipped up. I call this one 'Andy Gordon: Fat Guy, Little Talent.' Roll it, slaves!"

The mobility scooter man zipped past Andy's pals, faded the lights, and then headed to a bathroom. It was time for Nathan's unforeseen feature presentation. But what could Nathan possibly produce other than a teacher's aneurysm? About to find out, Andy stared from the worst seat in the house as *Space Fightin's* soundtrack stopped. Carnival music then swelled, as footage of Andy crashing through his classroom window played in slow motion. Morphing into a techno remix of the music, soundbites of Andy saying 'I suck' entered the song and formed an impressively catchy, auto-tuned composition.

With the new soundtrack, more footage continued on screen of reporter Gail Ellerbach kneeing Andy in the groin, his splash entrance into the chemical mud puddle, the reveal of his tattered Wacky Will boxers, and his barrage of bee stings outside the Spanish classroom. All edited to the beat, Nathan's footage then showed Andy breaking booths at Three-Fifth Chasers, hacking off the lumberjack's arm, and shooting down a paragliding Winslow at Pollen Valley Lake. Nearly all the tragedies that Andy experienced had been combined in a 10-minute montage of public shame. As the music faded, one last shot played on screen of Nathan humping the air in his cardboard hut as Tessa waved in front of him.

"And so concludes the pathetic tale of Andy Gordon," Nathan narrated on stage. "Let the disdain begin."

As the lights came back on, Andy slumped in his chair with an audience erupting in gut-busting guffaws. Seeing his results, Nathan cackled, removed his helmet, and laughed at Andy harder than the time he depantsed him in school. Fading in and out of consciousness, Andy considered all of the mountain shacks and arctic igloos he could relocate to and never show his face again. Yet all he could do was slouch over like a corpse. During the best of cons, it was now Andy's worst as Nathan and the crowd howled in knee-slapping hilarity.

Back in a ladies' bathroom, the wrinkly businessman cupped a hand at his ear as the explosion of chuckles struck his gold-plated hearing aid—the signal had arrived. Taking a few steps back from Nathan's gas canisters, he reached into his suit pocket, removed a match, and struck it upon his sun-scorched, wrinkly forehead.

"Time to shine," he said, staring into the flickering flame. "Match, meet your maker."

ANDY GETS CONNED

Just as the businessman began lowering his match to the ground, the bathroom door swung open. Janet then stomped up in a men's suit, now with a mascara mustache painted above her lip. Nearly slipping, she braced herself as the wrinkled man twisted his head around 180-degrees like a curious owl.

"Hey, ya schmuck," Janet grumbled in a baritone voice. "Nathan says the plan's off."

"I don't remember you, man boobs."

"Nathan's gonna be mighty pissed when he hears ya treated his number two henchman like this."

"I think that depends if you're an impostor or not, doesn't it? Stop blabbing. Just show me the handshake," said the wrinkled man, stretching his devil-horned fingers toward her.

Janet reached forward without hesitation, mimicking his wrinkled fingers for her first step in the convoluted, handshake process. For the second step, she kicked him square in the nutsack—twice.

"Was that it?" Janet asked, blowing the flame out as the wrinkled man fell into a pile of gas containers.

Meanwhile in the men's bathroom, the mobility scooter man lounged on a handicap toilet. But the commode seat was down and his pants were up, his feet resting on the scooter like a disability device hammock. Chewing an unlit cigar, he read the same issue of *Geriatric Dating* magazine that Mom had memorized long ago. And when the crowd's joyous reaction registered, he ignited his cigar. Belligerent fists then pounded his stall, so he stood up on his fully functional legs and opened the door. Awaiting in full salute was an amazing angel...sent directly from Heaven's smoking-only section.

"Hey, slick," Nurse Rosie barked with a cigar in her mouth, unbuttoning her uniform. "Can this old broad have a light or what?"

"Cancer ain't sexy, but you sure are," he said, flicking his lighter. "Haven't seen you 'round these parts before."

"I haven't seen you around *my parts* either. How about we puff each other's brains out?"

"You bet your bacon, I will," he said, leaning toward her as hundreds of cigars fell from his hat.

Seconds away from one of the most disgusting kisses imaginable, Nurse Rosie tilted her haggard face toward his, reached around his body for the toilet tank lid, and propelled that porcelain right into his pudgy, chicken-greased lips. When the mobility scooter man flew backward, his head splashed into the toilet. Her victim now gurgling in the germy waterpark, Nurse Rosie took the lighter and popped a row of cigars into her mouth.

"Thanks for the light," she snarled, igniting all her cigars. "Never saw somebody clean the latrine with their taste buds before. Interesting choice, soldier."

Meanwhile in a unisex bathroom, the businesswoman pulled out one of her linebacker-like shoulder pads and ignited it with a blowtorch. As the foam began blazing, student Emily bounded into the bathroom pushing a baby stroller. Inside, Fran poked her head out through the blankets while sucking a pacifier.

"Excuse me, Ma'am," Emily pouted. "I found this baby outside the bathroom. Is this yours?"

ANDY GETS CONNED

"I wouldn't birth any of you demons," said the businesswoman. "Go tell somebody who cares."

"All right, I'll go see if anyone's looking for her out there then. Her nametag says 'Fran Kirkpatrick,' and I think it's made out of gold. Hmm, a golden nametag, a diamond pacifier—I wonder if she's related to the billionaire Kirkpatrick family? Well, have a nice day."

"Wait! You're not going anywhere now!"

As the businesswoman removed handcuffs from her pocket and pounced, student Marcus stormed the bathroom and sprayed her face with a fire extinguisher. Her high heels never tested in a mixture of fire retardant and gas, the woman slipped. And when she plonked down to the floor, her flaming shoulder pad flew into the air. Spoiling her baby disguise to stop an inferno, Fran popped out from the stroller, caught the shoulder pad, and then doused its flame in the sink. But then, like a horror film villain who wasn't quite dead yet, the businesswoman sat back up.

"I've already shattered the glass ceiling," she growled, curling her fingers like a witch in business appropriate pantyhose. "But I think it's time to slit both your throats with a shard of that glass."

"Play Number 88, now!" shouted Marcus.

With the businesswoman lunging at Fran and Emily, Fran snatched Marcus's whiteboard from the stroller and held one side while Emily grabbed the other. Then like a game of bathroom chicken, they both ran at the businesswoman and pinned her against the wall. Behind them, Marcus palmed the fire extinguisher and tossed it like a 3-point shot. And everyone in the bathroom watched the extinguisher fly through the air, now seemingly in slow motion. Though the businesswoman managed to push Emily and Fran away and finally break free, the extinguisher had picked up the kind of speed that could crack a skull.

"Nighty night," said Marcus, his extinguisher then bonking the businesswoman's head and knocking her into the menstrual pad machine. "May your dreams be as dark as your incarcerated future."

As the businesswoman drifted into her concussion coma and slid down the wall, images of birds clutching money sacks flew around her head. And when her butt hit the floor, her disgraceful fall continued as a downpour of sanitary napkins rained from above. Piled-up pads now weighing her down, the businesswoman's slick pantyhose lost traction and she slid away from the wall. When her head slammed upon the tile, her legs flew upward and open for all to see. Then using the whiteboard for a different purpose, Fran thrust it upward and blocked Marcus's ogling eyes.

"She seems way more *down-to-earth* now, doesn't she?" quipped Fran, squinting. "But her vagina looks like a freakin' train tunnel."

Emily's snort-filled laughter then echoed through the bathroom. And the auditorium crowd, now regaining breath from their amusement, erupted into applause and whistles. Nathan's plan complete, he untied Andy and ripped the tape from his mouth. As his mind and lip throbbed with pain, Andy processed two important

ANDY GETS CONNED

lessons learned that day. One, that women put themselves through a hell of a lot of pain waxing their bodies like that. And two, that audiences can turn on you disturbingly fast.

"I'm done," announced Nathan, placing his Droid Blitzer helmet back on. "You can go home to your mom now, you fat, pathetic baby."

Having enough of this nonsense, Andy gritted his teeth, picked up the skateboard, and then battered Nathan's helmet with a brutal bash in full berserk mode. Consequently, Nathan's head rang like a gong and he collapsed backward. After dropping his wheeled weapon and hopping on, Andy skated toward his entrapped friends. But his rescue mission quickly failed when he struck a clump of electrical cords on stage. Now with the balance of a one-legged ballerina, Andy wobbled as if trying to surf in a tsunami. Then he lost control, crashing through the craft services food table without losing speed. While Andy wildly rode toward some equipment trunks, the food table's high-speed meats launched over the curtain and upon the audience. Thus, all vegetarians in the crowd had to hide under their seats for safety, dodging animal flesh like an active warzone.

"Free grub and a show?" screamed a hillbilly behind Winslow, both catching meat in their mouths. "Color me plumb impressed!"

"I can't stop," moaned Winslow between chews.

"This reminds me of when I blew up that orphanage in 'Nam," Zeus said, chomping down. "Nothin' beats airborne barbeque."

"I think I can stop now," said Winslow.

After passing the food table, history repeated itself as Andy struck more cords, flew off his skateboard, and flopped onto a wheeled equipment trunk. While the landing was soft, his trunk ride and crash into the wall felt more like a connecting flight with the side of a mountain. Upon impact, Andy tumbled off. But his camera flew up and then gently fell onto a backstage couch, still streaming Andy's crisis for all to see.

"I knew you'd agree with me," said Nathan, taking off his dented Droid Blitzer helmet. "I knew you'd reject the real Andy Gordon. So welcome, everyone, to today's much better event—the Nathan Hader Convention!"

CHAPTER 32

Upon hearing Nathan's intent to hijack Andy's convention, the crowd booed and pitched its partially eaten meats back at him. Now pelted by projectile beef and bologna, Nathan munched away on stage.

"I know, Andy sucks, right? Thank you, everyone!" Nathan exclaimed, as the audience ran out of meat and showered him with root beer bottles instead. "You're too kind! Way too kind."

Nathan then took a bow, and crowd members continued their bottle attack until Andy awoke from his collision. Now back in reality, Andy spotted his camera tipped sideways on the couch. And worse, it was pointed right at him—its red 'Recording' light still blinking.

"Oh no, everyone saw that," moaned Andy.

Andy's gaze became an intense glare, noticing Nathan on stage. He then switched focus to his captive friends, followed by the nearest exit. With two options available, Andy contemplated all of today's possible endings like a choose-your-own-adventure book.

"No, I'm not running away again!" Andy huffed, climbing to his feet. "I'm saving my samosas. It's time to make that android my bitch."

"Andy?" called a feminine voice, muffled through a mouth full of food.

From the shadows, Andy made out a thick, womanly silhouette. And her large chest blocked out most of the light behind her. With her frazzled hair, loud chewing, and breasts that could crush a bus, only one woman from Andy's past could fit that delightful description.

"Helga! Is that you?" Andy asked.

"No, but I totally see why you thought that," said Tessa, stepping into view with two 3-gallon tubs of AbsZero ice cream strapped to her chest. "Don't move. We settle this after one more bite."

Still in her onesie Wacky Will pajamas, Tessa plunged another spoonful of ice cream into her mouth. And then she ran at Andy like a suicide bomber.

"Andy!" she called, approaching. "Holy cow, you're looking svelte. Still jogging, huh?"

"You know I can get you and Nathan arrested for breaking into Leo's shop and stealing my memory card, right? How dare you show your face here!"

"What are you talking about?"

"I trusted you. I liked you! I finally thought there was someone out there with compatible quirks. And this was all some trick so you could shoot a video hit piece and then humiliate me in public?"

"I had no idea Nathan was making that."

"You were in the video for crying out loud."

"He asked me to be in his vlog, but he never showed me what he did with the footage. He didn't tell me that the video was about you either, Andy. I wouldn't want to hurt you like that—or at all, to be specific."

"Admit it, Tessa! You and your gorgeous boyfriend made that video together."

"Gross. I'm furious he put me in there, but I'm even angrier he did that to you. And until about 20 minutes ago, I thought he was homeless. Please believe me!"

"I can't trust you anymore."

"He concocted this whole story about you buying an audience to get in my pants at the speakeasy; he said you thought I wasn't funny! Then he started telling half-truths like changing his name to Nathan to escape his tragic past, putting all the blame on you. He said that you failed him after you brought a lion to class and he confronted you for it. He was playing us against each other the whole time! I was suspicious before, but after I watched your videos, I looked up his vlogs. He left one hell of a slimy trail. Here's my phone—look at his badly spelled texts!"

Every audience member now stared at the dorky soap opera unraveling on screen, the smart people tilting their heads sideways to adjust for such an odd camera angle. Nathan then faced the audience and stomped his foot, compacting the Droid Blitzer helmet just like most of the crowd wanted to do to his real head.

"Lies! These losers are liars!" Nathan fumed, as the show continued behind him.

"Are you kidding me? This is all real?" asked Andy, scrolling through Tessa's texts. "He failed my class three years in a row. And then he got expelled after he almost killed us with a lion, not me! This looks like Nathan used half-truths to seem credible? He accused me of his own crimes? He got us fighting with each other so we wouldn't see who was really pulling the puppet strings? I'll be damned—he paid attention to my politics lesson!"

"Nathan bragged about trying to split us apart in the videos he hid from me online; check my alphabetized bookmarks for more proof. He was using me to hurt you. And all because he failed your class? That's insane; he's a psychopath. He made me eat so much of this damned ice cream too," said Tessa, unstrapping the 3-gallon tubs from her chest. "He manipulated us to think we hated each other. Well I'm telling you the truth right now: I don't hate you, Andy Gordon!"

"And I don't hate you either," said Andy, returning Tessa's phone. "Not even close."

"I know; I saw your 'End of Jumbo Andy' video too. It was sweet. Experts say I might have cried like a baby. And then laughed like a baby followed by more crying—women are weird like that."

"Every word in that video about you is still true," Andy said, inching closer. "And making a funny lady like you laugh? Now that's an accomplishment."

Andy grasped Tessa's hand, interlocking their fingers together like fleshy zippers. Now having exchanged each other's sweat and initiating intimacy, Tessa responded with a sensual squeeze—a message far more important to Andy than even aliens' first contact with Earth.

"I really don't hate this either," Andy smiled.

ANDY GETS CONNED

"Why'd Nathan have to screw with this cute thing we have going on here?" Tessa asked, winking. "I'm not the only one who thinks this is totally cute, right?"

"No. Now how about you stop being hilarious so I can kiss you, dammit," said Andy, matching Tessa's smile.

The two, wide eyed and revealing more teeth than a dental examination, leaned toward one another. As they both closed their eyes, each lathered their lips with a coat of courtesy saliva. Then Andy pressed closer. Yes, with a bend of the neck to avoid any nose collisions, the nerdy pair shared a smooch. And it was so damned innocent that even the conservative parents still stuck in traffic would have approved.

As their eyes opened, they kept their lips locked. And they extended the kiss for as long as possible. Forgetting all their struggles and most trigonometry, the two shared a blissful moment with one man, one woman, and one jam-packed convention hall crowd watching them on screen.

"Awww," exhaled the audience, rivers of tears streaming down their tilted faces.

Right as the crowd grew silent, Robby's drunken father slammed open the entrance door. And then he stumbled back into the auditorium with an even larger keg strapped to his head.

"Yo, guys, what'd I miss?" he yelled. "I had to get a new keg since I sucked the other one dry. Are those two gonna bang? I like Andy, but I don't want to see him naked. I'd look at that lady with the red hair naked though. Oh, and while I'm talking and you're all being quiet for some reason, has anybody seen my brat kid

Robby? I want to give him one last beating before I put him up for adoption."

The nerve! The cluelessness! The inability to sense that he ruined perhaps the sweetest moment most people would ever see. With the wrong combination of words, Robby's drunken dad had pushed one particular audience member over the edge.

"Shut up, you prick!" bellowed Winslow, whipping around in his neck brace from the front row. "You need to shut the hell up now!"

As all other audience members stared forward at Andy and Tessa, Winslow took a deep breath and flexed every muscle with a herculean grunt. Fighting the forces of his own body wedged in three different seats, he popped free onto his legs. And he squeezed again, the casts exploding from his lumpy physique. Winslow then hurtled up the aisle with adrenaline-fueled fury, still somehow not gaining anyone's attention. Reaching his target at peak agitation, he tackled Robby's father, straddled him like a human hemorrhoid donut, and let loose a life's worth of pent-up frustration.

"You're an asshole!" Winslow screamed at the top of his lungs, punching the drunken father's face and cranial keg with 10 times the strength of a heavyweight boxer. "Asshole! Asshole! Asshole!"

Upon impact with Winslow's furious fists, the drunken father's head flew back and cracked upon the floor. As beer spurted out from the attached keg, Robby darted over and presented his dad with a fitting gift—one mighty kick to the weakened keg with his hamster-

ANDY GETS CONNED

costumed foot. He and Winslow then backed away while beer streamed out like a geyser, and the drunken father shot across the auditorium. Yes, they had created an intoxicated missile. Then Robby and Winslow stood in awe, watching as the projectile father tore a hole through the wall, flew down the sidewalk, and crashed into a storage pool at the sewer treatment plant.

As Andy and Tessa's lips slowly pulled apart, there wasn't a dry eye in the house or any houses of the online viewers either. Close by, Leo, Ben, and Peaches bawled with joy despite their captivity. And Mom joined in with leaky eyes from the audience, removing an elongated magician's handkerchief from her bosom to dab them dry. Not even Mr. Gentzel could hold back his emotional waterworks watching from the local hospital, defying both of his fire-seared tear ducts. And now seeing the endearing moment on screen, Nathan's eyes began dripping too—albeit for completely different reasons.

"This isn't right!" shouted Nathan. "Why are you all so damned dumb?"

"I wanted that kiss a long time ago," said Tessa.

"I know! I mean, I'm agreeing that I wanted it too, not that I knew that you wanted it," Andy said. "Because if I would have known you wanted it, I would have pounced on you the second you saved Jumbo from my mom's computer and said you liked dwarves."

"Speaking of, look who's been searching for rare earth minerals in my pajamas," Tessa said, reaching into her pocket and pulling out a familiar metal dwarf.

"You kept Jumbo?"

"Of course I did," Tessa smiled. "This thing's the equivalent of a diamond ring to a lady nerd."

"He's still in pristine condition. And the plastic axe condom's still on!"

"With all the running I did to get here, he would have sliced my clothes off without it. I know, I'm logical and funny, right? If you're impressed, how about a Round Two?" Tessa asked, moving closer.

Their second kiss then got slightly more aggressive when Tessa bear-hugged Andy and they joined tongues like two anteaters battling over the same hole. Round Two quickly escalated into a make-out groping session with more sucking sounds than R2CheeseDoodle trying to clear a cheese curl from Andy's throat. The crowd, now shocked and a bit randy, roared in support.

"Get a room!" shouted Andy's creepy mailman. "And then let me watch from the closet in that room!"

Hearing such a raunchy response to their private encounter, Andy and Tessa scanned the area. There, resting right on the couch, was Andy's streaming camera and its blinking red light.

"I forgot that thing was on," said Andy, pointing.

"Did we just make soft-core porn?" asked Tessa, then looking into the camera with a grin.

"Talk about a public display of affection!" added Andy, the crowd chuckling as he winked to the camera. "Hi, everyone. I'm Andy Gordon, and I'll be out there after I say something romantic to Tessa in private. Psst, I think she likes me. Keep the stage warm for us, Nathan, because we're about to come put you out of your misery."

ANDY GETS CONNED

"Yeah, and you're really gonna disdain this," said Tessa, as Andy powered off his camera and the projector screen went black.

"No! No! No!" Nathan whined, continuing to crush his helmet. "You're all stupid and gullible. Me! You want to watch me! Not this tubby teacher who ruined my life! Me, everybody! Me!"

"Before we start this adorable relationship, we have one more nasty thing to do," said Andy, pressing Tessa's body against his like the accordion pillows he practiced with. "And we have to do it right now in front of all those people out there."

"Geez, Andy. I figured we'd save that for the third date," she smiled.

"Let's pause the foreplay," joked Andy. "We need to finish taking Nathan down first."

"Yeah, let's humiliate him! Demoralize him! Let's make that bastard wish he were never born. You have a crowbar? I could totally break his legs with a crowbar."

"Maybe you shouldn't go near him just yet. How about you go untie my friends first and then I'll have you come out when you can crush Nathan emotionally—you know, the legal kind of crushing."

"That's probably a better idea. But I'll go find a crowbar just in case."

"Before you do that, one more of these."

Andy lifted Tessa by the armpits, and she wrapped her legs around his waist like a fire station pole. His hands then caressed her face and guided her lips forward, the two passionately swapping mouth DNA once more.

"Humina," said Tessa, melting and sliding down Andy, strengthening the fire pole simile.

"Let's go! We can do this! It's one cute couple versus one mean machine!"

"And one pissed off chick with a crowbar," Tessa said, somehow wielding one while crawling toward Andy's friends. "This is going to be brutal."

"Your con goes out of commission now, Nathan," said Andy, grabbing B-Fred's Pinnette costume from the floor. "You messed with the wrong nerd."

CHAPTER 33

With dopamine surging through his brain from all those smooches, Andy stormed the stage. But now, thanks to B-Fred's delivery, Andy strutted out dressed as *Space Fightin's* Pinnette. His jumpsuit's light-up spikes all flickering, he slid the three-lensed sunglasses down his nose to increase the cool factor. And his belly bounced considerably less, meaning that the sun on his shirt didn't look like it was exploding anymore. Having leveled up a number of traits and skills, Andy entered today's real-life 'boss fight' with an extra spring in his step. And as Tessa untied Leo, Ben, and Peaches, Andy planted his feet inches away from Nathan's flattened Droid Blitzer helmet.

"Come on, nerd, hit me again," said Nathan.

"No. We'll try my idea first. And if that doesn't work, you can take a free shot at me."

"Fine. What's your idea?"

"Let's have a little chat," Andy said, shifting his eyes to the crowd. "A little chat with a big audience. Just talk to me for a minute, then you can hit me."

"Even below the belt?"

"You can go as low as you want."

"Deal. I'll destroy you," Nathan said, winding up his fist in a circle. "I'll charge up enough power for this punch that your balls will shoot out from your butthole."

"Nathan, do you remember the final project I gave you every year in my history class?"

"This is stupid."

"Answer my question or you won't get to punch me in the junk. Oh, and this entire room will pulverize you worse than your helmet."

"Fine. Yeah, I remember all my final projects. They were the same presentation every year. You made me compare the evil scientists in *Space Fightin'* to some real scientists on Earth—the nerds who made all of those new and clear weapons."

"You mean *nuclear* weapons, but you were close."

"Whatever," grumbled Nathan. "Why are you bringing this up now? They were bad assignments, and you're an even worse teacher."

"Do you know why I kept giving you that project?"

"Because you're a nerd."

"That's one reason, yes. But I also wanted you to see how even geniuses can go down the wrong path in history—how these people regretted using their brainpower to harm others. I saw you putting zero effort into school, but you had this creativity and drive to terrorize me. So with that project, I was hoping you'd learn from the past; I was hoping you'd use some of that energy for good and turn your life around."

ANDY GETS CONNED

"Nonsense!" Nathan screamed. "If that was the lesson, you didn't need to put so much nerdy crap in it."

"I agree. You're right about that."

"Wait, what?"

"Yeah, you're right. I shouldn't have forced *Space Fightin'* into your topic. I shouldn't have shoehorned so many of my hobbies into the class either. Geeks like to share their passions with others, and I was trying to do that. But I didn't consider the students who weren't into the same things. So here's my real offer, Nathan: I'd like to give you a chance to do your project on any topic that you want. I'll tell Murray that I made a grading mistake when you're done, and he'll update your transcript. I'd like you to earn your diploma the right way."

"No! My deal's still on with Murray. Being a nurse's assistant is way easier than real work. It's too late. Your nerdy assignments made me fail. So you and all these nerds have to be stopped!"

"Yes, I'm a nerd. But this nerd just offered his rival a chance at redemption. We're a fairly friendly bunch like that, you know. A few hundred more nerds are in the audience right now, and they're not bothering you either. Through those doors and past those walls are millions of innocent dorks, some watching from home. There are sleeper cell armies of us everywhere around the world. And you know what most of us have in common?"

"Loneliness?"

"No, perseverance. We go through life judged by people like you. We're mocked. We're beaten up. We're depantsed in the cafeteria during Beans and Weenies

Wednesdays. But no matter how hard you try, we keep going and still find ways to be happy."

"No, you're not happy," Nathan balked, grabbing Andy's shirt collar. "I made your life way worse."

"That was only temporary though. Think about what you did for me. You put so many obstacles in my way that I had to break out of my rut to get over them. You helped me see a turbo speed shortcut that would have taken years to discover myself. And now I'm happier than ever before. So, I really owe you this," Andy said, embracing Nathan in a vice grip hug. "I still think you're an asshole, but thank you, Nathan."

"Eww. I'm covered in nerd germs. Get off me!"

"Okay, I figured you'd be this way. You've made your choice," said Andy, dropping Nathan to the floor. "I'm going to keep having fun with everyone in the room while you stay miserable. On our journey, we'll keep inventing spaceships and technology that advance humanity. And you can keep trying to harass us with that technology all you want. It's never going to work."

"It will. You're all pathetic. It has to work."

"No, I don't think so," Andy said, facing the crowd with a smile. "I think we're a hell of a lot better than this socially inept twat, right?"

A wave of agreement washed over Nathan like water hadn't in quite some time. Now ready for the final blow, Andy waved off stage. And then Tessa skipped over with a crowbar in each hand.

"My friends are here. My family's here. My fans are here. And now I can say that my lady friend's here too,"

ANDY GETS CONNED

said Andy, as Tessa snuggled him. "You can't do anything to ruin how great I am right now."

"This is way better than breaking his legs," said Tessa, lobbing the crowbars behind her.

"I've got nothing but time, lots of minions, and easy access to lions. I can make all of you miserable forever," Nathan shouted, as Mom and Chris rolled a stage trunk behind him. "And that's exactly what I'm going to do."

"That'll be pretty hard to accomplish from your next destination," said Andy.

"Where am I going?"

"That trunk," Andy said, head-butting Nathan in the face and sending him downward.

With the criminal disoriented, Chris slapped a pair of handcuffs on Nathan while Mom taped him to the trunk.

"Oh, and then jail," Andy added, patting Nathan's head. "You're going to jail too."

"No!" Nathan yelled. "You don't have any proof."

"I'm a cop. You think we need proof?" joked Chris.

"Let's see if this video changes your mind," said Andy, pointing to Peaches and Janet off stage. "Attention, ladies and gentlemen of the outcast jury. I present to you Damning Evidence: Exhibit A on screen!"

At the stage control panel, Janet inserted a memory card while Peaches pressed buttons. And they both worked safely, guarded by Ben and Leo wielding microphone stands like spears. Andy, Mom, and Chris then spun Nathan's trunk at the screen as testimonial booth footage played of Nathan and his business associates scheming inside:

"Andy should be on stage by now, so we need to work fast. Go wait in each bathroom on the main floor. When you hear the signal, torch the place," Nathan said on screen, the video then stopping.

"Now that's some proof," Chris said.

"But wait, there's more," said Andy, as Leo rushed over and handed him his camera. "I want to capture every second of your reaction to the next reveal."

"Remember this classic, Nathan?" Tessa asked.

On screen, a homeless-dressed Nathan picked his nose in the cardboard hut. And then he grabbed the pizza box TV, presenting it to his laptop's webcam:

"And before I end today's Nathan Says, I want to show you the bad gift that my worse girlfriend got me. She'll need to give me lots of sex to make up for this stupid thing. Am I right? Well, that's it for Nathan Says today. I'll speak at you all later," Nathan said, the box slipping from his hands, hitting the laptop, and crushing a couple maggots nibbling gunk off the keyboard. "Oh no, my maggots! My maggots!"

Reliving the tragedy, Nathan gulped on stage as he watched himself swat the TV away and click his mouse.

"Don't worry—Daddy powered off the camera before any people saw how pathetic we were."

Yes, mistaken again, Nathan had failed at deactivating his webcam in the hut. In his hurried reaction, Nathan had clicked the incorrect side of his computer mouse. Thus, the embarrassing video continued.

"Sorry, maggots, I didn't mean to drop the TV on you. Daddy's fingers are a little greasy from all that pizza *the bimbo brought. Now clean up your brothers' and sisters' bodies while Daddy relaxes, okay?" said Nathan.*

In the increasingly awkward video still rolling in the auditorium, homeless Nathan peeled off his downy coat. Then he removed his shirt, revealing a taut, male girdle around his stomach with three-dimensional abs printed on it. After unlacing the girdle, Nathan let his body do the work as a bulging, protein bar belly exploded outward. With relief down below, Nathan tugged upon his goatee, ripped it free from its adhesive, and exposed a double chin caked with cold sore scabs and a cyst the size of a golf ball. He then scooped out a set of pearly white dentures from his mouth, his gums as black as the night sky. In his final moment of liberation, Nathan reached up to his scalp and removed a gorgeous hair piece with a twist. And that's when he finally let his bald, hysterically misshapen head breathe.

"Ah, that's better!" exhaled Nathan, now unmasked on screen. "If Daddy's going to ride you into war, you're going to need stronger muscles and way more energy. Let's get our hearts pumping, okay?"

Nathan's webcam video then ended with him beatboxing his own sexy soundtrack while violating every piece of furniture with his crotch. Having seen all of the evidence, Andy's convention audience cackled with laughter even louder than they had before.

"How dare you steal footage of me?" shouted Nathan. "You had no right to do that!"

"Tell you what—I'll never play the video again," said Andy. "Because people are dying to see the live version instead. Hey, Tessa, can I borrow the Jumbo Shrimpit figure for a second?"

"My pleasure," said Tessa, handing him the dwarf.

In the only moment he'd ever body shame somebody, Andy removed Nathan's goatee, dentures, and hair piece on stage. After slipping off Jumbo Shrimpit's protective axe cover, Andy sliced Nathan's black shirt and man girdle in half. And that's when an even bigger Buddha belly appeared, Nathan clearly having put on more weight since he shot the video.

"Wow, that axe *was* sharp," said Tessa. "You could do surgery with that thing."

"Yeah, what do you say, Nathan? How about a tummy tuck?" asked Andy.

"No. Put my shirt back on, please," Nathan begged.

"So you're a failure *and* hideous," said Andy. "How'd you manage to get so ugly so young?"

"My mom smoked when she was pregnant. And I lived in a depleted uranium house surrounded by cell phone towers, so my body fell apart," pouted Nathan. "It's not my fault! Eating all those protein bars and never brushing my teeth are my fault, but not my childhood."

"You lose, Nathan Hader," said Andy, as Nathan squirmed on the trunk. "Okay, disposal team, it's time to get this garbage out of here!"

"Ten four," Chris responded, slapping a walkie-talkie into Andy's hand. "We'll keep you posted."

Nathan's black gums trembled as Peaches and Chris hopped off stage with the trunk. Unconcerned with their fragile Nathan load, the disposal team carried it down the

ANDY GETS CONNED

aisle as roughly as possible and banged against every armrest. Behind them, Andy and Tessa waved goodbye with their middle fingers as the crowd cheered.

"With the first video you made from Andy's footage, I can get you for burglary and theft," said Chris. "With the second video in the booth—arson. And with the sexy one of you humpin' the furniture with your clothes off, I can make you *very* popular in prison."

"Don't put me in jail! I'll rat out every slime ball I know in this town if you let me off the hook!" pleaded Nathan, Chris and Peaches then dropping the trunk.

"Andy! We got ourselves a squealer," Chris said through his walkie-talkie. "But I need your camera to capture his confession."

"Sure thing! Hey, everyone. I know this would be a perfect time to crowd surf back there, but I'm still a large man even with the weight loss and don't want to kill anyone. So how about you pass this camera back to the cop instead?" Andy asked, the fans then doing so until it reached Chris. "Anyone else with a camera should record the idiot and help spread the word too!"

"Okay, Nathan. Fess up," said Chris, streaming as hundreds of vloggers, indie filmmakers, and news crews surrounded Nathan's impromptu press conference. "This is your chance to start atonin' for your crimes against humanity and a few maggots. So spill your guts now or drop the soap later. Take your pick!"

Nathan shifted his eyes, taking a deep breath.

"My business minions are all crooks! The wrinkly guy doesn't pay taxes, the shoulder-padded lady uses child labor sweat shops, and the mobility scooter blob has been scoring great parking spots for 30 years even though he's not disabled," Nathan cried. "Oh yeah, and Principal Murray over at Bumble Ridge High violates every health code but doesn't fix anything because it's cheaper to bribe the local politicians instead. And he blows any extra cash on monkey teachers and security systems that take pictures of students that he then sells to lonely prison inmates! My god that felt good."

In the harrowing halls of Bumble Ridge High where Murray and his secretary watched the confession online, their mouths opened wide enough to fit a cantaloupe in each one. A second later, Murray then flopped his suitcase on the desk and loaded it with cash as his monkey helped pack the straw hats.

"Secretary, here's paperwork to replace the air-conditioning, fix the fire damage, and deactivate every patrol drone," Murray said. "But things are about to get messy around here, so you can take over while the monkey and I escape to Argentina."

"Sit down and shut your goddamn mouth!" growled the secretary, flicking open a switchblade and firmly pressing it against Murray's throat. "This job is mine! You're getting locked up forever, sleazebag! And if you or the monkey make one move, this secretary starts slicing."

CHAPTER 34

With Nathan's disclosure now over, Chris and Peaches lugged their criminal cargo through a group of Andy's old co-workers in the convention crowd. But when Andy's disposal team made it about halfway through the room, Bumble Ridge High School science teacher Mr. Schmidt stepped in front of them with his arms akimbo.

"Halt, Nathan Hader," Mr. Schmidt shouted, as his students handed him a bucket of mud. "It's time for my revenge. This is for screwing up my puddle experiment."

After lifting the bucket, Mr. Schmidt dumped its corrosive mud contents upon Nathan's leotard. As the fabric bubbled and fell off Nathan, a series of secondary leg and butt compression garments tore open too. And that sent another portly eruption of flesh outward.

"You're a loser, Nathan. Loser!" shouted Ms. Cartagena beside them, all her students recording with their phones. "Or, as we say in Spanish, 'perdedor.'"

"Perdedor!" the class chanted, as Chris and Peaches hustled outside with a semi-naked Nathan upon the trunk.

"I don't think Nathan will be showing his ugly face around Bumble Ridge again," announced Andy. "And I wouldn't have been able to do it without my samosas. I'd like to bring them on stage now if that's okay."

"You bet, Sergeant Andy!" Zeus shouted, as the crowd cheered. "Speech! Speech!"

"Thanks, Zeus. First, I'd like to bring up the special woman who led this convention and let me stay in her uterus for a whopping 13 months: my mother, Mom!" Andy said, as she walked on stage with a big bushel of red, white, and blue apples.

"I brought Flag Day apples, dear!" Mom said.

"Don't mind if I do," Andy said, taking a bite. "You have to be the most badass mom ever, you know? You've always been kind, even when I started bringing weirdos to the house like our next guest. Get up here, LSD-401K. Yes, he's the coolest robotic beatnik I've ever met, as well as our Reject Master. It's my dear friend Leo, everyone!"

"Hello, humans," Leo said in his robot voice, locking and popping on stage.

"Remember, he owns Leo's Larping & Comic Stash, so stop by and spend a few bucks. Or, all your bucks!"

"I'm comin' on stage too, sweetie!" Janet said, dashing out to Leo and matching his robotic moves.

"It looks like you bots are on the same operating system," said Andy. "I hope you have compatible parts!"

"Let's start plannin' some o' those promotions, Leo. Ya up for an all-nighter? A long and hard all-nighter."

"Righteous!" said Leo. "I have some transcendently comfortable bean bag chairs we can use."

ANDY GETS CONNED

As Leo's hippie heart pounded, Chris and Peaches loaded Nathan into Mom's flower delivery van parked outside the convention center. After rolling the trunk between a jungle of flowers that instantly made Nathan sneeze, Chris pulled out his walkie-talkie.

"The bald and fat eagle has landed!" said Chris. "He's red and sneezin' too. Looks like he's allergic."

"Peaches approves this torture, you line cutter," he said, glaring at Nathan. "Peaches really wants to slice Nathan in half with a samurai sword, but this is good too."

"I didn't hear that," said Chris.

"Thanks, guys," responded Andy on the other end. "Come back to the stage for the finale. Over and out."

Not taking any chances, Chris double cuffed each of Nathan's hands while Peaches added superglue as one last failsafe. Then Chris attached a series of other handcuffs, connecting Nathan's pair to the van's watering pipes.

"If you break these pipes, the van becomes an aquarium pretty quick. But since I'm a good cop, I'll let you watch TV to keep your mind off how screwed you are right now," Chris said, pulling up the vine blind and unveiling a TV with live convention footage on it. "Okay, I lied; I'm a bad cop. Enjoy!"

"What counts as news these days is really pathetic," Nathan moaned, then sneezing as Andy, Tessa, Mom, Leo, and Janet grouped together on stage.

"Thanks for joining us, Janet," said Andy. "She's the town's only progressive owner of a formerly racist speakeasy. The pentagram-shaped mozzarella sticks are to die for during Heathens-Only night too. So, Janet, with all the cameras here, does this count as the commercial I owe you? Or would you like an even more blatant plug?"

"This counts, sweetie," said Janet. "But I would like to announce that all o' the nights at Three-Fifth Chasers are Heathen friendly now since my co-owner Kirkpatrick croaked this mornin' in his iron lung!"

"Now *that's* some great news, isn't it, everyone? Let's keep the party going with another dead thing while we're at it. Get your butt on out here, ZomBen," Andy said, as Ben lurched over. "He's not only an original member of the samosas, but he's also an animal lover, particularly dolphins. And yes, ladies, Ben's still single somehow."

"I also help infertile families at the clinic," said Ben.

A loud whipping sound then cracked in the audience. Sauntering out behind the masses in her unforgettable black boots, the dominatrix pointed at Ben and cracked her whip once more. Ben then bulged his eyes out like a surprised cartoon character, motioning her up. And after the dominatrix joined Ben and put him in a headlock, Ben howled with glee at such a kinky lack of oxygen.

"Marry me!" yelled Ben.

"This is starting to sound like an award speech, so I'll pick up the pace," said Andy. "There are so many other people I want to thank too. Like Chris—he's a cop who's not only doing a bang-up job with security, but also my mom. Okay, that sounded dirty, but it's probably accurate so let's keep going. Then there's Peaches who filled in as our technician, and B-Fred who provided my wardrobe. Nurse Rosie, Emily, Fran, and Marcus all helped stop Nathan's crew from burning this place down. And then there's Winslow, the man who finally did what the rest of us wanted to do to Robby's drunken dad. Get up here!"

As Chris and Peaches tangoed onto stage, B-Fred clopped behind them in his Andy-branded clogs. Following, Emily pushed Marcus and Fran in the baby carriage. Yes, Marcus's butt was crammed in the seat sideways as Fran perched upon his chest and kissed him. And in the rear, Nurse Rosie still puffed on cigars as Andy's last two guests were nowhere to be seen.

"Winslow? Robby?" called Andy. "Where are you?"

The audience then separated in two and revealed a heartwarming truth. Behind them, Winslow and Robby now snoozed together near an exit—both pooped out from their climactic clash with the drunken dad.

"How cute! Let's pop some earplugs in those two so they can sleep while we cheer more," Andy said, embracing Tessa. "Because you're about to cheer a lot after I officially welcome this woman. Last but not least, the newest peep in our posse, and the lady who was awkwardly standing beside me this whole time—it's Tessa! She's one of my favorite comedians too. So if we're lucky, maybe she'll do her set for us tonight."

"Yes, I'll do stand-up!" Tessa said, jumping in Andy's arms. "But you're aware that, by dating a comedian, everything we do is fair game for material, right?"

"Like what?"

"Like how my boyfriend didn't realize how dirty 'peeps in our posse' sounded a few seconds ago. And that was right after he said a cop banged his mom on stage," Tessa said, then pecking Andy on the cheek.

"Humina," Andy gasped.

Back in Mom's delivery van, Nathan sneezed once more between the flowers. And this time he blew the few cloth particles off of his body. The naked Nathan then rocked on his trunk, inching as far as he could to the rear door while Andy and Tessa smooched on TV. His pockmarked arms still attached to water pipes with many handcuffs, Nathan stretched and frantically wiggled his big toe at the door handle. Then with a 4-inch toenail made sturdy from all those protein bars, Nathan opened the door as a slit of light blinded him.

"Ha! Nobody's going to drown me. I'll be out of here and releasing lions on those nerds in no time," Nathan said, then sneezing and losing leverage as the door closed again. "No! No! No!"

On his last scream, Nathan bashed the door with a double-legged shove. His escape now a little less bleak, Nathan popped the door wide open as harsh sun rays beamed upon his nude body.

"Success!" Nathan celebrated between sneezes, his greasy flesh sizzling in the sun. "I needed a tan anyway."

Nathan now tugging on water pipes with all his attached handcuffs, the van sounded like a blacksmith's shop. With a few forceful rolls of the trunk, he then cracked open a pipe as mineral water spurted everywhere. Fortunately for Mom, she had the exact insurance covering handcuff-related damage in the van. But unfortunately for Nathan, an extra-large dose of mineral water sent those plants into a feeding frenzy. And this released even more allergenic spores into his lungs. His sneezing becoming more frequent, Nathan continued denting the other pipe as reporter Gail Ellerbach appeared on TV outside of the convention. Though instead of her broadcast blazer, she wore a beekeeper suit with its hat tucked under her arm.

"We've recently gotten word that a large swarm of killer, Africanized bees has been spotted approaching the Zimmerman Convention Center," said Gail. "This particular swarm is said to be extra aggravated and accordingly lethal. Experts advise staying indoors and avoiding all flowery areas near water."

"Flowery areas near water?" Nathan cried, scoping out his current location. "Uh oh."

At that very moment, a family of comedically-timed crickets chirped while fleeing the van's formerly safe soil. Right as the crickets exited, a swarm of bees descended and blocked out the sun while packing inside their automobile grotto. After sucking up each blossom's nectar in seconds, the bees sensed another food source in the van—a dusting of protein bar crumbs on Nathan's skin.

Their tongues tickled Nathan until he squirmed, and the bees soon deduced that their protein plate was an impostor. Thus, they ramped up their gentle nibbles to aggressive stings. And when Nathan wildly shook the van, again witnessed by the conservative family still stuck in traffic, he yelped at the barrage of pointy bee butts plunging into his defenseless flesh. But then to make matters worse in a moment of questionable heroism, reporter Gail Ellerbach rushed over and slammed the van's rear door shut.

"Experts also say that trapping these bees makes them even more furious, which I'm sure you can hear behind me!" shouted Gail. "I'll be back with more bee tips soon, but we now return live to the captivating conclusion of The Andy Gordon Convention."

Now on the TV above Nathan's twitching body, Andy locked arms with his gang in front of the crowd.

"From the bottom of my heart, thank you all for coming today," said Andy. "The con's gone so well that we'll have to do it again next year! What do you say?"

The crowd erupted into the loudest applause yet, setting off most car alarms within a 2-mile radius. Now hearing this, the conservative family still stuck in traffic shook their heads in disheartening disappointment.

"Well great. It sounds like we missed a super special moment in there," said the conservative mother, as her daughter gazed outside.

"Mom? Dad? Who's that yellow person marching to the van where all the bees are?" asked the daughter.

"Sit tight, gang—now *this* looks interesting," said the father. "We still might get some entertainment after all!"

Passing by the family in a hazmat suit, Nurse Rosie approached the van, opened its doors, and revealed a tornado of bees inside. The bees, having delivered their pointy payloads and run out of protein crumbs, quickly swarmed away. And Nurse Rosie then removed her mask, still puffing a cigar underneath.

"Oh, Nurse Rosie, I could really use some medical attention," coughed Nathan, now looking like a squeezed stress ball from the swelling. "Please, help me."

ANDY GETS CONNED

"Quiet, blimpy. I came here to show you something," said Nurse Rosie. "We wanted you to see this."

From her suit, Nurse Rosie pulled out a rolled piece of paper wrapped with a red ribbon. As she unfolded the paper and moved it closer, Nathan's blurry eyes focused on the object she grasped—a Bumble Ridge High School diploma containing Nathan's name.

"My...diploma," said Nathan, peering through the small opening of inflamed flesh between his eyebrow and cheek. "You all figured I'd learn from my mistakes, and you're giving me a third chance?"

"Close," Nurse Rosie said, ripping the diploma in half and burning a hole through it with her cigar. "I came as the capper to your torment today."

"You bitch! You're getting two lions when I'm free."

"Let me help you cloak that porpoise paunch so nobody has to go blind today," Nurse Rosie said, pulling a bag of Nielsen's baked cheese curls from her suit and dumping them on Nathan's lumpy torso. "Except you, of course, after the bees come back for this grub."

When Nurse Rosie zipped her mask back on and retreated, an even larger bee swarm filled the van and ate each cheesy molecule on Nathan. Though Nathan remained motionless to not provoke them, the odd aftertaste of Nielsen's baked curls struck the swarm all at once. The bees now injecting enough toxins to take down three elk, Nathan hollered and wiggled so vigorously that Mom's van tipped over on its side.

"That...was...awesome!" shouted the daughter, as traffic finally thinned. "Can we come again next year?"

"Anything for you, darling," grinned the mother, as Nathan yelped in unfathomable pain. "Anything for you."

While Nathan's bee acupuncture stopped and the swarm left with their bellies full of cheese curls, above him on TV stood Andy and his samosas. Nurse Rosie soon returned to the stage, and all the misfits formed another celebratory kick line. Andy then nodded at the crowd, and his entire audience faced the news cameras to belt out their glorious goodbye—one last "Pop Goes the Weasel" parody designed for Nathan's ultimate destruction:

> *Nathan Hader's mean to nice geeks,*
> *Our dice are polyhedral,*
> *So we'll steal your cruel, bully techniques:*
> *Drop dead, you weasel!*
>
> *Your humor is a snooze fest,*
> *Your hygiene is medieval.*
> *You're one big, broke, bald, toothless pest,*
> *Drop dead, you weasel!*
>
> *Nathan has no friends—just regrets.*
> *His package size is fetal.*
> *He murders words way more than his pets.*
> *Drop dead, you weasel!*
>
> *Every nerd in this place,*
> *Hates you more than prequels,*
> *You're a waste of human space,*
> *Drop dead, you weasel!*

ANDY GETS CONNED

Hearing the catchy yet disparaging song, Nathan slammed his head backward and compacted a lone bee upon the trunk. And its crushed body then released a powerful alert pheromone into the air. A third swarm of bees arrived within seconds, hellbent for blood over their fallen bee brethren. And they all implanted enough stingers into Nathan to make him look like a pudgy porcupine. This time, without any nearby nourishment to refuel for their next assault, the furious and famished bees went for the last source of protein in the van—no plant or snack, but Nathan's own body. Concentrating on Nathan's appendages first so he couldn't fight back, the predatory bees tore apart Nathan's arm appetizers. They then went after Nathan's legs as their main course, topped off by one tragically disfiguring dessert—Nathan's crusty dong.

"Finish me off...you cowards," Nathan coughed, as his protein-rich blood quickly coagulated and kept him alive.

With Nathan fading in and out of consciousness, the bees suddenly stopped their woodchipper-like ways as 80,000 sour bee stomachs audibly churned. Their gurgles becoming gags, every single bee puked its bee guts out like a wretched waterfall upon Nathan. And then they left just as quickly as they arrived, now flying far past the horizon. Though Nathan had lost perhaps as hard as one could from Andy's role-playing plan, he did end up committing one good deed that day—unintentionally, of course. Because he had left his body in such a toxic state by refusing to bathe, word quickly spread throughout the killer bee community that food was no longer safe in the valley. And every angry buzzer evacuated en masse.

Yes, with Nathan's noxious side effects now known, killer bees would never flap their bird-sized wings in town again. And the peaceful honeybee industry could flourish once more. With Bumble Ridge now a little less scary, a little less corrupt, and a hell of a lot more friendly to nerds, its residents could return to their regular routine. Though considering how fucking weird the place was to begin with, regularity didn't mean a goddamned thing.

CHAPTER 35

Six months later, the morning birds seemed to be a little less torturous to Andy's ears and the sun not so invasive. As his creepy mailman delivered letters without reading them first, Andy buried his head under the dinosaur blankets yet again. Though, this time, his escape from sunlight brought him face to face with another human already doing the same—Tessa tucked tightly beside him in their blanket cocoon. Both misfits then snuggled and drifted back to sleep, now walled in by neatly arranged toys and collectables like a nerdy fortress.

"Andy, time for work!" Mom yelled from the kitchen.

Andy's feet immediately flung from the sheets, swinging down into wizard slippers while his bobbleheads danced under the bed. Tessa's feet then slid into her set of Pillow Kitty slippers. And though their footwear didn't come close to matching, their his-and-hers Wacky Will pajamas certainly did.

"Hi there," Andy said, hopping on the bed in pajamas so loose that he looked like a flying squirrel. "Want me to launch you to the bathroom so you don't have to get up? It'll only take one jump."

"Not if I catapult you there first," Tessa said, pouncing on the bed and then kissing him. "Good morning, handsome."

"Will mademoiselle require an expedient ride to 'ze café?" Andy asked in his over-the-top French accent.

"Yes, I 'vill need 'zat transport, French boy," Tessa responded in her ridiculous Russian accent. "Give me ride like horse, horse man."

Tessa latched onto Andy's back like a baby koala and rode him to their espresso bar beside the bed. Andy then picked up two cups of steaming caffeine and handed one to Tessa, the couple swigging them down. Now energized, they both bolted to the bathroom for some lustful loofah action. And after toweling off and blow drying each other like an automatic carwash, they applied their work-appropriate attire. Two T-shirts containing the text 'I'm With the Nerdy One' came first, featuring an arrow that pointed to the side. And then they both finished off their outfits with *Space Fightin'* blazers.

With Tessa now on Andy's back again, he dashed to his skateboard. And the mobile couple rolled past rows of meticulously hung Renaissance weapons and enough geeky collectables to start a museum. Andy then dismounted before the stairs and hustled down on foot as Mom sipped coffee in the kitchen. Not alone this morning, a number of guests ate breakfast beside her—Chris, Leo, Janet, Ben, and the dominatrix in a dolphin mask. While the guys and Janet munched away on

ANDY GETS CONNED

pancakes, the dominatrix downed a banana without chewing. And this meant that Ben could only stare at her lack of a gag reflex, getting no food into his own mouth.

"Andy! Tessa!" Mom shouted. "You'll be late!"

"Yeah, dammit!" added the breakfast crew in unison.

Now downstairs, Andy got back on the skateboard and passed through a living room filled with Tessa's computer parts. And then they zoomed by the historical marker sign noting that 'Andy and Tessa Met Here.' The kitchen now in sight, Tessa placed one hand over her eye while shifting her mouth to the side like a stroke victim.

"Are we thar yet, matey?" Tessa asked in her gritty pirate voice. "What be takin' so long?"

"If ye don't stop askin' questions, I'll turn this damned dinghy around," Andy said, mimicking her delivery. "Ye be the lookout. Are thar dangers ahead?"

"Aye, captain. Ye better slow down. Thar be landlubbers in the kitchen. Linoleum ahoy!"

As Andy and Tessa approached, the dominatrix finished her banana and swiftly raised its peel above her dolphin mask. Defying science, her motion somehow made the exact sound of a cracking whip.

"I bet I can make this into the trash can from here, piggies," toyed the dominatrix. "Any takers?"

"Right on," said Leo, pulling money from his pocket. "My intuition tells me you won't even slam the can; you'll miss. How about 100 bucks? No, retract that—500!"

"I say you're both wrong," Ben said, slapping cash onto the table. "I'm voting third party this time. Expect the unexpected!"

"Game on," said the dominatrix, chucking her peel.

Ben then won as the dominatrix's peel struck the can and slid down its side, plopping right in the pirates' path. As Ben celebrated, Andy and Tessa skated into the kitchen—both making engine sound effects with their mouths in harmonious pitches. Their flawless journey for breakfast booty now seeing its first hurdle, they struck the slimy peel upon Mom's polished floor. Andy then wobbled like an airplane going through turbulence in a typhoon. But when he applied his slipper landing gear to the floor, he smoothly dismounted without injury.

"You want some cereal, dear?" Mom asked.

"Nope. Two apples to go, please," said Andy.

"My brain still doesn't accept that," added Ben, the dominatrix then kissing his cheek with her dolphin snout. "Or that either!"

"Turn up the TV, will ya?" Janet asked, pointing. "There's breakin' news."

Mom turned up the kitchen TV, now displaying footage of reporter Gail Ellerbach in front of the Nielsen's Cheese Curl factory. On stage with CEO Lamar Nielsen grinning beside her, Gail held a poster-sized, orange check for five hundred thousand dollars.

"After months of searching, one lucky winner has finally found the elusive and life-changing Artificially Colored Orange Ticket," said Gail, as the winner emerged from a curtain. "Come on out here, sir!"

Andy and friends all twisted their heads in a double-take at the TV, now seeing the last person they'd ever expect to win anything. Yes, in his long-awaited moment of glory, Winslow strutted out in a fancy, orange suit. By his side hobbled the hunchback woman from Andy's convention, she and Winslow wearing golden wedding rings. No sadness in his eyes or signs of new wounds, Winslow grabbed the check and beamed with a smile.

"Welcome, Winslow!" Gail exclaimed. "As the winner, that means you get a tour of the Nielsen's factory, a dream job on the food tasting team, a lifetime supply of cheese curls, and a whopping five hundred thousand dollars. So, Winslow, what do you have to say?"

"Everyone in this town can go fuck themselves, Gail," Winslow said, flipping off the camera. "Except Andy Gordon and his samosas—the only people who ever gave a damn about me in this crap hole town."

"And do you have any idea how you'll spend all of the prize money?"

"Well, I have two big plans for the cash. First, my wonderful wife and I are going to give our new son the childhood he never had," Winslow said, as Robby the hamster-dressed boy skipped out and cuddled his leg. "We're going to pamper ourselves, avoid paragliding, and blow way more cash than any of you Bumble Ridge yokels will ever make in your lifetime. And while I have the mic, you should all be ashamed for what you did to us over the years. The mocking of Robby, the scorn for my wife's hump, the jumping into the air when I walked by to bring even more attention to my weight problem—it all ends now. So if you ever cross any of us again, you're dead. And that's not some figure of speech either; I mean strangled-with-my-bare-hands dead!"

"Good for him!" said Andy, catching two apples tossed by Chris in the kitchen. "It's nice to see the fat guy win every once in a while."

"Keep eatin' those apples and you won't be able to call yourself 'fat' much longer," said Chris, turning up the TV even more. "Now shush. No more talkin' until Winslow's done rippin' this town a new one."

"And what's your second plan for the money?" asked Gail. "Perhaps you'd like to donate some cash to your local, high-quality journalism outlet?"

"No way. You and your corporate-skewed network can suck it, Gail. But I did send Andy and his friends a special gift," Winslow said, holding Robby and the hunchback. "It should show up at their place sometime today. If you samosas are watching, I hope you like my present. Thanks for all your help! And I'll see you at the next *Rejects & Reptiles* session! The handicapped hippo must rise again!"

"Well that's mysterious," Andy said, picking up a briefcase and opening the door to his garage. "I guess we'll find out what it is after work."

"Be careful out there," warned Chris. "They're extra wild today."

Andy, Tessa, and Chris all filed through the door, passing its golden plaque etched with the text 'Samosas Studios: The Alvin Linda Gordon Room.' After crossing into the garage, Andy placed his briefcase on the floor and pulled out two wireless microphones.

"Boy, what a commute," said Andy, attaching his mic and handing one to Tessa.

ANDY GETS CONNED

"At least we carpooled though," said Tessa. "You're welcome, Earth."

Chris then led Andy and Tessa to a loveseat in front of studio cameras and lights, flanked by fervent fans behind a red rope barrier. After Tessa put on a golden crown, she and Andy crammed into the loveseat, nibbled their apples, and sipped from punch bowl-sized coffee cups on a table in front of them.

"Ten seconds to air, everyone," yelled Chris. "Don't touch the talent if you're plannin' on stayin' a *live* studio audience. Got it?"

As the crowd chuckled and Chris counted down, the rest of Andy's breakfast crew ran in. Janet and Leo came first with a stack of cue cards followed by Ben with his graphic design laptop. And finally, Mom guided the dominatrix out still in her dolphin mask, each taking control of a studio camera. Indeed, Samosas Studios' only employment qualification seemed to be knowing Andy—equal opportunity hiring be damned.

"Hi, everyone out there today!" said Andy. "You might know me as Andy."

"And you might know me as Tessa," she said.

"And welcome to today's episode of *Misfits in the Morning*. So, Tessa, I notice the crown. Who died and made you king?"

"Uh, the last king, actually. That's kinda how kings work, you know."

"Well I can't see how that's possible since I'm also the current king of this place," Andy said, placing a different crown on his head.

"No way, two kings? This isn't right."

"Come on, Tessa. Get with the times. It's perfectly fine for two males who love each other to hook up and—"

"No, not that. I mean, what could two ruling powers possibly do without fighting all the time?"

"We could redirect our frustration onto others," Andy suggested, winking at the camera. "How about we educate our kingdom through a series of vlog-style rants?"

"Oh, I like that a lot. The curvy King concurs!" said Tessa, nodding.

"What grievance shall we express first? Used car dealers? People who talk during movies? Maybe annoyingly cute couples?"

"That last one sounds like a good target. Listen up, annoyingly cute couples. Please approach the throne," Tessa said, as Mom rolled her camera closer. "We know you're happy and all, but you have to stop gushing about how perfect you are for each other. We really don't care how you met, and your life isn't a modern-day fairy tale."

"Unless you're us of course," Andy said. "Because we're kings!"

"Hypocritical kings!" Tessa added, then kissing Andy.

"For your punishment, we rule that you must help spread today's episode of *Misfits in the Morning*. It's the Season One finale, and we want to break records. So we order you to spam all your social media contacts right now! We have a great show somewhat planned, so what do you say? Is everyone ready?"

"Yes!" the audience responded, while Mom tilted her camera up and down as if agreeing.

ANDY GETS CONNED

"I don't know if they're ready enough," Andy sang, overacting. "I think we might have to stop the show."

"Maybe we should give them another chance?"

"The curvier king concurs!" said Andy. "So how do you feel about that, kingdom? Are you ready or not?"

Janet then spun her camera around with an epic swivel. With Andy's garage toys now organized and displayed in the house, his newest collection packed the place—a human audience. And, as the camera targeted them, they all jumped with excitement levels the garage hadn't seen since Andy was conceived there.

"On today's episode, we're going to get a safety lesson from Police Chief Chris on the proper way to bribe a cop. We'll chat about Winslow dropping a bevy of F-bombs on TV when he won Nielsen's prize and likely got Gail fired. We'll hear from Mom & Emily's Petal Peddlers about their new drone delivery service. Ben will unveil our next season's graphics he's been working on that likely contain dolphins. And then we'll wrap things up with a video we shot in the new disco tunnel connecting Leo's Larping & Comic Stash to Janet's Not-Racist Speakeasy. And, yes, that is the name of her establishment now. How's that sound, everyone?"

As the Alvin Linda Gordon Room filled with glorious applause yet again, Leo checked the show's live chat on his laptop and quickly scribbled '$300' onto a cue card. As he and Janet held the card up, Andy and Tessa both spat out their coffee in shock.

"Guess what?" Andy hyped. "We just received a $300 dance party donation! You're all amazing!"

"Ahoy, matey Peaches! Cue your finest sea shanty!" Tessa shouted.

"Peaches will get this garage yo-ho-hopping in no time," Peaches said at an audio station, his eyepatch now bedazzled with gems and sequins. "Chug ye grog and get on up here, ye scallywags. Peaches wants all hands on the poop deck. It's a cheese curl dance party!"

Samosas Studios' entire crew then hustled on stage, dancing to 8-bit video game pirate music as Nielsen's Cheese Curls rained from above. While wasteful, Andy figured that this cheesy confetti was the best way to blast through his stale basement reserves without putting on pounds. Plus, since it was inside, he wouldn't choke any more pigeons. With his teaching days now behind him, Andy happily escaped healthcare and retirement benefits in exchange for creative time with family and friends.

The show went on without a hitch, every segment running like clockwork despite each second not planned. From Chris's bribery lecture to Leo's disco tunnel segment, Andy and his samosa crew had managed to make work fun and profitable enough to never have to be a corporate slave again.

Later as the show wrapped, Andy and his gang gathered on stage once more—all stuffing into the final shot of a successful season. As everyone boogied, Andy's bots R2CheeseDoodle and R2CheeseToodle zoomed up on stage via ramp. And both circled the crew in their seemingly choreographed confetti removal. Tessa's Treb-Mew-Chet then joined in too, launching free T-shirts into the roaring misfit crowd.

ANDY GETS CONNED

"Thank you all for making the show a success," said Andy. "And we're not going away either. We have big plans next season like upgrading the entire studio, starting an internship program for outcast students, and raising enough cash to bring Wacky Will here for an interview."

"I think we can do better than an interview!" shouted a familiar voice from the garage door.

Andy whipped his head at the voice, as did everyone else in the garage. Now smirking at the door, with his rubber chicken suitcase and accordion in hand, stood Andy's long-time comedic hero Wacky Will Zimmerman.

"I'm way more than a guest now," said Wacky Will, dropping the suitcase and rocking out with his accordion onto the stage. "Winslow paid me enough cash to be your show's band leader practically forever. I was a little apprehensive when I recognized you as the guy who chased me down in parking lots for pictures over the years. But then I watched all your episodes and I changed my mind. I'm a big fan of both of you!"

Andy and Tessa's lower jaws then dunked into their coffee cups like dangling meat donuts. And Wacky Will blasted an accordion cover of the *Misfits in the Morning* theme song until his co-hosts recovered.

"How long were we out?" asked Andy.

"Long enough to call this show *Misfits in the Afternoon*, if you catch my drift," sang Wacky Will.

"Well let's wrap this up before it becomes *Misfits at Midnight* then," said Tessa. "So like Andy hinted at earlier, we have lots of reveals when we come back next season. We'll show you the fully upgraded studio. We'll give you all the details about our internship program. And it sounds like we'll have a ton of new Wacky Will Zimmerman tunes too."

"We sure will, Tessa," smiled Andy. "We'll answer all the questions you're dying to know. Just how much weight will I lose over the break? Which Ivy League college did B-Fred Barner get accepted to for his butter-based cooking? And are we really going to air a parody segment called *Nathan the Castrated Quadriplegic Says*? You better tune in one month from now to find out. We'll see you in Season Two, everyone!"

"Wait," said Tessa. "You can't leave our fans hanging like that. We have laws about that kinda torture."

"Well if they think that's a tease, then I can't wait to tell them about the ancient treasure map we found under the garage, my mom getting knocked up with triplets, Ben fathering enough kids to start a country, and maybe even more remarkable—the big, fat wedding ring that I hid in your pocket before the show," Andy smirked.

"Are you kidding?" Tessa asked, reaching for her pocket. "Andy, I can't tell if you're serious now or not!"

Andy launched up, starting Pinnette's classic peace dance from *Space Fightin'*. Curtsying twice while forming binocular shapes with his hands and wiggling his fingers, Andy delivered the character's message one last time:

"Dewem, Warpem, and Howem. To those who view the world askew, must warp together to pull through," shouted Andy. "Goodbye, everybody! Now roll the credits. Roll the credits!"

ACKNOWLEDGEMENTS

To my mom (Linda) and dad (Alvin) for not brainwashing me as a kid, but always encouraging my creativity. To Kate Fahey for letting me torture her with an early draft of this that I read out loud, as well as her helpful editing. To John Ellerbach for also giving feedback when I thought this book was close to being done 3 years ago. And finally to the formational comedians that I began idolizing as a kid like "Weird Al" Yankovic, Benny Hill, Monty Python, Mel Brooks, Norm Macdonald, The Three Stooges, Rodney Dangerfield, George Carlin, John Candy, Chris Farley, John Goodman, Leslie Nielsen, and the Zucker-Abrahams-Zucker filmmaking trio.

While it's debatable if I could have written this book without you, I know for sure the end result would have sucked a lot more. Like, way more. Smirk.

NOTE FROM THE AUTHOR

When I wrote this book, I wanted to create a universe without directly referencing much from the real world. A few historically significant people showed up—I'm looking at you, Benjamin Hitler—but that's about as topical as I went. Everything you saw was from my mind only. Thus, if any of my fake creations turn out to be real at some point, there are four ways that this could have happened:

(1) I thought that an idea was funny enough, or dumb enough, to expand into its own story myself.

(2) I created the same idea as another warped person and should be worried that I have an evil twin.

(3) People stole my work and are about to be contacted by my team of extremely litigious lawyers.

(4) I can predict the goddamned future and should be using my skills for something slightly more important.

OTHER BOOKS BY THIS AUTHOR

-Dolphin Cop: Maverick from the Sea (2020)

Dolphin Cop is one badass dolphin who squeals first and asks questions later. In this comic, Dolphin Cop struggles with one cold, hard truth—he killed so many perps in town that there's no crime anymore. So Dolphin Cop takes on a small case instead, searching for the pet store's lost aardvarks. Events escalate into a whale of a tale, becoming the biggest conspiracy that Earth has ever seen. As Dolphin Cop uncovers the mystery, he stays focused the only way he knows how—spewing sea puns and blowing a lot of heads off in the process. Can Dolphin Cop turn the tides? Or will his carcass sink to the ocean floor?

-Darker Truths: Extra Grim Fairy Tales of Even Grimmer Existence (2016)

Darker Truths will bombard your brain with thoughts of death and inescapable insignificance...but it rhymes, so it's funny! With over 40 full-page illustrations and nearly 100 pages of rhyming verse, this book contains five hilariously tragic tales. Matching the Seuss-like structure and wordplay, each illustration is packed with jokes. So take the plunge because, sometimes, everyone could use a little help making light of the darkness.

OTHER BOOKS NOT BY THIS AUTHOR

-War & Peace...But Mostly War

-Pride & Prejudice...But Mostly Prejudice

-Crime & Punishment...Though No Punishment If Rich

-The Catcher in the Sky: How One Landmine Changed Baseball Forever

-The Drakes of Wrath: These Ducks Are Socio-quacks

-Batch 22: It Took Me 22 Goddamned Tries to Successfully Make Brownies

-A Farewell to Arms: The Case of the Undiagnosed Leper

-Stein-en-Frank: I Think I Might Have Dyslexia

-Pair of Dice Lost: My d20s Rolled Under the Fucking Stove

-The Tragic School Bus: I'm Pretty Sure That My Bus Driver Is Suffering from Alcoholism and Somebody Should Probably Say Something About It

BUT SERIOUSLY

Reviews help. Your reviews bump my book up in the search results and push my weird work in front of more potentially weird people. So, could you do me one last favor and post a review? Take a minute and visit whatever the most popular online retailer is right now with my book on it. Then post a few words about your thoughts!

If that company happened to do something awful (perhaps related to dumping toxic waste on an orphanage) and you are rightfully protesting its website, then go to the second most popular site instead. Keep doing this as necessary until you hit the first website whose track record involves no toxic waste-filled orphanages.

Oh, and if websites don't exist anymore when you're reading this, then I'll assume that our reptilian overlords wiped most of us out and kept a few of us around to laugh and/or stare at like a human zoo exhibit. If I'm still alive, I greatly look forward to seeing what you think in those reviews! (Yes, even from you, reptilian overlords.)

ABOUT THE AUTHOR

Matthew T. McKeague became hooked on comedy when he was two years old, demanding that his mom show him how to use a VCR so that he could record *The Benny Hill Show*. Matt then taught himself how to create comedy sketch videos in his basement styled after Benny Hill, Monty Python, and *Saturday Night Live*. Using these skills after high school, he then studied media at the college level, becoming one of those academic doctors who can't save your life when you're choking on a hotdog.

Professionally, Matt has been a comedy writer and video editor in Los Angeles, as well as a journalist, film critic, and video game reviewer. In 2016, Matt released *Darker Truths: Extra Grim Fairy Tales of Even Grimmer Existence*, a collection of modern-day fairy tales for adults. The book quickly became a #1 Seller on Amazon in its Humorous Verse & Limerick category...likely due to a lack of competition. Then in 2020, Matt put out an absurdly silly comic book, *Dolphin Cop*, the same day he released his debut novel, *Andy Gets Conned*.

Photo by C. Reynolds

MORE ABOUT THE AUTHOR

In his creative work, Matt combines his passions for comedy and storytelling to create compelling tales of misfits, outcasts, and underdogs. Sardonic with a dash of intentional stupidity, Matt strives to make readers laugh at life's nonsense by showing how silly we can all be. His books aren't stories with just a few jokes in them—they take readers on a wild, comedic ride from start to finish.

Matt now spends his existence writing stories in darkened corners. He currently lives on a fictional farm with his imaginary wife and zero children. After recently announcing his run for Pope and dropping out 2.7 seconds later due to a lack of support, Matt abandoned his political aspirations forever. He's also not a platypus, in case you were wondering. His interests include some things while his disinterests include other things.
Matt is also a firm believer that people should make love while listening to polka music at least once in their lifetime.

"To those who view the world askew, must warp together to pull through,"

Matthew T. McKeague

www.ingramcontent.com/pod-product-compliance
Lightning Source LLC
Chambersburg PA
CBHW031558110426
42742CB00036B/115